The Plantation in the Postslavery Imagination

Imagining the Americas

Caroline F. Levander and Anthony B. Pinn, Series Editors

Imagining the Americas is a new interdisciplinary series that explores the cross-fertilization among cultures and forms in the American hemisphere. The series targets the intersections between literary, religious and cultural studies that materialize once the idea of nation is understood as fluid and multi-form. Extending from the northernmost regions of Canada to Cape Horn, books in this series will move beyond a simple extension of U.S.-based American studies approaches and engage the American hemisphere directly.

Millennial Literatures of the Americas, 1492–2002
Thomas O. Beebee

The Plantation in the Postslavery Imagination
Elizabeth Christine Russ

The Interethnic Imagination
Caroline Rody

The Plantation in the Postslavery Imagination

ELIZABETH CHRISTINE RUSS

OXFORD
UNIVERSITY PRESS

2009

OXFORD
UNIVERSITY PRESS

Oxford University Press, Inc., publishes works that further
Oxford University's objective of excellence
in research, scholarship, and education.

Oxford New York
Auckland Cape Town Dar es Salaam Hong Kong Karachi
Kuala Lumpur Madrid Melbourne Mexico City Nairobi
New Delhi Shanghai Taipei Toronto

With offices in
Argentina Austria Brazil Chile Czech Republic France Greece
Guatemala Hungary Italy Japan Poland Portugal Singapore
South Korea Switzerland Thailand Turkey Ukraine Vietnam

Published by Oxford University Press, Inc.
198 Madison Avenue, New York, New York 10016

www.oup.com

Oxford is a registered trademark of Oxford University Press

Library of Congress Cataloging-in-Publication Data

Russ, Elizabeth Christine.
The plantation in the postslavery imagination / Elizabeth Christine
Russ.
p. cm. — (Imagining the Americas)
Includes bibliographical references and index.
ISBN 978-0-19-537715-6
1. Plantations in literature. 2. Spanish American fiction—20th
century—History and criticism. 3. Caribbean fiction (Spanish)—20th
century—History and criticism. 4. American literature—20th
century—History and criticism. I. Title.
PQ7082.N7R89 2009
863'.609353—dc22   2009006266

9 8 7 6 5 4 3 2 1
Printed in the United States of America
on acid-free paper

To my parents, Kathy and Dan, for teaching me the power of stories.

ACKNOWLEDGMENTS

I am grateful to the many individuals whose insight, support, and friendship have helped bring this project to fruition. While at Columbia University, I benefited from the teaching and encouragement of many from within the university and without, including Gerard Aching, Bruno Bosteels, Deborah Cohn, Alfred Mac Adam, Nicole Marwell, Sintia Molina, and Gus Puleo. My special thanks go to Gustavo Pérez Firmat, for being a wise and witty advisor; and to Isabel Estrada and Chela Bodden, whose friendship through it all has been steadfast. A generous grant from the U.S. Fulbright Foundation allowed me to complete significant research in the Dominican Republic, and while there I received invaluable help and insight from Jeannette Miller, Ylonka Nacidit-Perdomo, and Alejandro Paulino Ramos. April Mayes, now in California, has also been most generous with her knowledge of the rich history of the Dominican Republic.

Since arriving at SMU, I have been invigorated and supported by wonderful colleagues, and would like to give special thanks to Denise DuPont, Luis Maldonado, and Francisco Morán, who have read and offered helpful comments on drafts of individual chapters. In addition, I am grateful to SMU for awarding me the University Research Council Travel Grant and the pretenure sabbatical, both of which allowed me to carry out additional research and writing. Completing this book would have been infinitely less joyful without my fellow Think-Tankers, especially our fearless leaders Richard Gordon and Bill Worden. Excelsior! I have also received much good advice, as well as timely encouragement, from Gordon Birrell, Olga Colbert, Marie-Luise Gaettens, and tireless help from our department's administrative staff, Debbie Garland and Rosemary Sanchez. Additionally, Suzanne Bost has been an able critic, intrepid collaborator, and dear friend.

At Oxford University Press, I would like to thank Caroline Levander and Anthony Pinn, the editors of this series, for their initial interest in my project, and

Shannon McLachlan and Brendan O'Neill for their helpful and timely responses to my questions. I owe a debt of gratitude, as well, to the three anonymous readers who provided careful, detailed comment on my manuscript.

Finally, I wish to express gratitude to my Spanish professors at the Claremont Colleges, whose passionate and honest teaching started me on this journey: Susana Chávez-Silverman, Grace Dávila-López, and Karen Goldman. My deepest thanks go to my first teachers, my parents, Dan and Kathy; to my siblings Marie, Will, and Harry; and to my husband, Sabri, *optum seni*.

I thank *Mississippi Quarterly* for allowing me to reprint a revised version of my article, "Intersections of Race and Romance in the Americas: Teresa de la Parra's *Ifigenia* and Ellen Glasgow's *The Sheltered Life*," *Mississippi Quarterly* 58.3–4 (2005): 737–59. Thanks, also, go to the *Revista de Estudios Hispánicos*, for their permission to reprint "The Author Bites her Tongue: New World Trauma and Testimony in Aída Cartagena Portalatín's *Escalera para Electra* and Gayl Jones's *Corregidora*," *Revista de Estudios Hispánicos* 40.3 (2006): 469–88. I gratefully acknowledge White Pine Press for allowing me to reproduce an excerpt from Dulce María Loynaz's poem, "Isla," and its translation, "Island."

CONTENTS

NOTE ON TRANSLATION

When reference is given only to a Spanish edition, the translation is mine. When using existing translations, I have indicated in brackets those passages I have modified or retranslated. I have included the original Spanish where the language is necessary to the understanding of my analysis. I have particularly relied on the following published translations: Onís's of *Contrapunteo cubano*; Acker's of *Ifigenia*; Maraniss's of *La isla que se repite*; Wing's of *Poétique de la Relation*; Lewis and Spear's of *Faulkner, Mississippi*; and Lytle's of *Sirena Selena vestida de pena*. Translations of *Jardín* and *Escalera para Electra* are mine.

The Plantation in the Postslavery Imagination

Introduction

The Paradoxical Plantation

Closed Place, Open Word: The Plantation and the New World Literary Imagination

The displacement and extermination of native populations, the forced exile and enslavement of millions of Africans, the tragedy of the Middle Passage, the ravaging of peoples and lands: these form the irreducible core of the legacy of the slaveholding plantation of the Americas, an institution that produced seemingly infinite riches for Old and New Worlds alike, and helped to fund the imperial projects of Europe and, later, of the United States. The present study proposes a model by which to evaluate the development, over the course of the twentieth century, of a trans-American poetic imaginary that has emerged from this brutal, dehumanizing past. It is an imaginary that the Martinican writer, Edouard Glissant, has disconcertingly likened to an "open word" that, always evolving, expanding, and questioning, stands in striking contrast to the tragically closed history it seeks to interrogate (*Poetics of Relation* 63–75). Throughout this book, I understand the plantation, in a literary context, to be not primarily a physical location but rather an insidious ideological and psychological trope through which intersecting histories of the New World are told and retold. Resituating it in a dynamic transnational context, the comparative analyses developed in the following chapters dislodge the literary plantation from stale rhetorics of nationalism, regionalism, and binary concepts of identity, thus altering its predictable contours and facilitating a reevaluation of its legacies.

As a great many historians and cultural critics have noted, the voices of those whose exploitation and loss were most intense under the plantation regime have, more often than not, been silenced or marginalized by the official archives of history. Consequently, our understanding of this history is far from complete. George

Handley, in his call for the nurturing of a "New World Poetics of Oblivion," observes that the unreliable, incomplete evidence to which we have access necessarily results in an image that is "fragmented, partial, and while undeniable, ultimately unknowable" (26). Moreover, because it is unknowable it is also unsayable: language, regardless of the skill or subtlety with which it is used, finally fails in its attempts to convey fully an unknowable past. What we say about the unsayable, in whatever context, can have far-ranging cultural, social, and even ethical consequences; and before we even open our mouths or laptops, we can be assured that the language we choose will be inadequate. Yet, Handley rightly asserts that this necessary failure "is not a cause for lamentation but rather an opportunity to pay homage to those histories that can never be summed up" (28). The ability of literary language, in particular, to recall the past and, at the same time, reflect on its own failings to articulate a complete or totalizing vision of that past, transforms it into a powerful tool for examining the traumas of history.

Even so, to focus, as this book does, on the relationship between the postslavery literary imagination and the slaveholding plantation, is to run certain risks. Leaving aside, for the moment, the dangers implicit in all comparative work and the particular perils associated with trans-American studies, it seems to me that perhaps the greatest hazard of a project such as this one is that it will reinforce, even exaggerate, the centrality of the institution and legacy it seeks to critique. In his 1975 essay, "Caribbean Man in Space and Time," Edward Kamau Brathwaite warns, "the plantation model ... is in itself becoming as much tool as tomb of the system that it seeks to understand and transform" (4). Nearly two decades later, Miriam Muñiz Varela levels essentially the same critique, complaining of "a monotonous history without ruptures" (106) and demanding "a critical appraisal" of "the fact that [the plantation] still occupies a central position in Caribbean discourse" (107).[1] What concerns Brathwaite and Muñiz Varela is that the ongoing dominance of the plantation in academic discourse about the Caribbean (both authors write expressly about the archipelago) largely silences the resistance of those who bore the brunt of the oppressive plantation regime and altogether ignores the historical and cultural developments that took place outside of it. As Brathwaite repeatedly reminds us, the plantation "does not contain all that is planted" (4). What role should the plantation play in the critical and literary imaginations of today? Is it possible to remember the devastation of the past without making the plantation a permanent center? At the same time, can we privilege multivalent forms of cultural and revolutionary resistance without falling into a simplistic celebration that claims to know the unknowable?

Glissant's theory of the open word allows us, not to resolve the tensions generated by these questions, but rather to navigate them productively, for two reasons. First, in contrast to the open word that emerges from it, he proclaims the plantation to be a "closed place," rubble and ruins incapable of regenerating. What is more, he argues that, despite claims to the contrary, it was closed from the very beginning, "functioning apparently as an autarky but actually dependent, and with a technical mode of production that cannot evolve because it is based on a slave structure" (*Poetics of Relation* 64). As a result, it "collapsed everywhere, brutally or progressively, without generating its own ways of superceding itself" (63). The resulting relationship between the plantation and the poetics that emerges from it is jarring, but also creative: "The place was closed but the word derived from it remains open" (75). As we shall see—and as the critiques by Brathwaite and Muñiz Varela suggest—Glissant's insistence that the plantation is in ruins, which is justified by his contention that it was "based on a slave structure," is far from universally accepted. Indeed, debates about the persistence of the plantation rage on, and form a central point of inquiry in this study. In *La isla que se repite*, or *The Repeating Island*, for example, Antonio Benítez Rojo flatly rejects the notion of the plantation as technologically stagnant and instead depicts it as a meta-machine capable of reinventing itself and devising ever more efficient forms of exploitation. Glissant, of course, hardly purports that all oppressive social and political structures died with the plantation. To the contrary, as Valérie Loichot has observed, he declares the plantation to be "one of the bellies of the world ... not the only one, one among so many others" and so suggests that "the literatures of the U.S. South and the Caribbean need to be extracted from the Plantation academic ghetto and cast as active agents of these other bellies of the world" (*Orphan Narratives* 198). Underscoring the closed nature of the plantation, Glissant imagines an open poetics that breaks free of the pull of the past, not in order to move beyond that past in some simplistic way, but rather to come to terms with it while, at the same time, confronting new challenges.

His theory is also useful because it disrupts the binary logic of the plantation by insisting that the open word is a product of both slave and master. In its earliest stage, it is elaborated through the oppositional, but always fragmented, oral traditions of the slaves and their descendants, who rely on "a symbolic evocation of situations" and the act of "saying without saying" (68). In its second stage, described as "a dead end or delusion," it takes on written form in the self-justifying texts of the master, who attempts to "blot out the shudders of life" by depicting the plantation as a tranquil Eden (70). It is therefore linked, not only to oral traditions, but also to the written canon; and not only to the struggles of slaves clamoring for freedom and justice, but also to the assertions of masters defending their right to human property. The open word thus describes a poetics born of perverse and bitter origins, which only achieves maturity in the wake of the plantation's collapse.

The word that emerges from the closed place of the plantation is open, but it is also dynamic, and I perceive its movement to be simultaneously pendular and spiraling. In regards to the former, we might look to Handley, who describes a "pendular swing between language's correspondence to its own rootedness in historical events and to its own self-referentiality" ("New World Poetics" 29). At the same time, the swing of the pendulum shares something in common with the movement of the counterpoint, as theorized by the Cuban anthropologist, Fernando Ortiz, in his *Contrapunteo cubano del tobacco y el azúcar*, or *Cuban Counterpoint: Tobacco and Sugar*. This movement, which Ortiz also describes as "transculturation," allows for negotiation between "the highly varied phenomena" that shape Cuba and other plantation regions, which are produced by "extremely complex transmutations of culture" (98). In the first case, then, the pendular motion refers to the capacity of language to reexamine the past even as it remains aware of its own representational limits. In the second, it describes the always provisional relationship between the multifaceted phenomena that have created plantation cultures. This book argues for the importance of both of these—that is, of discursive as well as cultural and socio-historical analysis—and, furthermore, attempts to imitate the swing of the pendulum or the rhythm of the counterpoint through its structure, by staging a series of dialogues. Each of the following six chapters pairs a text from Spanish America with one from the United States, and these pairings, multiplied across chapters, facilitate a proliferation of other dialogues between the first and second half of the twentieth century, female- and male-centered discourses, and continental and island poetics.

I have also organized this book in a roughly chronological order: chapters 1–3 are concerned with texts published in the second quarter of the twentieth century, which represent what I call "modern" plantation imaginations. In turn, chapters 4–6 examine works published from the 1970s to the turn of the twenty-first century, which correspond to "postmodern" imaginations. This division, which is described in more detail below, helps to illustrate the second movement of the open word, an eccentric spiraling through space and time that allows for a distancing from, as well as a decentering of, the plantation. By examining the continuities and the differences between its modern and postmodern manifestations, I argue that the open word is capable of transformation, but that its evolution does not follow a predictable course.

Plantation Paradoxes

In order to trace the trajectory of the open word, however, it is necessary to begin at the closed site from which it emerged—a site, as historians have long observed, that was built upon paradoxes. Perhaps the most fundamental of these results from its socioeconomic structures, which Eric Wolf has described as a principal cause for the plantation's "split personality" (138). These structures, on the one hand, are linked to the development and rapid expansion of global markets under European colonialism. On the other, they cannot be separated from what Eugene Genovese has called the "seigneurialism" of the slaveholding system. The unavoidable clash between the profit-centered, capitalist goals of the one, and the self-sufficient and feudal or semi-feudal tendencies of the other, leads to conflicts that play out differently in different regions. Genovese, for example, argues that in the U.S. South, the plantocracy self-consciously rejected the capitalist values of the liberal North in order to create "a distinct—or if you will, pure—slaveholding class" (101). According to Genovese, the success this class achieved in asserting its anti-bourgeois ideology is "the greatest paradox in a subject overflowing with paradox" because its members "emerged from the world's most advanced bourgeois society, adhered to a classically bourgeois religion, accepted liberal and democratic political principals, and were drearily repressed, guilt-ridden, and Anglo-Saxon in their sexual mores and attitudes toward miscegenation" (95–96). In *El ingenio*, or *The Sugarmill*, the Cuban historian, Manuel Moreno Fraginals, depicts a similar situation in tellingly different terms. Recounting the explosive growth of the sugar industry in eighteenth-century Cuba, he portrays the typical plantation master as an "economic entrepreneur" whose wealth was generated by slavery, an institution he nevertheless saw as "the chain shackling him to the past and preventing the leap into full capitalism" (18). As "a castrated, impotent, semi-bourgeois," the Cuban planter reluctantly accepted slavery as an economic necessity but longed to embrace the progressive, market-oriented values of "the revolutionary bourgeois who intellectually inspired him" (18). In contrast to its counterpart in the U.S. South, then, Moreno Fraginals holds that the Cuban planter class accepted slavery as an economic necessity but longed to embrace modern, capital-oriented values.

This distinction is mirrored in the terminology used to describe what in English is called the plantation, but in the Spanish Caribbean is more commonly referred to as the *ingenio*.[2] The former word, whose etymological root is the verb "to plant," is intimately tied to notions of rootedness, both literal and figurative. It can connote a variety of agriculturally oriented places and activities, including, according to the *Oxford English Dictionary*, "a cultivated bed or cluster of growing plants of any kind" and "an estate or large farm, esp. in a former British colony, on which crops such as cotton, sugar, and tobacco are grown (formerly with the aid of slave labour)." Another set of definitions, in their majority historical or obsolete, relates the plantation to the planting, not of vegetable life, but of various projects of civilization. It can mean, for example, "the settling of people, usually in a conquered or dominated country; *esp.* the planting or establishing of a colony; colonization." In contrast, the word *ingenio*, although most commonly translated as "sugar mill," encompasses both the fields where sugarcane is grown and the mills that process the raw material into a finished product. The *Pequeño Larousse* dictionary, for example, defines the *ingenio* as the sugar cane fields and the *ingenio de azúcar* as the industrial plant where the cane is ground into sugar. The dictionary of the *Real Academia Española* similarly defines *ingenio de azúcar* as both the machinery used to grind cane into sugar and the *finca*, or farm, containing the sugarcane fields and administrative offices. Thus while "plantation" depicts an essentially "rooted" site used for agricultural or colonial purposes, *ingenio* draws attention to the institution's "split personality" by highlighting the intimate relationship between its rural/agrarian and industrial/commercial nature.[3]

These brief examples demonstrate an important reality: although the plantation generated comparable—and comparably paradoxical—patterns of social and economic relations throughout the Americas, each region responded in distinct ways, and their varied responses are reflected in their literary imaginations. For example, the U.S. South has cultivated the notion of a "rooted" plantation, often depicted as the origin of the region's "civilized" institutions and autonomous communities. In contrast, the Spanish-speaking regions of the Caribbean and circum-Caribbean—especially Cuba, which had the most developed plantation society—have more often described the *ingenio de azúcar* as a modern invention that facilitates the exploitation of land and labor. In the first case, the plantation is imagined as an idyllic place. In the second, it is not a place at all but rather a system, a structure, or a machine.

I have presented these two concepts as characteristic, respectively, of the United States *or* the Spanish Caribbean, and I am not the first to have made this distinction. Deborah Cohn, for example, argues that the impulse to see the plantation as a paradise dominated the discourse of U.S. Southerners, who defended it "as an idyll emblematizing their (now fallen) way of life." In contrast, Spanish Americans in search of an originary site more often turned to "an idealized, primitivist vision of the pre-Columbian past, in which nature was still perceived to be inviolate" (20). There is much truth to Cohn's claims, particularly when one speaks, as she does, about a continental Spanish American imaginary. Within the plantation imaginary of the Spanish-speaking as well as the broader Caribbean archipelago, however, this opposition breaks down because the trope of paradise, wherever its imagined location, inevitably becomes entangled with the trope of the plantation. This is because paradise and the plantation, when the latter is understood to be an exploitative institution rather than "an idyll," are what Ian Strachan has called the "controlling metaphors" of a Caribbean discourse shaped by "the economics of imperialism." Despite their differences—paradise is "a myth made to cloud a particular reality" while the plantation is "a painful reality often mythologized"—they "rebuff and reinforce each other on the level of metaphor" (3). Thus, in the postslavery imaginary, the lush Edenic nature of the pre-Columbian past is only with difficulty separated from the plantation. As Sarah Casteel has argued, "in contemporary Caribbean writing, the paradisal landscape often is haunted by the historical legacy of plantation agriculture and the slave labor that sustained the plantation economy" (135). An idealized natural landscape, whether located inside or outside of the plantation, functions as a promised "sanctuary from history and a return to origins" and, simultaneously, as an evocation of that history (135).

If this complex landscape is one key site explored by the plantation imagination, the physical and metaphorical space that has come to be known, through the writings of the Brazilian anthropologist Gilberto Freyre, as the *Casa Grande*, or Big House, comprises another. Glissant has rightly declared that, when considering the legacy of the American plantation, Freyre's writings are "always relevant" (*Faulkner, Mississippi* 10) and I might add that Brazil is always pertinent as well. Although this study does not focus on the Portuguese-speaking behemoth of Latin America, the role it has played in the development of a trans-American plantation imaginary cannot be underestimated. While historians like Genovese and Carl Degler offer well-documented comparisons of the highly paternalistic plantation structures of northeastern Brazil and the southern U.S., the Cuban literary critic Antonio Benítez Rojo insists that the Brazilian plantation "might be taken simply as another Caribbean island" (72). Although less rigorous than his historian counterparts, Benítez Rojo's hyperbolic declaration captures the sense of a common imaginary that emerges from a shared, if not identical, past. Similarly, in the U.S., as Stelamaris Coser has observed, "because of its large size and its position as largest importer of slaves in the New World, Brazil has constantly played the role of foil to the U.S. system" (123). In particular, African-American writers have often looked to Brazil as a space of shared suffering and possible liberation, as both Gayl Jones's *Corregidora*, studied in chapter 5 of this study, and Toni Morrison's *Paradise*, examined in chapter 6, make clear.

For the purposes of this introduction, Freyre's *Casa Grande y Senzala* (1933), translated as *The Masters and the Slaves*, is especially relevant because it envisions the *Casa Grande* as binding together dueling concepts of the plantation: it is at once its main engine and its beating heart. On the one hand, it "represents an entire economic, social, and political system" that is highly technical and uniquely Brazilian: it includes, for example, everything from "a system of production (a latifundiary monoculture)" and "a system of labor (slavery)" to "a system of sexual and family life (polygamous patriarchalism)" and "a system of bodily and household hygiene" (xxvii). In this sense, it is a "total institution," as George L. Beckford has called the plantation. Yet it is also a rooted and rooting place that protects and nurtures the black-and-white Brazilian family: the same paragraph describes it as "a fortress, a bank, a cemetery, a hospital, a school and a house of charity giving shelter to the aged, the widow, and the orphan" (xxvii). Arguing that "the social history of the Big House is the intimate history of practically every Brazilian" (an exaggerated claim, to be sure, since the plantation thrived primarily in the country's northeastern regions), Freyre celebrates an imagined national family, and his embrace of its racially and culturally miscible nature has inspired many to recognize him as a model proponent of multiculturalism. Increasingly, however, critics have held him to closer scrutiny (xxxvii). Alexandra Isfahani-Hammond, for example, has argued that, by placing the Big House at the center of "the intimate history" of Brazil—and, implicitly, leaving the *senzala*, or slave shed, in the margins—Freyre reinforces the authority of the master and ultimately proposes "a symbolically Africanized, genetically white figure as the prototype for 'interracial' synthesis" (35).

Variations on Freyre's Big House, and on the family that dwells in it, play similarly powerful, and troubling, roles in the imaginaries of other regions as well. In Puerto Rico, for example, a metaphorical *casa solariega*, or patrician house, for many decades shaped a nationalist discourse that imagined a *gran familia puertor-riqueña*, or grand Puerto Rican family, living together in harmony under its gracious roof. But whereas Freyre celebrates, however problematically, the miscegenated nature of the Big House, Puerto Rican intellectuals from the same period envision a national harmony achieved through the unconcealed repression of cultural and racial difference and an attendant valorization of the island's inheritance from Spain. Since the 1970s, this old model of the *casa solariega* has been methodically deconstructed by new generations of Puerto Rican writers, perhaps most literally in the early fiction of Rosario Ferré, where it is transformed into a whorehouse, burned down, blown up, drowned in dust, or abandoned to the decay of time and neglect.[4]

In the United States, meanwhile, the white-columned mansions of the antebellum South continue to be objects of nostalgia, not to mention magnets for tourist dollars, as is demonstrated by online advertisements for plantation tours that encourage prospective customers to "feel the gentle breeze of Southern hospitality on a tour that takes you back to the glory of the Old South" (Gray Line New Orleans) or that promise "a visit to these stately plantations will make you think you are sipping a Mint Julep on the Veranda!" (Celebration Tours LLC). Parsing the enduring appeal of such tours, Jessica Adams observes that, by minimizing or erasing the presence of the slave and turning its main house into a domesticated container of romance and nostalgia, they transform the plantation into "an uncomplicated site of white achievement [that] offers solace in the face of civil rights or affirmative action" (87).

The Big House of Brazil, the *casa solariega* of Puerto Rico, and the nostalgia-soaked mansions of the U.S. South function as particular sites through which the plantation family and its postslavery descendants—that is to say, the imagined communities of those parts of the Americas most impacted by the plantation—are comprehended by the poetics of the open word. Once again, their differences reflect significant regional variations. In contradistinction to the houses of Brazil and the

U.S., for example, the *casa solariega* is not necessarily attached to the plantation, even though, as Juan Gelpí has shown, it always implicitly harks back to the *hacendados*, or great landowners, of the nineteenth century (22). Likewise, the imagined racial and cultural make-up of the metaphorical families that inhabit each iteration of the domestic space varies: in the manors of the U.S. South, tour guides sidestep the history of slavery in order to give "solace" to their white customers, while in the *casa solariega* the African presence is repressed in favor of the Spanish. Freyre's conception of the Big House seems distinct because, rather than attempting to conceal the existence of racial miscegenation, he writes about it openly and at length. Ultimately, however, as Isfahani-Hammond has argued, he too symbolically "whitens" the culture that emerges from this tangled network of often-violent intimate interaction. Regardless of their peculiarities, these metaphorical houses underscore what Michelle Wallace, writing about the U.S. context, has rightly asserted is the "hideously intertwined" nature of gender, race, and sexuality in plantation discourse (138).[5] Specifically, they expose the gender-inflected violence of the master-slave relationship by, however unwittingly, drawing attention to what Glissant has called "the damnation and miscegenation born of the rape of slavery" (*Faulkner, Mississippi* 88).

Of course, it is not only the house and the imagined community it shelters that become implicated in this tangled discourse. The landscape, as we have seen, is also caught up in the process. Even our notions of geography—of North and South, specifically—are caught up in its snarled web. In U.S. discourse, for example, the South has often been portrayed in eroticized terms, as a lushly sensual paradise or, alternatively, a sexually dissolute den of iniquity. When I write of the "South" here, however, an uncertainty arises: to which South do I refer? For if, on the one hand, southern states have been objectified by their northern neighbors, on the other, both the U.S. North and the U.S. South project strikingly similar fantasies upon Latin America and the Caribbean. As Frederick Pike reminds us, nineteenth-century Europe "divided the world into North and South spheres. Far to the south lay Africans, oversexed and not fully human; less far southward resided the Spaniards, Portuguese, and Italians, worthier than Africans but vitiated by their propensity for 'unmanly' conduct" (55). Moving to the United States, Pike continues:

> Americans tended to place the libidinous Other either in the West (Indians, Latin Americans, and the debauched elements of white society) or in the South. Within their own country, the South was home not only to the mythically lustful black but to sexually uninhibited white upper-class males as well as profligate white trash. Especially as the tide of abolitionist fervor rose, northerners eroticized the entire South, picturing it as one "great brothel." ... For many American northerners, the South lay also south of the border. (55)

Pike exposes the shifting "facts" of geography. The "North" may refer to Europe as a whole, to northern as opposed to southern Europe, to the northern U.S., or to the U.S. as opposed to Latin America or the Caribbean.[6] The "South," in turn, may be located in Africa, the Mediterranean, the lower regions of the United States, or below the U.S. border.

Pike also draws attention, at least implicitly, to the "hideously intertwined" nature of plantation discourse by suggesting that the "libidinous Other" is always darkened and feminized. The New World South, for example, is home to dark-skinned people as well as light-skinned ones, like the members of the master class and the "profligate white trash," who are (too) closely associated with their darker compatriots. Similarly, when not simply dehumanized, southern cultures are feminized in the crudest of senses; that is to say, they are depicted as closer to nature, irrational, unable to control base sexual urges, and generally guilty of "unmanly" behavior. Moreover, Pike underscores the centrality of the plantation in the context of the Americas when he asserts that the supposed licentiousness of this moveable South was symbolically associated with "plantation houses of shame where seminaked, dark-skinned sluts pranced about and competed for the honor of satisfying the master classes' animalistic urges" (55). Pike's grossly hyperbolic language draws attention, yet again, to the violent and oppressive dimensions of this highly eroticized, coarsely gendered discourse.

In this context, it is perhaps alarming that "southerners" of all stripes repeatedly appropriate the eroticized stereotypes imposed by the North, and transform them into positive assertions of cultural difference. As José Limón has noted, with reference to the Twelve Southerners, whose work will be examined in chapter 1, they construct "a profoundly eroticized and affirming vision of their cultures as more bodily intense, inherently 'artistic,' and sensuously spiritual" (19). Not surprisingly, such a strategy becomes problematic when we read it as another iteration of the plantation's entangled discourse of race, gender, and sexuality.

Each of the paradoxes I have enumerated in the previous pages—the "split personality" of the plantation; the dueling notions of plantation-as-paradise and plantation-as-machine; the "hideously intertwined" nature of the imaginary communities that dwell in the master's house and inhabit the landscape he pretends to shape; the shifting meanings of North and South; and the eroticization of land and culture alike—inform the plantation imaginary that gives shape to the poetics of the open word. The admittedly broad examples I have sketched furthermore demonstrate the need to read critically even those texts, like Freyre's, that seem to offer libratory, or at least productively unsettling, alternatives to the dichotomous logic of the plantation.

The Plantation, and the Nation, in a Trans-American Context

The dialogues staged in the following chapters stress approaches to transnational studies of the Americas that take nuance and difference seriously without reinforcing the stale binaries that too often dominate such discussions. They thus contribute to what has variously been called New World, Hemispheric American, inter-American, or trans-American studies.[7] As a relatively new field of academic inquiry, currently undergoing rapid growth at both the curricular and the investigative level, the methodologies and objectives of trans-American studies are much in debate, but the most useful attempts to characterize them resist monolithic definitions.[8] Roland Greene, for example, argues that what he calls New World studies "is neither unified (in the sense that any one of its projects must rehearse all the available standpoints) nor heroic (in the sense that its practitioners are understood to have New World studies itself, rather than more immediate outlooks, in mind)." Greene goes on to highlight what we might call the dialogic function of the "set of practices" that comprises New World studies: "It exists in the relations between discrete projects, and its only project is to put these into conversation with one another" (337). Claire Fox and Claudia Sadowski-Smith similarly envision "a framework that will enable scholars to explore hemispheric phenomena in depth, rather than a new paradigm that seeks to displace national (and other) geographic categories of analysis" (23). Sophia McClennen somewhat more concretely evokes the pendular or contrapuntal movement I have ascribed to the open word. Specifically, she advocates a "strategic counterpoint of a double consciousness" that, on the one hand, "stress[es] the dualistic, binary oppositions that dominate studies of North versus South and South versus south" and, on the other, "break[s] down those binaries into multiple dialectics that appreciate the complex web of relations that produce regional identities" (Review of *Look Away!* 189).

Each of these attempts to describe trans-American studies depicts, not a discipline seeking to claim new territories, but rather a flexible set of strategies capable of making theoretical, practical, or ethical interventions. Each also conveys, at least implicitly, conceptual and disciplinary tensions that include the ongoing conflict between "North" and "South" as well as the competing claims of transnational cultural studies versus traditional nation-based literature departments. While it is beyond the scope of this introduction to provide a thorough analysis of the debates stimulated by these tensions, I would like to consider one particularly salient example: the different trajectory of trans-American studies in the United States versus Latin America. Although it permeates an ever-wider swath of disciplines and departments, within the U.S. academy it is the field of (U.S.) American studies that has, in recent years, self-consciously positioned itself at the vanguard of trans-American discourse. As numerous critics have noted, however, while American Studies came into being during and because of the Cold War, its promotion of transnationalism coincides with the rise of NAFTA, globalization discourse, and the so-called New World Order. As a result, although its hemispheric turn is presented as radically decentering, skeptics have insisted on scrutinizing the broader institutional interests that drive it.[9]

While many of these skeptics have emerged from within American studies, others have come from without, particularly from Latin American studies, which, like its area studies counterparts, owes its existence to Cold War politics. Certainly, those Latin Americanists (myself included) who engage in such criticism are motivated, in part, by territorial self-interest. Nevertheless, many offer a valuable perspective on the debate, particularly those who reflect upon how and why the study of the Americas has developed differently in the United States versus Latin America. Again, a brief summary of a complex issue must suffice. Most critics concur that trans-American work in the U.S. tends to take place in the humanities and to draw from postcolonialism and poststructuralism, as well as from Chicano border studies, African and Latino diaspora studies, cultural studies, feminism, and queer theory. In contrast, Latin American-based intellectuals tend to view U.S. area studies programs in general, and trans-American discourse in particular, with deep suspicion. This is in part because their study of the Americas has traditionally emanated from the social sciences, and been grounded in Marxism and dependency theory. As such, it has been invested in understanding and resolving concrete political and economic problems, and has consciously distanced itself from postcolonial and cultural studies models of investigation.[10]

These different intellectual trajectories, in turn, imply divergent understandings of the role of the nation-state. While academics in the U.S. interrogate borders and deconstruct imagined communities, those in Latin America, as Fox and Sadowski-Smith note, "view the nation-state more positively as a potential vehicle for the protection of its citizenry against neoliberal forms of corporate globalism and as a guarantor of sovereignty from the United States" (8). In this context, the recent hemispheric turn in American studies is not understood as radical or libratory, but rather as a new form of intellectual imperialism that ignores the necessary role of the nation in developing countries, and attempts to define Latin America through a foreign theoretical lens. A paradox thus emerges. Trans-American discourse seems to employ a theoretical approach that fundamentally questions the nation. Yet, seen from Latin America, it does little more than repeat the old North-South dichotomy, and so reaffirm the domination of the United States. As Djelal Kadir argues, " '*post-nationalism*' emerges as a more capacious nationalism that reinscribes a nationalist project" (19).

In her essay, "US Americans and 'Us' Americans," Sonia Torres dramatizes the interrelatedness of geographical location and intellectual perspective by describing the double bind she faces as a scholar of American studies living and working in Brazil. On the one hand, she must contend with the suspicion of some Brazilian colleagues who cling to the "divide between hard core Marxists and cultural studies researchers or oral historians" (11). On the other, she faces the antipathy of some U.S-based scholars who resent an "outsider" invading their field (12). In response, Torres advocates a dialogic or contrapuntal model similar to those proposed by Greene, Fox and Sadowski-Smith, McClennen, and others. At the same time, she more specifically stresses the need for direct and sustained dialogue between scholars and critics from across the hemisphere.[11] Just as her own research employs the cultural studies models favored by the U.S. academy, so too she argues that U.S. academics could learn much from the always "implicitly" comparative gaze of "any non-US Americanist working in the humanities or social sciences" (13). Walter Mignolo echoes this assessment when he asserts that the fundamental difference between *Estudios de América Latina* in Latin America and Latin American studies in the U.S. emerges from the fact that the former are not restricted by "the obligation to think and write 'only about' Latin America but can think about the world (and Latin America) from a particular geohistorical location" (35). At its best, and despite its suspicious origins or practical and theoretical pitfalls, trans-American studies recognizes the specificity of its own location—as well as the fact, as Mignolo warns elsewhere, that "places of interactions are good and needed, but they do not imply common goals" (52)—while striving to look beyond itself in order to think expansively about the world, and also about itself.

Of the recent crop of trans-American publications, my own project is most closely aligned with Handley's *Postslavery Literatures in the Americas* (2000) and Loichot's *Orphan Narratives* (2007).[12] Both of these studies share, with my own, a similar focus on the postslavery literary traditions of the Caribbean (the Spanish Caribbean, mainly Cuba, in the case of Handley, and the French in that of Loichot) and the southern United States. Both dialogue with intellectuals and ideas located outside of the U.S. academy by drawing from theoretical models emanating from the Caribbean archipelago and, in the process, propose innovative critical models for navigating the historical, cultural, and poetic legacies of the plantation. Additionally, both are attuned to the gendered dynamics of the discourses they examine and do not exclude female voices: like me, they discuss Toni Morrison's fiction, and Handley also includes novels by Rosario Ferré (Puerto Rico) and Jean Rhys (Dominica). Yet they place a relatively greater emphasis on canonical male authors as well as on the genealogical and historical anxieties generated by what Loichot aptly labels "the double lack of origins—historical and familial—in postslavery cultures" (*Orphan Narratives* 18). These two threads of inquiry are, undoubtedly, connected. As Handley notes, genealogy is a central preoccupation of postslavery literatures precisely because it "serves to tell the story of the slave owner's aspiration to a clear and exclusionary line of descent and of inheritance from white father to white son." Of course, this unbroken paternal lineage comes under attack in the very same literatures, as Handley goes on to observe, for the focus on genealogy also "describes how transculturations on the plantation gave rise to an ultimately victorious and more persistent, even if unanticipated, inheritance" (14). Yet the privileging of male authors in this context can result in a hyper-attentiveness to anxieties of paternal origin that is so narrow as to distort our overall understanding of postslavery literatures. In this book, I actively challenge the assumption that the plantation imaginary has been shaped primarily by men, and seek to expand our notions of postslavery, postplantation fiction by focusing (although not exclusively) on female-authored texts that, on the one hand, display woman-centered perspectives and, on the other, dialogue with influential male voices. In doing so, I reveal understudied aspects of how the plantation imagination has been gendered, racialized, and eroticized in ways that oppose the domination of an ever-shifting "North" while also reproducing the subordinate place of female experiences and literary imaginings within the Americas. At the same time, I do not claim a monolithic feminine or feminist imaginary. Rather, I explore a variety of female voices, which, more often than not simultaneously challenge and reinforce the hegemonic discourses of the regions about which they write. I thus argue not only for a reconsideration of the relationship between the U.S. South and the Spanish Caribbean—and the place of female writers within the traditions of these regions—but also for a reevaluation of our critical understanding of these traditions as a whole.

Modern and Postmodern Plantation Imaginaries

The first three chapters of this book examine the development of the open word as articulated by intellectuals and artists of the southern United States and the Spanish Caribbean in the second quarter of the twentieth century. This period, which witnessed worldwide economic booms and busts produced by the unprecedented growth of industrialism and global markets, also saw the continuing decline of the landed aristocracies of these regions. Economic and social shifts, in turn, provoked a reassessment of established social hierarchies and official interpretations of the past. A climate of crisis and transformation thus stimulated the production of a rich body of written texts that attempted to reassert or, alternatively, redefine the narratives through which postslavery societies understood themselves as coherent imagined communities.

Although produced by diffuse cultural, intellectual, and linguistic contexts, each of the six texts analyzed from this period privileges a familiar plot of modernity: that of the traumatic transition from an agrarian order structured around the social and economic necessities of local communities, to a modern way of life organized to meet the needs of an increasingly industrialized society. Writing primarily from the point of view of the moribund landowning elite, they focus on intricate social and cultural negotiations unfolding at a local level. At the same time, they connect local concerns to broader dilemmas stemming from the aggressive intrusion of industrial powers associated with a North whose precise location shifts according to the national and ideological perspectives of the author in question. They thus expose the failures of their own cultures even as they critique an encroaching modernity that crushes both the positive and negative aspects of agrarian traditions. As a result, these texts tend to occupy an ambivalent position revealed in an unsettled and unsettling mixture of criticism of and nostalgia for old orders.

Chapter 1 considers two male-authored texts, *I'll Take My Stand* (1930) and *Contrapunteo Cubano del tobaco y el azúcar* (*Cuban Counterpoint: Tobacco and Sugar*, 1940). Written, respectively, by the collective known as the Twelve Southerners and the Cuban intellectual Fernando Ortiz, both are collections of essays that parse, almost always from opposing points of view, the socioeconomic and cultural paradoxes I have outlined above. For example, they promote competing notions of the plantation: for Ortiz, it is a monstrosity of imperialist capitalism; while for the Twelve Southerners, it is a bulwark against the spread of modernity. Despite their disagreements, however, both texts rhetorically oppose the advance of the industrialized North by depicting an idealized community rooted in a natural landscape (the plantation for the Twelve Southerners, the tobacco-cultivating farm, or *vega*, for Ortiz) organized and governed by a benign patriarchal authority. Moreover, both gender, racialize, and eroticize these landscapes and the metaphorical families that inhabit them in ways that uncover regional differences even as they draw attention to the hemispheric pervasiveness of the "hideously intertwined" discourse of the plantation. The Twelve Southerners and Ortiz admit the inevitability of modernity's triumph, but nevertheless succeed in rendering coherent communities that provide viable alternatives to the forces of the so-called North.

What kind of community, if any, might a female-centered poetics produce in similar circumstances? Like their male counterparts, the authors highlighted in chapters 2 and 3 interrogate the mores of modernity. But they also exhibit a sharp awareness of the dangers posed to women by the paternalistic paradises advocated by Ortiz and the Twelve Southerners. While the male voices in chapter 1 laud a "southern" landscape that has been feminized and eroticized, the female voices in chapters 2 and 3 worry that the sumptuous pleasures of such a landscape are most often denied to women, or are generated at their expense. At the same time, preoccupied as they are by what Handley has identified as "the postslavery placelessness of the white

Creole woman" (*Postslavery* 151), they are unable to make a clean break from the racial hierarchies and prejudices put in place by plantation discourse. As a result, although they struggle to imagine a different kind of community, they repeatedly fail in their quest.

Chapter 2, which investigates *Ifigenia* (*Iphigenia*, 1924), by Teresa de la Parra, and *The Sheltered Life* (1932), by Ellen Glasgow, focuses on the role that family histories and notions of genealogical "purity" play in the lives of young women. More specifically, the novels in question link the romantic desires of the daughters of the landowning elite to a past, which, although seemingly remote from the urban spaces inhabited by these heroines, reveals itself in a constant pressure to conform to romantic ideals shaped by the socioeconomic dynamics of the plantation. Even though they are primarily concerned with the plights of their light-skinned protagonists, both novels also suggest through important subplots the ways in which black women, too, are trapped by these dynamics. While shown in a sympathetic light, the novels' non-white characters are nonetheless constrained by pressures exerted through the plot and through language itself, which, I argue, are shaped to a surprising degree by the different concepts of race that prevailed in Glasgow's Virginia and Parra's Venezuela.

Although hardly unconcerned with genealogy, it is geography that dominates my readings of the novels presented in chapter 3. Unlike *Iphigenia* and *The Sheltered Life*, which are largely urban in setting, *Delta Wedding* (1946) and *Jardín* (*Garden*, 1951) return us to premodern landscapes that simultaneously evoke Eden and the plantation. Significantly, it is only *Delta Wedding*, written by the Mississippian Eudora Welty, that takes place on the plantation. In contrast, the Cuban poet, Dulce María Loynaz, emphatically distances *Garden* from that site. Nevertheless, as we have seen, in a Caribbean context the manor house and paradisiacal garden, which order the landscape of Loynaz's novel, inevitably refer back to a plantation past. Despite their consciously different relationships to the actual site of the plantation, both novels create multivalent terrains that reveal the frustrated subjectivities of their upper-class protagonists and redefine the relationship between the nation, gendered as masculine, and the feminine land it seeks to occupy. More specifically, they propose that the ethos of a "feminine" wilderness, interpenetrated with the domestic space of an equally feminized manor house and garden, might counterbalance the "masculine" values heralded by the modern nation. By embracing conventional associations of the feminine with myth, cyclicality, and space, however, they reenact a problematic relationship between female identity and historical agency that threatens to trap women forever in a position of ahistorical passivity.

Taken together, the texts investigated in chapters 1, 2, and 3 belong to what might be labeled—somewhat ironically, given their unrelenting critique of modernity—a modern plantation imaginary. The six works paired in chapters 4, 5, and 6, in turn, tap into the concerns of our so-called postmodern age and, in doing so, expand the possible avenues that the open word may take. Unlike their earlier counterparts, the authors of these later works are no longer consumed by the binary, agrarian versus industrial. Nor do they show much concern for the plight of the plantocracy or the "placelessness" of white women. Instead, they turn their attention to the short- and long-term effects of the violence, humiliation, and loss suffered by the descendants of those who served that once-powerful elite. Abandoning the mix of criticism and nostalgia toward the past so characteristic of the earlier works, they struggle to resist the silencing effect of what Glissant has called "History with a capital *H*, " by representing a variety of "particular histories" that disrupt monolithic "official" versions of the past (*Caribbean Discourse* 248). At the same time, they also engage the present by probing, directly or indirectly, the impact of emerging sociopolitical movements and technological advancements that transform notions of the self, the nation, and the multifaceted relationships between these entities. In all of the texts considered in the second part of the book, the Glissantian concept of the "imaginary construct of Relation" predominates (*Poetics of Relation* 131). This concept, which will be discussed in more detail in chapter 4, entails what we might imagine as a pendular swing between the desire to uncover linkages and the need to respect the opacity of the other as well as the self. The first of these, the need for connection, is particularly apparent in a strategic transnationalism that directs the movements of the protagonists and shapes the structures of the texts. The second, the respect for opacity, reveals itself in a reticence or refusal to produce (through withholdings of effort or information) or reproduce (through a kind of self-imposed sterility).

Chapter 4 scrutinizes two texts to which I have previously alluded: *La isla que se repite* (*The Repeating Island*, 1989), by Benítez Rojo, and *Faulkner, Mississippi* (1996), by Glissant. The latter is the only book chosen for this study that was originally written in French, and the only U.S.-centered text not written by a U.S. American. Perhaps for this reason, more than any other work I examine, Glissant's essay liberates the U.S. South from the myth of southern exceptionality, not by arguing against that myth but rather by shifting the terms of the debate. Placing this contested region into a radically transnational context, he argues that it must be understood as part of an expansive but coherent hemispheric plantation experience. Benítez Rojo, likewise, taps into a transnational imaginary, dramatically introduced by the titular metaphor that describes the Caribbean as a "repeating island." Yet, in contrast to Glissant, he remains silent about linkages between the plantation histories of the U.S. South and the Caribbean. Moreover, as I mentioned earlier, he defines the plantation as an indestructible, consummately modern machine from its inception, while Glissant, as we have seen, depicts it as a self-destructing institution doomed, in large part, by its inability to adapt to the technological demands of modernity. Despite these discrepancies, both writers draw from a common arsenal of metaphors—including rhizomes, disordered archives, and aquatic voyages—that signals their shared interest in articulating a poetics that interprets the plantation past through a postmodern critical perspective.

Written almost two decades earlier than the texts analyzed in chapter 4, *Escalera para Electra* (*Stairway for Electra*, 1970), by Aída Cartagena Portalatín, and *Corregidora* (1975), by Gayl Jones, do not define themselves as postmodern, nor do they focus on the site of the plantation with the same intensity. Jones's protagonist, for example, is separated from that site both physically and chronologically: her great-grandmother and grandmother worked as slaves in Brazil, where her mother was conceived; she, in contrast, was born and raised in Kentucky. There, she labors not in cotton fields but in smoky bars where she sings the blues. The distance from the plantation in *Stairway for Electra* is more radical still, not only because its Dominican narrator is traveling in Greece, but also because the role of the slaveholding plantation in shaping the imagination of the Dominican Republic is tenuous, since its sugar industry did not flourish until the 1870s, well after the legal end of slavery, which occurred in 1822. Indeed, Cartagena's novel is more immediately concerned with the legacy of three decades of dictatorship under Rafael Trujillo, and the trauma of an ensuing civil war and military occupation by the U.S. Despite a dearth of white columns or sugar mills, however, the plantation asserts its presence in these novels, as a real or metaphorical site of trauma that only the arduous process of bearing witness can begin to heal. The self-awareness with which both authors describe this process can be attributed to the moment that they were writing, the 1970s, which saw the development of the *testimonio* in Latin America and the neo-slave narrative in the U.S., genres that arose in response to the social and political upheavals of the era. As they invoke the rhetoric of witness bearing, these novels, like the essays by Glissant and Benítez Rojo, construct transnational imaginaries that disrupt established political and generic boundaries and question the premises upon which national and cultural autonomy are based.

Transnationality and, indeed, traversals of all kinds, give shape to the pairing of novels featured in chapter 6: *Paradise* (1998), by Toni Morrison, and *Sirena Silena vestida de pena* (*Sirena Selena*, 2000), by Mayra Santos-Febres. At first glance these novels would seem to have little to do with the plantation or with each other: the former unfolds in an all-black hamlet isolated on the sweeping plains of Oklahoma, while the latter occurs in the luxury hotels and underground gay bars of the tropical metropolises of San Juan and Santo Domingo. Yet both strive to subvert conventional racial or gender identities—Morrison refuses to disclose the race of key characters, Santos-Febres' protagonist is a teenaged drag queen—and both emphasize transnational movement. Ultimately, however, they return to that center of patriarchal power, the Big House, in order to transform it. Santos-Febres imagines a transvestite mansion, redressed and so revealed to be a parody of a parody whose authentic forms cannot, and perhaps should not, be recovered. Morrison, in turn, has described her desire to convert what she calls the "racial house" into "a race specific yet nonracist home" ("Home" 5).

That novels as divergent as *Paradise* and *Sirena Selena* would engage in such a strikingly similar project—that of transforming the Big House—serves to underscore the increasingly expansive, but nevertheless intersecting, trajectories available to the open word. At the same time, however, it is important to recognize that the differences between these texts reflect profound cultural, linguistic, geographical, and historical disparities that reverberate in different ways throughout this study. One brief example must suffice: regardless of the time period or region in which they were written, or the racial or ethnic affiliations of their authors, the Spanish (and French) Caribbean texts chosen for this study are consistently more global, transnational, and transcultural in scope and vision than their U.S. counterparts (although it should be noted, with reference to my previous discussion of the different ways that trans-American studies have been understood in each region, that most of them resist or reject extending these connections to the United States). For example, while the young protagonists of the U.S.-centered novels, *The Sheltered Life* and *Delta Wedding*, make vague references to future or past trips abroad, the heroines of *Iphigenia* and *Garden* spend years living in Europe and make extensive comparisons (if only to prove fundamental differences) between their host countries and homelands. *Corregidora* and *Paradise* self-consciously invoke a hemispheric imagination by envisioning an interpenetration of the histories and peoples of the U.S. and Brazil. Yet their transnational visions are remarkably limited in comparison to the more radical movement that organizes *Stairway for Electra* and *Sirena Selena*, which not only hop from island to island—from the Dominican Republic to the Greek archipelago in the first case, and Puerto Rico to the Dominican Republic, in the second—but, in the process, create fluid circuits of migratory movement and so disturb the North-South binaries that have ordered the spatial imagination of the plantation. Moreover, like Loynaz's *Garden, Stairway for Electra* and *Sirena Selena* display an island imagination whose concepts of space, borders, insularity, and movement differ fundamentally from their continent-bound counterparts. These differences, along with others, are important for many reasons, not the least of which is that they direct our gaze *beyond* the borders of the plantation, and remind us that, despite its lasting impact, the history of the plantation is not the only one that has shaped this New World, nor can its reverberations be understood in isolation. By looking at other factors, we not only guard against the danger of reasserting old hierarchies, but we also allow ourselves to recognize that, however horrific, the plantation's reach is limited and we might one day escape from its grasp.

Modern Plantation Imaginaries

I'll Take My Stand and *Cuban Counterpoint*

The present chapter considers how issues of modernity and national identity were linked to the plantation past through anti-imperialist, masculinist discourses that arose during the first half of the twentieth century. In particular, it examines two texts that, reacting against industrialization, global capitalism, and northern stereotypes of southern regions, looked to the site of the plantation as a means by which to redefine the relationship between South and North. The first of these, *I'll Take My Stand: The South and the Agrarian Tradition*, was published in 1930 by the Twelve Southerners, a group of poets, literary critics, and other intellectuals from the U.S. South who would later be known as the Southern Agrarians. The stated goal of their manifesto, which takes the form of a carefully orchestrated collection of essays, was to define "a Southern way of life against what may be called the American or prevailing way; and all as much as agree that the best terms in which to represent the distinction are contained in the phrase, 'Agrarian *versus* Industrial'" (xxxvii). Ten years later, the Cuban anthropologist and ethnologist Fernando Ortiz issued his *Contrapunteo cubano del tabaco y el azúcar*, or *Cuban Counterpoint: Tobacco and Sugar*, a comprehensive study of tobacco and sugar cultivation in Cuba, which begins with the immodest claim, "in the universal history of economic phenomena and their social repercussions, there are few lessons more instructive than that of sugar and tobacco in Cuba" (5).

Published at opposite ends of a tumultuous decade, these seminal texts share points of contact grounded in the paradoxical nature of the plantation, which I have described in my introduction. Both stress the link between economic and cultural development, and challenge hegemonic notions of regional or national identity by critiquing industrial capitalism, opposing South to North, and positing the plantation as a central site of inquiry. Moreover, they claim to present pragmatic agendas for reform, but do so by employing remarkably literary, even poetic, language that invites a wider spectrum of interpretation by calling attention to subtle discursive techniques, complex metaphors, and richly racialized, gendered, and eroticized imagery.[1]

Despite their similarities, however, the two texts differ fundamentally. Not only do they offer competing definitions of basic terms, including South, North, and plantation; they also utilize opposing rhetorical strategies to shape their arguments. This second difference is apparent by glancing at the main title of each book. The defiant *I'll Take My Stand* lays bare a Manichean dilemma that demands the endorsement of one way of life and the condemnation of another. The articulation of the book's central opposition "Agrarian *versus* Industrial" thus encapsulates an argumentative structure built on absolute difference. In contrast, *Cuban Counterpoint* privileges the model of the counterpoint, a musical technique that layers two melodies over each other to create a more complex composition. Although Ortiz relies on oppositions to construct his arguments, he introduces elements that play against, but also with, each other in a mutually transformative process. As a result, he suggests the creative (as well as destructive) potential of conflict and contradiction, while the Twelve Southerners, in order to maintain the inflexible binaries that direct their project, must depend on silences, gaps, and other evasive maneuvers, which allow them to suppress or gloss over complexity.

Plantation as Paradise, Plantation as "Cyclopean Machine"

The lacunae in *I'll Take My Stand*, and the deliberateness with which they are employed, reveal themselves most conspicuously in the first and last essays of the volume, which define plantation culture through negation. Underscoring what it is *not* (modern, industrial, complicit with northern capitalism), both pieces express unwillingness to say what it *is*. In their collective opening statement, for example, the Twelve Southerners proclaim that agrarian society "does not stand in particular need of definition" (xlvi). In his closing essay, Stark Young goes a step further: not only does it not *need* to be defined, it simply *cannot* be defined. Referring specifically to the aristocratic culture of the antebellum era, Young argues: "It is a thing forever annoying to those who, from the outside of such traditions, wish to put them into reasonable terms, and it will never be understandable by those born in a different scheme of life" (350). Plantation culture thus remains perpetually inaccessible to the outsider who seeks understanding through logical reckoning or "reasonable terms." The effect of such negative argumentation is to imply inevitability and naturalness. As Michael Kreyling has asserted, "Like all dedicated elites, the Agrarians more or less manipulated the image of the problem their time and place embodied so that their solution seemed unavoidable" (5). The South they invoke is not, they declare, an ideological construct—that is, an imagined community—but rather a *natural* reality that can only be comprehended by those already in the know.[2]

Despite their reluctance, the Twelve Southerners finally must define agrarianism. They do so, on the one hand, by continuing to insist upon its naturalness and, on the other, by emphasizing two essential attributes: origins and order. At the most literal level, they contend that the cultural origins of the U.S. South lie in Europe, and that its order is agrarian, patriarchal, and, informally at least, aristocratic and even feudal (several of the essayists employ the term "squirearchy" to describe the non-hereditary nature of the plantocracy). In his contribution to the volume, for example, Allen Tate contrasts the historical roots of the U.S. North and South in this way: "If New England's break with Europe made her excessively interested in the European surface, the ignorance and simplicity of the South's independence of Europe, in the cultural sense, witness a fact of great significance. The South could be ignorant of Europe because it was Europe; that is to say, the South had taken root in a native soil" (172). Here, antebellum southern culture was the product of an effortless, even unconscious, transplanting of the values of the Old World to the New, where they grew in a different, yet still native, soil. Declaring the South to be the direct offspring of Europe, Tate reclaims as positive negative stereotypes of southern simplicity, which merely reflect the region's "natural" spontaneity. Furthermore, he suggests that New England's preoccupation with Europe is an *unnatural* consequence of an embittered colonialist mentality not experienced in the southern states.[3]

Like Tate, John Crowe Ransom asserts a singular connection between Europe and the U.S. South, affirming "a thesis which seems to have about as much cogency as generalizations usually have: The South is unique on this continent for having founded and defended a culture which was according to the European principles of culture" (3). He goes on to describe the order that emerges from these cultural origins: having rejected the "insatiable wanderlust" celebrated by northern hegemony, southern states nurture settled communities that tie them to ancient values and mores:

> In most societies man has adapted himself to environment with plenty of intelligence to secure easily his material necessities from the graceful bounty of nature. And then, ordinarily, ... he and nature seem to live on terms of mutual respect and amity, and his loving arts, religions, and philosophies come spontaneously into being: these are the blessings of peace. (7)

Here and elsewhere, Ransom signals his poet's lack of faith in scientific rationality and official historical discourse by using insistently tentative language, exemplified by his ironic introduction of "a thesis which seems to have about as much cogency as generalizations usually have." Subsequent descriptions similarly employ equivocating words such as "most," "ordinarily," and "seem," which cast doubt upon the literal, if not the symbolic, truth of his words. Initially, he does characterize the origins and order of the plantation in a relatively straightforward manner: as European and agrarian. Concrete definitions, however, bleed into abstract notions. The resulting image of a peaceable civilization that effortlessly generates organic and artistic bounty is explicitly utopian. Drawing together various connotations of the word "order," Ransom indicates that the traditional hierarchical *organization* of the plantation produces a profound spiritual and moral *orderliness*. Suppressing debates and dissent—most notably about slavery and its legacy—Ransom implies that the origins of this order must also be understood on two levels: in tangible terms, as

European; and in symbolic terms, as Edenic. Glossing over the murky complications of history, he embraces the elusive certainty of myth. Such strategic elusiveness, evident throughout *I'll Take My Stand*, seeks to avoid what Kreyling terms "the trap of definition," but ultimately traps the plantation in static binaries (16). When viewed through the lens of history, it is a site of unrecoverable loss; when formulated symbolically, it becomes an impossible paradise. Either way, it remains just out of reach.

While the Twelve Southerners structure their discourse through elision and evasion, Ortiz noisily draws attention to the gaps and silences in his text. He introduces the multi-chaptered second part of *Cuban Counterpoint* with a brief note clarifying that part 1, a shorter, more unified essay, "makes no attempt to exhaust the subject" of tobacco and sugar (97). The resulting incompleteness, although it will be partially remedied by the "supplementary chapters" that comprise part 2, is an unavoidable upshot of "the variety of factors that determine [sugar and tobacco, and] cause them to vary greatly in the course of their development; at times there are similarities that make them appear identical; at times the differences make them seem completely opposed" (97). This passage is one of many in which Ortiz deliberately questions the stability of the "amazing contrasts" between sugar and tobacco that he promises to reveal in the second paragraph of his book (3). The resulting disruption of an opposition he himself establishes reminds the reader of the book's title and the strategy of the counterpoint it implies, which we might in turn relate to the pendular swing and eccentric spiraling of the open word (described in this book's introduction), whose movements seek to evade the strictures of the plantation's binary logic.

Ortiz supplements the concept of the counterpoint with the neologism "transculturation," which is intended to convey "the highly varied phenomena that have come about in Cuba as a result of the extremely complex transmutations of culture that have taken place here, and without a knowledge of which it is impossible to understand the evolution of the Cuban folk" (98). Underscoring diversity and complexity yet again, Ortiz identifies "the Cuban folk" as his object of study. "El pueblo cubano" in the Spanish original (254), this phrase implies the inclusion of all social and economic groups on the island. Indeed, the author quickly lists over two-dozen specific ethnic groups that have contributed to Cuba's "evolution," making it immediately evident that the pueblo is heterogenous and evolving. Moreover, he accentuates the violent loss experienced by each of these groups, no matter where they come from or how they arrive: "all of its classes, races, and cultures, coming in by will or by force, have ... been torn from their places of origin, suffering the shock of this first uprooting and harsh transplanting" (100). Ortiz's portrayal of disparate peoples brutally uprooted and transplanted into an inhospitable new environment differs sharply from Tate's description of European culture thriving in the "native soil" of the U.S. South. Both writers employ metaphors of roots, but to different ends. Tate insists upon an effortless, culturally homogenous transplantation from which springs a new Eden. Ortiz, in contrast, stresses the pain produced by the thorny multiplicity that Tate and the other Twelve Southerners deliberately suppress, and so suggests the destructive potential of transculturation. Moreover, he deliberately calls attention to the unequal effects of such destruction. Europe, for example, is a "hurricane" that "shook the Indian peoples of Cuba, tearing up their institutions by the roots and destroying their lives" (99). Africans, in turn, are "the most uprooted of all" for having been forced into "conditions of mutilation and social amputation" even more severe than those of European and Native American peoples (102).

Yet, even as he points to its legacy of inequality and injustice, Ortiz insists upon the creative possibilities of transculturation, as when he describes successive groups of immigrants arriving "in sporadic waves or a continuous flow, always exerting an influence and being influenced in turn" (98) ["en oleadas esporádicas o en manaderos continuos, siempre fluyentes e influyentes" (255)]. Here, disorientation and loss are accompanied by a process of mutual transformation represented, tellingly, in marine terms: as each group arrives, "in sporadic waves or a continuous flow," it surges into and merges with others—as the Spanish text states, it is simultaneously *influyente* ("exerting an influence") and *fluyente*, or flowing and open to change ("being influenced"). By tapping into the aquatic imagery of an island imaginary unavailable to the Twelve Southerners, Ortiz is able to mitigate the rigidness of the root with the fluidity of the sea, which allows for movement without dismemberment. As we see here, and shall see again in future chapters, such interactions between landscape and seascape play an important role in shaping a sense of place inextricable from a discourse of island insularity that vacillates between rootedness and fluidity, nationalism and transnationalism, openness and reticence. As Elizabeth DeLoughrey observes in *Routes and Roots*, "the ocean's perpetual movement is radically decentering; it resists attempts to fix a locus of history" (21).

The counterpoint, transculturation, and aquatic imagery: all of these are used by Ortiz to illustrate the inexhaustible complexity that for him characterizes the *pueblo cubano*. Benítez Rojo argues that this insistence on complexity distinguishes Ortiz's project from those of other modern historians of the plantation who, reliant on rigid oppositions, "show the seams of their own arbitrariness, their own self-segregation, their own self-censorship. ... Furthermore, they construct themselves astutely within a 'coherent' and 'authentic' fable of legitimation which inserts them directly into the discourse of power, either to repeat its statements or to displace them" (*Repeating Island* 156). Benítez Rojo lists as examples several twentieth-century treatises on the Cuban sugar plantation, including Ramiro Guerra y Sánchez, *Azúcar y población en las Antillas* (1927); Raúl Cepero Bonilla, *Azúcar y abolición* (1959); Manuel Moreno Fraginals, *El ingenio* (1964); and Juan Pérez de la Riva, *El barracón* (1978), all of which profess positivist and/or Marxist ideologies. Given the scientific objectivity to which these texts aspire, it is ironic that Benítez Rojo's description applies equally to *I'll Take My Stand*. Despite their often aggressively anti-scientific rhetoric (and although they never mention sugar in Cuba), the Twelve Southerners likewise expose the "seams" of their arguments even as they endeavor to present a "fable of legitimation." Although Ortiz is similarly invested in countering northern hegemonies and offering alternative theories about the past, much of his originality derives from the obvious pleasure he takes in accentuating arbitrariness.

It is this same quality that explains the ongoing appeal of *Cuban Counterpoint* to contemporary critics, who revel in its evocatively poetic, radically decentered discourse (not to mention its piquant celebration of sensual pleasure). As Benítez Rojo indicates, these elements imbue Ortiz's text with "a possible proto-postmodernity" (156). Roberto González Echevarría likewise suggests that the author of *Cuban*

Counterpoint was ahead of his time due to his self-conscious recognition that "he was incapable of being an anthropologist studying himself," which led him to understand "what anthropology would only gradually later acknowledge: that as a discourse it was part of the modern and contemporary mythology from which it emerged" (215). Yet for the latter critic, Ortiz was not possessed of a proto-postmodern mindset. Rather, it was his embrace of literary language that allowed him to recognize the limitations of his scientific practice. Without the influence of imaginative writers like the Afro-Cuban poet, Nicolás Guillén, and the acclaimed Cuban novelist, Alejo Carpentier, Ortiz "would have been confined to writing solemn prose, a mixture of patriotism and academics" and, furthermore, may never have broken with the racism-inflected biological determinism that typified much of his earlier work (213).[4] Moreover, González Echevarría asserts that *Cuban Counterpoint* is "anchored undoubtedly by the imperative of identity" and, as such, "is an archetypal work of modernity" (216). González Echevarría's warning serves as a valuable reminder that, although he seeks more flexible models by which to do it, Ortiz's driving concern, like that of the Twelve Southerners, is to produce a viable imagined community, a coherent notion of national identity.

He develops this notion primarily through the titular counterpoint of sugar and tobacco. This counterpoint, in turn, entails a second one, that of the *ingenio*, or sugar mill, and the *vega*, or tobacco farm. Ortiz introduces this second pairing by tracing the development of the *ingenio* from the simple water- or horse-powered mills set up by early colonists, to the steam engine of the nineteenth century, and finally to the rise, in the twentieth century, of the enormous industrialized agricultural complexes he calls "super-centrals." Representing "a complete victory" for the machine, the super-centrals comprise "monstrous iron octopuses" and "Cyclopean machines" connected to "great tentacles of railways," which "gave rise to the occupation of virgin lands" and "have created the demand for more and more land to feed the insatiable voracity of the mills with canefields, pasture land, and woodland" (51–52). Here, the Cuban author exploits monstrous imagery that might be taken straight from a horror movie to convey the shocking conditions inflicted upon his island-nation by the super-central: rhetorically transforming the mill and the railroad into unappeasable monsters, he imagines the Cuban landscape as a virgin in distress, violated by a phalanx of one-eyed machines and crushed in the greedy embrace of an iron octopus.

At the same time, he employs the drier language of social science to enumerate the basic structural characteristics of this monstrous entity: "mechanization, latifundism, sharecropping, wage-fixing, supercapitalism, absentee landlordism, foreign ownership, corporate control, and imperialism" (51). This catalogue of the social and economic conditions created by the twentieth-century *ingenio*, which links the modern phenomenon of supercapitalism to the feudal system of latifundism, suggests another important difference between Ortiz and the Twelve Southerners. As his metaphors of voracious monstrosity evince, he depicts imperial—what the Twelve Southerners would term "northern"—aggression in consistently negative terms. Yet he rejects the feudalism that both he and the Twelve Southerners associate with the plantation in order to embrace a struggle for liberty explicitly linked to modernity:

On the heels of the mechanization came the great latifundism—that is, the use of a great extension of land by a single private owner. Latifundism was the economic basis of feudalism, and it has often reproduced this state. The struggle of the modern age has always been, particularly since the eighteenth century, to give man freedom and sever him from his bondage to the land, and for the freedom of the land, liberating it from the monopolistic tyranny of man. (52)

Paradoxically, then, the modern process of industrialization produces "great latifundism," a repetition of old feudal patterns that undermines the freedom for which modernity has fought. This freedom, significantly, is defined as freedom *from* and *of* the land. Ortiz resembles the Twelve Southerners in his advocacy for a non-exploitative relationship between humanity and nature. He identifies the potential for such a relationship, however, not with ancient customs but rather with the libratory projects of modernity. In contrast to the Twelve Southerners, who idealize an antebellum squirearchy, Ortiz rejects latifundism as fundamentally abusive toward human communities and nature alike.

It is in tobacco—whose fumes, as we shall see, have fired the revolutionary imagination of modernity—and in the *vega*, where tobacco is grown, that Ortiz finds a compelling, and compellingly *modern*, alternative to the super-central. And yet, perhaps contradictorily, both tobacco and the *vega* are intimately tied to premodern ways of life: just as smoking has its origins in the ancient rites and rituals of indigenous Americans, so the *vega* is rural and agricultural rather than urban and industrial in nature. Indeed, the *vega* seems to serve many of the same symbolic functions as the plantation does for the Twelve Southerners. A garden-like site, it fosters a mutually beneficial relationship between the natural world and the human communities that inhabit it. Those communities, moreover, esteem a patriarchal and familial work ethic: "The personal element always predominated in tobacco-growing, and there was a patriarchal, intimate quality about its work" (65) ["En el tabaco la producción ha sido más personal y su trabajo tuvo patriarcalismo y familiaridad" (214)]. As a result, the *veguero*, or owner of the *vega*, maintains "a strong attachment to his land, as in the rancher of old" (56). Like the plantation imagined in *I'll Take My Stand*, the *vega* is an Edenic space (in the sense of being both a garden and a utopian site) in which members of a patriarchal community work together, in harmony with each other and the land. Yet Ortiz insists that the *vega* shelters, not an aristocratic plantocracy, but rather a vital middle class that disdains the large landholdings so necessary to the *ingenio* (65).

In "Novel and History: Plot and Plantation," Sylvia Wynter demonstrates that the opposition represented by the binary between the *ingenio* and the *vega*—what she more generally defines as the antagonism between the industrialized plantation and the small cultivated "plot"—lies at the heart of the pan-Caribbean experience. Like Ortiz, Wynter links the plantation to the systematic exploitation of labor and land and the plot to a community-centered, profoundly ecological folk ethos. She also argues, "if the history of Caribbean society is that of a dual relation between plantation and plot, the two poles which originate in a single historical process, the ambivalence between the two has been and is the distinguishing characteristic of the Caribbean response" (99). Wynter's plot and Ortiz's *vega* are different in essential regards: most crucially, the former emerges from the African slave experience while the latter, with a few caveats, is associated with a Europeanized peasant culture. Yet the above quote brings to light two points that link the plot and the *vega* together. First, although it remains outside of the circuits of global capitalism, the plot (or *vega*) nevertheless derives from the same historical process that created the plantation. Despite what might be considered its traditional characteristics, it is not a throwback to premodern times but rather is as much a product of modernity as its more grandiose counterpart. Second, both writers understand the tense interactions between plantation and plot to be central to the formation of Caribbean identity. Indeed, it is notable that, unlike most of the competing pairs established in the pages of *Cuban Counterpoint*, such as tobacco and sugar, the *ingenio* and the *vega* are without fail represented in starkly oppositional terms. Locked in combat, they symbolize two distinct options for the nation.

The division between plantation and plot quietly infiltrates *I'll Take My Stand* as well. Although the Twelve Southerners never articulate the opposition, a silent (or silenced) friction emerges between those who, like Ransom or Young, praise the aristocratic planter as the maker of "Southern civilization" and others who, like Andrew Nelson Lytle, exalt the humble yeoman farmer as the guardian of the same. Since the late 1980s, revisionist critics have made much of this underlying strain, and have demonstrated that the members of the Twelve Southerners who were most con-cerned with formulating a practical economic program for reform eventually resolved it in favor of the small farm.[5] In other words, whether out of deep conviction or for pragmatic purposes, they ultimately became proponents of the plot (or, more accu-rately, another, even more blatantly Europeanized, iteration of the plot). Within the pages of the volume itself, though, the underlying ideological conflict is suppressed or ignored.[6] Like other gaps in the text, this one is caused by a determination to main-tain the book's dogged assertion, "Agrarian *versus* Industrial." Rather than consider the socioeconomic and cultural differences between subsistence farms and large-scale plantations, all agrarian spaces, when considered in the light of history, become equal victims of northern aggression. Likewise, when presented symbolically, they all are charged with positive value and linked to the Edenic plantation. Ironically, then, the plot-plantation binary is upheld in *Cuban Counterpoint*, a text that normally revels in undermining or complicating oppositions; and suppressed in *I'll Take My Stand*, a work that typically labors to maintain its rigid dichotomies.

Gender, Race, and the "Erotics" of the Plantation

Yet again, unlike the homogenous, harmonious plantation envisioned by the Twelve Southerners, the *vega* is permeated by the paradoxes of tobacco, which, according to Ortiz, has been praised as "a very holy thing" (57) and denigrated as "a thing for sav-ages" (57). Rooted in the communal, magical rites of ancient tribes, it helped spark revolutions in France as well as Cuba, where "the riots of the tobacco-growers and the Cuban middle class against the tobacco-monopoly holders might be considered the beginnings of national consciousness" (252). Holy and devilish, ancient and modern, peaceable and revolutionary, the opulently heterogenous nature of this intoxicating substance exemplifies Ortiz's penchant for employing subversively sensual imagery to distinguish the lush grounds of the *vega* from the mechanized site of the *ingenio*. Although generally more restrained, the Twelve Southerners employ similar strategies when they depict plantation society as leisurely, natural, and spontaneous. Both texts thus respond, implicitly or explicitly, to northern stereotypes of southern cultures as intellectually unsophisticated, less civilized, and more inclined to sexual excess. Confronting the cultural and economic marginalization of the South for which each respectively speaks, Ortiz and the Twelve Southerners demonstrate keen awareness of the degrading images circulated by the industrialized North that they defy; but, rather than refute these images, they reclaim them and, in the process, reconfigure the racialized and gendered language that helps to shape them. At the same time, however, they reassert problematic links between race, gender, and sexuality in context of the New World plantation.

This is true of *I'll Take My Stand*, despite the fact that its authors rarely pause to consider the contributions, literal or figurative, of white women or African Americans to the "bodily intense, inherently 'artistic,' and sensuously spiritual" plantation utopia they construct (Limón 19). Even the southern lady, central to so many nostalgic descriptions of the U.S. South, makes only occasional appearances, usually as the staid matriarch rather than the vivacious belle, and invariably as a peripheral character.[7] Although the volume does not ignore slavery and race entirely, it acknowledges African Americans only so as to reconcile them with its idealized vision of the plantation. Ransom, for example, asserts: "Slavery was a feature monstrous enough in theory, but, more often than not, humane in practice; and it is impossible to believe that its abolition alone could have effected any great revolution in society" (14). This is the essay's only mention of slavery, and Ransom's language, once again reliant on obfuscating qualifiers, typifies the oblique rhetoric employed throughout. Even Frank Lawrence Owsley, whose essay engages ugly stereotypes of Africans as cannibalistic savages, nevertheless attempts to circumvent the ethical dilemmas of slavery by asserting that the institution "was no essential part of the agrarian civilization of the South" and "was practically forced upon the country by England" (76).

Paradoxically, the only essay in the collection devoted to examining the place of blacks in the (postbellum) South also most vividly dramatizes this elusive language. "The Briar Patch," by Robert Penn Warren, offers an admittedly tepid defense of racial segregation—which its author later publicly disavowed—and eschews the racial vitriol of Owsley.[8] Warren does not pit blacks against whites or justify slavery by invoking African "barbarism;" nor does he interrogate white racism or explore the moral evil of slavery. Rather, he attempts to tell a history of slavery in the United States that deflects questions of victimization, violence, and guilt. This effort is apparent not only in the essay's overarching argument but also in its language, including its frequent recourse to conditional verb forms and the passive voice. For example, the opening sentence declares: "In 1619 twenty negroes were landed at the colony of Jamestown and sold into slavery" (246). Employing the passive voice, Warren erases responsibility. The African men and women in question simply "were landed ... and sold." Indeed, the only active agent in this scenario is the ship, ironically named the *Jesus*, which "touched history significantly but only for a moment" before "she disappeared forever into the obscurity from which she had brought those first negroes to American shores" (246). Warren thus ascribes the origins of slavery in the United States to a ghostly ship that unloads its human cargo before vanishing "forever" over the far horizon of the sea. Similar symbolic and syntactic displacements mark the entirety of the essay, which ultimately marginalizes the question of race altogether: efforts to end racism "are only palliatives that distract the South's attention from the main issue"—that is, the threat of industrialism and modernity (264). Although his approach to the race question is more progressive and more firmly rooted in history than those of his fellow contributors, Warren's conclusion fails to depart from the central thesis of *I'll Take My Stand.*[9] The institution of slavery is too closely associated with "the Southern way of life" to be forthrightly condemned. Moreover, both Ransom's assertion that abolition was incapable of producing "any great revolution" and Warren's dismissal of civil rights reveal an undemocratic and anti-revolutionary bias that contrasts sharply with Ortiz.

If the Twelve Southerners marginalize flesh-and-blood African Americans, they nevertheless symbolically darken certain aspects of southern society while lightening others. They also invariably masculinize what they lighten and, inversely, almost always feminize what they darken (from this perspective, the otherwise conventional feminization of the slave ship *Jesus* may take on unexpected significance). Thus their often-subtle use of racialized language cannot be separated from their figurative representations of gender. Such is the case in John Donald Wade's "The Life and Death of Cousin Lucius," a fictional biographical sketch that briskly follows its title character from childhood to old age and death. Early on, two brief images of place serve to delineate the maturation of this character, presented as one of the last genteel patriarchs of the Old South. The first scene depicts a young Lucius during the Civil War, observing his mother in her garden as she supervises "a number of negro women who were gathering huge basketfuls of vegetables" (269). The second imagines him as a young man studying "Vergil and Horace and other Romans" on a campus covered with "countless great oaks, lightened by countless white columns" (272). Both of these moments delineate spaces in which culture and nature interact in harmony, but their racial and gendered meanings vary. Cultivated by female slaves who labor under the direction of their white mistress, the maternal garden of Lucius' boyhood is a fertile site exemplifying the hierarchal, peaceable coexistence of black and white as well as wild and domestic. The patriarchal grounds of his intellectual apprenticeship, in turn, are studded with great oaks, virile symbols of nature brought under control and "lightened" by the civilizing presence of the equally virile columns. Both the garden and the campus demonstrate a hallmark of the plantation community as imagined by the Twelve Southerners: the orderly subordination of nature to culture. However, the former, visually dominated by dark female bodies at work, remains a lush but threatening childhood recollection: it is tellingly linked to Lucius's memories of the U.S. Civil War, in which the absence of his father and the death of an uncle loom large. The garden's femininity, while capable of producing great bounty, is further darkened by the lack of male presence. In contrast, young (white) men, engaged in intellectual rather than physical labor, populate the illuminated environs of the college. Wade lightens the intrinsically masculine space of the campus—metonymically, the space of transplanted European culture—on a number of levels: aesthetically, through the architectural feature of the Romanesque columns; racially, because its students hail from various strata of the white plantation squirearchy; and intellectually, by placing the Western canon at its philosophical core.

The pattern apparent in these images pervades the imaginary of *I'll Take My Stand:* spaces dominated by (domesticated) nature are darkened and/or feminized, while spaces representative of culture are lightened and masculinized; but, within the confines of a romanticized South, they are rarely if ever in conflict. To the contrary, their relationship is hierarchical, harmonious, and, above all, productive. Good husbandry on the part of masculine culture fosters an idealized relationship with feminine nature. The soil submits willingly to caring cultivation, and produces abundant crops so that human settlements might prosper.

This model of voluntary compliance with patriarchal rule contrasts vividly with what Ransom calls the "insatiable wanderlust" of a U.S. North that takes the feminine land by force, brutally exploits her resources, and then abandons her in its endless pursuit of more fertile ground (7). Once again, another salient comparison with Ortiz emerges, for the North's "insatiable wanderlust" directly recalls the "insatiable voracity" of the *ingenio*, which similarly devours virgin territories. For the Twelve Southerners, however, the plantation is the defense against, rather than the catalyst for, such activity. If, as Pike has suggested, the North envisioned the South as "one 'great brothel,' " the Twelve Southerners reverse the terms of the argument by conflating northern wanderlust with lust and, conversely, portraying the U.S. South as a gentlemen who woos rather than rapes, and nurtures rather than abuses (Pike 55). As a result of their fixation on expansionist projects, northern progressives are little more than "men in a state of arrested adolescence" (5) whereas southerners (like Europeans) have "founded and defended" a unique culture (7). Far from exemplifying a weak, effeminate domesticity, the South's settled nature represents an identity at once robustly masculine and powerfully erotic.

Ransom and the others thus embrace a sensuous vision of plantation culture by inverting stereotypes to suggest that the frontier machismo of the North is sexually stunted and even perverse. The South may be more static, but it is for this very reason more profoundly masculine. At the same time, however, the essays in *I'll Take My Stand* studiously avoid licentious stereotypes—Pike's "mythically lustful black" and "sexually uninhibited white upper-class males" (55)—in order to underscore what might be called a chaste eroticism. Avoiding overtly sexual themes, they bind erotic activity to the (re)productive potential of matrimony. More frequently, they eschew even metaphorical sexuality in order to emphasize the aesthetic and unhurried nature of southern living. Tate, for example, claims that the U.S. South "was sensuous because it lived close to a natural scene of great variety and interest" (172), while Donald Davidson asserts the inherent creativity of an agrarian lifestyle "congenial to the arts which are among the things we esteem as more than material blessings" (59). It is, however, Stark Young's closing essay that most openly celebrates the opulent excesses of the squirearchy, which are juxtaposed with the "degradation" of northern piety (337): "The aristocratic implied with us a certain long responsibility for others; a habit of domination; a certain arbitrariness; certain ideas of personal honor with varying degrees of ethics, *amour propre*, and the fantastic. And it implied the possession of no little leisure. Whether that was a good system or not is debatable" (350). Gathering under a single rubric a variety of not-always-compatible characteristics made more tenuous by his refusal to judge the merits of the system, Young evokes exotic notions of otherness to suggest a romantic world of chivalry and violence, hot-blooded rivalries and baroque revelries. At the same time, he portrays a vigorously masculine society that thrives on shows of strength and domination, pride of self, and bold trips of the imagination. In this passage and elsewhere, Young's essay, more than any other in *I'll Take My Stand*, approaches the counterpoint's strategic ambiguity.

It is true that Young narrowly ascribes "Southern characteristics" to "a life founded on land and the ownership of slaves" (336); and that, like his fellow writers, he remains silent regarding the ethical questions surrounding slavery and race. Nevertheless, unwittingly or not, he employs racialized language that suggestively darkens southern culture. On the one hand, he argues that the "family traditions" of the U.S. South endure, in part, due to the racial and ethnic "purity" of the plantocracy, which "came from the British Isles, with Scotch clannishness plentiful enough, and remained unmixed with other bloods, as did the French and Spanish of Louisiana, for a long time" (347). On the other hand, his cryptic reference to "the French and Spanish of Louisiana," punctuated by the phrase "for a long time," implicitly acknowledges a tradition of intermixing not only amongst European "bloods" but also between them and their slaves. This suggestion of miscegenation is amplified by his previous comparisons of the solidly British plantocracy to a variety of "dark" European southerners, including Jews (336), Italians (342), and Russians (342). Most striking, however, is his association of the plantocracy with the Spanish. Attempting to define the cultural pride expressed by southerners, he contends "it is not pride in the boasting sense" but "a sort of mad self-respect and honor complex, such as the Spanish traditionally have, though as a rule not so strong, foolish, and magnificent" (351–52). Evoking the exotic Spanish other, Young simultaneously invites comparison and asserts difference as he describes a foreign excess that borders on mental imbalance: southerners, like the Spanish (but less so) suffer from a "complex" that makes them marvelously "mad" and "foolish." Young's evocations of cultural stereotypes, at once simplistic and complex, subtly threaten to collapse the binary between dark and light, if not black and white, and intimate that the agrarian South might better oppose the industrial North by creating alliances with other Souths, whether they be located in southern Europe or, perhaps, south of the U.S. border.

But if Young opens the door, however narrowly, to the possibility of a cultural alliance between the Anglo and Spanish Souths, Ortiz decisively slams it shut again by emphatically opposing the Cuban *vega* to the tobacco plantations of the United States: "Tobacco, instead of encouraging the small farm or holding in Virginia, gave rise to a growing appetite for land, and the planters who cultivated tobacco with slave labor kept pushing westward in search of new lands, thus increasing the territory and pushing back the frontiers" (60). Contrary to the Twelve Southerners, Ortiz associates Virginia tobacco and, by extension, the U.S. plantation system in general, not with agrarianism but with industrialism; and not with settledness but with wanderlust. That is to say, he makes no distinction between the U.S. North and the U.S. South. Both regions are industrial and imperialistic and, whether for regional gain or broader national interests, both have historically acted as aggressors toward their southern neighbors. Underscoring the power imbalance between his South and the U.S. South, Ortiz contends that the plantation so idealized in *I'll Take My Stand* does not resemble the garden-like *vega* so much as the monstrous super-central.

A second distinction between Young and Ortiz is that the former eroticizes the U.S. South in an abstract sense only. Carnal relations play no role in his essay and the only mention of women involves his rather prudish disapproval of ladies who have, he suggests, prostituted themselves and tarnished their family names by appearing in "advertisements confessing their addiction to some face cream or some mattress" (332). Ortiz, in contrast, constructs a vision of Cuba that is not only eroticized but also unmistakably sexualized. He does this through the personified figures of tobacco and sugar, "Don Tobacco" and "Doña Sugar," who he introduces in the book's opening paragraphs. Although he initially posits them as adversaries, the dynamic that develops between them never mimics the rigid dichotomy maintained between the *vega* and the *ingenio*. Rather, it echoes the movement of the counterpoint, or the complex dance of transculturation: sugar and tobacco, representing different yet related facets of Cuban culture, interact with each other, as well as the institution of the *ingenio*, in ways that change through time and space. As Fernando Coronil insightfully observes: "Their qualities are contradictory and multiple, carrying with them the marks of their shifting histories. In an encompassment of diverse attributes typical of the baroque, tobacco and sugar incorporate multiple meanings and transform their identities" (xxii). Firmly embedded in history, yet also highly aesthetic and erotic, Doña Sugar and Don Tobacco make culture even as they are made by it, in a delicate, sensual give-and-take.

Although they are "all contrast" (6), they share much in common, a paradox revealed through the racialized language used to describe them:

> Tobacco is dark, ranging from black to mulatto; sugar is light, ranging from mulatto to white. Tobacco does not change its color; it is born dark and dies the color of its race. Sugar changes its coloring; it is born brown and whitens itself; at first it is a syrupy mulatto [who, being dark, abandons itself to] the common taste; then it [bleaches and refines itself] until it can pass for white, travel all over the world, reach all mouths, and [be paid more] . . . . (9)

> El tabaco es oscuro, de negro a mulato; el azúcar es clara, de mulata a blanca. El tabaco no cambia de color, nace moreno y muere con el color de su raza. El azúcar cambia de coloración, nace parda y se blanquea; es almibarada mulata que siendo prieta se abandona a la sabrosura popular y luego se encascarilla y refina para pasar por blanca, correr por todo el mundo, llegar a todas las bocas y ser pagada mejor . . . . (143)

What is most remarkable about this passage is not the basic distinction of tobacco as "dark" and sugar as "light," but rather the lack of racial purity ascribed to both, and their differing reactions to this. Don Tobacco is proud of his darkness, while Doña Sugar artificially lightens herself to appeal to universal ("northern") tastes. This difference allows Ortiz to develop the national allegorical dimension of his text. Tobacco, the elite child of the *vega* and symbol of an independent national identity, celebrates his color. Sugar, churned out by the exploitative *ingenio*, lightens herself into an object of desire in order to attract the attention, and pocketbooks, of rich northern suitors. Both are Cuban, as their mulatto colors show; but tobacco is natural and native, and sugar is imitative of all that is foreign.

Ortiz's racialization of tobacco and sugar cannot be separated from his gendering of them, which adheres to traditional notions of sexual difference that also advance the text's national allegory: the defiant, virile maleness of tobacco embodies the authentic Cuban character while the victimized, but also imprudently wanton and opportunistic, femaleness of sugar represents the weak, exploited body politic.[10] Indeed, while his presentation of race differs significantly from the Twelve Southerners, Ortiz's delineation of gender is quite similar. Like the former, and to an even greater extent, he relies on images of debased womanhood to describe the dangerous effects of industrial capitalism: Young may imply that southern belles are figuratively prostituting their good names by hocking creams and bedding, but Ortiz goes a step further. His sugar may be exploited, but she is eager to be exploited, first as a sugary sweet mulatta "abandoning" herself to the common taste, and then as a bleached-out globetrotter whose goal is to "reach all mouths" and "be paid more." Indeed, Doña Sugar comes dangerously close to embodying uglier stereotypes of mixed-race women as sexually insatiable and complicit in their own abuse, stereotypes manifested, with different variations, throughout the postslavery Americas. As Vera Kutzinski reminds us with reference to Cuba, "the iconic mulata ... is a symbolic container for all the tricky questions about how race, gender, and sexuality inflect the power relations that obtain in colonial and postcolonial Cuba" (7).[11]

The racially inflected misogyny of Ortiz's imagery is clear, but it is important to recognize that, when it is linked to an "authentic" Cuban identity, Ortiz celebrates the erotic nature of sugar and, especially, tobacco. For example, he playfully compares tobacco's coloring, which comprises seventy-eight variations, to Cuba's female beauties, who "cannot be simply reduced to blondes and brunettes" (22). At the same time that he revels in the amazing variety of Cuban tobacco and women, however, he decries foreign "tobaccologists" and "race theorists" who, dismissive of this bountiful diversity, foist artificial blends onto an unsuspecting public:

> It is not to be wondered at that there are "tobaccologists" ... who, for the sake of defending the tobacco interests of their own countries, have created varieties, blends, names, and brands as absurd and artificial as the imaginary races invented by the race theorists of the present. And the races of tobacco, as well as its mixtures and adulterations, are so on the increase at present that outside of Cuba there are hybrid cigars, of unconfessable ancestry [*mestizajes inconfesables*], some not even of tobacco; and the Havana cigar of good family has always to be on the alert for innumerable and hateful bastards who would usurp the legitimacy of his good name [*nombre puro*]. (23)

> No es de extrañar, pues, que por esos mundos haya tabacólogos ... quienes, so pretexto de defender las condiciones del tabaco según los egoísmos y banderas de sus países, han creado razas, ligas, nombres y marcas de vitolas tan fantásticas y artificiales como las mitológicas razas inventadas por los racismos del día. Y ahora van de tal modo en aumento las razas de tabaco, así como sus mezclas y sus adulteraciones, que ya fuera de Cuba hay cigarros híbridos, de mestizajes inconfesables y hasta sin tabaco alguno, y el habano de abolengo tiene que renegar continuamente de las infinitas y abominables bastardías que le usurpan la legitimidad de su nombre puro. (161–62)

Once again, Ortiz portrays Cuban tobacco as natural, racially mixed, and proud. Here, however, it is not sugar, with its dubious external alliances, but the foreigner himself, masquerading as an expert, who represents a dangerous, degraded artificiality. Playfully exploiting the double meaning of *puro* ("pure" and "cigar"), he accuses outsiders of usurping the *puro*'s "pure" name, while he usurps racist discourse by refusing to define purity in terms of genealogy or "blood" (or, for that matter, of sexual chastity). Rather, he argues that true purity emerges from cultural and economic practices that reflect the values of the *vega*. Mulatto Cuba, he implies, must protect its honor and decency—that is to say, its *purity*—from foreign interests who hypocritically define themselves as experts on purity while spewing out synthetic monstrosities that struggle to hide their "unconfessable ancestry." Race, gender, erotic play, cultural production, and sexual reproduction thus become hopelessly intertwined.

Within this context, Ortiz's comparison of multihued tobacco and women, although hardly qualifying as a subversive feminist trope, does threaten to overflow the boundaries of the gender binary established in the opening pages of his text. Elsewhere, his physical descriptions of tobacco boldly, even bawdily, illustrate its masculine strength. Its leaves are described as "hairy" and "weathered and tanned by the sun" (150) and when smoked as a cigar or in a pipe it is "a boastful and swaggering thing, like an oath of defiance springing erect from the lips" (15). Not surprisingly, given the sexual urgency of the previous description, "virile tobacco calls for delicate hands, those of women or those having a woman's soft touch" (84). At the same time, as we have seen, he compares its seventy-eight shades to a lineup of women being carefully appraised by male admirers. And although it "is born a gentleman" (43) its plants are "like lovely ladies" (28). Each of these images depicts tobacco as a body caught up in desire that is, to a certain extent, predictable: "male" tobacco is most often portrayed as a sexual aggressor and "female" tobacco as a seductive, but passive, object of beauty. Yet, by shifting between the male and female, Ortiz destabilizes tobacco's masculine identity and, at times, seems to celebrate the resulting fluidity as illustrative of tobacco's deeply erotic nature—after all, the "delicate hands" tobacco craves may belong to a woman, but they may also belong to a man with a "woman's soft touch."

Ortiz quickly abandons any suggestion of playful gender ambiguity, however, when the patriarchal order of the *vega* is threatened by foreign industrialism. Implicitly censuring tobacco's ability to move between male and female poles of identity, he complains that it has been emasculated by the popularity of cigarettes, which are "the babies of cigars, of embryonic masculinity, all wrapped in rice paper, and with gold tips, and even perfumed, sweetened, and perverted like effeminate youths" (15). Unadulterated, tobacco (especially the superior varieties from Cuba) exudes sensuality and attracts desire, in both masculine and feminine guises. When foreign capitalist interests debase the pure *puro* with the prissy cigarette, however, it turns into an "effeminate youth," an undeveloped embryo, or a castrated "eunuch" (77). The erotic nature and productive capacity of tobacco is thus directly linked to its proximity to the *vega*. Sugar's proximity to the *ingenio* transforms her from a sweet, if slightly slutty, mulatta to an artificially whitened whore; likewise, as tobacco moves away from the *vega*, his legendary virility disappears in a puff of smoke.

Conclusion

Ortiz's argument that the super-central degrades the erotic impulses of both sugar and tobacco approximates the Twelve Southerners' insistence that the North's imperialist wanderlust leaves it in "a state of arrested adolescence" (5). But while both *Cuban Counterpoint* and *I'll Take My Stand* counter sterile images of northern modernities with richly eroticized visions of their own southern cultures, Ortiz embraces an eroticism that is not only productive but also excessive. At the end of part 1, Ortiz concludes sugar and tobacco's allegorical debate by declaring that what appeared to be enmity was in fact "just a bit of friendly bickering, which should end, like the fairy tales, [... with t]he marriage of tobacco and sugar, and the birth of alcohol, conceived of the Unholy Ghost, the devil, who is the father of tobacco, in the sweet womb of wanton sugar. The Cuban Trinity: tobacco, sugar, and alcohol" (93). Thus the story of tobacco and sugar concludes with a familiar fairy tale marriage and the promise of a child to come. However, as Gustavo Pérez Firmat has observed, "the Holy Spirit has been replaced by unholy spirits" and "the birth of alcohol parodies the doctrine of the Virgin Birth" (64). Stark Young may intimate that ethically questionable behavior, self-love, and "no little leisure" are integral to the southern culture he lauds, but he hedges his bets with his use of the past tense and the coy assertion, "whether that was a good system or not is debatable" (350). In contrast, Ortiz subverts the conservative nature of the fairy tale—not to mention of religious orthodoxies—in order to praise impurity, heresy, intoxication, and revolution, and to propose these as the foundation upon which to build the *future* Cuban family.

Despite the sensuous nature of the U.S. South they imagine, the Twelve Southerners strive to present the plantation as a site of origins and an unchanging paradise. As a result, their vision is forever backward glancing.[12] Ortiz, in contrast, rejects static, exclusionary visions of paradise, never more explicitly than when he proclaims, "mankind is coming to the conclusion that good and evil are to be found in all plants, and that if there was a Paradise it included the whole world, which must be completely made over if we are to find and enjoy it once more" (202). Here, utopia lies not in the recovery of the past or a repetitive return to origins but rather in the innovations of the future and a remaking that multiplies rather than excludes. Unlike the Twelve Southerners, Ortiz consistently approaches the legacies of modernity from a nuanced perspective. His striking proposal of an all-inclusive global Eden, however, lives in tension with his nationalist construction of the patriarchal, dominantly Creole-European *vega* as an idealized site of Cuban culture.

Both Ortiz and the Twelve Southerners articulate radical critiques of industrial capitalism, which are grounded in nationalist or regionalist projects that express themselves through eroticized language. Like *I'll Take My Stand*, which concludes with Stark Young's paean to the "mad self-respect" of the southern aristocracy, *Cuban Counterpoint* challenges middle-class piety and the restrictions of the modern industrial order by extolling pleasure and leisure while exhibiting a general disdain for the efficiency of machines and markets. At the same time both texts locate their sensuous, unhurried imagined communities in an explicitly patriarchal agrarian space that—be it the plot-like *vega* or the grand antebellum estate—inevitably, ironically links earthly paradise to hierarchies of gender and race that cannot be separated from the complex, often horrific, legacies of the New World plantation.

Race and Romance in the Americas

Iphigenia and *The Sheltered Life*

Part 1 of Teresa de la Parra's novel, *Ifigenia*, or *Iphigenia* (1924), is a long letter written by María Eugenia Alonso to a former classmate and friend, Cristina de Iturbe. Although María Eugenia, sixteen years old and recently orphaned, is Venezuelan, she has been living in Caracas for only a few weeks after spending ten years of her childhood in Europe with her father. She writes in the bedroom that her grandmother has prepared for her, from which she has a view of the house's enclosed patio and gardens. As its title, "A Very Long Letter Wherein Things Are Told As They Are in Novels," indicates, the letter is novelistic in form and content. It is modeled, María Eugenia explains, after the fairy tales and romantic novels that she and Cristina read in boarding school. The young author emphasizes not only the structural parallels between her letter and those novels but also the similarities between herself and their heroines. Like many an enchanted princess, she is imprisoned—although not by an evil sorceress, but rather by boredom and the four walls of her grandmother's house. She has also, like the traditional female protagonist, suffered betrayal at the hands of her family, in particular her father's brother, Eduardo, who has stolen her rightful inheritance. Finally, as she is not too shy to point out, she is sophisticated, intelligent, and beautiful. In short, she is an ideal heroine: "I no longer consider myself a secondary character at all … and I have, moreover, the presumption to believe that I am worth a million times more than all the heroines in the novels we used to read" (10). María Eugenia thus does more than assert a likeness between herself and the fairy tale characters she invokes; she proclaims a difference—her own superiority—and, in doing so, claims the power to shape her life story through the written word. Her writing, however, remains a hidden activity: she pens the letter to Cristina and, later, a series of journal entries, only in the protected solitude of her bedroom.

The first chapter of *The Sheltered Life* (1932), by Ellen Glasgow, begins with its protagonist, Jenny Blair Archbald, sitting in the dining room of her grandfather's house in the fictional town of Queenborough, Virginia. She reclines at a French window that overlooks the garden and reads Louisa May Alcott's *Little Women*. Unlike María Eugenia, Jenny Blair does not compare herself to this novel's heroines. To the contrary, she judges the March girls to be "pokey old things" and only forces herself to read because her grandfather is paying her a penny a page. After concluding that "nothing happened" in the lives of the March girls, she proclaims: "Mamma may call the Marches lots of fun, but I'm different. I'm different" (3). This proclamation of difference leads to an epiphany she only vaguely comprehends, but which, the third-person narrator tells us, holds profound significance because the protagonist is "discovering her hidden self": "But all she knew was 'I am this and not that.' All she felt was the sudden glory, the singing rhythm of life. Softly, without knowing why, she began crooning, 'I'm alive, alive, alive, and I'm Jenny Blair Archbald'" (3). Jenny Blair's response to this moment of discovery is to sing a spontaneous, self-affirming refrain. However, just as María Eugenia hides her writing, so Jenny Blair does not share her song with anyone; instead, she guards it "jealously" and invokes it only when she is alone (4).

In these opening scenes, the protagonists sit alone, inside an old family house, behind a window that frames a garden and offers a glimpse of the outside world. Although they long to explore that world, they are forbidden from leaving the domestic space. Instead, they interact with what might be termed conventional female literature. Rather than passively consuming these stories, however, they react to them by producing their own texts: María Eugenia rewrites fairy tales with herself in the role of heroine, while Jenny Blair rejects the heroine altogether and affirms her uniqueness in song. Each girl thus initiates a creative and critical process through which she imagines herself freed from the traditional "female plot," and full of potential for growth and adventure. This potential, however, is doomed to remain unfulfilled. As she matures, she becomes increasingly aware of a contradiction between societal demands and her own desire for freedom and growth. When this happens, she retreats into romantic fantasies and channels her once-defiant creative energy into the task of dissimulating to family and friends, especially as her fantasies develop into a dangerously real flirtation with a married man.

The downward trajectories of María Eugenia and Jenny Blair are all too familiar to readers of nineteenth- and twentieth-century fictions about women; and, as their opening allusions to conventional women's literature illustrate, the authors of *Iphigenia* and *The Sheltered Life* self-consciously participate in a wider tradition, which some have called the "failed female *Bildungsroman*" and others the "female tale of development."[1] Like their counterparts in fictions written by women across the Americas, such as Edna Pontillier in Kate Chopin's "The Awakening" (U.S., 1899) or the anonymous narrator of María Luisa Bombal's *La última niebla* (*The House of Mist*, Chile, 1935), María Eugenia and Jenny Blair learn that they cannot be accepted as members of their societies and also be free or whole in the ways that they wish.[2] Thus, while their protagonists proclaim their individuality, Parra and Glasgow link their stories to those of other modern women, real and literary. By carefully delineating political, socioeconomic, and historical context, however, the authors also underscore the cultural specificity of their stories. In doing so, they reveal how the apparently individualistic strivings of the young women represented are inseparable from, and profoundly shaped by, the legacy of the plantation, as it manifested itself, respectively, in Venezuela and Virginia.[3] Moreover, like the Twelve Southerners and Ortiz, they understand this legacy to be fundamental to arguments about national and regional identity, and place their protagonists at the center of these.

"Dethroned Scions": Daughters of the Plantation Past

Parra, née Ana Teresa Parra Santoja, was born in Paris in 1889, to Venezuelan parents. She published her first novel, *Iphigenia*, in 1924, to wide acclaim in Europe as well as Venezuela and Colombia. Although she maintained a vast written correspondence with family, friends, and critics, Parra would only complete one more novel before succumbing to tuberculosis at the age of forty-seven. In contrast, Glasgow, born in 1873 in Richmond, Virginia, was already well known when, in 1932, she published *The Sheltered Life*, which was reviewed in almost fifty North American newspapers and journals.[4] A prolific writer, she produced twenty novels, as well as short stories, poems, essays, and an autobiography, in a career that began in 1897 and ended just a few years before her death in 1945. Despite this difference, Parra and Glasgow were both popular authors whose work received extensive, if decidedly mixed, critical attention during their lifetime, and has continued to inspire passionate debates to the present day.

Many of these debates center on how they depict political, economic, social, and cultural shifts that took place during their lifetimes. In the Venezuelan context, Parra grapples with substantial changes brought about during the long dictatorship of Juan Vicente Gómez, which extended from 1908 to 1935, a period that also witnessed the establishment of Venezuela's oil industry. Among other things, her writing betrays an intense preoccupation with social instability and the breakdown of traditional class and racial hierarchies, results of the increased economic and social mobility facilitated by the modernization of the nation's economy. For her part, Glasgow, born less then ten years after the end of the Civil War, was apprehensive of the volatility that affected all strata of U.S. southern society in the wake of Reconstruction. Like the Twelve Southerners, whose *I'll Take My Stand* was published just two years before *The Sheltered Life*, she was worried by the increasing influence of economic models imported from the U.S. North, but the deepening racial prejudice of the post-Reconstruction era also troubled her.

Both writers were sensitive to the fact that these upheavals, imposed by the processes of modernity, impacted people from all classes, races, and ethnic groups. Yet, as the novels under consideration make clear, they were also profoundly influenced by their personal backgrounds and experiences. On the one hand, Parra and Glasgow were unconventional, modern women by the standards of their day. Unmarried and childless, they participated in prominent intellectual and artistic communities and frequently critiqued the patriarchal traditions of the cultures into which they had been born.[5] On the other hand, they remained proudly aware of family histories that connected them to the exceptionally deep-rooted landowning aristocracies of their respective societies: Glasgow's mother, Anne Gholson Glasgow, was a descendant of the illustrious landed gentry of Tidewater, Virginia. Parra's family identified itself as *mantuano*, a title claimed by the Caracas aristocracy who traced their ancestry to the Spanish conquistadors and leaders of the Independence movement and their wealth to the cultivation of the land.

Glasgow and Parra thus grew up hearing stories that lauded the glorious deeds of their ancestors and, like their protagonists, grappled with the ways in which their familial ties influenced their lives and work. Although in *The Sheltered Life* and *Iphigenia* it is critical ambivalence, rather than pride or collusion, that dominates, it is nevertheless important to recognize that both women at times demonstrated a conservatism in concordance with values inherited from their families. For example, Parra frequently expressed fears about the unstable social and economic situation in her country, and lent public, if lukewarm, support to Gómez's dictatorship.[6] Glasgow, in turn, shared some of the viewpoints evinced by the Twelve Southerners in *I'll Take My Stand;* and, despite the fact that Allen Tate had described her, in a letter to Donald Davidson, as one of "the worst novelists in the world" (Fain and Young 872), cultivated personal and professional relationships with Tate, Davidson, and others during the period in which she was writing *The Sheltered Life.*[7]

Given Glasgow and Parra's intimate and troubled connections to the plantocracies of their respective nations, it is hardly surprising that the plantation remains a powerful symbolic force in the lives of their protagonists, who, as daughters of the proprietary elite, remain under the sway of the past by virtue of a genealogical continuity established, first and foremost, by the strong presence of María Eugenia's grandmother in *Iphigenia* and Jenny Blair's grandfather in *The Sheltered Life.* Both grandparents are products of the nineteenth century, and their defiantly anti-modern worldviews dominate the households in which they live. The idealized order of the previous century is thus preserved within the tightly controlled domestic spaces depicted in the novels' opening scenes, as well as by the older generation's carefully manipulated family histories. The commanding figure of the grandparent, as a synecdoche for the larger community, seeks to harness the protagonist's creative, or procreative, powers, in order to reproduce the old order.

Despite its symbolic significance, however, the physical site of the plantation is largely absent from these novels, which emphasize industrializing urban settings.[8] The first chapter of *The Sheltered Life*, for example, opens by invoking "a breath of decay from the new chemical factory" that invades the once genteel neighborhood where the Archbalds live (5). Similarly, María Eugenia's initial glimpse of Caracas is dominated by the hustle-and-bustle of a dock filled with laborers loaded down with goods from Europe.

In the rare moments they do exit the city, these novels represent the plantation as a refuge from the hazards of modern urban life but, at the same time, as a static manifestation of the past. In *The Sheltered Life*, for example, the family plantation— whose name, Stillwater, underscores its stagnation—appears only in the ambivalent memories of Jenny Blair's eighty-three year old grandfather, General Archbald. On the one hand, as a poetically inclined boy, he was tormented there by his grandfather, who labeled him a "milksop" and gleefully smeared him with the blood of his first hunting kill. On the other hand, like the Twelve Southerners, he wistfully marvels at the plantation's rootedness: "No other way of living had ever seemed to him so deeply rooted in the spirit of place, in an established feeling for ... the whole fresh or salty range of experience" (104). Unlike *The Sheltered Life*, *Iphigenia* does return to the present-day plantation. Halfway through the novel, María Eugenia's grandmother whisks her to the family's hacienda, of which the protagonist proclaims, it "has received me with great affection and great melancholy. It undoubtedly knows that I am the last child of its ancient owners, and it shelters me with veneration and pity like one of those poor dethroned scions who vegetate sorrowfully in some corner of their lost domain" (156). Now a source of debt rather than wealth, the hacienda becomes for the narrator a potent symbol of familial decline and personal loss, and she depicts it as a lush, but unproductive, garden whose old sugar mill lies in ruin (159).

In both novels, then, the plantation functions as a symbol of an irretrievable order. In *The Sheltered Life*, however, it is virile and masculine. No place for a "milksop," it encompasses a "fresh or salty range of experience" that would be (at least in its salty form) forbidden to proper young ladies. In *Iphigenia*, in contrast, Parra feminizes the hacienda by turning it into a fertile, if unprofitable, Eden tenderly embracing a teenaged girl. The relative "hardness" or "softness" of these images should be understood as a consequence, not only of General Archbald and María Eugenia's very different personal and generational perspectives, but also of the distinct models of the plantation that flourished in Virginia versus Venezuela.

Virginia, as we have seen, developed a system that relied on slave labor and rarely allowed for self-sustaining economic activities. As Herbert Klein verifies, the Virginian tobacco plantation required "the simple monoproduction of a staple crop and the wholesale importation of manufactured goods for all the luxuries and many of the necessities of plantation life" (183). In contrast to Virginia and the rest of the southern United States, Venezuela developed what Rafael Herrero labels the "plantation-hacienda" (14–18) and Josefina Ríos de Hernández calls the *plantación-conuco* (14–15), which featured a greater range of agricultural diversity than its Virginian counterpart and encouraged the cultivation, by peasant labor, of smaller fields (*conucos*) whose produce was used for profit as well as personal consumption. Thus, as Herrero's terminology suggests, the "plantation" in Venezuela resembled what many historians have called the "hacienda."[9] According to these historians, the economic structures of the hacienda are, in practice, less capitalistic and more self-reliant than those of the plantation, and both Herrero's model of the "plantation-hacienda" (14–18) and Ríos de Hernández's concept of the *plantación-conuco* (14–15) would suggest that the great estates of Venezuela conformed to this pattern.[10]

In the introduction to this book, I underscored the etymological difference between the English word, "plantation," which portrays an essentially "rooted" site used for agricultural or colonial purposes, and its rough Spanish corollary, *ingenio*, which undermines the agrarian-industrial binary by drawing attention to its dual nature. Parra's novel reminds of this third term of significance, "hacienda," which in both Spanish and English (and, indeed, at key moments in *Iphigenia*) may elicit nostalgic visions of country retreats or family-owned ranches and farms. The Spanish etymology of hacienda, however, does not suggest the relatively more humane, less capitalistic model of production proposed by historians. Rather, it traces back to the verb *hacer*, which means "to do" or "to make." More specifically, the dictionary of the *Real Academia Española* highlights the action of making wealth: in addition to describing a farm, "hacienda" may refer to a business transaction, the "total wealth or riches that someone has," or a "work, action, or event."

Despite her nostalgic rapture over her return to her family's "ancient" domain, María Eugenia simultaneously emphasizes the economic function of the hacienda and laments its inability to do what its etymology suggests it should do: make money and add to the family's wealth. This inability, it is suggested, results precisely from the hacienda's lack of capitalist vigor. In a modernizing Venezuela, capital and industry, not land and agriculture, offer the best methods of accumulating wealth. In contrast to María Eugenia, who longs for economic independence, General Archbald, like the Twelve Southerners, marginalizes the material order of his capitalistic plantation in order to memorialize its "spirit" and "feeling," as well as its "zest" and "mellow flavour" (104).

The distinct inflections taken on by the plantation in Glasgow and the hacienda in Parra reflect cultural differences we have already seen played out: the penchant in the U.S. South to repress the economic function of the plantation, and the tendency in Spanish America to do precisely the opposite. Yet the same inflections also suggest a more literary difference, rooted in the poetic strategies of each work. Both authors employ irony as the primary tool through which to reveal the dearly held beliefs and romantic memories of their characters to be fraudulent, superficial, and even immoral; but only Parra utilizes language that actively undermines stable notions of gender and race so as to imagine an (ultimately failed) alternative to the old order of the patriarchal plantation.

As we have seen, Glasgow uses the memories of General Archbald to represent the plantation in masculinist, eroticized terms that strikingly resemble those employed by the Twelve Southerners. Ultimately, however, she exploits his foolishness and vanity to reveal the illusory nature of his remembrances. Throughout her novel, she similarly delves into the psyche of the town's once-dominant landowning class, and shows how its members understand—and misunderstand—themselves, not in relation to the changes brought on by modernity, but in continuity with their clinging interpretations of the antebellum past. The resulting vision is of a hopelessly insular community that, refusing to acknowledge its profound connections to either the distant "North" or the nearby non-white "other," demands the sacrifice of its own women to reproduce itself. Despite its ironic perspective, the novel ultimately submits to the strictures imposed by the society it critiques, and so remains mired in the static worldview of its characters.

Unlike Glasgow, Parra pushes against such constraints by underscoring their inherent instability. Everything in her protagonist's world is in flux: her racial identity, her economic standing, even her geographical and national status are brought into question by her long years in Europe. This volatility is echoed in the language of the novel, which constantly disrupts predictable notions of femininity and masculinity, darkness and lightness, and sexuality. In its exploitation of the topsy-turviness of language, *Iphigenia* resembles Ortiz's *Cuban Counterpoint*. Both authors revel in the uncertainty of the written word, and use it to open up more flexible ways of thinking about racial, sexual, and national identities. Yet Ortiz finally celebrates the marriage of devilish tobacco to victimized sugar as a triumph of *cubanidad;* Parra, in sharp

contrast, presents the marriage of her equally victimized female protagonist as, perhaps, a victory for Venezuela; but also as a tragedy for María Eugenia, who unlike
Jenny Blair, is sacrificed, not to the old order, but to a new, although equally (perhaps
more) exploitative one.

Parra's "Simple Chronicles of Love"

Writing to a critic of *Iphigenia*, Parra declared that the most important content of her
novel "is what is not written, what I traced without words" (*Obra Escogida* 2: 214).
Narrated from the perspective of a teenager who is intelligent but prone to exaggeration and misinterpretation, *Iphigenia* is full of ironic gaps and silences.[11] One of
the stories that lies in these gaps is that of Venezuela at the beginning of the twentieth
century. Rather than recount it directly, Parra conveys this history via the political
and economic concerns of Caracas's *mantuano* class. Their concerns are most often
articulated in dialogue-heavy after-dinner debates, which María Eugenia faithfully
transcribes. Although she rarely participates in these grown-up conversations, the
protagonist filters their meaning through her limited understanding and adds little
expository commentary to remind the reader of the concrete facts that inform the
speakers' debates and arguments. A careful reading, however, reveals that, behind
these often heated, sometimes veiled exchanges, lies a series of historical facts:
Cipriano Castro's usurpation of the Venezuelan presidency in 1899; an ensuing
transition from regional rule by local *caudillos* to a centralized, authoritarian form of
government; the Gómez dictatorship, which lasted from 1908 to 1935 and so was
well into its second decade when *Iphigenia* was published; the development of
Venezuela's oil industry; and, as a consequence of all of these events, a profound
transformation of the social and economic structures of the nation. By telling this
history indirectly, through the disjunctures in María Eugenia's narration, Parra binds
her protagonist's fate to that of the nation, but in a reciprocal, mutually dependent
fashion: neither narrative can exist without the other. The private world of an impoverished *mantuana*, circumscribed within the domestic sphere, becomes the other face
of a public life organized by dictatorial rule and capitalistic pursuits.

    Indeed, María Eugenia's first attempts to articulate her personal situation are
grounded in those most material terms of economic modernity: capital and consum-
erism. Soon after her return to Venezuela, she discovers that her father's fortune has
been turned over to Uncle Eduardo, an arrangement that thrusts her into financial
dependence. Sitting in her bedroom, she compares life in her grandmother's house to
the one brief taste of freedom that she experienced in Paris, where she spent several
weeks before her voyage back to South America. There, under the benign neglect of
her chaperones and with an inheritance of twenty thousand francs in her pocket, she
explored the boutiques and beauty salons of the city and experienced, for the first
time, the intense joy of spending her own money. Like Cinderella, she is transformed—or rather, transforms herself—from a plain schoolgirl into a young woman
"radiant with optimism and looking like a very elegant Parisian" (7). When she enters
her grandmother's conservative household, however, she reverts to the status of an
"object that people pass about, lend or sell to each other" (14). As she moves from

consumer to object of consumption, her identity as an "elegant Parisian" without ties to family or nation is thus revealed to be a cruel joke.

María Eugenia's analysis of her economic position once again provides a salient contrast with Ortiz, allowing us to reconsider the latter's description of Doña Sugar's circulation within foreign economies. When he declares that sugar "[bleaches and refines itself] until it can pass for white, travel all over the world, reach all mouths, and [be paid more]," he not so subtly condemns her globetrotting as a form of prostitution (*Cuban Counterpoint* 9). Rather than throw herself at foreign markets that only want to use her, she should marry Don Tobacco and give birth to the Cuban family. Yet María Eugenia's grasp of her situation is quite different: Europe does not exploit her, but rather offers the possibility of independence. It is her own nation that longs to take advantage of her. Moreover, as we shall see in the second part of this chapter, it is her "whiteness" that makes her so valuable an "object" within this national, rather than global, context. In *Cuban Counterpoint*, the feminine, embodied by Doña Sugar, is a (sometimes complicit) victim of global capitalism; *Iphigenia*, in contrast, understands female sacrifice as necessary to the survival of the nation. The first two parts of *Iphigenia* develop the issues raised in this passage by tracing the protagonist's relationships with two very different female role models: her grandmother, who stands for family, patriotic nationalism, and economic pragmatism; and her friend, Mercedes, who represents romance, Parisian sophistication, and consumption.

The grandmother (called Abuelita, or "Granny," by the narrator) is portrayed as an authoritative figure endowed with the masculine power of oratorical persuasion, which she acquired from her late husband: "From her contact with my grandfather, her husband, who was a poet, a historian, a minister in the government, and a professor, she acquired a distinguished grace in her speech and ease and elegance in all her words" (52). Focusing on Abuelita's mastery of language, inherited from a patriarch whose résumé imbues him with broad institutional authority, Ileana Rodríguez argues that hers "is the masculine voice in a woman's mouth," devoted to defending the interests of the *mantuanos* (64). While she wields words skillfully, however, it would be misleading to think of the grandmother's language as purely masculine, for she convinces by softening the sharp edges of her words with the comforting contours of maternal love. In this sense, her authority is portrayed as deeply feminine, located in her position as honored matriarch and in her ability to persuade by twisting facts, pleading, and inspiring profound feelings of guilt in her orphaned granddaughter. Her linguistic strategies resemble not so much the polished oratory of the accomplished statesman, as the subtle doublespeak described in Josefina Ludmer's classic essay as one of "the tricks of the weak."

Abuelita patiently cajoles with a pragmatic objective in mind: to transform María Eugenia into a "mujer virtuosa," a virtuous woman, so that she can secure a marriage with a wealthy man and, in doing so, ensure the continuance of the family line. To this end, she insists that, in Venezuela, a young woman in search of a suitable husband need only be pretty and, more importantly, morally irreproachable: "Our men truly worship virtuous women, and when they are going to marry they never look for a wealthy companion, but rather for an irreproachable companion" (59). Therefore, she encourages the protagonist to abandon reading and writing; to be chaste, pious,

and devoted to the home; and, above all, to embrace her fate by practicing the feminine art of resignation: "We women, my dear, were born to forgive" (54). The grandmother's use of a feminine second person plural ("We women," or "las mujeres ...
hemos nacido" in the Spanish [1:100]) reflects her (tricky) tendency to speak in terms
that depict abnegation as an intimate, communal activity. In order to illustrate the
connection between virtue, self-sacrifice, and family, she recites a matrilineal genealogy that begins with her own fortuitous marriage and extends backward through the
generations:

> "Look, I was poor when your grandfather fell in love with me and ... I was happy ...
> oh, so happy! ... Your paternal grandmother, Julia Alonso, married Martín, a mil-
> lionaire, when she and her family were living in utter poverty. They had to work just
> to be able to eat! ... Rosita Aristeigueta, a relative of none other than Bolívar and of
> the Marquis del Toro ... the Urdaneta girls ... the Soublettes ... the Mendozas ...
> María Isabel Tovar, my cousin ... ."
>   And going back again seventy years in time, Grandmother, with her very soft,
> caressing voice, began to weave, one after another, simple chronicles of love,
> in which, without monetary interest, marriages of idyllic, patriarchal happiness
> appeared. (59–60)

The foundations of family and nation merge in this litany of famous names, great
fortunes, and humble women, murmured in the seductive tones of affection and interrupted constantly with ellipses that act as subtle reminders of all that remains unspoken. The grandmother feminizes and eroticizes (albeit chastely) the past by narrating
it as a collection of "simple chronicles of love"—national history wrought small, in
which women become the central players and struggles for power or money are replaced with scenes of domestic harmony.

It is a strategy that brings to mind Parra's concept of the Spanish-American
colonial era as presented in a series of lectures she gave in Bogotá in 1930, under
the title, *The Influence of Woman on the Formation of the American Soul* [*Influencia
de la mujer en la formación del alma americana*]. In the second installment of
this three-part series, she describes the colony as intensely feminine and argues that
for this reason no written history can truly capture its essence, which is accessible
only through an oral tradition whose gentle tones echo Abuelita's: "In order to speak
about the Colony, one must take the plain and familiar tone of conversation and of
storytelling" (*Influencia* 78). Parra (mis)characterizes the colony as existing outside
of history—in part, because it predates (Spanish-American) nationhood—and therefore outside of the masculine realm of authority.[12] Abuelita similarly tells appealing
stories about a female-centered past. The happy world she describes, however, is
"idyllic" and "patriarchal," adjectives that ironically emphasize the trap laid by her
seemingy simple chronicles. It is idyllic (*idílica*), which is to say simple and rustic,
but also constructed (like the chronicles) with poetic artifice; and it is patriarchal
(*patriarcal*). Despite her feminizing rhetoric, the order Abuelita supports is, finally,
that of tradition and patriarchy. This is the first of many times that *Iphigenia* presents
a failed attempt, by a character or by the author herself, to articulate a feminine alternative to patriarchal society.

The author seems to locate another such alternative in Mercedes Galindo, a wealthy friend and mentor to María Eugenia who is in her thirties and married but childless. Characterized by none of the authority associated with Abuelita, Mercedes embodies a sensuous, sophisticated femininity coded as both exotic and cosmopolitan. She and the protagonist spend many afternoons in her extravagant *boudoir*, which the latter describes in the following passage:

> Mercedes has built an Oriental setting for her Creole indolence, and instead of swinging in a hammock to the whispering breezes and the waving palm trees, as celebrated in the music of the *habaneras*, she rests on her huge, low Turkish divan, pale [*blanquísima*], stretched out, surrounded by a multitude [*sinfín*] of pillows, among whose soft mounds, shaded by curtains, she reads, dreams, mediates, sips tea, feels bored, and sometimes, too, she cries. (126)

> Mercedes ha querido orientalizar su indolencia criolla, y en lugar de mecerla en una hamaca bajo un susurrar de brisas y un abanicar de palmas, como en las habaneras, no, la cultiva en su bajo e inmenso diván turco, alargada y blanquísima, rodeada por un sinfín de cojines, entre cuyas suaves abolladuras, bajo la penumbra de las cortinas, lee, sueña, reflexiona, duerme, toma té, se aburre y a veces también llora. (1: 208)

Although she embodies "Creole indolence," Mercedes deliberately exoticizes habits and characteristics that would otherwise suggest a conventional *mantuana* identity. By replacing the indigenous hammock with a Turkish divan, she imitates the metropolitan obsession with all things "Oriental" and so transforms her *boudoir* into a multivalent transnational space, in which symbols of Parisian sophistication, Eastern extravagance, and *criollo* mysticism pile up like the endless supply of pillows on the divan. The resulting room is sensual—it is, after all, a *boudoir*—and its eroticism is explicitly feminine, as is signaled by the "soft mounds" (in Spanish, *suaves abolladuras*, or soft hollows) of the cushions and the prominent figure of Mercedes, her pale (*blanquísima*, or "very white") body languidly reclining. As a space where Mercedes can indulge in everything from boredom to tears, and as the site of secret conversations with her young protégée, it is also coded as a feminine enclosure where female intimacy is established and female desire can circulate freely. It is, in sum, a refuge from the rigid patriarchal order, and a site of transgressive excess that overflows the boundaries of nation, family, and conventional morality.

Although Mercedes and María Eugenia discuss their romantic and erotic yearnings in explicitly heterosexual terms, it is also a place where the open secret of Parra's lesbian desire collides with her fictional creation's yearning to be liberated from familial obligations and pecuniary restrictions. In "Reading Lesbian in Teresa de la Parra," Sylvia Molloy argues that expressions such as "freedom," "independence," and "without rules" appear in Parra's writing as "coded words" that convey "a lifestyle and, yes, a sexuality over which 'they'—family, institution, modern national state—have no authority" (249). Significantly, when María Eugenia speaks such "coded words" in the *boudoir*, she does so precisely to articulate her wish to control her sexuality by rejecting heterosexual marriage: "after all, I understand why some women don't want to get married! If I were a man, I wouldn't want to get married either! Think what a delight and how splendid it must be to be free and roam the world, having adventures and spending thousands and thousands and millions!" (133). For María Eugenia, personal freedom implies not only the ability to choose a husband, but to choose *not* to have a husband. Such freedom, however, must be achieved through financial independence, the only means by which to loosen ties to family and nation in order to "roam the world."

Mercedes responds to her young friend's outburst by rebuking her fixation on wealth and returning to the more conventional topic of romance. On the surface, Mercedes' concept of love seems to be quite modern compared to Abuelita's, for she portrays courtship and marriage, not as a means of continuing the family line, but rather as a path to individual happiness. Yet her scheme to make a love match between María Eugenia and Gabriel Olmedo, an impoverished *mantuano*, reveals Mercedes to be far from the liberated role model that María Eugenia seeks. Furthermore, Mercedes' analysis of her own marriage, which she describes as humiliating, teeters between progressive and traditional points of view. On the one hand, she blames her inability to end it on the restrictions imposed by "conventions and laws" (137). On the other hand, she claims to remain married by choice and because of a moral superiority which leads her, like the women of Abuelita's chronicles, to noble self-sacrifice: since she does not possess a soul that is "as selfish as some women" (136), she cannot divorce a husband who, however despised, would become dissolute without her. Although elsewhere she goes so far as to articulate a modern critique of marriage as a form of slavery or prostitution, Mercedes cannot act, or even contemplate acting, on that critique. María Eugenia is quick to identify Mercedes' contradictory outlook with her grandmother's "simple chronicles of love" and to insist once again on the importance of economic independence: "'I think all these chains are just romantic and poetic notions very similar to those that Grandmother and Aunt Clara [forge] in their imagination. Actually you could break them very easily. Don't you have money of your own to live on? Don't women in other countries get divorced? Why, you don't even have any children, Mercedes!'" (136). Latching onto the metaphor of slavery, which she will reemploy at key moments to describe her own situation, the protagonist suggests that the "chains" that bind *mantuana* women are forged in their own overripe imaginations, and that they can achieve true independence by abandoning "romantic and poetic notions," looking to "women in other countries," and addressing the material circumstances of their lives.

Parra dedicated *Iphigenia* to Emilia Barrios, a friend, mentor, and patroness who was the real-life inspiration for the character of Mercedes, and who died shortly before the publication of her protégée's first novel. When Barrios invited Parra to move with her to Paris, the aspiring writer eagerly accepted. When Mercedes offers the same opportunity to María Eugenia, she rejects it. In her own life, Parra left Venezuela for Europe in order to loosen, if not escape, the bonds of family and nation. Her protagonist, ironically unable to break the very chains she has denounced as false, cannot do the same. As Sylvia Molloy poignantly observes, "what had been achieved, surely not without effort, in life, could not be repeated, at least in the Venezuela of the 1920s, in literature" (250). Soon after her offer is declined, Mercedes returns to Paris and disappears from the novel. In one respect, her removal from the plot simply helps to drive it forward; but it also quietly signals that the feminine alternative to nation that she ostensibly represents, epitomized by the (homo)eroticized transnational space of her *boudoir*, is untenable. As a result, in the final half of the novel, María Eugenia must learn to negotiate the risky world of romance, and the concomitant demands of family and nation, alone.

Glasgow's "Most Extraordinary" History

Jenny Blair's quest for independence, like María Eugenia's, ends in tragedy; and many of the struggles she confronts parallel those faced by her Venezuelan counterpart. Yet her story unravels in a different fashion, in part due to issues of perspective and narrative voice. In *Iphigenia*, a teenaged María Eugenia narrates her own life, and so the novel's point of view is limited by its narrator's age and the use of the first person. Moreover, since the novel's dramatic tension arises from María Eugenia's active struggles against the expectations of her community, and since her writing is itself an act of rebellion, those struggles only cease when she puts down her pen—that is to say, when the novel ends. *The Sheltered Life*, in contrast, features a third-person narrator whose perspective changes frequently, juxtaposing the young protagonist's point of view with those of other characters, especially her grandfather who, like María Eugenia's grandmother, embodies the old order. As a result, Jenny Blair's development is mapped within, rather than against, the traditions of her community, and the dramatic structure of the novel rests not on defiance but compliance.

Such tonal and structural differences signal thematic distinctions as well: although both narratives comment on larger cultural and economic transitions, *Iphigenia* represents the traumatic change itself, while *The Sheltered Life* dramatizes an entrenched, if ultimately futile, resistance to change. This resistance takes the form of a carefully constructed myth of historical continuity enforced by the Archbalds and the Birdsongs, which is illustrated in an early description of their refusal to move out of the old neighborhood:

> The Birdsongs stayed because, as they confessed proudly, they were too poor to move and the Archbalds stayed because the General, in his seventy-sixth year but still incapable of retreat, declared that he would never forsake Mrs. Birdsong. Industrialism might conquer, but they would never surrender.
>
> One by one, they saw the old houses demolished, the fine old elms mutilated. Telegraph poles slashed the horizon; furnaces, from a distance, belched soot into the drawing-rooms; newspapers, casually read and dropped, littered the pavements; when the wind shifted on the banks of the river, an evil odour sprang up from the hollow. Still undaunted, the two families held the breach between the old and the new order . . . . (5–6)

Written to highlight the perspective of General Archbald, this passage elicits comparison with the Twelve Southerners. Not only does it pose the binary "Agrarian *versus* Industrial" as an irreducible difference, it also employs metaphors of war to contend that said difference can only be resolved through violent confrontation. As Michael Kreyling observes, from its title onwards, *I'll Take My Stand* makes plentiful use of "martial rhetoric ... to ratchet-up the tension" and so underscore the urgency of its intellectual agenda (168). Glasgow, however, imbues her bellicose images with irony. Living on a shabby street and breathing in the toxins from the nearby factory, her protagonists imagine the forces of industry as a second invading army from the North, and their refusal (or financial inability) to move as a brave act of noble sacrifice. Yet, while this passage conveys nostalgia for beauty lost, its language also suggests, too casually, an exact correspondence between the violence of the Civil War and that of industrialism: both demolish, mutilate, slash, belch soot, strew garbage, and fill the city with evil odors. That the war mutilated flesh and littered battlefields with bodies, while industrialism mutilates trees and litters sidewalks with newspapers seems to be a difference that matters little.

Moreover, the passage's militarism, especially its insinuation that industrialization comprises a second Civil War, underscores the hard line drawn between South and North. A few characters do appear to represent positive aspects of northern culture, most notably the Birdsong's nephew John, a student of science who frequently articulates a modern point of view. Yet, unlike *Iphigenia*, where the North in the guise of Europe performs a critical role, in *The Sheltered Life* it appears only as a two-dimensional scapegoat. Parra's novel shows how modern European values and trends influence the thoughts, feelings, and imagination of the protagonist. In Glasgow's, in contrast, the U.S. North may be instinctively blamed for the blight of industrialism, but it plays no vital part in shaping the narrative or the lives of the southern protagonists. This almost absolute absence calls attention, yet again, to the static, inward-looking nature of the South.

The sentences immediately following the above citation draw the reader's attention to the gendered nature of this South by implicitly contrasting the ravages of industrialism to the mythical splendor of Eva Birdsong, who "had been a famous beauty in the eighteen nineties; and the social history of Queenborough was composed wherever she decided to live that history. As late as the spring of 1906 [when the novel opens], she was still regarded less a woman than as a memorable occasion" (6). As her name indicates, Eva/Eve stands outside of history, at the origins of the (antebellum) world. Only in her mid-thirties, she embodies an idealized past: "she had already passed into legend. Romantic stories were told of her girlhood" (6). As indicated by General Archbald's vow to "never forsake Mrs. Birdsong," the survival of the legend depends upon the "romantic stories" her beauty generates. From its opening pages, then, *The Sheltered Life* opposes North to South. Yet it diminishes the concrete presence of the former while connecting the latter, not to the chastely erotic culture evoked in *I'll Take My Stand*, but rather to rigid concepts of (upper-class white) femininity. Moreover, by tracing the moral and social educations of its dual protagonists, General David Archbald and Jenny Blair, the novel underscores the ways in which such concepts of femininity are inseparable from complementary ideals of (upper-class white) masculinity.

While *Iphigenia* explores (ultimately ephemeral) alternatives to the *mantuano* patriarchy, *The Sheltered Life* lays bare the limits of the patriarchal imaginary through the character of General Archbald, whose memories comprise part 2. Entitled "The Deep Past," this section begins with his recollections of being called a "milksop" by his grandfather, a slave owner who exemplifies eroticized northern stereotypes of the southern gentleman. On the one hand, General Archbald remembers his grandfather as a chivalrous romantic who remained "devoted" to his "fragile" wife even after she went mad; on the other, he recalls him to have been an uninhibited sadist: "He could no more look at a wild creature without lusting to kill than he could look at a pretty girl without lusting to kiss" (103). In order to measure up to the demands of his grandfather's code of masculinity, the general suppresses his artistic nature, just as Jenny Blair suppresses her creativity to conform to the corresponding code of femininity. He becomes a war hero and emulates the chivalry of his grandfather, but also tempers the older man's violent embrace of conquest with a deep philosophical bent. As a result, he is, in many ways, reminiscent of the genteel southern gentleman glorified in *I'll Take My Stand*, and is infinitely more complex and sympathetic than his grandfather. At the same time the ironic undertones of the narrative refuse to let him off the hook: Julius Rowan Raper observes that the "drama of the general's mind is a story of self-deception" (*From the Sunken Garden* 147) and Helen Levy states more bluntly that Glasgow "makes him look more than a little ridiculous" (260).

Particularly revealing of his moral failure are his judgments regarding the women in his life, which consist almost exclusively of merciless evaluations of their physical appearances: he thinks his unmarried daughter Etta to be "scarcely more appealing than some heartless caricature of feminine charms," breathes a sigh of relief when "the sheath skirt, so cramping to [his daughter] Isabella's voluptuous style" goes out of fashion, and admires Jenny Blair as "a pretty little thing in her way, fresh, sparkling, dewy with innocence" (176) while also concluding that "she would never have been called a beauty" in the more discerning nineteenth century (125). Eva Birdsong is the standard by which he measures all other women, and he idealizes her beauty with macabre exaggeration: " 'Even when she is dead,' he thought, 'her skeleton will have beauty' " (139).

While obsessing over their exteriors, however, the general dismisses their interior development. He derides his daughters, for example, as "little deeper than airplants by nature" (131) and remains baffled when he does intuit the emotional depth of a female character. Upon catching a "look of defeat" in Eva's face, he proclaims: "I've seen that look often before, but there was always some cause I could explain. I saw it in many faces after the war, and in many more faces while Reconstruction lasted. But those were times that shattered men's nerves" (222). Eva has been defeated by the very societal pressure that the general, perhaps more than anyone else, exerts upon her; but because he so values the symbolic significance of her beauty, he cannot fathom her human affliction, which he associates only with the male experience of war. Although he ponders his own (male) suffering incessantly, Archbald fails to recognize the female potential for similar philosophical and emotional struggle. Moreover, despite the fact that he often expresses frustration with what he perceives as the frivolous nature of women, he perversely values his granddaughter precisely for the "sentimental appeal" of her shallowness, which functions as a verification—ultimately false—of her innocence (131).

The general's perceptions are inextricable from the myth of the southern lady, who, as Anne Goodwyn Jones asserts, "embodies virtue, but her goodness depends directly on innocence—in fact, on ignorance of evil. She is chaste, because she has never been tempted" (9). Describing the antebellum U.S. South, Anne Firor Scott affirms, moreoever, that southern ladies, like children, slaves, and other dependent members of the plantation's social hierarchy, "were expected to recognize their proper and subordinate place and to be obedient to the head of the family. Any tendency on the part of any of the members of the system to assert themselves against the master threatened the whole" (17). In the postwar era, the southern lady continues to fulfill a similar role, helping symbolically to legitimize and stabilize patriarchal power relations. She is thus necessary for the preservation—real or illusory—of old hierarchies, including, as we shall see below, racial ones. As Glasgow makes clear, however, women like Eva, Jenny Blair, and even the homely Etta, are not simply victims of General Archbald's sexist judgments. Just as Abuelita, in *Iphigenia*, weaves idylls of female submission and patriarchal happiness, so too the female characters in *The Sheltered Life* are complicit in sustaining the myth of southern womanhood.

In tracing the process through which her young protagonist is initiated into this myth, Glasgow focuses especially on two cultural categories, described by Carol Manning as "the cult of beauty and the school of evasive idealism" (310). Both of these categories highlight the hypocrisy of the paradigm of the southern lady and, by extension, southern culture as a whole. While the cult of beauty compels women to conform to a narrow definition of physical attractiveness, the school of evasive idealism teaches them to ignore or explain away unpleasant truths. Distinct yet interrelated, they are most fully embodied by two characters: Jenny Blair's mother, Cora Archbald, and her neighbor, Eva Birdsong. Cora and Eva are, in many ways, counterparts to Abuelita and Mercedes in *Iphigenia*. Cora, like Abuelita, is a widow and the matriarch of the home she shares with her father-in-law and two unmarried sisters-in-law. Eva, like Mercedes, is an unhappily married woman with no children of her own, who acts as friend and confidante to the protagonist. Unlike the older women in Parra's novel, however, Cora and Eva are never opposed to each other. Matron and belle, they exemplify complementary facets of southern womanhood.

In a 1916 interview, Glasgow described evasive idealism, a phrase she employed often, as "a whimsical, sentimental, and maudlinly optimistic philosophy of life" that avoids a "straightforward facing of realities" (*Ellen Glasgow's Reasonable Doubts* 122). It is a philosophy that rises not out of genuine optimism, but rather from a determination to avoid difficult truths—a determination that, to sustain itself, must rewrite the past to suit the needs of the present. While all of the white characters in *The Sheltered Life*, regardless of age or gender, live by the rules of evasive idealism, the concept is most thoroughly explored through the figure of Cora. Cora's especially durable brand of evasive idealism is born of a deep cynicism, a fact revealed when she warns Jenny Blair: "It is only by knowing how little life has in store for us that we are able to look on the bright side and avoid disappointment" (240). Cora protects her daughter from such disappointment by teaching her to repress her innate creativity and curiosity. When, as a nine-year-old, Jenny Blair describes the world in precociously poetic terms, Cora chides "you see entirely too much" (10). When she asks questions about sensitive family matters, she is ordered to repeat a revised and improved version of the event. The lessons are all too effective: by the time she is a teenager, Jenny Blair silently scolds the Birdsong's progressive, perceptive nephew,

John, for "seeing too much" (249) and excuses her own moral failures by repeating the mantra, "I didn't mean anything in the world" (164, 292).

In her capacity as a mother, Cora teaches her daughter to become an evasive idealist; as matriarch of the Archbald household, she insures that the family genealogy conforms to societal expectations. Thus, when Isabella becomes engaged to the working class Joseph Crocker, Cora worries about the effect the match will have on the family name and quietly pays a genealogist to trace—or, more accurately, create—a past for the Crockers that includes a respectable 1635 arrival to the United States and a distant relative who was "one of the barons of Runnemede." Like the Twelve Southerners, Cora insists on the "aristocratic" nature of the southern squirearchy and observes without irony: "Everyone thinks the Crockers' family history has been most extraordinary" (173). Unlike María Eugenia's grandmother, who persuades actively and authoritatively, Cora alters perception through whispered rumors meant to evade confrontation and debate. Nevertheless, both women manipulate genealogies to preserve a false history.

If Cora sustains the official version of the past through dissimulation, then Eva, as we have already noted, embodies that past through her unchanging beauty. Although the community idolizes this beauty, the narrative voice underscores its falsity: Eva is not "natural" but rather a creation of art and will. When she first appears, she is described in rapid succession as an allegory, a muse, and "a new Juliet." Her radiance looks like "it might have been painted" and her gestures are "faintly theatrical" (15–17). Glasgow implicitly contrasts Eva's rehearsed theatricality with nine-year-old Jenny Blair's authentic creativity, while also accentuating the symbolic importance of the former's artifice. As Levy argues, Eva allows the Queenborough elite to "reinforce an idea of their social arrangements as unchanging. To implicate the female ideal in matters of sexuality and maternity is to immerse, by consonance, the social circle itself in passing time and thus mortality" (257). As a girl, Eva dreamed of being an opera singer. As a woman, she channels her artistry into the task of preserving the illusion of her beauty. She neither creates nor procreates; rather, she reproduces the old order. Unlike the Twelve Southerners, who depict that order as nurturing a productive relationship between the masculine and the feminine, Glasgow's portrayal of Eva suggests quite the opposite.

The simultaneous disintegration of her marriage and her body underscores Eva's corporal and spiritual sterility. The former is destroyed when she finally admits that her husband, George, is chronically unfaithful; the latter is ravaged by an unnamed illness that necessitates a hysterectomy. As a result of these crises, she undergoes a personal transformation, revealed by two conversations that articulate her changing attitude toward romantic love. In the first part of the novel, she tells her nine-year-old neighbor that "'a great love doesn't leave room for anything else in a woman's life. It is everything'" (55). In the final part, however, she warns the protagonist, now sixteen, that love does not bring happiness: "'I wish I could tell you the way to feel a great love and still be happy. But I cannot. I have never learned how it can be. I staked all my happiness on a single chance.... Never do that, Jenny Blair'" (210).

Unlike Mercedes in *Iphigenia*, Eva finally rejects the values of the old order. Her transformation, however, comes too late: Jenny Blair has already fallen prey to the romantic notion of a "great love." Like *Iphigenia, The Sheltered Life* suggests that friendships forged between generations of women might create bonds that will break, or at least reconfigure, old chains. But, although their relationships suffer for different reasons—María Eugenia recognizes Mercedes' hypocritical adherence to the conventions she claims to abhor, while Jenny Blair embraces the conventions that Eva begs her to rebel against—both novels ultimately caution that the transformative capacity of such friendships is limited in the face of a powerful past. Thus Jenny Blair rejects Eva's advice and pursues a flirtation with Eva's husband, while the other characters ignore her involvement with her married neighbor. Describing her as "vague," "vacant," "shallow," and, above all, "innocent," they prefer to see her as an attractive, empty page on which they can write the future as yet another repetition of the past.

Intersections of Race and Romance

Although Jenny Blair and María Eugenia are mostly confined to the domestic realm, the outside world comes to them in many shapes and forms, but is most compellingly embodied by the laundress Gregoria in *Iphigenia*, and the laundress Memoria in *The Sheltered Life*, women of color who play small but crucial roles in revealing how the protagonists' lives and (potential) romances connect to a past and present indelibly marked by the atrocities of slavery. In both novels, the laundress inhabits an ambiguous textual space. On the one hand, her white employers draw the broad strokes of her character in a self-interested fashion, claiming a thorough knowledge of her even as they refuse intimate connection with her. On the other hand, within the larger patterns of the narrative, she functions as a stubbornly unknowable symbol, an insistent memory/*memoria* of those aspects of the past some would prefer to forget. As a trusted household servant—a washer of dirty laundry—she is simultaneously inside and outside of the family and has access, metaphorical and literal, to its secrets. Because of this knowledge, she might to bear witness to events that would otherwise be written out of history. But, in these novels anyway, she remains silent.[13] Describing the role of black characters in Faulkner's fiction, Glissant argues that, although he avoids the most offensive stereotypes, Faulkner fails to "render the 'real' situation of Blacks. Rather, he describes Blacks in a situation that suits his purpose. This is why their presence is so important: as a generalizing 'signified,' they embody a position (as people) that is weighty and substantial" (*Faulkner, Mississippi* 57). Similarly, neither Parra nor Glasgow emphasizes the "real" situation of Gregoria or Memoria. Rather, they use these characters as enfleshed symbols of that which remains unspoken.

Iphigenia, for example, does not expose how the instabilities and uncertainties of modernity affect Gregoria's life, even though it hints that these transformations led the elite to support Gómez's dictatorship to protect themselves from the non-white "masses" of which she is presumably a member. Parra frequently alludes to *mantuano* hypocrisy, as her characters deny their own mixed-race ancestry while decrying the decline of the "white" elite to which they belong. Winthrop Wright confirms this hypocrisy when he describes the common belief that "mestizos, blacks, and Indians needed an authoritarian government. Order and progress necessitated the implementation of a white dictatorship, even if the dictator, like Gómez, was probably a mestizo" (81). Yet, despite a few hints and glimpses, Gregoria's private thoughts about this situation remain impenetrable.

Likewise, *The Sheltered Life* never depicts Memoria's struggles with the racist society in which she resides, even though its timeframe (1906–1914) coincides with a deepening of racial prejudice throughout the U.S. South, which not only manifested itself in an increased violence toward blacks in daily life but also in the legal codification of discrimination. As Glasgow's biographer, Susan Goodman, notes: "In the years following Reconstruction, local governments supported a tacit policy of general intimidation, as Southern states rewrote their constitutions to rescind most of the rights of black citizens. By the turn of the century, three-quarters of the black population had become tenant farmers or domestic workers, their economic condition not substantially improved since antebellum days" (*Ellen Glasgow* 91). As a character, Memoria is undeniably sympathetic; but we are told nothing about her struggles in such an environment. Rather, like Gregoria, she "embod[ies] a position that is weighty and substantial."

This position is initially established by color. More specifically, Memoria's lightness and Gregoria's darkness, repeatedly emphasized, reflect the different racial preoccupations of each novel. These, in turn, are dictated by the specific historical contexts described above, as well as by the distinct concepts of race and miscegenation that have tended to dominate racial discourse in the U.S. and Venezuela. While the former has tended toward the notorious "one drop rule," the latter has distinguished between its "pure" black citizens and those of mixed race, as Wright observes:

> Venezuelans consider only those individuals with black skin as blacks. Thus, a mulatto became a *pardo*, a nonblack, and therefore more acceptable. By the same token, Venezuelans did not adhere to the Anglo-Saxon belief that a drop of African blood made an individual black. Actually, they altered the perspective: they considered individuals with a drop of white blood superior to blacks. (3)

Individuals of mixed race who were culturally and, very often, legally denied the privileges of whiteness in the South were thus granted them in Venezuela, at least to a certain degree. Although Venezuelan society was not, as a result, free of racial prejudice, its concept of race was relatively more flexible. This flexibility influences Parra's language, which emphasizes the subjectivity and instability of racial identity while also using Gregoria's darkness, repeatedly described in terms of its "brilliance" and "purity," as a symbol of the Venezuelan elite's longing for an unmixed racial order. Light-skinned Memoria, in contrast, calls into question the U.S. South's rigid concept of race by embodying the repressed history of miscegenation. Although she is clearly identified as "black," Cora describes her as "nearly white" (22) and Jenny Blair identifies her as "very nearly but not quite colored" (38). Glasgow thus ironically employs a "nearly white" African-American woman to examine the unbending notions of black versus white that dominate her portrayal of race; in contrast, Parra uses a character described as "pure" black to highlight the instability inherent in Venezuelan concepts of race.

Between Black and White in *Iphigenia*

As the first half of *Iphigenia* comes to a close, María Eugenia reacts with grief to the departure of Mercedes and the sudden marriage of her love interest, Gabriel Olmedo, to a member of the nascent commercial class that prospered as a result of the economic and political changes that took place during Gómez's dictatorship. The second half of the novel picks up two years later, after a period of silence during which the protagonist quits writing in order to submit to her grandmother's wishes that she be a *mujer virtuosa*. For her efforts, she is rewarded with a fiancé, the successful, overbearing César Leal, who is also a member of the rising commercial class. Although they recognize the need to make alliances with this class, however, the novel's *mantuano* characters disparagingly identify its members with the nation's mixed-race population.

Venezuelan society, as depicted in *Iphigenia*, comprises three distinct racial and socioeconomic groups: a "pure" white upper class, a "pure" black servant class, and a vast mixed-race population whose members resist both racial and class categorization.[14] Each group plays a particular role in the text, but María Eugenia's depictions of white Gabriel, mixed-race César, and black Gregoria—and, ultimately, her understanding of her own place in Venezuelan society—are primarily shaped by her ambivalent attitude toward the mixed-race majority. Her ambivalence, in turn, reflects the Venezuelan elite's understanding of miscegenation in the late nineteenth and early twentieth centuries, which was mired in a pseudoscientific positivist discourse that equated the white race with progress, labeled non-whites as inherently inferior, and associated racial mixing with mental and physical degeneration. According to Wright, the resulting concept of race was characterized by a fundamental contradiction: while vehemently rejecting the more virulently racist theories associated with the European and North American positivism they otherwise embraced, the country's intellectuals did believe that the progress of a nation could not be separated from the whiteness of its people. This belief led them to promote a policy of *blanquimiento*, or whitening, of the populace through immigration from Europe and continued racial mixing, a policy that "depended upon the assimilation of nonwhites into a *café con leche* blend" (74). Miscegenation was thus viewed as the cause of Venezuela's lack of progress, because its *pardo* population was blamed for its economic and cultural shortcomings. At the same time, a certain type of racial mixing, one that would lead to the "whitening" of the race, was understood as the key to the nation's eventual progress.[15] Within such a paradigm, light-skinned women like María Eugenia functioned as symbolic and literal potential mothers of a future "white" nation.

Parra plainly acknowledges the falsity of the Venezuelan elite's claim to its own "pure" whiteness by making several references to its racially mixed past; but she also shows how its privileging of whiteness contributes to the protagonist's sense of self and her way of seeing the world around her. Perhaps most important for the vain, pretty narrator is the cultural equation of beauty with light skin. From the opening pages of *Iphigenia*, María Eugenia explicitly links images of whiteness with beauty, taking great pride, for example, in her own exaggerated paleness. In contrast, she is deeply troubled by any sign of darkness marring an otherwise light complexion. Describing a group of mulatto dockworkers, she notes with dismay: "none of them had the unity of characteristics or the uniformity of appearance that I had seen in pure blacks. Rather each one individually and all as a group constituted a variegated mixture [*abigarrada mezcla*] of races, where white prevailed, but distorted [*desprestigiada*], as in caricatures the likeness prevails in spite of distortions [*deformidades*]" (27). The protagonist and her family and friends repeatedly employ similar images of deformity and caricature to differentiate mixed-race individuals from "pure" whites as well as "pure" blacks. In doing so, they betray their fear that this population, with its increasing numbers and economic potential, will upset the traditional balance of power.

Unsettled by such uncertainties, the protagonist and her community are keenly cognizant of their own declining economic situation. Thus, the more pragmatic members of María Eugenia's family urge her to accept Leal's offer of marriage, in spite of the contemptuous remarks that they make about his lineage. Uncle Pancho, for example, observes of Leal's sisters: "They are tall, skinny, dark-complexioned girls [*trigueñas*] with pimply faces. It's quite possible that his not taking them to the club dances is because of how ugly they would look in evening dresses" (225). Although he does not directly state that the family is mixed-race, his labeling of the sisters as "dark-complexioned" and "ugly" is reminiscent of María Eugenia's description of the dockworkers. María Eugenia's grandmother is even more veiled in her assessment: "Leal ... Leal ... these Leals were not around in my day! It seems to me I've heard of the name, but like ... really second-rate ... no, they're a long way from first-class ... But it's true, too, that things have changed today!" (225). Abuelita's pauses, emphasized through the frequent use of ellipses, are more significant than her words, for they gesture toward the deliberately unspoken, yet ever-present issue of Leal's race. Nevertheless, although he hails from a "second-rate" family, the Alonsos must be prepared to sacrifice their racial and class purity in order to adapt to their reduced economic power. In response to the duty pressed upon her to contribute to the process of *blanquimiento*, María Eugenia clings fiercely, and fearfully, to her "pure" white identity. Resisting the notion that, in order to progress economically, she must "regress" racially, she takes comfort in the "pure" black visage of Gregoria, which she repeatedly associates with romantic notions of nature, oral tradition, and a harmonious balance between untainted black(s) and white(s) familiar to readers of *I'll Take My Stand*.

María Eugenia's fascination with Gregoria's blackness should be understood within the context of her family's slave owning past, alluded to when she visits the old hacienda and speculates that its manor house might have been "built by the family slaves, who would also be called 'Alonso' like their masters" (156). This allusion is especially significant because the institution of slavery was historically weak in Venezuela. According to John Lombardi, from "about 1824" onwards there was an "almost total unanimity of opinion [on the part of landowners] against the servile institution," and free labor gradually replaced slavery, which was formally abolished in 1854, to little resistance from local landowners (6). By emphasizing the Alonso's slaveholding past and, more generally, by giving disproportionate attention to the European and African elements of Venezuelan society while essentially ignoring its large and vital indigenous population, Parra hones in on the aspect of racial mixing that caused the Venezuelan elite the most discomfort. As Wright observes, members of the elite tended to claim that *mestizos* (people of indigenous and European descent) rather than mulattos (African and European) or other racial mixtures "made up the bulk of the population," although there was no evidence to support such a belief (54). Similarly, more than one critic of *Iphigenia* has assumed that Leal is *mestizo*, even though Parra never gives him any specific racial label. Asserting her aversion to labels of any kind, Parra declares in *Influencia de la mujer* that "while politicians, military men, journalists and historians spend their lives putting antagonistic labels on things, youngsters, common people (*el pueblo*), and above all we women, who are numerous and very disorderly, busy ourselves with shuffling those labels to once again establish cordial confusion" (62). By "shuffling" racial labels in *Iphigenia*, Parra underscores their arbitrary or perceived nature.

For María Eugenia, however, Gregoria's blackness functions in quite the opposite manner: it creates an illusion of racial certainty. Throughout *Iphigenia*, with few exceptions, any mention of Gregoria is accompanied by almost fetishistic references to "pure" blackness: her black skin, her black handkerchief blending with her black hair, and, above all, her black hands. In a passage dedicated to the "blanquísimo poema de la batea," or "the whitest poem of the tub," María Eugenia admiringly describes how these hands contrast with the white suds of the laundry tub: "How her black hands shine on the immaculate whiteness! Sometimes they seem like two enamored swallows frolicking and chasing each other on the same little cloud" (102). Imagining a dull domestic task as a poetic interaction between the "pure" blackness of the laundress's hands and the "pure" whiteness of the foam in her tub, the protagonist betrays a profound longing for a world in which whites and blacks live together but unmixed. Moreover, she suggests that it is the loyal servitude and nurturing of black hands that allows whiteness to prosper and multiply, just like "the richness of the white foam, that grows and grows, eternally, with the continual beating and rubbing" (103). This "poem," shaped by its fictional author's desire for an impossibly unblemished racial order, exemplifies Parra's tendency to tweak Venezuela's already highly developed racial lexicon, rejecting stable meaning in favor of irony and ambiguity. As Wright asserts, the verb *blanquear*, "to whiten," in the context of the day, signified the idea of "whitening as a prerequisite for social and political mobility" and "suggest[ed] the antithesis: black characterized backwardness, ignorance, poverty, and failure" (6). Parra pushes this ambiguity further, endowing the concept of *blanquimiento* with meaning at once more pliable and more personal. Gregoria, through her (apparently) untainted blackness, reaffirms the whiteness of the family for whom she works. In doing so, she comes to symbolize, for María Eugenia, a romantic ideal of a stable racial order unimpeded by the volatile racial identities that actually characterize Venezuelan society.

Parra does not reserve her flexible employment of the concept of *blanquimiento* only for discussions of race as it relates to social and economic status. Images of blackness and whiteness, as well as darkness and lightness, are also linked to gender and sexuality, as Rodríguez implies when she asserts that the men in *Iphigenia* are "physically and morally lacking" and that, as a result, "the masculine occupies the same places as the grotesque and the ugly ... the place of mestizaje and mulataje" (68). While Rodríguez's observation holds true at times, Parra's penchant for irony and ambiguity prohibits her from embracing a straightforward opposition of masculine and feminine: indeed, the very idea that the masculine would occupy the same rhetorical position as the miscegenated already undermines any clear dichotomy. Furthermore, it is not the masculine in general, but rather the threat to (white) female beauty and autonomy by male economic and sexual power that locates some men, some of the time, in this denigrated category. The young diarist does paint a few male characters—notably Uncle Eduardo—in a consistently unflattering light. Most, however, move with startling ease from "blackness"—or, more accurately, "mixed-ness"—to "whiteness," depending upon their perceived alliance with or against female interest and desire.

For example, the first time María Eugenia meets Gabriel Olmedo she fixates on his physical darkness: "he's not bad looking if you happen to like [dark] men, but ... I don't like jet-black hair except in a cat's back, and on people it irritates and displeases me" (109) ["no resulta mal para aquellas personas que encuentran agradable el color trigueño, pero ... a mí no me gusta ver el pelo negro azabache sino en el lomo de los gatos, y ... en las personas me crispa y me desagrada" (1: 179–80)]. When she is reunited with him two years later, however, she finds him transformed. Not only does she praise him for his moral goodness as he cares for her dying uncle, but she also observes that he is whiter than she thought: "Judging by his face I thought he was [darker], but no, he is white, white, very white" (273). Engaged to a man she does not love, watching her favorite uncle and her grandmother slowly die, María Eugenia's perception of Gabriel is so transformed by her circumstances that her first reaction is to "whiten" him. Such inconsistent perception of fairness and darkness reveals that her judgments are based on emotion and circumstance rather than racial origin or even physical appearance.

Nowhere is this more vividly portrayed than in her self-descriptions. Although she most often portrays herself as "blanca y bella," or white and beautiful, this assessment falters at key points, such as when, depressed by her financial dependence, she looks at her white hands, mottled by shadows and pressed against her black dress, and imagines them to be "living symbols of my submission and my resignation" (78). A similar, more intense, destabilization occurs in the novel's last chapter. Waiting for dawn, when she plans to flee with Gabriel to Europe, María Eugenia examines her image in the mirror: "since I was dressed in white, and since inside too I was full of white happiness, in the silent room, the soul of night that surrounded me melted into me so that for a moment, my silhouette and my bright soul were a single brightness fused with the bright moonlight" (330). The extreme whiteness of this moment is reminiscent of her earlier description of the whiteness of Gabriel; but, as the dreamlike nature of the language suggests, it is impossible for so much whiteness to retain so much positive value for long.

Indeed, in the next moment, she is gripped with fear and her whiteness becomes a pale reminder of her uncle's recent death. Quickly, she puts on a black velvet coat and hat just as a cloud covers the moon, causing her reflection to darken into the shadows and turn her into "the horrible vision of death" (332). When she turns on the light to alleviate her fear, her reflection is again transformed: "at that cruel instant, between the black velvet of my cloak and the black velvet of my hat, my frightened face, pale and worn out, looked completely faded, with the hollow-eyed fatigue of sick people and the funerary marble of withered roses" (334). Her first reflection, "pure" white, delights her until it reminds her of death. Her second reflection, "pure" black, seems to her the very vision of death. It is this last reflection, however, forcing black and white together in her exhausted face, which is the most horrible of all.

As the novel concludes, images of black and white regain a kind of stability, but one that is founded upon a new symbolic order: white, although still associated with female beauty, represents a violated and ultimately dead form of that beauty. Black has lost whatever benign associations it once held, and becomes a symbol of violence and destruction. Having decided to marry Leal, María Eugenia sits in her room, staring at her wedding dress, which she imagines is being attacked by the black chair on which it lays: "how the black chair silently speaks, and how the limp whiteness screams in its black arms! The chair seems like a sadistic lover embracing a dead woman" (353). María Eugenia's vivid language unites the racial, sexual, economic, and political concerns implicit in her situation. She, a white woman and a virgin, is the white dress; Leal, a sexual predator of mixed race and economic means, is the black chair. This disturbing scene precedes María Eugenia's final (and characteristically dramatic) submission: she proclaims herself a modern Iphigenia, ready to sacrifice her "docile, enslaved" body to the "Sacred Monster with seven heads that are called society, family, honor, religion, morality, duty, conventions, and principles" (353). Recognizing the futility of her longing for a stable racial order or even a fixed personal racial identity, she capitulates to her family's desire for a respectable marriage and to her "blackening," both symbolic and real, by this union.

The final pages of *Iphigenia* stress that a social order founded upon racially mixed alliances will prevail in Venezuela. At the same time, they emphasize the protagonist's belief that she is a victim of this order, which forces her to sacrifice her beautiful white body. As she does throughout *Iphigenia*, Parra uses these final scenes to reveal how her protagonist is defined, and so bound, by established racial, economic, and social categories. At the same time, however, by employing images that destabilize notions of black and white embedded in the history, culture, and language of Venezuela, she lays bare the subjective nature of these categories.

Remembering (through) Memoria in *The Sheltered Life*

Glasgow does not embrace such radical ambiguity and instability, because racial identity in the fictional realm of her novel, as in the historical world and legal rhetoric of the U.S. South, is negotiated in black or white, with no middle ground. Thus the light-skinned Memoria, whose "black" identity is brought into question by the casual comments of Jenny Blair and her mother, is a notable anomaly. Within the historical and cultural context of the novel, the ambivalence of her physical presence is especially provocative. Joel Williamson observes that between 1850 and 1915, southern attitudes toward racial mixing became increasingly intolerant "as the dominant white society moved from semiacceptance of free mulattoes ... to outright rejection." Accompanying this rejection was "an almost total commitment to the one-drop rule. In white eyes, all Negroes came to look alike" (62). Throughout the U.S. South, including Virginia, legal definitions of "white" and "black" reinforced changing social attitudes. Whereas in eighteenth-century Virginia individuals who were at least three-quarters "white" were considered to be white, by 1910 an individual with one-sixteenth "black blood" was classified by law as black. In 1924, Virginia passed the "Act to Preserve Racial Integrity," which, according to Werner Sollors, "extended racial definition to an almost mystical level by suggesting that 'the term "white person" shall apply only to the person who has no trace whatsoever of any blood other than Caucasian'" (6). In a society struggling to preserve the strictly segregated racial hierarchy of the antebellum era, the threat of miscegenation was confronted through laws that circumscribed "whiteness" and "blackness" so as to deny, both legally and symbolically, the biological and social fact of racial mixture.

A similar dynamic of denial is described in *The Sheltered Life*, although it is made manifest through the evasive idealism of the characters rather than through legal maneuverings. The members of María Eugenia's family in *Iphigenia* reluctantly but pragmatically accept the need to "blacken" themselves in order to survive economically and socially. Such a solution, it goes without saying, would be unthinkable for the Archbalds and Birdsongs. Even their genteel poverty becomes a badge of honor, a sign of their refusal to surrender to industrialism. Although they cringe at Isabella's marriage to the working-class Joseph Crocker, they can create a false genealogy for his family and turn a pedestrian pedigree into an "extraordinary history." But even though Memoria, too, shares blood ties to their family, they can never openly acknowledge that they are bound to her in any relationship other than that of employer-employee. Memoria, neither black nor white, may function for the *reader* as a textual reminder of the place where blacks and whites meet in intimacy and violence. However, the white characters—whose point of view the narrator always privileges—refuse to acknowledge this history. As a result, the novel can only gesture obliquely toward the legacy of slavery that the laundress represents.

In *Iphigenia*, Gregoria provides a comfortingly visible—although entirely imaginary—barrier of "pure blackness" between the protagonist and the poverty of the racially mixed "unsheltered" world that encroaches upon her. Memoria's mute presence, in contrast, is subtly, almost invisibly, woven into the text; and her influence, like that of memory itself, is easily overlooked. She is referred to only four times, twice in the novel's first fifty pages and twice in its third and final section. In three of these scenes, she is not present but merely a topic of conversation. Despite her peripheral position, however, Memoria plays an essential role in the lives of the novel's characters and in the movement of the narrative. If it could be argued that the events of *The Sheltered Life*—and the moral and emotional development of Jenny Blair—are driven by the love triangle that forms between her and the Birdsongs, it could also be argued that Memoria is the unacknowledged fourth presence in this dynamic.

She is George's long-time mistress and the catalyst for both Eva's and Jenny Blair's love for George. Eva first falls for her future husband when, as a girl of eight, she witnesses him rescue three-year-old Memoria from a burning shack in Penitentiary Bottom, the heart of Queenborough's black neighborhood. Jenny Blair realizes that she loves George "best of all" when, at the age of nine, she roller-skates into Penitentiary Bottom, hits her head, and is rescued by Memoria. When she awakens from her fall, she sees George, who promises not to reveal her misadventure if she keeps secret his presence in his lover's house. These two events reflect each other in significant ways. Both involve a rescue—the first of Memoria, the second by her—that takes place in Queenborough's black neighborhood when Eva and Jenny Blair are pre-adolescent children. Both also represent a high point of excitement in the privileged women's lives, the first and last time they venture out of their neighborhood into the outside world in search of new experiences. Soon after the rescues, they lose interest in everything but George and their love for him.

The novel shows how, as soon as George asks her to share a secret, Jenny Blair forgets her desire for adventure and surrenders to him: "she yielded completely to the charm of the moment. Even if nothing exciting ever happened to her in the future, this one day would be always brimming over with thrills" (43). Describing her response as a drugging, a drowning, captivation, and intoxication, the passage highlights not just the helplessness but also the thoughtlessness with which she succumbs to a situation fraught with danger. Eva's experience was much the same, as she reveals when describing George's rescue of Memoria: "'nothing so exciting ever happened to me again. But I fell in love with George then, and I never got over it'" (147). For both women, the beginning of romance marks the end of their yearning for personal adventure and creative action. Neither Eva nor Jenny Blair ever get over it.

The location of the rescues is also important: both occur in Memoria's poor, black neighborhood and, indeed, inside her home; yet, in both cases, Memoria's presence is of secondary importance from the perspective of the newly infatuated girls. She is observed only as she relates to George—or, more accurately, as George relates to her. Eva recalls how George carelessly tosses the rescued baby into her waiting mother's arms before resuming his ball game. Rather than censuring him, however, she reads his striking nonchalance as a further sign of bravery: "I think the thing I really loved him for was his courage" (147). Lying in a hospitable bed, emaciated from illness, Eva continues to cling to the illusion that her husband—who, as she speaks, pursues his seduction of Jenny Blair—is a man of valor. As a girl, Jenny Blair also notes George's treatment of Memoria: he looks "in the most careless way at [her]" and, before leaving, "called back to her so indifferently" (42). Unlike Eva, Jenny Blair vocally disapproves of his behavior. As soon as he turns his back on the laundress, however, she forgets her admonishment and basks in "the look of tender protection in his face" (43).[16] Excusing or dismissing George's apparent indifference toward a woman whose significance they refuse to acknowledge aloud, Eva and Jenny Blair, first as girls and then as women, yield to the charms of one who embodies the ideal of southern manhood.

In doing so, they symbolically accept the duty of the southern belle to remain silent about her knowledge of the violent sexual history between white men and black women. Thus the refusal of Eva and Jenny Blair to see George accurately is connected to the same discourse of race, gender, and sexuality that perpetuates the ideals of the gentleman and the belle. As Goodwyn Jones notes: "southern womanhood has from the beginning been inextricably linked to racial attitudes. Its very genesis, some say, lay in the minds of guilty slaveholders who sought an image they could revere without sacrificing the gains of racial slavery" (3–4). Likewise, the ideal of the southern gentleman is inseparable from the history of slavery and racism. Moreover, both rely on opposing stereotypes of black men and women established during slavery. Thus, the virile white master opposes the weak and emasculated black male slave. Similarly, the beautiful but sexually pure belle contrasts with the so-called black Jezebel, whose aggressive, degraded sexuality makes her complicit in her own violation. Each element of the discourse—the powerful male master and the powerless male slave, the pure white woman and the perverse black woman—feeds into what Wallace calls the "hideously intertwined" system that entangles and entraps blacks and whites, men and women, long after the legal end of slavery (138). Glasgow's novel offers a scathing critique of this dynamic, but the gentleman and, especially, the belle are her focus. Black men and women all but disappear. She decries destructive silences even as she relegates black characters like Memoria to secondary roles or symbolic functions. In this sense, Glasgow could be considered guilty of perpetuating the very system she critiques.

Indeed, a number of critics have condemned her portrayals of black characters as racist. Elizabeth Ammon, for example, declares that, even though she spoke out against racism, it is "imperative to recognize the damage done to Glasgow's art by her class privilege and racism" (175–6). David Coffey similarly argues that she "was unable to break with the prevalent attitudes on race of her time and place" (124). Evidence of these attitudes can be found in *The Sheltered Life*, which contains portraits of black characters that are, at best, troubling. The Birdsong's maid, Maggie, for example, is described as a literal throwback to the pre-Civil War South, "blacker, as Mrs. Birdsong once remarked, then God made them now" (242), and as a servant who "adored the ground her master walked on" and "never minded slaving over her stove on hot summer evenings" (243). Such a stereotypical characterization is deeply problematic. At the same time, Maggie is described from the point of view of Jenny Blair, who observes the servant while remembering what various white adults have said about her. In this sense, we might argue along with Raper, "when Glasgow exercises restraint in her presentation of Southern race relations, she is following the conventions of realistic fiction; that is, she is mirroring the denial of her characters" ("Ellen Glasgow" 130). Regardless, the result is an ambiguous perspective best illustrated by the narrator's use of the anachronistic "master" and the demeaning descriptor "slaving," which can be read as either a grossly insensitive use of language or a subtle reminder that Jenny Blair's relationship to Maggie is warped by the slave-holding past.

The effect of such ambiguity, however, is markedly different from the "cordial confusion" established by Parra's constant disruptions of black/white and light/dark binaries. Although both novels emphasize the point of view of the elite, *Iphigenia* disorders the dichotomous language of race to draw attention to the impossibility of maintaining static difference. Glasgow's imagery, in contrast, intentionally or unintentionally reinforces racist stereotypes that privilege absolute racial difference. Although Parra's strategies are in some ways more radical, each woman's language is ultimately rooted in the concepts of race that prevailed in their respective cultures. Just as Parra highlights the fluidity inherent in the Venezuelan rhetoric of *blanquimiento*, so the unbending notion of "one-dropism" reverberates profoundly in Glasgow's plot and poetry.

Despite her obvious sympathy for her character, this is ultimately true of Glasgow's depiction of Memoria as well. Goodman asserts that the author "not only gives Memoria her own plot—something she herself had not chanced before [with black characters]—but she also makes her the novel's unsung heroine, its resolute survivor" ("Memory and Memoria" 244). I would argue, however, that the plot bestowed upon Memoria is limited by the novel's restricted point of view and, perhaps, by constraints imposed by the author's personal ties to the Tidewater plantocracy. Memoria's character is fleshed out only insofar as it relates to the white protagonists (particularly to Jenny Blair and Eva Birdsong's relationships with George). Her more personal story remains largely an untold potential, and she a praiseworthy but passive "resolute survivor."

At the same time, the textual space occupied by Memoria does allow Glasgow to connect silences about race and slavery to other silences, including those surrounding issues of womanhood and female sexuality. Furthermore, it reveals how the accumulation of such silences distorts broader concepts of innocence, guilt, and justice.[17] The novel exposes these distortions most clearly in the final scene, when Eva, upon discovering her husband in an intimate embrace with Jenny Blair, fatally shoots him. Immediately after the shooting, General Archbald insists that Eva is innocent and proclaims the cause of death to be accidental suicide. He even persuades the Birdsong's nephew John to turn away from his progressive or "northern" perspective in order to assist with the cover-up. Both men embrace the old code of honor, which the general, in an earlier passage, recalls as "the heroic pretense that plain murder was pure accident. By force of superior importance, [the old families of Queenborough] had ignored facts, defended family honour, shielded a murderer for the sake of saving a name, turned public execration into sympathy, and politely but firmly looked the law out of countenance" (128–29). Representing the old and new generations, the two men stand in the presence of Eva's emotional and physical devastation, Jenny Blair's moral corruption, and George's murdered body, and proclaim not only their innocence but also their superiority.

Like *Iphigenia, The Sheltered Life* ends with a sacrifice, although who is sacrificed, and for what purpose, remains unclear. Eva, who has sacrificed herself almost to the point of death, now sacrifices her husband, and potentially her own freedom, in an attempt to avenge herself. Or, perhaps realizing it is too late for personal vindication, she commits murder in order to free Jenny Blair and the future generations she represents from the romantic ideal and violent reality that George symbolizes. Jenny Blair's response, like John's, however, suggests that Eva acts too late not only for herself but also for the younger generation. Fleeing the scene of the crime, Jenny Blair insists on her innocence: "I didn't mean anything ... I didn't mean anything in the world!" (292). This mantra, which she repeats throughout the final part of the novel, contrasts sharply with her youthful declaration of selfhood—"I'm alive, alive, alive and I'm Jenny Blair Archbald" (3)—and so signals her willingness to sacrifice her intellect and creativity to the deception that pervades her society.

Conclusion

Jenny Blair and María Eugenia live, as Glasgow declares, the sheltered life, and neither is able to connect herself or her actions to the wider world. Thus Jenny Blair retreats into a self-absorption that strips her of compassion for those who suffer: "she couldn't (and it wasn't her fault) find the poor interesting. She loved life, and wanted to be happy" (220). Despite a relatively more critical understanding of her society and the changes it is experiencing, María Eugenia's ability to move beyond herself is likewise limited. In the final pages of *Iphigenia*, she claims to be, like Venezuela's black slaves, scarred by centuries of abuse and forced servitude; yet, in the very next paragraph, she admires herself as white and beautiful. Identifying with the poverty and exploitation of non-white women, she still insists upon the privilege of racial difference.[18] Like Jenny Blair, she is unable to imagine a true alliance with the unsheltered people of the world.

Despite this similarity, many of the restrictions and expectations imposed upon Jenny Blair differ from those that María Eugenia experiences. The latter is bound by the project of *blanquimiento*, which teaches her to disdain racial mixing while simultaneously demanding that she sacrifice her own racial "purity" for the sake of the nation, whose economic progress is dependent upon the "whitening" of the population. The former, in contrast, is confined by the ideal of southern womanhood, which claims to shelter her but also requires that she guard the open secret of miscegenation. María Eugenia fears becoming like the mixed-race women of her society. Jenny Blair has no such worries. Indeed, her tragedy is that, apart from her naive romantic pining for George Birdsong, she has no worries at all. Trapped in the distorting silences of her culture, she has matured into a young woman incapable of reflection. Thus, while María Eugenia mournfully, but deliberately, sacrifices her "beautiful white body" to a new national order, Jenny Blair placidly surrenders to the ideal of the southern belle. In both cases, however, the protagonist's understanding of the world around her, and her value in it, is predicated upon dubious notions of genealogical exceptionality, which are implicitly reaffirmed by the lack of genealogy or history ascribed to the characters of Gregoria and Memoria.

Writing about María Eugenia and the protagonist of Dulce María Loynaz's *Garden*, which will be analyzed in the following chapter, Rodríguez affirms, "These white women have a history" (98). The same could be said of the women in *The Sheltered Life* and Eudora Welty's *Delta Wedding*, also studied in chapter 3. All of these characters are members of landed aristocracies that once shaped a history intimately linked to the genealogies—and, as we shall see, the geographies—of a plantation past. In turn, that history shapes them. In a letter written to a critic of *Iphigenia*, Parra addresses the irresistible hold of the familial past. Accusing the critic of needing "to know at any cost the logical and concrete reason for each one of my heroine's acts," she warns, "but you will never know because she is illogical, and she is illogical because in spite of that ultramodern mentality, which sweeps her up in revolutionary exaltation, she is controlled, and will always be controlled, by her ancestors" (*Obra Escogida* 2: 214–15). Parra describes a fundamental struggle between the "illogical" call of genealogy and tradition and the "logical" and revolutionary appeal of modernity.

If *I'll Take My Stand* and *Cuban Counterpoint* articulate a similar impasse (although from opposing ideological points of view), the four female-authored novels studied in this chapter and the next domesticate and feminize the dilemmas they present. Each novel struggles to free its protagonists from what Glissant, in his brief account of the open word, calls the "delusion" of the master, which "blot[s] out the shudders of life, that is, the turbulent realities of the Plantation, beneath the conventional splendor of scenery" (*Poetics of Relation* 70). For Parra and Glasgow, the "splendor of scenery" that dazzles and blinds their protagonists is located in the metaphorical realm of the past, where the dead order the living. Welty and Loynaz engage that scenery on a literal level, fashioning complex landscapes that reflect the frustration of their protagonists while, at the same time, challenging conventional concepts of the "masculine" nation and the "feminine" land it seeks to control. Regardless of their different narrative trajectories, however, the characters who populate these exemplars of the modern plantation imaginary finally remain immobile, fixed between the intoxicating promises and poisonous hazards of modernity, on the one hand, and the lure of a paradisiacal past that threatens to entrap them forever, on the other.

Women, Nation, and the "Problematic of Space"

Garden and *Delta Wedding*

T he novels examined in the previous chapter, Parra's *Iphigenia* and Glasgow's *The Sheltered Life*, are plot-driven: harnessing the forward-moving energy of the conventional chronological story, they narrate the lives of protagonists who, trapped between modern industrialism and the traditional hierarchies associated with the plantation, are pushed helplessly toward an unhappy ending. In contrast, *Jardín*, or *Garden* (1951), by Dulce María Loynaz, and *Delta Wedding* (1946), by Eudora Welty, are notable for their very lack of plot. Loynaz's novel spans more than a decade of its protagonist's life, but dedicates the bulk of its pages to describing Bárbara's solitary days, spent wandering through her family's abandoned house and garden or examining old letters and photographs. *Delta Wedding* takes place over a much shorter period of time, a little more than a week, and relates a series of mostly unremarkable events preceding the marriage of Dabney Fairchild, favorite daughter of a large Mississippian family, to the overseer of her father's plantation. The author's preface to *Garden* contains a warning that would serve the potential reader of *Delta Wedding* equally well: "[the book's] plot has proven to be so spread out and weak, so lacking in coherence, that it barely manages to hold up the frame of the book's chapters" (9). Each novel has a plot, weak and scattered though it may be. Neither, however, is driven by it. Rather, they deliberately interrupt the inexorable forward movement that impels *Iphigenia* and *The Sheltered Life* to their tragic ends.

They do so, in part, by drawing from the strategies of the so-called lyrical novel, a literary form that first emerged in the nineteenth century and retained its popularity through the first half of the twentieth century.[1] Juxtaposing lyric and narrative modes, the lyrical novel disrupts the flow of chronological or historical time. While preserving the basic function of narrative—the representation of a fictional world that is comprehensible to the reader—it strives to create its world, not from a series of actions that takes place over time, but rather from a series of images whose meaning emerges through structural and linguistic patterns. The result, according to Ralph Freedman, is a genre that generates "an immediacy of portraiture, an availability of themes and motifs to the reader's glance without the interposition of a narrative world" (9). The phrases "immediacy of portraiture" and "the reader's glance" suggest meaning that is organized spatially rather than temporally; and, indeed, the lyrical novel tends to understand time in terms of space. Or, as Ricardo Gullón argues, it extends the instant by "eternalizing it, which is to say, spatializing it. To eternalize the instant is to turn time into space, detaining and isolating one of its beats" (21). Isolated and immobilized, the "instant" can be seen and touched, and eternity is brought within human grasp. Yet, as Gullón recognizes, the glory of immortality and the trap of timelessness are difficult to distinguish because the eternalized instant generates a "constant return in which, once again, eternity and timelessness draw close to each other, rub against each other, and are ... two names for a single sensation" (46). Seeking to disturb the relentless march of time, the lyrical novel runs the risk of trapping itself and the reader in a miasma of timelessness, a cycle of eternal return, or death itself. For this reason, even as it favors lyrical time, or timelessness, the genre depends upon the dynamism of narrative time to bring itself back into the flow of history, and of life.

Articulated in gendered terms, the lyrical novel facilitates a confrontation between what has been traditionally conceived of as masculine time—that is to say narrative, linear, or historical time—and so-called feminine time, which is paradoxically the absence of time, or the privileging of space over time. As Julia Kristeva observes "when evoking the name and destiny of women, one thinks more of the space generating and forming the human species than of time, becoming or history" (63). Within this symbolic matrix, the feminine is outside of, and antithetical to, historical time, and women are identified with the ahistorical, precultural realms of mythology and nature.[2] The resulting "problematic of space," as Kristeva terms it, takes on particular meaning in the context of the New World novelistic traditions to which *Delta Wedding* and *Garden* respond, traditions that often narrate the nation in terms derived from the symbolic conflict between feminine space and masculine time. That is to say, they allegorize national history as a struggle between historical culture and ahistorical nature, in which the heroic (male) founders of the new nation toil to possess untamed (female) territories, settle them, and make them productive.

Although they are not novels, both *Cuban Counterpoint* and *I'll Take My Stand* draw from elements of this discourse. The latter, for example, imagines the order of the plantation as based upon a productive, but always hierarchical, partnership between a lightened, masculinized culture and a darkened, feminized nature. As we saw in chapter 1, Ortiz's racialization and eroticization of the relationship between culture and nature is less predictable. His gendering of it, however, is quite similar: decrying the mechanized plantation as a monstrous cyclops that devours virgin territory, he upholds the tobacco *vega* as a model of good husbandry and productive, patriarchal community. Despite their differences, both texts demonstrate how woman comes to be identified with and symbolically bound to the land; and, as a result, how she is unable to participate as an active subject in the creation of the modern nation. Unlike these male-authored essays, the novels discussed in chapter 2 do not focus on the physical space of the plantation: in *Iphigenia* and *The Sheltered Life*, it is not virgin territories that are devoured by modernity or tamed by an idealized community, but rather virginal young women who must sacrifice their creative and procreative energies in order to reproduce old imagined communities or give birth to new ones.

Like the novels by Glasgow and Parra, *Garden* and *Delta Wedding* feature female protagonists who struggle with issues of sexuality, romance, and love. Yet, like *I'll Take My Stand* and *Cuban Counterpoint*, they imagine a deeply eroticized natural world in the heart of the plantation. In the process, they confront the quandary described by Jean Franco: "Women's attempts to plot themselves as protagonists in the national novel become a recognition of the fact that they are not in the plot at all but definitely somewhere else" (146). Loynaz and Welty respond to this dilemma, not by forcing their protagonists back into the plot or rejecting the traditional association of women with nature. Rather, they represent Franco's "somewhere else" as a landscape simultaneously sculpted by history and charged with lyrical desire. That is to say, they unite what Glissant calls the "closed place" of the plantation with the expansiveness and mutability of the open word.

Although their strategies for shaping space are similar, the spaces they shape diverge in significant ways: *Delta Wedding* is located on a working plantation in the Mississippi Delta, while *Garden* takes place in an almost abandoned house and garden located on the coast of an unnamed island. This difference reflects, in part, broader differences in fictions from the U.S. South and Spanish America concerned with the search for national and cultural origins. As I commented in the introduction to this book—and as *I'll Take My Stand* amply demonstrates—writers from the U.S. South have tended to privilege the plantation. The novelists of Spanish America, in contrast, have more often set their works in a virgin wilderness. In *Delta Wedding*, Welty engages, but ultimately subverts, the imagined community of the Edenic plantation. In *Garden*, Loynaz conjures a primitive natural world that improbably survives on the very edge of a modern city. In contrast to *Delta Wedding*, and to an even greater extent than in *Iphigenia* and *The Sheltered Life*, the literal space of the plantation is absent from the pages of *Garden;* indeed, as we shall see, the problematic of island insularity is in many ways her central focus. Yet the plantation's presence, although deliberately marginalized, is undeniable when the historical forces that constructed the house and garden are taken into account.

Notwithstanding their differences, the landscapes imagined by the two authors are both dominated by gardens and houses, which in turn are surrounded, penetrated, and transformed by the historical forces of modernity, on the one hand, and the eternal rhythms of the natural world, on the other. The resulting terrains, at once closed and open, reveal the frustrated subjectivities of their protagonists. But they also attempt to redefine the relationship between the modern masculine nation and the primitive feminine land it seeks to occupy in such a way that woman is not sacrificed for community.

Insularity and the Plantation Landscape

It is hardly surprising that both Loynaz and Welty would privilege the lyric along with the landscape. As artists, they were acclaimed for the lyrical qualities of their writing; personally, they were devoted to the regions of their births and their familial homes throughout their long lives. Loynaz, born in 1902, in Havana, Cuba, to an illustrious literary family, is best known for her poetry, often written in free verse and abounding in intimate yet concrete images from the natural world and daily life. *Garden*, which was written between 1928 and 1935 but not published until 1951, is her only novel; and, in its preface, she questions whether it is a novel at all, finally determining that it might be more accurately called a lyrical novel: "I have wanted to add to the word 'novel' the adjective 'lyrical,' which, more than a paradox, serves as a mitigating factor, as an explanation" (9). Always loyal to her ancestral heritage and proud of her father's service in Cuba's wars for independence, Loynaz nevertheless remained aloof from national politics. She stayed on the island after 1959, but ceased publishing until the mid-1980s and withdrew from civic life almost completely. Her withdrawal, however, did not represent an abrupt change in behavior prompted by Castro's revolution. Rather, it reflected a natural aversion to public life and a deep attachment to the solitude provided by the memento-filled home she refused to abandon. After decades of self-imposed isolation, she experienced renewed interest in her work after being awarded the Premio Nacional de Literatura in 1987 and the Premio Miguel de Cervantes in 1992. She died in her beloved home five years later, at the age of ninety-three.

Born in 1909, in Jackson, Mississippi, Welty had already garnered critical acclaim for her short stories when she published *Delta Wedding*, her first novel, in 1946. Unlike Loynaz (or Parra and Glasgow), she was not a daughter of the local elite; her father and mother were middle-class and hailed from Ohio and West Virginia, respectively. Like her Cuban counterpart, however, the Mississippian avoided implicating herself and her work in political debates, and famously articulated her dislike of literary didacticism in 1965, in the midst of the Civil Rights Movement, when she argued that "writing fiction places the novelist and the crusader on opposite sides" (*Eye* 147). Welty's long, active career as a writer of novels, short stories, essays, and memoir brought many accolades, including a Pulitzer Prize in 1969. Like Loynaz, despite her far-reaching fame, Welty maintained close ties to home. She died, in 2001, in the family house where she had lived for seventy-six years.

In contrast to Loynaz, Welty never directly employed the term "lyrical" to describe her prose; more than one critic has, however, and Welty's own meditations on writing lend validity to such an understanding of her work.[3] Fiction, she wrote, is "fuller [of mystery] than I know how to say. Plot, characters, setting, and so forth are not what I'm referring to now; we all deal with those as best we can. The mystery lies in the use of language to express human life" (*Eye* 157). A palpable aura of mystery permeates both *Delta Wedding* and *Garden*, informing a distinctive sense of place that reflects the authors' artistic philosophies as well as their profound loyalty to community, house, and home. Both women grapple with complex political, historical, and sociological questions but avoid didactic commentary and rely instead on a lyrical exploration of their protagonists' experiences of space and time, or of place and history.

Reflecting upon the place of place within this mysterious dynamic, Welty, in an essay entitled "Place in Fiction," asserts: "Place in fiction is the named, identified, concrete, exact and exacting, and therefore credible, gathering spot of all that has been felt, is about to be experienced, in the novel's progress. Location pertains to feeling; feeling profoundly pertains to place; place in history partakes of feeling, as feeling about history partakes of place" (*Eye* 122). Emphasizing its particularity and materiality, Welty defines place as an identifiable "spot" filled with solid beings and recordable actions. It is the ground upon which the novel's plot and, she suggests in the second sentence, history itself unfold. Yet the reassuring solidity of this "spot," its apparent knowableness, is complicated by an insistence that place and history are inseparable from the experience of emotion, and the intuitive knowledge that this experience grants. Three elements—place, history, and feeling—thus participate in an enigmatic communion, and it is through their intermingling or interpenetration that the precise, poetic space of the landscape comes into being.

Welty questions the "knowable" quality of history by bringing it into a non-hierarchical contact with the closed place of the "spot," on the one hand, and the open word of emotion, on the other. The result is a vision of the past, not tragically closed but, as she affirms elsewhere, intimately linked to the present: "Whatever is significant and whatever is tragic in its story live as long as the place does, though they are unseen, and the new life will be built upon these things—regardless of commerce and the way of rivers and roads, and other vagrancies" (*Eye* 299). Employing the freer movement of the open word, she succeeds in doing what neither the Twelve Southerners nor Glasgow could accomplish: she disrupts the dichotomous logic of plantation history through the articulation of a landscape in flux, reshaped and renewed by the peoples and actions that flow through it.

In *Delta Wedding*, Welty applies her dynamic vision to the Mississippi Delta, whose fertile territory was historically dominated by cotton plantations and whose imagination was governed by what Albert Devlin terms "the informing myth" of the Delta as a place of "timeless bounty"—a myth espoused, for example, in a 1923 article from in Jackson *Daily News* that presented " 'the theory that the Yazoo Delta was the original Garden of Eden' " (91).[4] By setting her story on the ground of the plantation, and then prying that ground open, Welty self-consciously evokes, and then undermines, this myth along with the conventions of the Plantation School of fiction, which was largely responsible for popularizing images of columned mansions, vivacious ladies, dashing gentlemen, and simple, happy slaves.

Although early (non-novelistic) examples of this genre date back to the first half of the nineteenth century, it attained broad appeal only in the post-Reconstruction era, when writers such as Thomas Nelson Page and Joel Chandler Harris published books that were read, in the United States, by masses of northerners and southerners alike.[5] Lucinda Mackethan, among others, has asserted a direct link between its rise in popularity and the collapse of the old plantation system: "a popular literature stocked with belles and cavaliers, courtships and duels, mansions and cotton blossoms, and, at the heart of the scene, wistfully reminiscing darkies, had to await the actual demise of the plantation world" (209). Writers of the so-called New South thus produced a literature celebrating an Old South that, they recognized, would never be regained. The resulting vision of the plantation as an antidote to the dehumanizing demands of modern life bears a hardly coincidental resemblance to the agrarian paradise portrayed by the Twelve Southerners in *I'll Take My Stand*.

The plantation novels of the late nineteenth century, in particular, tend to conform to other conventions as well: most locate the "Big House" at the physical and metaphorical heart of the plantation; valorize the leadership of a patriarch who embodies chivalric virtue and traditional values; portray slaves as loyal and contented subjects; and develop a tragic notion of history that arises, inevitably, from the comparison between old and new orders. Of this last characteristic, in particular, Devlin observes, "only the memory of a golden time ... could provide ample solace for the benighted present and still more unpromising future" (119).

On its surface, *Delta Wedding* reproduces many of these of conventions. Yet, as Devlin argues, Welty's novel "possesses a different attitude toward time and historical process" (119). This attitude, I would argue, is inextricable from her "sense of place" and her employment of lyrical strategies. In the previous chapter, we saw how Glasgow harshly critiques the cultural paralysis of the U.S. South even as she recreates the very dichotomies that keep it mired in the past. Although Welty likewise rejects the insularity of southern culture, the structure and style of her novel do not mirror, however ironically, its paralysis. Instead, she employs subtle linguistic shifts, considered repetitions, and accumulated images and tones to fashion a lyrical or open landscape of endless variation and constant change.

In *Garden*, Loynaz also moves within the confines of a carefully constructed landscape. Yet, if Welty forces open the sealed parameters of the plantation, Loynaz compresses untrammeled nature into the intimate space of her titular garden, creating an enclosed atmosphere at once claustrophobic and vital. According to the Cuban critic, Fina García Marruz, in its wildness the garden bears a striking resemblance to the sprawling natural environments that dominate many canonical Latin American novels:

> [Critics] speak of the "jungle" of José Eustasio Rivera, of the "pampa" of Don Segundo Sombra, of the prairies of Doña Bárbara, of the Great Savannah of Alejo Carpentier, but they never relate any of this to the *Garden* of our Dulce María Loynaz. Yet couldn't one say that from the outset all of these stories share a common link? That they center themselves in one space, in nature—our American nature—, which serves not as a stage or a background, but rather as a rooting theme? (549)

Like the male contemporaries referred to above, Loynaz analyzes the confrontation between premodern and modern orders and explores a foundational link between national identity and natural environment in the Americas.[6] However, by replacing the unknown vastness of the *selva* or the *pampa* with the enclosure of a garden, she draws nation *and* nature into a constricted, traditionally feminine realm.[7] Additionally, by attaching the garden to a house, she appears to domesticate these entities even as she feminizes them. Comprising three elements—the garden, the house, and the surrounding sea—the novel's terrain is inherently limited and endlessly expansive, modestly domestic and explosively fecund. As such, it replicates ambiguities that infuse not only *Garden* but also many of Loynaz's poems, in which images of house, garden, and sea are similarly prominent. Like Welty's essays, Loynaz's poetic work reveals a well-defined sense of place. Hers, however, is shaped not by the encounter between place, history, and feeling, but rather by the paradoxical nature of island insularity, which is conveyed through the variations of these three recurring elements.

Her 1947 collection, *Juegos de agua*, exemplifies some of these tendencies. A series of short poems, it catalogues water in its many forms: flowing through a sea or river, contained in an aquarium, distorted by the machinery of a fountain, moving through the atmosphere as rain or fog. Shifting shape from page to page, alternately confined and unleashed, water is a conduit through which to meditate upon the possibilities of transformation and variation, the encroachment of modernity, and the relationship between human civilization and the natural world. When, on several occasions, it is imagined as a sea existing in a tense, erotic relationship to land, it becomes a means by which to contemplate the dynamics of insularity. Loynaz often, in these cases, conforms to a conventional description of the sea, with its cycles, tides, and undulating flows, as feminine. In her poem "Isla," however, it is the *island* that is feminine, and under siege by an aggressive masculine sea. Barely audible above the howling winds, the besieged landmass declares herself to be the Ouroboros, swallowing her own tail: "I fly or collapse,/ I swallow my tail/ like a sign of the Infinite" (*A Woman* 95) ["Puedo volar o hundirme ... Puedo, a veces,/ morder mi cola en signo de Infinito" (*A Woman* 94)]. An archetype, according to Jung, of primordial unity and cyclicality, the Ouroboros functions as a vivid reminder that life feeds on death; and the poem underscores the interpenetrating danger of the self-devouring serpent and the violent attacks by the sea:

> I am earth broken away. Sometimes
> water blinds me and I cower,
> water is the death I float in.
> But open to tides and cyclones,
> my shattered breast takes root in the sea.   (*A Woman* 95)

> Soy tierra desgajándose ... Hay momentos
> en que el agua me ciega y me acobarda,
> en que el agua es la muerte donde floto ...
> Pero abierta a mareas y a ciclones,
> hinco en el mar raíz de pecho roto.   (*A Woman* 94)

Using the progressive, reflexive form of the verb "desgajar," or to break off (translated as "broken away"), Loynaz extends the metaphor of the Ouroboros: the island depicts herself as earth eating away at itself. At the same time, the sea attacks at regular intervals, further unnerving her.

This bleak stanza ends, however, with an oblique gesture of hope, signaled by the ellipses, in the Spanish original, that immediately follow the image of the sea as "la muerte donde floto ...", or "the death I float in." On the one hand, these ellipses suggest continuation, and so a deferral of the finality of death. On the other hand, they emphasize the recurring threat of the sea, which lingers and lurks. The death begot by the sea is not absolute; but, like the tide, it always returns. Thus the "Pero," or "But," that begins the following line does not negate this death but rather denotes a tentative strategy for confronting it, one that involves both a feminine vulnerability, captured by the island's openness, and a masculine aggression, suggested by the verb "hincar," which is translated as "takes root" but literally means to thrust, plunge, or plant one object into another. The island, initially gendered as feminine, now takes on characteristics of both genders in order to survive and grow. The image of a shattered breast thrusting itself into the depths of the sea fuses vulnerability with forceful action, and attests to a longing for wholeness and stability as well as an attendant recognition that this is impossible. The poet, nevertheless, does not seem to mourn this impossibility. Rather, she understands the dual nature of the island, its feminine penetrability and its masculine penetrativeness, to be the source of its redemption as well as its ruin. Employing erotically charged and fluidly gendered imagery, Loynaz suggests that, by simultaneously opening up to the sea and drawing into itself, the island can create an insularity that accepts death even as it nurtures growth and creativity.

Welty's open sense of place is a strategic response to the relentlessly closed, backward-looking vision of the U.S. southern imaginary as it is exemplified in *I'll Take My Stand* and the Plantation School of fiction. Loynaz's sense of place—which, unlike Welty's, valorizes both closedness and openness—similarly engages a well-known cultural discourse, that of island insularity. A proper account of this pan-Caribbean discourse, both broader and deeper in scope than that of the Plantation School, is beyond the reach of the present study.[8] Its significance as well as its complexity, however, is hinted at by a brief comparison between *Garden* and *Cuban Counterpoint*, both of which emerge from the Cuban context of the 1930s and grapple with Cuba's vulnerability to, and need for, the outside world.

Ortiz, as we have seen, commemorates the contributions of dozens of national and ethnic groups to Cuban culture, even as his concept of transculturation emphasizes both the generative and the destructive potential of such cross-cultural contact. At the same time, Ortiz's critique of imperialism and industrialization lead him to indict those who have exploited Cuba *without* participating in the process of transculturation. He singles out the imperialist projects of Spain, England, and the United States, presenting each as more dangerous than the last, in part because of their ever increasing reliance on absentee landlordism, a system that maximizes economic exploitation while minimizing participation in the reciprocal process of transculturation (63–64). Pointing to the destruction inflicted upon the nation by such outside aggression, he longs for Doña Sugar to stop wandering the globe in order to settle down with Don Tobacco. Likewise, he urges his readers to abandon the foreign-owned super-central and support the local *vega*. The outside world never ceases to be vital to his vision—he declares, after all, that "if there was a Paradise it included the whole world" (202). Yet he argues that Cuba cannot take pleasure in a global paradise without first nurturing its own plot, and its own family.

If Ortiz describes Cuba's vulnerability to outside influences in terms of historical and cultural processes, Loynaz, in "Isla" and *Garden*, represents island openness in primarily geographical terms. Although *Garden*, like *Cuban Counterpoint*, unequivocally condemns the encroachment of the industrialized world onto the island, it refuses to articulate an alternative historical trajectory or to imagine a different kind of national community. Indeed, in contrast to both Ortiz and Welty, Loynaz seems to question the very possibility of community. Ortiz's *vega* may be "like a garden" (56), but Loynaz's garden is no idealized *vega*. Instead, it reveals itself as a lonely landscape that exposes the damage that untrammeled patriarchal control has wrought upon the island even as it lays bare the irresolvable conflict at the heart of island insularity: the tension between the yearning to break free of isolation and interact with the wider world, and the need to protect oneself from constant invasion, be liberated from dependency, and develop a richly autonomous identity. Although Loynaz seems largely uninterested in judging the relative merits of isolation versus openness, she finally insists upon the indispensability of seclusion and intimates that Cuba might resolve its eternal dilemma by embracing a lonely woman and a garden that have, for too long, been ignored.[9]

Sea, House, Garden: Island Insularity in Verdant Green and Shades of Gray

Garden's dual protagonists, the titular garden and its inhabitant, Bárbara, are barbarous, as the woman's name suggests, and their primitiveness emerges, not only from their mythical connection to nature, but also from their complicated relationship to history, modernity, and the insular space of the Cuban nation. In her brief "Preludio," or "Prelude," Loynaz declares that her novel contains "neither time nor space, as in the theories of Einstein. The garden and the woman are in whatever meridian of the world—the most curved or the tautest—. And at whatever degree—the highest or the lowest—of the circumference of time" (9). Although she claims a broad universality, however, the author's invocation of Einstein's theory of relativity ironically undermines this possibility. Because her understanding of time and space depends upon her chronological and spatial location in the world, Bárbara's perception is shaped by her identity as a young woman, a white Cuban, and an impoverished daughter of the declining aristocracy, as well as by her view of the modern world, which is circumscribed by the limited perspective her garden allows.

This perspective is established in two brief vignettes, untitled and without chapter numbers, that bookend the main text of the novel. The first opens: "Barbara pressed her pale face to the iron bars and looked through them. Automobiles painted green and yellow, shaven men and smiling women, were passing very nearby, in a luminous parade cut at regular intervals by the interwoven railing of the grille" (14). The protagonist, her view dissected at regular intervals by iron bars, stares out from her rambling house and lush gardens onto a cityscape that does not know, or care, that she exists. This image is repeated, almost verbatim, in the novel's final paragraphs, underscoring Bárbara's exclusion from the mechanized metropolis that functions as the novel's central symbol of modernity, much the way the super-central does in Ortiz.[10]

Like Caracas in *Iphigenia* and Queenborough in *The Sheltered Life*, the city in the opening and closing scenes of *Garden* epitomizes modernity's invasive, dehumanizing nature. Its negative function, however, is mitigated by a chapter in the second part of the novel, "La ciudad," which divulges Bárbara's desire to escape the garden and flee to the city. In this dreamlike chapter, the protagonist stumbles upon a mysterious spiral staircase in her house and climbs it until she has an unobstructed view of the entire island. Relieved to find the garden shrunk down to the size of an impotent "floral rug" (104), she shifts her gaze to a metropolis identifiable by its stony whiteness: "whiteness of polished paving stones, of chips of living rock cut at angles, grown into points" (105). The narrator—sounding very much like the Twelve

Southerners disparaging "the shop-girl [who] reads the comic strip with her bowl of patent cereal" (*I'll Take My Stand* 35)—warns that the city is filled with "thousands of Bárbaras" who exist "without a story to tell" (105). Yet the rhythms of this tropical urban space entrance the protagonist. As she imagines its residents listening to the tales of sailors from faraway places, or selling pineapples, oysters, and herbal remedies, she yearns to see the city victorious over the garden: "if it would only grow at once, if it would finish swelling up like a piece of ripe fruit, and its new houses would reach Bárbara's old house! And if only the houses would take over the garden, and the garden would disappear, devoured by stone" (107). The final words of the chapter, however, indicate the futility of her desire by emphasizing the menacing vitality of the garden, which "laughed softly … quickly stifling the sound under the harboring wind" (107).

Iphigenia and *The Sheltered Life* openly acknowledge the triumph of the modern city, even as they at times convey nostalgia for a more traditional past. *Garden* does something different: it recognizes the threat as well as the promise of both the city and the garden, portrays their embattled interactions, and depicts Bárbara as trapped between the white stone of the one and the lush green of the other. At the same time, however, the novel plainly privileges the garden over the city and, employing the subterfuge of the lyric, pushes the invasive urban space to its margins. Technological advancements, historical time, and official records disintegrate and disappear, while the garden, with its old-fashioned house and obsolete inhabitant, takes center stage.

Yet *Garden* does not, and cannot, completely isolate its island or its protagonist from the outside world. In *Cuban Counterpoint*, Ortiz describes Cuba's history as a process dependent upon the constant, violent uprooting and transplanting of peoples; *Garden* alludes to a similar method of development, but in environmental, rather than human, terms. The weather patterns on Bárbara's island, for example, are both tropical and temperate: sudden rainstorms abound and a hurricane erupts to alter the course of the protagonist's life; yet spring, summer, fall, and winter pass in regular succession, with snow occasionally dusting the ground. Likewise, the garden's vegetation is not stereotypically Caribbean, although it does include specimens native to the Antilles and referred to by their common Cuban names, like *yagruma* and *miraguano*. These, however, grow alongside boxwood, native to Africa and Eurasia; fig trees, indigenous to western Asia but long cultivated in the Mediterranean; and, of course, the proliferate rose, whose varieties are found all over the world, but much more commonly in the northern hemisphere than in the tropics. Such botanical diversity reflects real events, as Elizabeth DeLoughrey observes: "The colonial process involved a simultaneous uprooting of plants *and* peoples, reminding us that the etymological root of the word 'diaspora' is 'seed.' Often the same ships contained flora and fauna as well as human beings for transplantation to colonial botanical gardens and sugar plantations across the Atlantic" (*Caribbean Literature* 18). The varied plant life in Bárbara's garden echoes the human diversity depicted by Ortiz; confirms the archipelago's insular openness; and shows how, whether by force, accident, or design, outside elements transform the landscape.

Like its sense of place, the novel's notion of time, intentionally disorienting, reveals the persistence of the past in the present, but also strategically exacerbates the difficulty of comprehending the significance of that past. Although Bárbara is a young woman at the beginning of the story, she struggles to remember her own child-hood. References to real-world historical events are vague and, at times, misleading. Names of cities and important people are excluded or deliberately misidentified. Chronological confusion is further heightened by the seventeen-year gap between the time Loynaz completed the novel in 1935, and its eventual publication in 1951. Yet hints dropped here and there establish a veiled timeline for Bárbara's life: nine-teen or twenty years of age at the beginning of the novel, she was born in the early 1880s. After spending two decades isolated in the confines of her house and garden, a hurricane shipwrecks a blue-eyed navigator, a scientist whose name is never revealed, on her beach, and she flees the island with him at the turn of the century. They marry, have two children, and live abroad for about twenty years before return-ing to the island, where Bárbara meets her tragic death shortly after the end of World War I.[11]

A search for chronological clues thus reveals that the three defining moments in Bárbara's story—her birth, her exit from the island, and her final return to it—coin-cide with three distinct periods in Cuban history. Her life begins in the midst of an era of intense *independentista* activity: she is born just after the end of the Ten Years War (1868–1878), an ultimately unsuccessful struggle for national independence, and be-fore the abolition of slavery, decreed in 1886. She flees around the time of Cuba's final war for independence and the United States' 1898 intervention in that war. That is to say, she flees at a moment when her nation's history teetered between the opti-mism inspired by a patriotic struggle that united Cubans across race and class; and the pessimism that emerged when the United States occupied the island, negotiated the terms of peace with Spain, and, in 1902, used the Platt Amendment to force the fledging government to sign away its sovereignty. Finally, Bárbara returns to the is-land, and her death, at a time of disillusionment and outright despair, when the Cuban nation faced economic instability, rampant political corruption, and dictatorial rule.

The span of Bárbara's life, however, represents only one dimension of the nov-el's begrudging timeline. *Garden* encompasses a second chronology that reaches back to the mid-nineteenth century, a temporal regression confirmed by two sets of documents discovered by the protagonist: a series of newspaper clippings and a cache of love letters. The clippings, almost the only fragments of official history to pene-trate Bárbara's world, are dated "Thursday, September 10, 184 ..." (84). They thus provide objective evidence for establishing the second timeline. Meanwhile, the let-ters, which are also from the nineteenth century and play a more significant role in the plot, function quite differently: far from imparting objective information, they produce a magical bond between the protagonist and the great-aunt, also named Bárbara, to whom they are addressed. While they generate a supernatural temporal link capable of (con)fusing the identities of the two Bárbaras, however, these more personal documents also reveal historical differences between the mid- versus the late-nineteenth century.

For example, they reveal that the house, almost completely abandoned at the dawn of the twentieth century, buzzed with activity a few decades earlier, playing host to fancy balls, literary salons, and political gatherings. Peppered with references to classic Western artists like Virgil and Bach, and contemporary ones like Carolsfeld and Pierrot, the missives expose the distinct social and economic situations of each

Bárbara. The first comes of age in a time when the Cuban elite was made wealthy by a booming plantation economy: between 1778 and 1846 the number of Cuban sugar mills more than tripled.[12] The second, in sharp contrast, grows up in a period when the same elite suffered severe economic decline. As Louis Pérez recounts, after the end of the Ten Years' War, "Sugar planters everywhere in Cuba were in crisis. 'Out of the twelve or thirteen hundred planters on the island,' the United States Consul in Havana reported early in 1884, 'not a dozen are said to be solvent'" (98). In gesturing toward the distinct fortunes of the two Bárbaras, the letters thus evoke the island's plantation past, which is otherwise conspicuously absent from the novel. Depicting a bucolic world of refined European taste, they offer a romantic portrait of Cuba in the mid-nineteenth century, when the sugar industry was at its peak and a homegrown aristocracy grew wealthy from its profits.

Yet, throughout the novel, this history remains a buried subtext, deliberately diminished by an author who, as we have seen, begins by proclaiming to have written a story that could take place anywhere at anytime. The contemporary critic's desire—my own desire—to uncover clues in order to establish a firm timeline echoes, on some level, Bárbara's futile struggle to understand herself through the concrete facts of history and genealogy. In turn, both the critic and the protagonist battle the novel's lyrical impulses, which insist that the significance of its heroine's life, and of its own pages, escapes historical comprehension. At the same time, *Garden* cannot escape history altogether. Just as it provides Bárbara with photos and papers that offer fragmentary but tangible glimpses of her past, so it grants the reader just enough information to orient herself chronologically. Despite the documentary evidence provided, however, in this lyrical novel the secrets of the past reveal, and conceal, themselves more completely and complexly through the natural and architectural features that comprise the landscape.

Ironically, these features initially come to the reader's attention through yet another form of documentary evidence: the old photographs that the protagonist examines in the first part of the novel, in which the same backgrounds turn up behind her frozen figure again and again: "The sea, the house, the garden … The garden, the house, the sea. A succession of grays in every gradation" (57). The spaces that define Bárbara—sea, house, and garden—merge together in monotonous shades of gray. Yet their merging is the result, not of sameness or a harmonious blending of distinct elements, but of the struggle for dominance between the sea and the garden, which are described with deceptive simplicity: "the sea was good" and "the garden was bad" (57). The "good" sea combats the "evil" garden, but such dichotomous descriptions belie their complex relationships to each other and to historical time, relationships hinted at by their interactions with the manmade elements contained within them.

The sea, for example, regularly washes objects onto Bárbara's beach, but strips them of chronology, and therefore of narrative or historical coherency. A waterlogged shoe, an empty bottle, a lifejacket emblazoned with the mysterious word "Southampton": all of these are "ambiguous things, detached and disconnected things; they gave no idea of anything or anybody, and were barely useful for dreaming a little. They were just the dark remains that the sea is always bringing and taking, without direction or owner, detritus of cities, vestiges of shipwrecks, sediment of anonymous lives and deaths" (39). The isolation and insularity of Bárbara's island only amplifies the anonymity of these remnants of the past, which inspire dreams but not logical narratives. The sea thus destabilizes history, allowing the protagonist to imagine herself in new ways. Bárbara views it as "good," a friend and ally, and it is associated with roads and the horizon, and so also with freedom and escape. It remains a neutral conduit for the artifacts of history and the people who make or flee that history. It brings the blue-eyed man to Bárbara's shore and carries her away with him into the modern world, but it also provides a route back to the island and, ultimately, to the protagonist's death. It thus facilitates dreaming and self-examination, as well as movement and narrative, but creates none of these.

The garden, in contrast, is not neutral in the face of time and history. To the contrary, it actively opposes them. Its opposition, however, is complicated by an ambiguous nature, which is partially revealed through its relationship with the third element of Bárbara's landscape: the house. After proclaiming the sea to be good and the garden to be evil, the narrator ominously declares: "And the garden was already everything ... Only the sea valiantly resisted its invasion. The garden was the house, a white, petrified garden" (57). The house, then, is simultaneously equated with, and differentiated from, its immediate surroundings: it *is* the garden but—like the gleaming city of stone—it is also "white" and "petrified," void of the overabundant life that surrounds and threatens to destroy it. It is victim, rival, and double of the garden. Moreover, both house and garden are, on the one hand, intimately connected to Bárbara and, on the other, tentatively linked to the historical space of the nation. In addition, just as the house, in some sense, functions as a double of the garden, so too it has its own double: a pavilion, half-buried by lush vegetation, whose domiciliary identity is confirmed by the Latin inscription above its entrance: *Parva domus, magna quies*, or "Small house, great quiet" (77). Both domiciles, big and small, are white and stony like the city, and littered with objects that Bárbara scrutinizes as she struggles to piece together a chronology of her life.

The bigger house holds objects that gesture toward the hidden plantation past alluded to in the letters: heavy antique furniture, medieval tapestries, stuffed birds poised to sing in dusty gilded cages, gold-leafed books. In their solid physicality and ornate familiarity these objects "connote epoch and history," and recall the wealth generated by the nineteenth-century sugar industry and the luxury goods from Europe favored by the plantation elite (Rodríguez 102).[13] Despite being displayed in the ancestral house, however, they are not beloved totems of some carefully preserved tradition, but rather abandoned theatre props surrounded by "silence interrupted from time to time by noises made by fallen set pieces, by side flats coming apart, by an entire forest of cardboard in pieces on the boards of the stage" (98). Although, in contradistinction to the miscellany washed ashore by the sea, they are capable of eliciting specific memories, these "props" remain disconnected from a comprehensible family history.

The house's other living inhabitant, Bárbara's black nanny Laura, is also described as an abandoned prop, "indistinguishable from the furnishings" (92). If the house's decor evokes the previous prosperity of the plantation, however, Laura functions as an inert reminder of slavery and, in doing so, reveals the house to be an oblique facsimile of the Big House. A reliable servant—and, given her age and the late date of emancipation in Cuba, likely a former slave—she appears rarely, but when she does her presence is solid, unlike the ghostly aura of the great-aunt Bárbara. Tellingly, she seems to form an essential part of the house itself: she is "so rigid and so black that, if it weren't for the slight trembling of her rosary, made of terebinth seeds, she might have been confused for one of the carved stone figures that … with great anguish supported the architraves of the large front door" (91). Like the figures that anguish under the heavy beams they support, Laura labors under the weighty history of the house. Refusing (or perhaps unable) to leave, she continues to care for her white charge without dissimulating her malice. When Bárbara is a sick young girl, Laura tells her nightmare-inducing tales of "goblins and demons;" when she is a young woman, she accuses her of having "the devil inside her body" (93). The only active inhabitants of the house, the two women share no sense of community or solidarity. A key to their estrangement can be found in the novel's descriptions of their strange physical appearances: the protagonist is represented in soft, bland images— she is "a delicate fungus" (200) and "a smooth and slack thing" (201)—while the servant is stony and intractable. That is to say, Bárbara is allied with the vegetal realm of the garden, while Laura's flinty nature links her to those spaces associated with history and modernity: the city, the house, and, as we shall see, the pavilion. Yet Laura is not white like the city or house. Instead, she is black like a "small pile of coal" that is "always staining [Bárbara's] landscape" (96). A blot on the protagonist's, and the novel's, memory, she symbolizes the dark underbelly of Cuban history.

The women's mutual distrust climaxes when Bárbara begs Laura to show her the way back to the small pavilion, which she has recently discovered, only to have the old woman decline to assist her. Pointing to the pavilion as the principle source of historical knowledge in the novel, Ileana Rodríguez argues that Laura is, on the one hand, "the only person who knows [its] secret." On the other, because she "barely occupies textual space," she "serves only as a negation" (100). Like Gregoria in *Iphigenia* and Memoria in *The Sheltered Life*, Laura acts as a stubborn reminder of that which is excluded from official narratives about the past. But, like the untold history she embodies, she is pushed so far to the margins of the narrative that the protagonist simply wishes her away: "Laura doesn't think, Laura doesn't exist" (218).

Despite Laura's refusal to help, Bárbara finally makes her way back to the half-buried pavilion, which she first discovers after accidentally falling asleep in the garden. Upon awakening, she strips off her clothes and tears through layers of dirt and rock to uncover the structure. Naked, weak, and without memory, she reenacts her birth in reverse, for she struggles not to exit her mother's womb but to enter history's tomb, a rebirth inscribed as death. The pavilion's interior obliterates the fecundity of the garden: "the last trace of organic life seemed to disappear; and neither grasses, nor insects, nor moss could be seen anywhere" (82). In contrast to the house, it is not ornately decorated, but it does contain a collection of antique weapons, a small whip fashioned from Caribbean sugar cane, and hundreds of dried ears of corn, stacked against one wall and blackened with age. Seemingly random, these artifacts quietly symbolize Cuba's ethnic and economic origins. The guns and swords hearken to the Spanish Conquest, the whip evokes sugar cane fields and slave labor, and the corn recalls, not only the indigenous peoples who first grew the crop on the island, but also the people of African descent who gave it an important place in the religious rituals of Santería.[14] Moreover, the whip, whose handle is incrusted with turquoise stones that form a "B," once again links Bárbara to her great-aunt and, by extension, to Cuba's plantation past.

If the pavilion's objects suggest a deeper past, its two sets of documents reveal the modern history of the nation. Although the newspaper clippings preserve public discourse while the love letters divulge private passion, both sets of papers are authored by nineteenth-century males and narrate stories that remain incomplete. The clippings, dating to the 1840s, recall a period that, although preceding the great patriotic struggles of the Cuban nation, was marked by incipient calls for independence.[15] Age has faded some of their words; others are difficult to decipher because of jagged tears in the paper. Bárbara, who has never seen a newspaper before, struggles to stay awake while attempting to read their fragmented, frequently illegible content:

> The words, nevertheless, said nothing. There were names of countries and of men, some perhaps read before in the History bound in blue lambskin; the word liberty [*libertad*], to muster greater transcendence, was written at times in all capital letters … But her eyebrows kept arching until they formed two sharp angles, under which the fatigued butterflies of her eyelashes trembled darkly … . (84)

The newspapers record names and dates to tell a piece of the official history, here literally a History with a capital "H," which Bárbara has also seen in her family's library, bound in blue lambskin. Yet her ongoing inability to understand the cries for liberty reinforces the novel's marginalization of the history of the nation, even as it underscores the protagonist's alienation from modernity's libratory projects.

Like the newspapers, the letters, also from the 1840s, tell a fragmented story. Faded, torn, and eaten by insects, they represent only the voice of the male lover, never that of the older Bárbara to whom he writes. Unlike the newspapers, however, these documents do not induce a soporific stupor. To the contrary, they unleash the supernatural presence not only of the great aunt but also of their young author, the mysterious "A…". Filled with passion and foreboding, their prose satisfies the "traditional requirements" of a nineteenth-century Romantic novel (an impossible romance, unexpected obstacles, the final escape, etc.), as García Marruz has observed (553–54). Augmenting the theatrical tension inspired by this familiar context, A … first appears, before Bárbara discovers the letters, in a yellowed photograph, as a well-dressed dandy with strangely imprecise, delicate features: "A loose silk dickey blurred the contours of a somewhat frail body, the body of a boy who grew too quickly" (19). The earliest epistles he pens to the protagonist's great aunt, filled with feverish expressions of devotion, would seem to confirm his identity as a vaguely unformed man-child. Soon, however, he reveals a darker side, dominated by jealous rages and an obsessive need for control. His letters grow longer, terrifying the younger Bárbara and stifling even the novel's empathic narrator, who fails to intervene for paragraphs and then pages at a time. As it becomes more and more strident and aggressive, A …'s voice threatens to suppress all of the female voices in the novel: the nineteenth-century Bárbara, the twentieth-century Bárbara, and the feminine narrator.

Although he fails to do so—at least, perhaps, until the novel's conclusion—his increasingly frightening presence imbues the text with psychosexual significance and further complicates Bárbara's relationship to the garden, which seems to act in complicity with the demon lover.[16]

Indeed, the contradictoriness of the garden (already apparent in its complex relationship with the house and pavilion) takes on a new dimension when A ... reveals himself to be its creator. Eager to control his beloved, he confesses that he has aided an assembly of workmen in constructing the garden's thick white walls, and boasts:

> As the years pass by and other lovers pass next to your garden walls, which I have wanted taller (and which by then will be worn-out and covered with moss), they won't know that the burning, suffocating anxiety with which I wanted to subdue you germinates in each grain of sand that holds the rock in place, that the passionate obstinacy that I put into your life oozes from each deep joint in the brick, the unsleeping desire of all my days to keep you, to keep you [*de guardarte, de guardarte*] ... . (148)

> Cuando pasen los años y otros enamorados se paseen junto a esas tapias de tu jardín, que yo he querido más altas—ya entonces gastadas y verdosas—, no sabrán que de cada grano de arena que sujeta la piedra brota el ansia ardiente y sofocada con que yo quise sujetarte, que cada juntura honda del ladrillo rezume la apasionada obstinación que yo puse en tu vida, el desvelado afán de todos mis días de guardarte, de guardarte .... (148)

Here we discover that the enclosure that surrounds the garden and traps the second Bárbara, was built to control and confine the first Bárbara. Moreover, it was constructed by laborers who, with their "blue shirts stained with plaster" (147), bear a striking resemblance to the "men with blue shirts, brushes and buckets, and many papers printed with words" (83) who pasted the newspaper clippings onto the pavilion walls. Loynaz thus establishes an unexpected link between the pavilion and the garden wall, and by extension between the newspapers and the letters: they are all products of male labor and a nineteenth-century masculine imagination.[17] The white garden walls at which Bárbara stands in the opening and closing scenes of the novel thus unexpectedly align themselves with the gleaming city and its concrete projects of making history and marking territory.

At the same time, the garden's organic elements remain intimately tied to the endless cycles of nature and the intangible world of myth and archetype, which are described as profoundly feminine: "The earth is the proliferate mother, fecund, untiring, the perennially horizontal mother receiving the seeds of life, which are the dead, giving birth to the sprouts of death, which are the living. The earth. The earth like the earth of the garden ..." (140). The earth, like the island in Loynaz's poem "Isla," is an Ouroboros, extending life through death and death through life. Unlike the erosive soil of the island, however, this mythically feminine garden is not vulnerable but strong and even malicious; and, like A ..., it seeks not simply to control Bárbara but to possess her completely, to annihilate her. "*La* tierra" (the feminine land), "*el* jardín" (the masculine garden), and A ... (the architect of the garden's wall), are thus inextricably connected.

Unable to evade the grasp of A ... by breaking down the walls of the garden, Bárbara chooses an alternate route of escape: the neutral sea, through which she flees in the boat of the blue-eyed foreigner, an emissary, at least symbolically, of a modern and developed North. As many critics have noted, her exit from the island seems to signal the beginning of a happily-ever-after ending, which is foiled only in the final chapters of the novel.[18] The failure of the fairytale finale is foreshadowed, however, by a pointed change in the novel's language, which becomes strident and even didactic as it describes countries where "Progress" and "Futurism" reign supreme (280), and where myths, legends, and other ancient forms of narration are abandoned in favor of the latest trend: "they followed or grew tired of following the apostles of recently arrived gods, the preachers of new doctrines, new freedoms, and new servitudes" (281).[19] It is perhaps not surprising that the narrative invites us to read these, its most unlyrical pages, not as a dreamlike fairytale or scary ghost story, but rather as an uncomplicated national allegory in which Bárbara, conforming to traditional gender roles, plays the part of Cuba torn between two potential lovers: A ..., a nineteenth-century romantic visionary, whose passion for the island nation is profound but annihilating; and the blue-eyed man, a rational scientist representative of a cosmopolitan twentieth-century modernity. Bárbara yearns for freedom and so chooses the latter, only to discover that he, too, longs to control her. Uninterested in the personal history she has struggled to claim, he instead invents a simple, socially acceptable past for her. He teaches her speech, but then tells her what to say. Indeed, the principal difference between the two nameless men who vie for the woman's (or nation's) affection may be this: one employs the poetry of Romanticism to isolate her in the garden, while the other uses the rhetoric of progress to separate her from it.

Comprehended through this lens of allegory, Bárbara's experience of modernity acts as a critique of the patronizing attitudes of cosmopolitan nations toward their "underdeveloped" neighbors. The sophisticated northern circles in which she moves view her with a mixture of salacious curiosity and bored disdain as they gossip about her origins. Drawing from a predictable list of faraway (invariably "southern") locales, some suggest that she is from the Persian Gulf or a small island in the Indian Ocean, while "others, more sensible, shrugged their shoulders, saying they had bought mangos from many similar Creole girls, who arrived barefoot to receive boats in the ports of La Guayra and Pernambuco" (271). While Bárbara's husband invents a past for her, his coterie engages in jaded speculation, and their dismissive skepticism is reiterated by the narrative voice, which, earlier silenced by A ... 's obsessive rage, now sheds its customary lyricism and acquires a detached, objective, and even objectifying tone.[20]

As a response to these experiences, Bárbara's return to the island signals an unarticulated, but unshakeable, need to reconnect with the realm of her garden, which, although dangerous and often hostile, nevertheless possesses an insular nature that offers refuge from the turmoil of the industrialized world. Marked by the reemergence of the empathic, lyrical narrator, the final scenes of the novel describe Bárbara's homecoming and death in densely poetic, richly ambiguous language. Upon reaching shore, she meets a fisherman who informs her of the presence of a nearby pueblo and asks her if she prefers to go to it or to her former place of dwelling. Bárbara reacts with incredulity to his reference to the pueblo, and silently wonders if it is the city she gazed upon decades before. When she fails to respond aloud to his query, however, he guides her to the site of the house, which has disappeared under the voracious growth of the garden. As day breaks, she sees her young guide's face for the first time: "it was a pale face, almost without contour, that seemed to be molded from soft wax, half melted in some places" (313). Frightened by his strange appearance, she draws back as a remnant of white wall begins to crumble. Large pieces of it fall on top of Bárbara and the fisherman, apparently killing them— although a yellow lizard escapes from the rubble as the sun rises and the novel's final page, like its opening one, shows Bárbara still trapped inside the garden: "from behind, from below, forever ..., she pressed her pale face to the iron bars" (316). The island has changed in significant ways: the ancestral abode has fallen into ruins and, apparently, a new pueblo has been founded. At the same time, the garden, more powerful than ever, decisively connects the landscape she fled to the one to which she returns.[21]

So, too, does the mysterious figure of the fisherman, whose voice, "distant and monotonous, could have been the voice of a child or of an old man. Even of a woman; it was a voice without sex and without age" (307). The uncertainty caused by his intonation is simultaneously relieved and intensified when the sun reveals his half-formed features. The ambiguity of his physical appearance links him to A ..., who, in the photograph Bárbara discovers earlier, has blurred features and an oddly un-formed body (19). It also connects both him and A ... to Bárbara, who the blue-eyed man initially perceives as almost primordial in her formlessness: "everything seemed liquid, blurred, diffuse in her; she was like a smooth and slack thing" (201). That all three of these amorphous figures dwell in the garden further reinforces their correla-tion, for the garden, as we have seen, is similarly indefinite. Like the island in the poem "Isla," it is capable of masculine penetration and feminine openness and, like the Ouroboros, it is inextricably linked to the cycles of life and death. Which is to say, it possesses a divided or, perhaps more compellingly, androgynous nature. This po-tential for androgyny extends to A ..., with his soft, adolescent features, and the fisherman, whose voice is ageless and sexless. It also, perhaps, applies to Bárbara herself, whose name not only indicates her barbarous attachment to nature, but also contains the possibility of gender ambiguity. For Catholics, Saint Barbara is a virgin martyr imprisoned and later killed by her pagan father for converting to Christianity. In the practice of Cuban Santería, however, it is the name given to Changó, a power-ful male Orisha, the god of thunder represented by the ram. Thus the protagonist's name—which in the final pages of the novel appears in its masculine form, "El Santa Bárbara," as the name of the husband's yacht (298)—hides within it multiple identi-ties: man, woman, African, European, Catholic, pagan, virgin saint, African warrior. Incomplete or too complete, she and her barbarous companions remain undefined and, in rational scientific terms, indefinable.

Throughout *Garden*, Loynaz traces Bárbara's stymied attempts to define herself and her relationship to the natural and manmade landscapes that surround her. Yet even in the moment of her (possible) death, the relationship remains unclear: true, it is the manmade wall that kills her, but does it collapse of its own volition, or rather because it has been undermined by the encroachment of the garden? At the same time, however, the author asserts a correspondence between persecutors and persecuted: Bárbara *is* the garden, and she is like A ... and the fisherman. Moreover, she is also mysteriously connected to her great aunt as well as her reticent servant, Laura. By establishing tenuous but traceable links between her solitary protagonist and other inhabitants of the garden, Loynaz insinuates a shared identity that might form the foundation for a different kind of imagined community. This insinuation has led at least one critic to suggest the fisherman-guide as a redemptive figure.[22] Certainly, his final words to Bárbara resonate with religious significance: "Fear not, I will show you the path ... Look: the sun is already rising" (314). His admonition to "fear not," his promise to show her the way, his assurance of the arrival of the light of dawn: these biblical professions, along with his half-finished features, mark him as Christlike, a new Adam who will lead the heroine from the solitary garden to the community of the pueblo. Yet, characteristically, the novel frustrates the generative potential of this relationship: instead of the pueblo, the fisherman leads her to the garden wall, and so the new Adam is usurped by the old Adam—which is to say, by A ... . The question arises: do his half-finished features represent newness and potentiality, or decay and demonic depravity? Like the Ouroboros, Bárbara's story thus circles back to its own beginning, where it ends not in death but in stasis. Neither alive nor dead, the protagonist looks out from behind the garden's gate to her island landscape, now modernized for the pleasure of tourists: "The din of civilization grows all along the bewildered beach" (315). Perched at the edge of the sea, this civilization is oriented toward the outside world. It does not, therefore, cultivate the thriving insular community hinted at in Bárbara's earlier visions of the city or in her strange guide's promise of a pueblo. Rather, its ports and highrises welcome outsiders who are eager to gaze upon barefoot *criollas* bearing mangos. Thus the novel closes with a glimpse of a developing tourist economy that—as we shall see in chapter 6—contemporary writers like Ian Strachan and Mayra Santos-Febres have likened to a new iteration of the plantation. Deprived of the fortunes of the sugar plantation, estranged by nineteenth-century cries for freedom, bereft by cosmopolitan modernity of her productive insularity, Bárbara is deemed irrelevant by a nation that looks forever to the sea, turning its back on her insular world—and so, Loynaz suggests, on the source of its true identity.

"An Iridescent Life": The Undulating Underbelly of the Plantation

In contrast to *Garden*, *Delta Wedding* features multiple protagonists and a sprawling cast of intensely communal characters. Published at the end of World War II, it takes place in September of 1923, on the prosperous Fairchild Plantation. Welty explained on numerous occasions that she chose a year in which "nothing" happened on the Delta: no natural disaster, no depression, no war. This allowed her to keep male family members at home and "concentrate on the people without any undue influences" from the outside world (Bunting 49–50). As her biographer Suzanne Marrs argues, however, Welty's choice of chronology did not arise from a desire to avoid the traumas of recent history, but rather from a need to engage them from a distance but in an intimate context:

> Two paradoxes of the United States' war effort [during World War II]—an attempt
> to protect the sanctity of nations and individuals from arbitrary assertions of power,
> even as it employed tremendous power itself, the criticism of reductive stereotypes
> abroad, even as such stereotypes persisted among its own citizens and institutions—
> these paradoxes, Eudora believed, must be confronted in the private place where life
> is lived. (137)

For Welty, the Mississippi Delta provided an ideal setting precisely because these
paradoxes so closely mirrored the contradictions of the plantation. The United States
defended national sovereignty while imposing its will upon other nations, and
espoused freedom abroad while upholding legal and social systems at home that
discriminated on the basis of race or ethnicity. Similarly, the plantation had long
portrayed itself as simultaneously egalitarian and aristocratic, a realm of individual
opportunity and a highly structured, hierarchal community that, while supposedly
fostering harmonious relationships amongst all of its members, relied on social coercion, racist dogma, and brute physical force to maintain the order necessary for the
production of wealth.

In *Delta Wedding,* Welty knowingly and critically engages these inconsistencies.
Nevertheless, because of its familiar plantation setting and gentle lyrical tones, many
early reviews of the novel accused it of perpetuating the self-mythologizing conventions of the Plantation School of fiction (described in the first pages of this chapter).
For example, Diana Trilling argued that Welty fell into "myth and celebrative legend
and, in general, to the narcissistic Southern fantasy" and so revealed herself as "just
another if more ingenious dreamer on the Southern past" (105). Trilling indicts Welty
for rejecting social transformation in favor of anachronistic mood. Yet the superficial
archaism and insularity of the plantation are precisely the elements that allow Welty
to lay bare the fallacy of the "narcissistic Southern fantasy" by exposing the conflicts
that arise between the rigidity of tradition and the irrepressible dynamism of a wilder,
more personal landscape.

Indeed, the pages of *Delta Wedding* abound with subtle signs of restlessness,
indications of imminent social and economic change even in the seemingly tranquil
year of 1923. Black laborers and household servants engage in small acts of violence
or brazenness. Although most of these seem innocuous and are ignored or dismissed
by the white protagonists, they accumulate over the course of the novel, acquiring
symbolic weight. More explicit (although almost as ignored) are the rebellions of the
Fairchild daughters. Shelley, the eldest at seventeen, yearns to be a modern woman:
she refuses to attend the Delta's famous dances, sneaks cigarettes, reads Fitzgerald's
The Beautiful and the Damned, and loudly proclaims her intention never to marry.
Meanwhile, Dabney, a year younger, defies the class-based prejudices of her peers
and becomes engaged to Troy, the plantation overseer, who hails from a poor mountain family. Perhaps more telling than the young women's unconventional behavior
is the response of their family. In more traditional plantation literature, the marriage
of the planter's daughter to the overseer would constitute a threat against the old
order, precipitating a grave crisis that would only be intensified by the longstanding
rivalry between the Delta and the hill regions from which Troy hails.[23] The Fairchilds, however, may express gentle disapproval, but they do nothing to prohibit either

Dabney or Shelley from acting on her desires. Nor do Troy's plans to diversify and modernize the plantation's business model elicit much protest; to the contrary, they meet with the enthusiastic approval of at least one Fairchild brother.

These glimpses of agitation, shifting alliances, and openness to new ideas allude to the sweeping transformations that would affect the Delta in the two decades after 1923. The devastating flood of 1927, the Great Depression and its New Deal reforms, World War II: all of these would alter the world portrayed in the novel. In the 1930s, encouraged by federal programs and subsidies, the region's plantations initiated the process of modernization hinted at by Troy.[24] The war brought even greater changes, which extended from the economic into the social realm. As the historian James Cobb observes, during these years wages for cotton picking rose significantly, union activity increased among farm workers, and the rural population began to migrate to cities and towns. Moreover, black men and women increasingly expressed their discontentment in public forums, and racial anxiety among whites became more pronounced. Cobb argues that, despite the economic growth of the thirties and forties, "the transformation of Delta agriculture left the region's planter-dominated social and political framework fundamentally intact" (207). Nevertheless, he concludes, at the end of World War II it was primed for greater social and economic reform: "Delta planters seemed to be confronting a future in which they would be forced to fend off the civil rights initiatives of the same federal government whose agricultural and relief policies had thus far helped them to sustain their social and political dominion" (208).[25]

Thus by 1946, the year that *Delta Wedding* was published, the public would have read Welty's lush descriptions of Fairchild, Mississippi, knowing that the supposedly unchanging world of the Delta was in the process of irrevocable change. Such knowledge would have contrasted jarringly with the self-conscious sameness that structures life on the Fairchild plantation. On the evening that nine-year-old Laura arrives from the city to spend the summer with her dead mother's family, for example, she observes that "boys and men, girls and ladies all, the old and the young of the Delta kin—even the dead and the living, for Aunt Shannon—were alike—no gap opened up between them" (14). The three dashes in this sentence, however, visually contradict the little girl's observations: they open up gaps between the very words that proclaim their absence. Two paragraphs later the narrator confirms that, although "Laura from her earliest memory had heard how they 'never seemed to change at all,'" she in fact "could see that they changed every moment. The outside did not change but the inside did; an iridescent life was busy within and under each alikeness" (15). This image of iridescence, of solid light refracted into an array of colors, captures perfectly the external fixedness and internal flux that characterizes Welty's vision of the plantation. It also contrasts sharply with the interaction of the various elements in Loynaz's landscape in *Garden*. Although the house, garden, and sea sometimes blend together, the result is not dynamic but deadening: far from generating a unpredictable burst of rainbow colors, they form a dull "succession of grays in every gradation" (57). More frequently, however, they interact as adversaries, and their contact is bereft of creative potential. By applying the image of iridescence, not only to its geographical but also to its human protagonists, *Delta Wedding* attempts to break this stalemate.

Before depicting Laura's arrival, the opening scene of the novel describes her journey to Fairchild, on "the 10th of September, 1923—afternoon." She travels on the Yellow Dog, a "mixed train" that runs between Yazoo City and the town of Fairchild (3). As soon as the train enters the cotton fields of the Delta, the landscape dominates the nine-year-old's attention as well as the narrator's: "Thoughts went out of her head and the landscape filled it. ... The land was perfectly flat and level but it shimmered like the wing of a lighted dragonfly. It seemed strummed, as though it were an instrument and something had touched it" (4). The Delta, like the Fairchild family, is always the same, "perfectly flat and level," and always changing, "shimmer[ing] like the wing of a lighted dragonfly." As the sun dips below the horizon, the uniformity of the scenery reasserts itself even as the hearth, a classic image of domesticity, is invoked: "The sky, the field, the little track, and the bayou, over and over—all that had been bright or dark was now one color. From the warm window sill the endless fields glowed like a hearth in firelight" (5). Just as the tender yet stifling embrace of the family inhibits individual difference, so the homey light momentarily homogenizes and tames the diverse, if repetitive, landscape, merging together bounded and unbounded space, cultivated and uncultivated wilderness, and preindustrial and industrial life.

The journey through the landscape, enacted here by Laura, becomes a familiar motif in *Delta Wedding*. The featured traveler, usually a Fairchild woman by blood or marriage, is, most often, performing some kind of domestic task: paying a pre-wedding visit to the maiden aunts, delivering a cup of soup to a sick servant, reconciling with a spouse. Her physical movement, in turn, indicates a spiritual quest; as she moves through the land, she contemplates the terrors and joys of marriage, sexuality, and duty to family and self. The terrain through which she journeys includes natural or semi-natural spaces, like the fields and bayous that Laura sees from the window of the Yellow Dog, as well as the forest and the Yazoo River; but it also encompasses domestic, manmade sites. Indeed, houses and gardens lie at the center of the landscape, and the natural areas—the fields, bayous, forests, and river—act as the borderlands that define the outer limits of the plantation and of the narrative itself. It is in the borderlands that Laura's journey begins, and through them that she and the others travel.

More specifically, Laura passes through "endless fields" that serve as the starting point of the Delta: "And then, as if a hand reached along the green ridge and all of a sudden pulled down with a sweep, like a scoop in the bin, the hill and every tree in the world and left cotton fields, the Delta began" (4). Rarely dwelled in but constantly traveled through, not fully wild or completely domesticated, the fields—like the sea in *Garden*—offer the possibility of free movement. Unlike Bárbara's sea, however, which contains only disordered debris, these fields also help shape the history of the Delta into an orderly narrative. The land they now occupy was once forest inhabited by Native Americans whose presence, although not specifically mentioned here, permeates the novel's sense of place, a reminder that "though they are unseen ... new life will be built upon these things" (*Eye* 299). The fields themselves come into being when the forests are "pulled down with a sweep," cleared by the first white settlers, and worked for generations by African slaves and their descendants. The final words of the sentence, "the Delta began," emphasize that the fields mark geographical as well as historical beginnings. At the same time, by identifying what came before them, the novel quietly disrupts the mythology of the unchanging plantation. Welty further underscores the historical (and economic) significance of the fields by setting *Delta Wedding* in September, at harvest time, and using the songs of field workers, clattering of wagons, and vibrations of the compress as the constant background noise of the narrative. The individual quests undertaken by the Fairchild women cannot be separated from the accumulated history of these open spaces, which tie the journeying protagonists to the plantation past and present, as well as to the other women they encounter in their wanderings.

One of these women is Pinchy, a black adolescent on a journey of her own. Throughout *Delta Wedding*, Welty registers the presence of African Americans, whose labor in the houses, gardens, and fields comprises another type of background noise.[26] Pinchy's role is distinctive, however, because she spends most of the novel undergoing a mysterious rite-of-passage referred to only as "coming through." The details of the ritual remain unknown, but in addition to spiritual conversion and sexual coming-of-age, the phrase "coming through" connotes motion, transition, and transformation—and, in fact, Pinchy is always on the move. Like the Fairchild women, she journeys unceasingly through the borderlands. The first time she appears, early in the novel, India, the nine-year-old Fairchild daughter, spots her: "'There goes Pinchy, trying to come through,' said India, to make Dabney open her eyes. Sure enough, there went Pinchy wandering through the cotton rows, Roxie's helper, not speaking to them at all, but giving up every moment to seeking" (32). As will happen repeatedly, Pinchy appears just as a Fairchild woman is traversing the land, allowing Welty to register subtle parallels between shifting pairs of questing female figures. In this case it is Dabney, on her way to visit her aunts, who is depicted in relation to Pinchy. As she travels, she turns inward, closing her eyes and contemplating her courtship with Troy, and her hopes and fears for their future. When India indicates Pinchy's presence, in order to rouse the older sibling from her reverie, they are in Mound Field, whose name evokes a sensual fertility appropriate to the coming-of-age questing of Pinchy and Dabney. The name also commemorates the Native American burial mounds found on the site, and so explicitly ties the field, which bustles with harvest-time activity, to the history of the Delta before "the Delta began." Although Dabney, like Pinchy, is "not speaking ... at all, but giving up every moment to seeking," she does not recognize any similarity but rather disapproves of the other girl's condition, declaring with a frown, "'I hope she comes through soon'" (32). Dabney's eyes remain figuratively and literally closed to the connection between them: "Blindly and proudly Dabney rode, her eyes shut against what was too bright" (34).

In the second half of the novel, Robbie Reed, the estranged wife of George Fairchild, also interacts with Pinchy, this time in the Deadening, a field whose name, like Mound Field, holds multiple meanings. Metaphorically, it warns of the physical and psychic dangers that each character risks when crossing it. Yet it also recalls, yet again, that the cotton plantations of the Delta were founded through the destruction of life: this is the site "where the old Fairchilds had started, deadened off the trees to take the land" (144). Braving this bleak terrain under an oppressive sun in order to reconcile with her husband, Robbie encounters Pinchy inside a small cotton shed.

The novel clearly delineates the similarities between the two women: both are alone and unprotected, dwarfed by the immensity of the landscape, and in search of answers and, more immediately, relief from the blazing heat. Furthermore, both are excluded from the inner circle of the Fairchild family, Pinchy because of her skin color and Robbie because she hails from a working-class family. Like Dabney, however, Robbie is blind to what she shares with the young girl and so banishes her "from inside to outside, to the strip of shade under the doorway" (147). Ironically mimicking the power structures that make her an outsider at Shellmound, the house where her husband awaits her, Robbie turns the shed into her own insular shell(mound): "It was nice in here. She felt as if she were in a shell, floating in that sea of light" (147).

In *Garden*, Loynaz places a white woman and a black woman in the same landscape, only to emphasize their utter isolation from each other. In contrast, Pinchy's recurring presence in *Delta Wedding* suggests a meaningful connection, both spiritual and historical, between blacks and whites—but one that remains stubbornly unacknowledged by the Fairchild clan, whose attitude is reinforced by Troy when he shoos the girl away: "Go on! I get tired of seeing you everywhere!" (149). Troy's assertion that he is "tired of seeing" Pinchy recalls Dabney's earlier refusal to look at "what was too bright." Although she is "everywhere," Pinchy, when she is seen at all, is seen in negative terms. As Barbara Ladd remarks, her "absence from the moral world of the Fairchilds" indicates a collective denial of the need for, and inevitability of, social transformation (546). Unlike Bárbara, who makes Laura vanish from Loynaz's novel with the mantra "Laura doesn't exist" (218), the Fairchilds may close their eyes to her presence, but they cannot make Pinchy go away.

To the contrary, from beginning to end Pinchy is associated with several acts of violence or potential violence. Shortly after seeing her in Mound Field, Dabney remembers a knife fight between two black boys that she once witnessed Uncle George break up. Later, for unexplained reasons, Pinchy causes a second knife fight between the same boys, now grown men, which results in Troy shooting one of them in the hand. And, in the final pages of the novel, she appears again, just after Dabney's mother, Ellen, is left "trembling" because her black gardener, Howard, has asserted his dislike of roses (226). Ladd argues, "Welty seems consistent in her determination to call attention to the potential for violence in the seemingly intact Fairchild circle, and she does so by using the presence of this unobtrusive young girl" (548). Her language is apt. Like Parra, Glasgow, and Loynaz, Welty "us[es] the presence" of an "unobtrusive" black figure "to embody a position ... that is weighty and substantial," as Glissant observes of Faulkner's black characters (*Faulkner, Mississippi* 57–8). But the roles played by Parra's Gregoria and Glasgow's Memoria are positive, if inherently limited. In contrast, Pinchy, like Loynaz's Laura, is subtly threatening. Her very name connotes, albeit in a mild fashion, pressure, privation, and violence. She signals unacknowledged commonalities between blacks and whites while also laying bare the hollowness of the harmonious racial hierarchy so central to the U.S. South's postbellum myth of the plantation.

Welty also intimates that, while the Fairchilds remain blinded by pride and self-imposed insularity, Pinchy possesses a clearer vision: "Her eyes were wild but held a motionless gaze on the white fields and white glaring sky and the dancing, distant black rim of the river trees" (147). Pinchy's gaze fixes equally on two very different landscapes. The first, "the white fields and white glaring sky," is uniform, dangerous, and oppressive (and the link between oppression and whiteness is surely not coincidental). The second, "the dancing, distant black rim of the river trees," although still out of reach, promises freedom, joyful movement, and relief from the tyrannical glare of the sun. Inevitably, these landscapes generate different visions for different women—for Pinchy the remote river trees may bring to mind a route of escape for ancestors fleeing slavery, or a sheltered place from which she cannot be summarily ejected. Regardless of individual perception, however, certain constants hold true. The fields remain scorched by history: their very names, Mound Field and the Deadening, link them to a deadly past (the burial of indigenous peoples, the clearing of the fields), as well as to death itself. In contrast, the undomesticated places—the forests, the bayous, and the Yazoo River—are sites of heightened emotion, unknown peril, and intense mystery in which "feminine" time holds sway.

Like the fields, these wilderness areas are borderlands; but they are not the product of human labor. Dense and labyrinthine, they encourage circuitous movement rather than direct routes. The river winds its way through the landscape and the bayous curl in and out of the river. The forest, too, is a twisting maze, full of intertwined branches and tangled underbrush. These spaces offer shelter from the relentless heat of the sun—or the relentless vigilance of the community[27]—but (like Loynaz's garden) they harbor more enigmatic dangers, a fact revealed in the revelation that "Yazoo means River of Death" (194). While tapping into the mortal fears of those who travel through them, they also provide a needed space for the contemplation of "inward, uncomforted thoughts." As Shelley, the oldest Fairchild daughter, recognizes, death can be conceived of in more than one way:

> "River of Death" to Shelley meant not the ultimate flow of doom, but the more personal vision of the moment's chatter ceasing, the feelings of the day disencumbered, floating now into recognition, like a little boat come into sight; and tenderness and love, sadness and pleasure, being let alone to stretch in the shade. ... River of the death of the day the Yazoo was to Shelley, and their bayou went in and out of it like the curved arm of the sleeper, whose elbow was in their garden. (194)

Here the linear movement and unrecoverable losses of history do not order time; rather, the cyclical rhythms of nature and the longing of the lyric do. These feminine forms of time comprise "the more personal vision," where knowledge is not dictated by official history or romantic family lore but rather revealed gradually, through repetition, or suddenly, in the disarticulated moment of epiphany. As such, the wild borderlands intimate alternative ways of knowing and relating—available through dreaming, contemplation, and "being let alone to stretch in the shade"—that bear a striking resemblance to Bárbara's solitary life in her garden. The question here, as in *Garden*, is whether or not it is possible to generate a productive relationship between these new ways of knowing and the ongoing demands of history and community.

The tension between the ethos of the wilderness and the order of the plantation is revealed most clearly in the novel's architectural landscapes, its houses and gardens, where feminine and masculine, or lyrical and historical, time constantly invade each other, just as the wild bayou weaves in and out of the carefully tended garden at Shellmound, the novel's principal domestic domain. Like those other mounds on the plantation, the Indian burial mounds, Shellmound is a "great fortress grave," a fossilized shell into which the family withdraws to ward off the outside world (Griffin 530). Even in its defensive insularity, however, the house overflows with abundance: vines on the stable wall are "elbow deep," desks are "paper-crammed," and porches are "full of late sleepers" (8). The environs of the house thus embody "the informing myth" of the Delta as "the original Garden of Eden" (Devlin 91). The dining room at Shellmound, described in strikingly organic terms, exemplifies both this paradisiacal bounty and the complex interpenetration of the natural with the historical characteristic of Welty's domestic landscape. Fashioned from or imitative of natural elements, the room's decor brings the wilderness into the home: it contains, for example, "walnut-and-cane chairs," "some shell-patterned candlesticks," a Victrola that looks "like a big morning-glory," and "oil paintings of split melons and cut flowers" (18). While they are evocative of nature, these furnishing and decorative pieces also help to tell the personal, political, and economic history of the Fairchild family. Great-Grandfather made the chairs from "his walnut trees when he cut his way in to the Yazoo wilderness" and Aunt Mashula painted the colorful still lifes (18). The rich details and brand name cachet of popular luxury items like the Victrola or a Port Gibson epergne attest to the wealth that the family has accumulated, while a collection of firearms (not unlike the antique guns that Bárbara, in *Garden*, discovers in the pavilion) traces their continuous participation in conquests and wars, from early skirmishes against Native Americans, to the Mexican-American War of 1848, and the Civil War two decades later.

Like the furnishings that fill Bárbara's house, these objects "connote epoch and history" (Rodríguez 102); but, unlike their counterparts, they are not abandoned props. To the contrary, each holds a special place in the family lore. Gaston Bachelard observes that such beloved household items are imbued with generative powers: "they take their place not only in an order but in a community of order. From one object to another, housewifely care weaves the ties that unite a very ancient past to the new epoch" (68). Bachelard implicitly identifies the "housewifely" cultivation of this "community of order" as women's work. Similarly, although men are the protagonists of the Fairchild legend —as Laura notes, "it was the boys and men who defined the family always" (14)—the task of preserving the past falls to the women. Nevertheless, as Aunt Tempe's ever-critical eye discerns, the order established in Shellmound is fragile: "the high, shabby old rooms went unchanged, for weddings or funerals, with rocking chairs in them, little knickknacks and playthings and treasures all shaken up in them together" (98). Expensive collectibles are cracked, while paintings and photographs hang at haphazard angles. One of the guns, given to Grandmother Laura Allen, has "a flower scratched with a little penknife along the pearl handle, and … little toothmarks in it" (99). Signs of individual difference and indifference erupt in every corner, and the organic imagery of the flower etched on the handle of the lady's gun indicates that these disruptive elements are allied with a natural order that relentlessly reveals the iridescent underbelly of plantation life. Thus Shellmound's feminine energies—although not always the women and girls themselves—are pulled in two directions: on the one hand, they are charged with maintaining a "community of order" in which they are denied full participation; on the other, they are sympathetic to the impulses of the wilder landscape, which remain unimpressed by human history and progress.

The tension between these two impulses might be compared to the struggle that Bárbara faces in *Garden*, as she strives to grasp history and nation from within the confines of the garden. Yet the relationship between the manmade and natural elements of Loynaz's landscape is quite different from that of Welty's. In *Garden*, the house, pavilion, garden walls, and city are stony and void of life, while the garden is verdantly prolific; and these opposing spaces are locked in deadly combat. The latter, in contrast, represents a dynamic merging: civilization transforms nature, scooping up forests and depositing cotton fields; and nature reinvades civilization, playfully wreaking havoc upon the order it attempts to establish.

The mutuality of this second relationship is explored from a distinctively female perspective at the Grove, the plantation's oldest abode. "A dove-gray box with its deep porch turned to the river breeze" that stands "under shade trees with its back to the Shellmound road," the Grove, even more than Shellmound, is identified with the natural world. Its "sun-faded" garden runs close to the riverbank and its chimneys and brick pillars are painted green to match the surrounding scenery (37). Facing toward the Yazoo, the River of Death, and away from the road that bustles with family and commercial activity, the Grove is, as Griffin notes, "constructed out of nature, offering the same primal image of security as the nest;" it also acts as a reminder that the nest is merely "a dream of security in a precarious reality" (529). Nest-like, natural, and fragile, the Grove is a feminine domain inhabited by women, with each generation more secluded from the world of men than the last. Its first resident is the founding matriarch, Mary Shannon, who "lived in a house all alone and away from everybody with no one but [her] husband" (41). Later, the great aunts, Mac and Shannon, arrive to raise their orphaned nieces and nephews after their own husbands are killed in the Civil War. Finally, the maiden aunts, Primrose and Jim Allen, inhabit the house, living without the company of men or children. The Grove's architectural harmony with the river and the forest suggests a harmonious relationship between human community and nature that is quite different from the conflictive dynamic at play in Shellmound; yet its almost complete identification with the wilderness places it outside the flow of history and threatens to sever it from community altogether. This is not to say that the Grove is isolated from history. To the contrary, it is packed with reminders of the past. Its halls are haunted by the ghost of Aunt Mashula, who died waiting for her husband to return from war, and its rooms decorated with mournful portraits of Mary Shannon. Indeed, it is the birthplace of the Fairchild legacy and the womb of its matrilineal inheritance. Primrose and Jim Allen use recipes from Aunt Mashula's cookbook, read Mary Shannon's diary, preserve the history of each frilly knickknack, and invoke the names of the dead because, as Primrose observes, "Jim Allen wants all the ghosts kept straight" (45). The "community of order" established by the maiden aunts' "housewifely care," however, resembles the timeline of the conventional plantation novel: it looks only backward and remains irrelevant to the present. That is to say, it is order without community. If the Grove represents the possibility of a mutual, non-exploitative relationship between the community and the natural world, it also symbolizes the dangers of female isolation, the marginal status

of women in historical discourse, and the ongoing difficulty of establishing a productive relationship between nature and history.

In contrast, a third and final house, called Marmion, embodies the most grandiose and romantic visions of the southern masculine imagination. Named for a poem
by Sir Walter Scott, whose historical romances inspired many of the conventions of
the plantation novel, Marmion overpowers the surrounding landscape with its redun-
dantly impressive "temple-like, castle-like" architecture and its viscerally virile "pillars springing naked from the ground" (122). Unlike the Grove, it refuses to blend
into nature. Even its garden, which features a playhouse and a maze, privileges human ingenuity over natural form. The house's interior reaches toward the heavens
with twin spiral staircases "winding into depths of light" from whose upper levels
eight-year-old Roy Fairchild claims to "see the whole creation" (176). Deliriously
hubristic, like the Tower of Babel or the romantic legend of the South, Marmion is
doomed to fail on a grand scale:

> Marmion had been empty since the same year it was completed, 1890—when its
> owner and builder, [Laura's] grandfather James Fairchild, was killed in the duel he
> fought with Old Ronald McBane, and his wife Laura Allen died broken-hearted very
> soon, leaving two poor Civil War-widowed sisters to bring up the eight children.
> They went back, though it crowded them, to the Grove, Marmion was too heart-
> breaking. (120)

The "heart-breaking" tale of Marmion is, of course, as elaborate an edifice as the
house itself, and both evoke the rhetorical structure of the plantation novel—the very
structure that *Delta Wedding* seeks to undermine.[28] Like the Grove, Marmion is cut
off from the flow of narrative and historical time. Unlike that little gray house, however, this gleaming white mansion resists relationship with the natural world.

When Laura and Roy explore the abandoned house, they encounter Aunt
Studney. Another inscrutable black woman inhabiting the landscape, Aunt Studney
always carries a sack, whose contents she refuses to divulge, and responds to her
white interlocutors with a terse "Ain't studyin' you." When the children enter, they
find her "in the middle of the room ... standing over her sack and muttering" (175).
As an outsider to the plantation, Laura's unsure, almost frightened, reaction is
tellingly different from that of her male cousin, who "acts as if Aunt Studney were
always here on his many trips to this house" and imperiously invites Laura to make
herself at home (175). As Roy climbs to the top of the staircase to enjoy the commanding view, Laura stays on the ground floor, where three events happen in short
succession: Laura strikes a key on a small piano, Aunt Studney cries out "high and
threatening like the first note of a song at a ceremony," and bees emerge from every
corner of the house "hum[ming] everywhere, in everything" (176). The silent house
suddenly vibrates with strange, almost ritualistic tonalities produced by a triad
of female figures—a young girl, an old crone, and the bees, ancient symbols of
matriarchal power—each of which stands progressively further outside the center of
Fairchild family life and thus potentially embodies an ever-greater threat to it.

Oblivious to the moment, Roy descends the stairs, demands to know why Aunt
Studney has let bees into *his* house, and tauntingly asks her to show him the contents

of her sack. Despite his airs, however, as he exits the premises the narrator exposes a startling reversal of roles: "Aunt Studney watched him swagger out, both hands squeezing on her sack; she saw them out of the house. Outdoors it was silent, a green rank world instead of a playhouse. 'I'm stung,' said Roy calmly" (177). In this scene, Roy emphasizes that Marmion is *his* house no less than four times, yet it is Aunt Studney, already present when he arrives, who sees him out when he leaves. Moreover, he and Laura return to a landscape that has been utterly transformed, the ingenious playhouse and maze having disappeared into "a green rank world." This space, now intensely feminine, shows itself hostile to the masculine pretensions of Marmion.[29] Literally an impenetrable wilderness, its hermetic nature is symbolized by Aunt Studney's perpetually sealed sack, which functions (like the coal-like features of the old servant, Laura, in *Garden*) as a symbol of a reticence that is at once sexual, racial, and historical. As Laura intuits, "Aunt Studney was not on the lookout for things to put in, but was watching to keep things from getting out" (177). This hermetism is also underscored by the bees, traditionally associated with parthenogenesis, female purity, and self-regeneration, which are impenetrable and penetrating, as their attack on Roy demonstrates. Buried beneath green rank nature, Marmion's legend—that is to say, the plantation legend—has been annihilated by a curtain of green. In order to reemerge as a vital force, it must make itself vulnerable, not only to history but also to nature, and to the painful friction that signals the potential for a different kind of interaction based, not on the subordination of one order to the other, but rather on a dynamic, generative interpenetration of the two.

Conclusion

Nathaniel Hawthorne's forests, Domingo Faustino Sarmiento's pampas, Willa Cather's deserts, José Eustacio Rivera's jungle, Antonio Pedreira's insular islands, Faulkner's Big Woods: imaginative renderings of the natural world appear repeatedly in literary texts of the Americas that engage the problems of modernity. The resulting landscapes vary as much as the topography of the regions that inspire them, but questions about the origins and nature of imagined communities, when not displayed prominently on their surfaces, inevitably lurk in the shadows of these untamed American spaces. Welty and Loynaz participate in this tradition, but their landscapes insist upon the interplay of an archetypal feminine wilderness with an enclosed domestic realm whose ancestral manor houses and fertile gardens permit the exploration of the fraught relationship between an agrarian past and a modern present. Although their stories center upon the experiences of women, these authors do not attempt to subvert the representational link between women and the land, or the opposition between feminine and masculine time. To the contrary, they embrace this conventionally gendered imagery, a strategy that leaves them vulnerable to accusations of essentialism.[30] Certainly, their respective endings lend credence to such a claim. *Delta Wedding* concludes with a kind of marriage feast, a post-honeymoon picnic on the grounds of Marmion, during which members of the Fairchild family, served by a passel of black servants, eat, laugh, and talk with the same self-satisfaction they have displayed throughout the novel. *Garden*, in contrast, closes with the scene of Bárbara's apparent death followed by a vision of her immortal form, seemingly passive, trapped in the garden—a repetition of the very image with which the book opens. Although it contains subtle hints of change, Welty's comic ending seems to belie the social and economic transformations that will soon befall the Delta region. Loynaz's vision is darker, although it stops just short of tragedy by denying the reader the catharsis of death and suggesting that the true calamity is not Bárbara's fate but the modern world's refusal to acknowledge her.

At the same time, by returning obsessively to the ancient associations of women with mother-earth, these authors do more than offer an essentialist portrait, be it light or dark in tone, of insular landscapes. They also assert the devalued ethos of the feminine wilderness as a needed supplement to the masculine values and patriarchal order heralded by supporters of the traditional plantation and the modern nation alike. In her persistent privileging of insularity, Loynaz differs from Welty, who actively, if gently, rejects the myth of southern isolation. Yet both authors propose solitude and contemplation as ways of knowing inextricable from a different kind of landscape. By gathering the outside world into densely compressed lyrical terrains, *Garden* and *Delta Wedding* attempt to reconfigure the topography of the plantation so as to imagine a still unimaginable order in which both women and men may find freedom as well as community.

Postmodern Plantation Imaginaries

The Repeating Island and *Faulkner, Mississippi*

As we have seen, the characters that populate the novels studied in chapters 2 and 3 remain immobile, trapped between the romantic tales of the past and the revolutionary lure of modernity. Despite their critical engagements with the plantation, they are finally unable to escape its dichotomous logic. The texts examined in the remainder of this book, representatives of what I am calling a postmodern plantation imagination, approach the risks of stagnation and immurement from a different historical perspective and with a different set of strategies. Published between 1970 and 2000, they possess a greater temporal distance from the plantation past, which allows them to confront its horrors with less ambivalence. No longer concerned with the opposition between industrial and agrarian orders or the fate of the plantocracy, they are instead consumed by the problems and possibilities posed by anticolonial revolutionary movements, international struggles for the rights of women and other marginalized peoples, massive changes brought about by technological advances, ever more rapid migrations of peoples around the globe, and myriad other challenges associated with our so-called postindustrial, postmodern age.

Reacting to these circumstances and events, the texts studied in the following three chapters attack fixed notions of "History with a capital 'H'" by presenting multiple, often contradictory, histories that undermine the possibility of a unified, coherent narration of the past. They also subvert or reject traditional concepts of gender, race, and sexuality by conjuring characters that are at once vulnerable and reticent, withdrawing and powerful. In certain ways, these characters resemble Loynaz's Laura and Welty's Aunt Studney, black women who use their reticence as a means by which to withhold knowledge: just as Aunt Studney will not reveal what is in her sack, so Laura refuses to show Bárbara the way to the pavilion. In contradistinction to Glasgow's Gregoria and Parra's Memoria, they are threatening figures, and their threat lies precisely in their refusal to cooperate with their white counter-parts. But whereas Laura and Aunt Studney are tertiary figures at best, the marginalized histories and strategic withholdings they embody take center stage in the postmodern imaginary. Reticence may reveal itself through subtle evasion, aggressive silence, or even biological sterility, but the refusal to produce or reproduce becomes an impor-tant means by which to refute the delusional discourse of the master.

The narrators and protagonists of these texts, moreover, publicly exhibit both their words and their bodies. Performances that are simultaneously oral and corpo-real become an indispensable means by which to confront and bear witness to the past. Finally, they counter immobility and unproductive insularity by exploring the libratory potential of movement within and between nations, communities, races, genders, and individuals. In doing so, they strive to break down the confining walls of official history and, at the same time, to recognize—but also, perhaps, redirect—the internal and external migrations, forced or voluntary, that have shaped the plantation landscapes of the Americas. Words and body, rhythm and performance, traversals and testimonies, language and silence: all of these become important means by which to confront the past.

The two texts highlighted in this chapter—*La isla que se repite: el Caribe y la perspectiva posmoderna*, or *The Repeating Island: The Caribbean and the Postmod-ern Perspective* (1989), by Antonio Benítez Rojo, and *Faulkner, Mississippi* (1996), by Edouard Glissant—exemplify these strategies, although often to quite different effect.[1] As the subtitle of *The Repeating Island* makes clear, Benítez Rojo overtly claims the label "postmodern," and both he and Glissant employ a familiar set of postmodern metaphors that evoke fragmentation, multi-directionality, and fluidity, in order to deconstruct official narratives. *The Repeating Island* has been included in countless graduate school syllabi and received extensive scholarly attention; and while much of this attention has been markedly critical, the book's influence has endured in large part due to its evident ambition; its audacious, if at times haphazard, application of postmodern theory; and its skillful, often idiosyncratic, analyses of canonical Caribbean texts. *Faulkner, Mississippi* has received less attention from the U.S. academy, perhaps because of its apparently narrow (not to mention already ex-haustively studied) focus, which belies its baroquely transnational perspective. It is, after all, a book about Faulkner written in French by a Martinican poet and postcolo-nial critic who reads that most inextricably "Southern" and "modern" of writers in a thoroughly global, markedly postmodern context.

Given their elaborate narrative structures, self-consciously polemic stances, and expansive agendas, it is not surprising that many critics have underscored the perfor-mative qualities of both *The Repeating Island* and *Faulkner, Mississippi*. As one reviewer observes of the latter, Glissant "glid[es] from novel to novel in search of evidence for a thesis that is endlessly deferred—precisely the technique he praises in Faulkner's modernist invention" (Goldstein 729). The result, according to Loichot, is "an incessant call and response, each rereading of Faulkner via Glissant (or vice versa) creating a new text" ("Glissant, Yoknapatawpha" 100). As they examine a series of mostly canonical literary works that exemplifies a modern plantation imaginary, Glissant and Benítez Rojo textually perform, in a very postmodern way, an "endless" or "incessant" deferral of meaning, a reticent withholding of answers that allows them to return to the site of the plantation without—perhaps—becoming mired in its dichotomous logic.

Benítez Rojo's Proliferating Plantation Machine

Benítez Rojo begins *The Repeating Island*, which he tellingly dedicates to Fernando Ortiz, by defining the plantation as a machine: "The machine that Christopher Columbus hammered into shape in Hispaniola was a kind of *bricolage*, something like a medieval vacuum cleaner. The flow of Nature in the island was interrupted by the suction of an iron mouth, taken thence through a transatlantic tube to be deposited and redistributed in Spain" (5–6). Benítez Rojo depicts a crudely pieced together apparatus—a Frankensteinian creation, one might say—that deforms nature, interrupting and, more precisely, redirecting its flow from the Caribbean to Spain. It thus facilitates the destructive work of colonialism: from its "mercantilist laboratory," Europe "conceived the project of inseminating the Caribbean womb with the blood of Africa" (5) and, having forcibly impregnated it, used its "medieval vacuum cleaner" to suction out the fruits of that womb for its own consumption. In this passage, the author exploits intertextual references, including both Ortiz's evocation of "Cyclopean machines" and Deleuze and Guattari's theory of the machine, as well as richly and not unproblematically gendered language, to generate a foundational image of a suffering, feminine Caribbean repeatedly violated by a rapacious masculine Europe.[2]

Perverse though it may be, however, Columbus's prototype was, according to Benítez Rojo, merely a feeble first attempt. Once perfected, it reemerges, first on the sea, as the famed Armada of the Spanish empire, and finally on land, as the fully developed plantation. In each iteration it is, emphatically, an invention of modern Europe: "I want to insist that Europeans finally controlled the construction, maintenance, technology, and proliferation of the plantation machines, especially those that produced sugar. (This family of machines almost always makes cane sugar, coffee, cacao, cotton, indigo, tea, bananas, pineapples, fibers and other goods whose cultivation is impossible or too expensive in the temperate zones . . .)" (9). In this, his initial attempt to define the plantation, Benítez Rojo describes it in the language of industry and technology. Yet he also depicts its development in surprisingly familial or genealogical terms: "born in the New East" (8), its proliferation engenders "a family of machines." Although, as we shall see, he consistently questions notions of origins when interrogating the history and development of Caribbean cultures, Benítez Rojo ironically echoes the plantocracy's obsession with genealogy by insisting upon a "pure" European lineage for the plantation.

This plantation, like Ortiz's super-central, is proliferating and insatiable. Moreover, it is highly adaptable: "ever since it was put into play, this powerful machine has attempted systematically to shape, to suit to its own convenience, the political, economic, social, and cultural spheres of the country that nourishes it until that country is changed into a *sugar island*" (72). Although inextricable from the histories of slavery and colonization, its influence does not end with abolition or independence. To the contrary, "there are changes and adjustments to go with this new situation, but the plantation machine in its essential features keeps on operating as oppressively as before" (73). Imposing itself upon island after island, in century after century, this "machine of machines" (72) churns out "imperialism, wars, colonial blocs, rebellions, repressions, sugar islands, runaway slave settlements, air and naval bases, revolutions of all sorts, and even a 'free associated state' next to an unfree socialist state" (9). The output of the plantation machine is not limited to agricultural products; it also manufactures political structures, violent conflict and repression, and a variety of oppositional resistance movements.

After offering up this strikingly undifferentiated catalog of the products, or byproducts, of the plantation, however, the author recoils from its polarizing implications. First, he implies that each of these products, regardless of its nature, serves merely to reinforce the plantation's power. More tellingly, he declines to expound upon his pointed pairing of the "'free associated state'" of Puerto Rico and the "unfree socialist state" of Cuba. Instead, he demurs: "You will say that this catalog is unnecessary, that the whole subject is already too well known"; and then redirects the conversation from politics to poetics: "Let's talk then of the Caribbean ... of sentiment and pre-sentiment" (9–10). Nevertheless, his linking of Cuba with Puerto Rico, and his insinuation that the political status of each emerges from and reproduces the plantation, marks a rare moment of (almost) overt political commentary that serves to underscore the deliberate lack of such engagement elsewhere in the text. As a Cuban living in exile since 1980, Benítez Rojo's opinion of Castro's regime is encapsulated in the phrase, "unfree" ("no libre" in the Spanish original).[3] Yet, even though *The Repeating Island* consistently privileges Cuban cultural production, it touches only briefly on the theme of post-1959 Cuba, most notably in a chapter on the poetry of Nicolás Guillén, and never refers to Castro by name.

How should we understand the author's silence, or reticence? It is a question that acquires additional urgency in light of the author's acknowledged indebtedness to Ortiz, who rejects many aspects of modernity but unequivocally embraces its revolutionary spirit and even intimates that it is precisely this spirit that will save Cuba. Santiago Colás intriguingly suggests that this silence may be an "uncanny" product of a "fear of 'being cut off' from the utopian culture of the People of the Sea ... a fear complicated by Benítez Rojo's own complicity (as exile) in the cutting off" ("There's No Place" 213). Colás' proposal is lent credence by a second "uncanny" silence: the almost total absence of the United States, the country in which Benítez Rojo, the exile, made his (non-)home almost ten years before the publication of *The Repeating Island*.

Certainly, one might intuit a critical attitude toward U.S. imperialist activity in some of the author's comments. For example, it is possible to read his coupling of the "free associated state" of Puerto Rico and the "unfree socialist state" of Cuba as an ironic commentary rather than a straightforward juxtaposition. This possibility is heightened when we consider certain discrepancies between the 1995 reprint of the English translation and the book's first edition in Spanish (1989). For example, the "catalog" quoted above includes "imperialism, wars, colonial blocs, rebellions, repressions, sugar islands, runaway slave settlements, air and naval bases, revolutions of all sorts." The Spanish original, however, lists "guerras imperialistas," or imperialist wars, rather than imperialism and wars, and additionally mentions banana republics, interventions, dictatorships, and military occupations (xii). Each of these elements, omitted in the English translation, points more clearly to the interference of outside powers in Caribbean affairs—interference that, in the twentieth century, has come overwhelming from the United States. Elsewhere in his original introduction, Benítez Rojo suggests that he is, in fact, deeply invested in exploring and redressing this imbalance of power: "las Antillas constituyen un puente de islas que conecta de 'cierta manera', es decir, de una manera asimétrica, Suramérica con Norteamérica" (iii). Yet again, the English translation reads differently: "the Antilles are an island bridge connecting, in 'another way,' North and South America" (2). The difference lies in the middle clause, which in the original translates as "in a 'certain way,' that is, in an asymmetrical manner," but which in the translation has been condensed into the much vaguer "in 'another way.'" This difference, I maintain, intimates a hesitation to exploit the full implications of his original contention regarding the relationship between South and North. One the one hand, "asymmetrical" describes an unequal relationship; on the other, as we shall see, "in a 'certain way'" is used throughout *The Repeating Island* to describe an indefinable mode of Caribbean cultural resistance to the plantation machine. By replacing these two descriptors with "in 'another way,'" the English text mutes its critique of the "assymetrical" nature of North-South relations, even as it subtly excludes the United States from the possibility of participating in the cultural performance of resistance to the plantation suggested by the phrase, "in a 'certain way.'" I suspect that the incongruities I have pinpointed between the Spanish and English texts are due, not to the translator taking liberties, but rather to changes made by Benítez Rojo in later editions of his book.[4] Either way, however, they are symbolic of his "uncanny" reluctance to offer any sustained analysis of the connection between the U.S. and the Caribbean and, more specifically, the possibility of articulating a *productive* relationship between North and South.

The few direct references to the United States that he does make comprise, not a unified argument, but a series of fragmented insinuations. He indicates, for example, that traces of the repeating island may be found in Miami (3) or "a cafe in a barrio of Manhattan" (4); and, from time to time, he associates certain aspects of African-American and Native American culture (jazz, the Harlem Renaissance, the history of the Seminoles in Florida) with Caribbean cultural production. These examples imply that, to connect the regions in question—be it "in a 'certain way'" or "in 'another way'"—one must look to geographical and cultural spaces in the U.S. shaped by a diasporic confluence of non-European peoples and traditions. At the same time, however, Benítez Rojo seems to assert the limitations, even the irrelevance, of such spaces. Since attaining political independence, the United States has "assumed its role as a nation in European terms, and under the canons of European thought and traditions. ... The North American nation regards its own African, Asian, Latin American, and even Native American populations as 'minorities,' that is, as ethnic groups alien to its essentially European nature" (201). This insistence on its "European nature" suggests that the behemoth to the north is in fact not absent from the pages of *The Repeating Island*. Rather, it is called by a different name: Europe. That is to say, it is an unsullied descendant of the bloodline that invented the plantation machine, not the one that suffers under it. Benítez Rojo thus reemploys the genealogical rhetoric of the Twelve Southerners, who claim "the South could be ignorant of Europe because it was Europe" (172). Both he and they insist on an unbroken continuity between Europe and the United States, embodied in the space of the plantation. But while the Twelve Southerners use the plantation to differentiate the traditional (U.S.) South from the modern (U.S.) North, Benítez Rojo presents the United States as a monolithic North that denies the contributions of its "minorities" and devotes itself to the perpetuation of the "machine of machines."

The result is a more pointed condemnation of U.S. imperialism than is found in the introduction, but also a curious sort of double erasure in which, on the one hand, the U.S. becomes conflated with Europe and, on the other, its "minorities" are denied the power to disrupt this "European" identity in a national, transnational, or diasporic context. Nowhere is Benítez Rojo's ambivalence more evident than in his description of Martin Luther King Jr., who he praises as "able to be a Caribbean person without ceasing to be a North American, and vice versa" and "fill[ing] the space in which the Caribbean connects to the North American" (24). Yet he fails to articulate *how* King fills this space. Instead, he enumerates King's various "Caribbean" qualities, such as his "African ancestry," "ancient wisdom," and "improvisatory vocation," before concluding that he was "unquestionably idiosyncratic in North America" (24). Benítez Rojo thus undermines the very connection he asserts: the resonance between Martin Luther King and the Caribbean is explained through personal idiosyncrasies rather than deeper cultural, historical, or political linkages.

Other critics who have commented on the author's refusal or inability to carry through on his initial promise to explore the linkages between the U.S. and the Caribbean have focused particularly on the way he downplays the influence of diasporic movement in the shaping of Caribbean identity. Frances R. Aparicio, who concurs with Colás' notion of the uncanny, argues that Benítez Rojo does not pay sufficient attention to the flow of historical and artistic exchange between the Caribbean and the United States, and concludes: "Perhaps what is most uncanny about this text is precisely the repression or total absence of U.S. Caribbean cultural and literary productions" ("Performing the Caribbean" 642). To Aparicio's focus on diaspora in a U.S./Caribbean context, Silvia Spitta adds the role of Africa, arguing "Africa, even though written in as trace or desire, nevertheless remains absent as signifier and diaspora. With his choice of 'chaos' and privileging of rhythm, Benítez Rojo constructs an ever-vanishing Caribbean, a nostalgic mirage of everything the United States is not and can never be for a Cuban academic living here, now" (171). Spitta's line of reasoning is especially helpful for understanding Benítez Rojo's inability to pinpoint King's connection to the Caribbean: by seeing Africa only as "trace or desire" and failing to underscore the concrete, historical migrations of African peoples through the New World, he is unable to articulate the abiding correspondences between North and South. It is not surprising then, that he never mentions the ubiquitous presence of the plantation in the U.S. South. In *Cuban Counterpoint*, Ortiz vehemently rejects similarities between the history of the plantation in the U.S. and Cuba. Benítez Rojo would seem to agree, but rather than explain why, he simply extends his uncanny silence.

Glissant and the Death of the Plantation

In contrast, in *Faulkner, Mississippi*, Glissant traverses the landscapes, literary and real, of the U.S. South in order to argue for a common trans-American past. His book opens in the mode of a travel narrative, as he describes a road trip through Louisiana and Mississippi, on which he embarks with "three Antilleans and a very slight French woman" (16). From the beginning then, the location of his narrative in the U.S. South and the composition of his little group, which unites the Antilles to Europe, signals that Glissant's conception of the Caribbean will be different from Benítez Rojo's. The group tours two historical domiciles that embody distinct facets of the planta-tion. The first, Rowan Oak, is William Faulkner's home in Oxford, Mississippi; the second, Nottoway Plantation, is a restored antebellum mansion on the banks of the Mississippi River near Baton Rouge, Louisiana. Weaving together his impressions of the two houses, Glissant begins by likening Rowan Oak, "imposing but neglected," to New York City: "This is characteristic of the United States, both North and South: glitter and glamour are always side by side with ruin and dilapidation. (Tourists in New York, for example, expect to be awed.) As if even in famous places, like Rowan Oak, the ephemeral lies in wait ..." (10). Glissant establishes his intention to disrupt tourist-book truisms by impudently equating New York City and Rowan Oak as "famous" attractions that embody a "glitter and glamour" mixed with "ruin and dilapidation" typical of the U.S., North and South. In the passage immediately following, he makes another, perhaps more expected, comparison when he links Faulkner's ramshackle residence to the Caribbean plantation system:

> [Rowan Oak] itself is at once a Plantation manor (*casa grande*) and family home. We discover later that the stable is a pathetic little structure, weather-beaten and rusty, like the ones we can find next to the Black slave sheds (*sencillas*; the title of Gilberto Freyre's work is always relevant). The configuration of the Plantation was the same everywhere, from northeastern Brazil to the Caribbean to the southern United States: *casa grande e senzala*, the big House and the slave hut, masters and slaves. (10)

In contrast to Benítez Rojo, Glissant explicitly includes the U.S. South in his elabora-tion of the plantation's geographical and historical development; moreover, through-out the pages of *Faulkner, Mississippi*, he intentionally complicates notions of South and North. On the one hand, Rowan Oak is like New York: both are quintessentially U.S. American in both their dazzle and their decay. On the other hand, Faulkner's residence is like any other plantation, echoing (if only symbolically; the stable, after all, is not located next to an actual slave shed) the architectural model that extended the length of the trans-American landscape.

The multivalent geography of the (U.S.) South is further complicated by the theme park glitter of Nottoway Plantation. If Rowan Oak lures visitors with the gritty appeal of New York, Nottoway, "cleaned, sanitized, pasteurized," promises the syn-thetic entertainment of Las Vegas' New York, New York Hotel and Casino (11). Like a buffed-and-polished version of Bárbara's manor in *Garden*, it substitutes the lived-in feel of a family home with a strangely hollow simulacrum that denies the

specificities of history. While Bárbara's home summons up images of a dusty abandoned theatre, however, Nottoway recalls "a slave-era film set" (13) whose rooms are
decorated with carefully chosen, meticulously arranged objects that shape a "memory [that] is selective, rid of the whiff of slavery" (12). Each display strives to erase
the horrors of the past. By their bodily presence, however, Glissant suggests that he
and his fellow travelers challenge their intent: "What fascination had drawn us to this
place? Perhaps only the unconscious knowledge that it remained a spectacular theater
for great tragedy whose plot we carried inside us" (14). A collective, incarnate "we"
disturbs the calculated artificiality of the film set with the subversive immediacy of
guerilla theatre. Historical and geographical boundaries are thus further destabilized,
this time through a human corporality that testifies to the horrors of the past.

As he travels the U.S. South searching for transnational connections, Glissant
notes that he is often met with a resistance he links to the myth of exceptionality:
"one emphatically says 'the South,' with a capital 'S,' as though it represents an absolute, as though we other people of the south, to the south of this capitalized South,
never existed" (30). Benítez Rojo responds (if only indirectly) to this erasure through
an unspoken refusal to name the South. Glissant, in contrast, insists on uncovering
volatile yet physically palpable linkages between south and South. At the same time,
he repeatedly signals the latter's intimate connection to the imperialistic North
(Rowan Oak is "like" New York, after all) and, at the same time, its penchant for
simultaneously obliterating and romanticizing the slaveholding past.

Glissant's focus on the Big House also distinguishes him from Benítez Rojo, for
whom the domestic space of the plantation remains a largely absent site, subsumed
under the all-encompassing machine. At the same time, it allies him with the female-
authored novels studied in chapter 3, which similarly stress the house's symbolic role
in maintaining the official version of the past. Like Bárbara's abandoned manor in
Garden or the vacant Marmion in *Delta Wedding*, Rowan Oak and Nottoway are not
living, breathing spaces. They are undoubtedly charged with meaning, but they are
monuments and museums that tell, however falsely, about what has come before. The
past hides in plain site in Nottoway: its truth, however, is not contained in its rooms
but rather carried as "unconscious knowledge" in the bodies of Glissant and his
friends. In this sense, Glissant's vision differs from those of Welty and Loynaz, both
of whom imbue natural and manmade landscapes with mythical power. Glissant certainly recognizes the intensity of the American landscape, which he describes in
Caribbean Discourse as "open, exploded, rent" (145). Yet elsewhere in the same
book, he argues, "Our landscape is its own monument: its meaning can only be traced
on the underside. It is all history" (11). If Welty and Loynaz emphasize the ability of
the landscape itself to contain, form, and deform community, Glissant draws attention to the human capacity to redefine their relationship to that landscape by tracing
a different path of movement through it.

The industrial scenery surrounding Nottoway also underscores the temporal
mutability of the plantation: in nearby fields, where cotton used to grow, a gas
refinery "glimmer[s] in the fullness of day" and "huge tractors and machinery now
cultivate fields of sugarcane" (12). Glissant's juxtaposition of the plantation myth
that Nottoway strives to preserve and the mechanical realities of modern agroindus-
try suggests an additional difference between Glissant and Benítez Rojo, one that I

hinted at in my introduction: the latter defines the plantation as a machine from its inception; the former, in contrast, conceives of it as a self-destructive institution defined by slavery and doomed by its inability to adapt to the technological demands of modernity.

Glissant delineates his notion of the self-limiting plantation in *Poetics of Relation*, a book whose theories plainly inform the pages of *Faulkner, Mississippi*, which was published six years later. We have seen that Glissant defines in more expansive terms the boundaries of a trans-American region that shares a common legacy based on the history of the plantation. At the same time, he echoes his Cuban counterpart in his insistence that, everywhere it spread, the plantation imposed similar social and economic structures: "despite very different linguistic areas engaged in very divergent political dynamics, the same organization would create a rhythm of economic production and form the basis for a style of life" (63). When he turns to the temporal or historical dimensions of the plantation, however, he does not describe a powerful, proliferating institution but rather the opposite: "The Plantation system collapsed everywhere, brutally or progressively, without generating its own ways of superseding itself" (63). At the same time, he stresses the plantation's enduring influence in the realm of cultural formation: "How did a system that was so fragile give rise, paradoxically, to what are seen as the modern vectors of civilization ...?" (63–4). This paradox emanates from the contradictions generated by the plantocracy's tendency to imagine the plantation as an enclosed, self-sufficient garden when, in practical economic terms, it was absolutely dependent upon the capital and technology of modernity (67). The fantasy of autonomy, coupled with a continued reliance on the exploitative and anachronistic system of slavery, results in the plantation's collapse. Yet the same factors that reduce the plantation to rubble paradoxically engender the open word.

In *Faulkner, Mississippi*, Glissant traces the emergence of the open word through the figure and fiction of Faulkner, whom he imagines in the dual role of unreconstructed planter and visionary artist who dwelled "on the edge of a caste, in a space where all is about to crumble ... on a margin where it is very hard to evaluate or trace any connection with the Other" (3). Faulkner's reluctant engagement with the other focuses Glissant's rereading of him. On the one hand, Glissant credits him with forging a new mode of the epic that questions and ultimately rejects the possibility of genealogical purity and filial order: "Epic song and tragic disclosure have traditionally had as their purpose a restoration of a lost unity. Through their intervention, we are guaranteed to regain it. The Faulknerian intervention accepts the impossibility of a return to equilibrium. This is the source of its originality and force" (98). On the other hand, he stresses Faulkner's inability or refusal to depict his African-American characters—as well as white women, children, and other marginalized people—as active participants in the making of history. This, in turn, signals a rejection of what Glissant calls creolization: "Creolization is the very thing that offends Faulkner: *métissage* and miscegenation, plus their unforeseeable consequences" (83). *Métissage*—literally translated as miscegenation—here represents the idea of a simple mixture; creolization, in contrast, complicates the process by underscoring the "unforeseeable consequences" of such mixing. As Valérie Loichot observes, its "result, which is not a synthesis, but a coalescence, bears the marks of the initial violence of the encounter, and the present distance which keeps these elements apart" (*Orphan Narratives* 191).[5]

Comparable to Ortiz's transculturation, Glissant's creolization accepts both the creative and destructive potential of the encounters of peoples within the space of the plantation, without reducing such encounters to biological, genealogical, or linguistic categories. It is only by embracing mixture, despite its risks, that new and vital cultures can be forged; its refusal, in contrast, "leads toward this new abyss: the ramblings of the Southern world as well as those of the world as a whole are wrought by the same refusal and the same disturbance—namely, that of the Other" (*Faulkner, Mississippi* 98). Here again the correspondence between Ortiz and Glissant is illuminating. In 1940, the Cuban ethnologist imagined a lost paradise that "included the whole world, which must be completely made over if we are to find and enjoy it once more" (*Cuban Counterpoint* 202). Almost sixty years later, the Martinican poet envisions a "new abyss," an inferno that threatens to devour "the world as a whole." In both cases, the key to finding paradise—or, what amounts to the same, avoiding a hell of our own making—is the acceptance of the disturbance created by the other.

A Postmodern Poetics (Out) of the Plantation

As J. Michael Dash has observed, creolization is not a "happy hybridity but an explosively baroque ground that is neither foundational nor originary" ("Martinique/Mississippi" 103). It is precisely upon such ground, whose volatility was once obscured by the illusory order of the plantation, that Glissant envisions the materialization of the open word, which takes the form of a "poetics of Relation" that rejects filial origins and uncomplicated ideas of *métissage*. Benítez Rojo similarly asserts a mode of creative expression that, although inseparable from the plantation, resists the desire for origins and biologically based notions of *mestizaje*: "it is not a 'mulatto' mixture, if that term is meant to convey a kind of 'unity'; it is a polyrhythmic space that is Cuban, Caribbean, African, and European at once, and even Asian and Indoamerican" (81). Despite their opposing images, of the plantation in ruins versus the plantation as indestructible machine, both Glissant and Benítez Rojo conceive an anti-foundational poetics that emerges from, and also combats, the plantation.

Both also suggest an unbreakable link between the physical site of the maroon or *palenque* (communities established by runaway slaves) and the emergence of their poetics. Glissant, for example, compares the oral traditions of slaves to the "discontinuity the Maroons created through that other detour called *marronnage* [slave flight]" (*Poetics of Relation* 68). Stated differently, "historical *marronage* intensified over time to create creative *marronage*"—which is to say, the open word (71). Benítez Rojo similarly asserts a link between the *palenque* and an alternative literary tradition: "I think that the Caribbean's 'other' history had begun to be written starting from the palenque and the maroon, and that little by little these pages will build an enormous branching narration that will serve as an alternative to the 'planter's histories' that we know" (*The Repeating Island* 254). Like Ortiz before them, these authors identify two distinct historical spaces: the totalitarian and mechanistic plantation or *ingenio*, on the one hand, and the decentered and aesthetic *vega* or maroon, on the other. However, unlike Ortiz's *vega*, the maroon is made by and for slaves; in this sense, it resembles the small plot that Wynter writes about in "Novel and History: Plot and Plantation." Both Glissant and Benítez Rojo seem to agree with Wynter that "the ambivalence between the two has been and is the distinguishing characteristic of the Caribbean response" (99).

In each text, this ambivalence is made visible through an imagined circularity of the plantation. Their respective models of circularity, however, once again point to significant differences. As we have seen, Glissant imagines a closed circle that struggles to contain the bodies of runaway slaves as well as the dispersed openness of "creative *marronage*," and finally collapses in the very moment that the open word (a product of both "creative *marronage*" and the delusional fantasies of the master) escapes its premises. For Benítez Rojo, in contrast, the plantation imposes an unending cycle of oppression whose "circular death" compels flight: "Thus to the circular death that the Plantation inflicts one must oppose an attempt at flight: the metonymical unfolding of a prevailing and vital culture" (149). Glissant's open word emerges from both the maroon and the plantation. Benítez Rojo's sense of poetics, on the contrary, presents the *palenque* as a mobile site of perpetual resistance to, and flight from, the plantation. Like the open word, its "metonymical unfolding" generates constant motion, but while the former strategically combines a pendular swing with an eccentric spiraling, the latter takes a more erratic course, whose horrifying dictate is to keep fleeing the grasp of the immortal plantation.

These distinct concepts of circularity should be understood as products, not only of the different models of the plantation proposed by each author, but also of their diverging attitudes toward history and, in particular, toward the history of modernity. Certainly, the circularity described in both texts rises from the historical institution of the plantation, and so is quite different from the feminized mythical and natural cycles that predominate in *Garden* and *Delta Wedding*. Yet Glissant's contention that the plantation was a closed, self-destructing circle is explained by his insistence on defining it specifically as a slaveholding institution; with abolition, the plantation must meet its end. This does not, of course, mean that Glissant purports that all oppressive social and political structures died with the plantation. Yet he asserts the necessity of understanding the historical plantation in order to better analyze the problems confronted by our globalizing world:

> The Plantation, like a laboratory, displays most clearly the opposed forces of the oral and the written at work—one of the most deep-rooted topics of discussion in our contemporary landscape. ... It is also within the Plantation that the meeting of cultures is most clearly and directly observable, though none of the inhabitants had the slightest hint that this was really about a clash of cultures. (*Poetics of Relation* 74)

If, for Benítez Rojo, the plantation is a diabolical creation of Europe's "mercantilist laboratory," for Glissant it functions, paradoxically, as an unintentional laboratory in which both its own historical legacy and the dynamics of the "contemporary landscape" might be better understood.

Yet the plantation's value is only partly historical: the poetics of the open word that emerges from it in its dying moments also proves to be a uniquely flexible tool with which to probe both the past and the present. This poetics, in turn, is linked to the Glissantian concept of Relation, an "imaginary construct" that identifies "the acknowledged validity of each specific Plantation yet at the same time the urgent need to understand the hidden order of the whole—so as to wander there without becoming lost" (*Poetics of Relation* 131). Shifting between "domination or liberation," the "near and deferred," dream and action, Relation represents "the possibility for each one at every moment to be both solidary and solitary" (131). Like the open word, Relation takes on the movement of the pendulum, recognizing the specificities of each plantation while also revealing a "hidden order" (very different from the order imagined in *I'll Take My Stand*) that unites them. In its valorization of dream and solitude, it bears a striking resemblance to the lyrical longing embedded in the landscapes produced by Welty and Loynaz in *Delta Wedding* and *Garden*. Yet it acts in solidarity to confront, rather than to marginalize or evade, the horrors of the past, and so envision a vital community.

The poetics imagined by Benítez Rojo, in contrast, is founded on the need to evade or flee the circular death of the plantation. It necessarily expresses resistance that, according to the Cuban critic, takes two basic shapes: polyrhythmic performance and a longing for nonviolent union with the other, both characteristic of the cultures of the "Pueblos del Mar," or Peoples of the Sea, his term for the inhabitants of the Caribbean archipelago:

> Certain dynamics of their culture also repeat and sail through the seas of time without reaching anywhere. If I were to put this in two words, they would be: performance and rhythm. And nonetheless, I would have to add something more: the notion that we have called "in a certain kind of way," something remote that reproduces itself and that carries the desire to sublimate apocalypse and violence; something obscure that comes from the performance and that one makes his own in a very special way; concretely, it takes away the space that separates the onlooker from the participant. (16)

Although intimately related, the dynamics he describes are also contradictory. The first, "performance and rhythm," engages an endless play of difference, a daring overlap of dissimilar rhythms, and a volatile exchange between performer and spectator; and it is this mode that, Benítez Rojo suggests, most accurately represents the condition of a peoples defined by the "will to persevere through flight" (25). The second, on the contrary, expresses a mystical and erotic longing to merge completely with the other. Tellingly, the author's description of this longing relies on a series of reticent phrases such as "in a certain kind of way," "something remote," "something obscure," and "a very special way." The effect is to distance the reader from the concept described, even though that concept is "concretely" an obliteration of such distance. The skepticism inherent in his language suggests that the vicious circle of the plantation cannot be conquered through impossible dreams of peaceful resolution. Instead, it must be resisted through a particular kind of flight, a voyage of difference as unending as the plantation itself.

Despite his valorization of dynamic difference, however, Benítez Rojo is not immune to reductive desires, as exemplified in this and other descriptions of the so-called "Peoples of the Sea." Indeed, the taciturn language of the above quotation harkens back to Stark Young's contribution to *I'll Take My Stand*, which depicts the U.S. South's squirearchy as "difficult to explain" and "never ... understandable by those born in a different scheme of life" (*I'll Take My Stand* 350). Benítez Rojo similarly emphasizes the "obscure" and "remote" traits of Caribbean peoples and poetics, while rhetorically insisting that he "cannot describe [the] 'certain kind of way' " in which they manifest themselves (10). Responding, for example, to the commonplace that the region's novels are "excessive, baroque, grotesque," he affirms: "I think that all this is true, but only when it's seen from Europe." Behind the "West's idea of the Caribbean [... t]here lie codes that the Caribbean people alone can decipher. These are codes that refer us to traditional knowledge, symbolic if you will, that the West can no longer detect" (220). Like Young, Benítez Rojo thus imagines a plantation-based culture inaccessible to outsiders, particularly those who rely on "modern," which is to say "Northern" or "European," patterns of knowledge. Certainly, these authors represent perspectives that are, in most ways, opposed: the former invokes ancient Roman, Greek, and Anglo-Saxon civilizations and the latter non-Western traditions; the former defends the beneficiaries of the plantation system and the latter its victims. Yet both inscribe a site of resistance that stands firmly outside of modernity.

In this way, too, Benítez Rojo differs from Glissant. As we have seen, the latter not only explicitly recognizes the historical value of the plantation as "laboratory," but also argues, like Wynter, that the plot/maroon and the plantation are "two poles that originate in a single historical process" ("Novel and History" 99). Both, that is, are products of the same modern moment. In contrast, Benítez Rojo implicitly associates the vital culture of the *palenque* with an order, at once premodern and postmodern, that remains inexplicable and inaccessible to modernity. Critiquing this aspect of his argument, Román de la Campa contends that Benítez Rojo jumps from "oral, preindustrial temporalities to postmodern discursivity" in a strategy "aimed at erasing the cultural legacy of modernity as historically specific and variegated" ("Mimicry" 547). Certainly, Benítez Rojo depicts the legacy of modernity as an overwhelming—one might even argue foundational—presence. However, because that legacy is represented through the monolithic model of the plantation machine, he fails to recognize the particular and irregular impact of modernity in the Caribbean. One result of this is his "uncanny" silence regarding the Cuban Revolution, U.S. imperialism, and diasporic movement: despite their obvious differences, all of these can simply be lumped together as byproducts of the plantation.

Benítez Rojo's sublimation of modernity is further complicated by his reliance on two of it principle authorizing discourses: history and science. With regards to the former, de la Campa insightfully observes that his text contains "large sections of traditional historicism that although quite informative in their own right, evidently betray the author's commitment to novel modes of narration" ("Mimicry" 540). Similarly, the scientific discourse of chaos theory serves as a foundational metaphor for his "repeating island," which emerges from "the (dis)order that swarms around what we already know of as Nature" and, concomitantly, the "dynamic states or regularities that repeat themselves globally" (2).[6] By refusing to engage modernity fully, or to recognize as legitimate any form of resistance that emerges from its multivalent legacy, Benítez Rojo paradoxically deprives the "Peoples of the Sea" of historical agency. Instinctual and indefinable, they remain outside the flow of history, inaccessible and unintelligible to anyone but themselves. At the same time, like Benítez Rojo himself, they are beholden to the very discourses that marginalize them. I would agree with de la Campa, then, when he argues, "conjuring the idea of a living community from this theoretical cul-de-sac becomes unlikely, if not irrelevant" ("Mimicry" 549).

"A Certain Kind of Way": Female Flesh, Exposed and Closed, in *The Repeating Island*

The "theoretical cul-de-sac" that Benítez Rojo creates for himself is also apparent in his recourse to another strategy familiar to readers of both the Twelve Southerners and Ortiz: he strategically eroticizes the oppositional culture he depicts. In particular, he establishes a deliberately gendered discourse detailing three images of femininity that reverberate throughout the book. I have already alluded to the first of these, his foundational image of a suffering, feminine Caribbean, which is graphically reinforced by his portrayal of the Atlantic as "the painfully delivered child of the Caribbean, whose vagina was stretched between continental clamps ... ; all Europe pulling on the forceps to help at the birth of the Atlantic: Columbus, Cabral, Cortés, de Soto, Hawkins, Drake, Hein, Rodney, Surcouf ..." (5). Juxtaposing an active masculine agency, represented by a cadre of famous men, with a passive feminine victimization, the author represents the Caribbean as a symbolic woman reduced to her grossly distended genitalia. The Caribbean machine begins to work precisely at the sexual and reproductive center of this grotesque being whose vagina becomes a site of spectacle and speculation for the men who struggle to claim for themselves the life that they have planted within her. The "circular death" of the plantation, although a product of historical processes, parasitically feasts upon the gynopoetic circularity of the female reproductive system.

Benítez Rojo's other evocations of the Caribbean as a female body implicitly refer back to, but also revise, this initial image. The first is a much-commented upon passage in which he describes "the moment at which I reached the age of reason," on a "stunning October afternoon" during the Cuban missile crisis, when, in the empty streets of Havana, "two old black women passed 'in a certain kind of way' beneath my balcony." He continues:

> I cannot describe this "certain kind of way"; I will say only that there was a kind of ancient and golden powder between their gnarled legs, a scent of basil and mint in their dress, a symbolic, ritual wisdom in their gesture and their gay chatter. I knew then at once that there would be no apocalypse ... for the simple reason that the Caribbean is not an apocalyptic world; it is not a phallic world in pursuit of the vertical desires of ejaculation and castration. (10)

This passage draws a telling distinction between Benítez Rojo's narrative of the origins of the Caribbean machine and his attempt to define "the Caribbean of the senses, the Caribbean of sentiment and pre-sentiment" (10). If the plantation emerges from the monstrously misshapen vagina of a victimized mother, two old women evade "the vertical desires of ejaculation and castration" of European modernity and so bridge the temporal gap between premodern mysticism and postmodern performance, even as they facilitate the author's movement toward intellectual maturity.[7]

In both images, the feminine fulfills a traditional mediating function, but in different ways. The earlier passage depicts a symbolic feminine that embodies collective suffering. The second, in contrast, describes concrete female bodies that, although ultimately serving in a symbolic capacity, are individualized and contextualized: they are two old black women walking down a Havana street on a sunny afternoon in October of 1962. Although still explicitly sexed by a masculine observer, they are not portrayed as victims. Instead, they project an intense eroticism that is at once exposed and concealed, blatant and mysterious. On the one hand, the author presents them unabashedly as spectacle—as literal streetwalkers—whose rhythmic gait entails an archetypal Caribbean performance. On the other hand, their fascination reveals itself ephemerally, as an "ancient and golden powder" emerging from between gnarled legs. Moreover, their advanced age is hardly irrelevant, for it implies that their sexuality is unproductive, excessive, abnormal, or even grotesque. The suggestion that their sterility is actively *desired* by the male spectator is confirmed by the fact that they initiate him into the "age of reason," an intellectual rather than erotic coming-of-age whose appellation self-consciously references a Sartre novel in which the protagonist's quest is to terminate his lover's pregnancy.[8] Provoking yet impenetrable, erotic yet infertile, these women personify the tension without consummation, the desire that neither recreates nor procreates, that lies at the heart of Benítez Rojo's poetics.

The third female figure, the Virgen de la Caridad del Cobre, "proposes a fusion of the cults of Atabey (Taino), Oshun (Yoruba), and Our Lady," and so epitomizes "the creoles' integrationist desire" and the impulse to nonviolence that is also central to his poetics (52). It is true that the old women conquer apocalypse through their audacious performance and rhythmic gait; and the virgin, too, incorporates aspects of polyrhythm and performance. Nevertheless, her primary function is to incarnate the integrationist longing. If the previous female figures are intrinsically sexed from the moment of their appearance, the virgin, by virtue of her name (and the virtue it implies), is unsexed but nevertheless inevitably defined in sexual terms. Like the feminized archipelago, she is a suffering mother; yet like the old women, she refuses phallic desire. Benítez Rojo recounts the tale of her miraculous rescue of three seafaring men who, according to Cuban oral tradition, were named Juan Criollo, Juan Indio, and Juan Esclavo, which, he argues, "conveys mythologically the desire to reach a sphere of effective equality where the racial, social, and cultural differences that conquest, colonization, and slavery created would coexist without violence. This space ... is repeated time and again in the diverse expressions that refer to the Virgen, such as images, medallions, prints, lithographs, printed prayers, songs, popular poetry, and even tattoos" (52–3). Throughout *The Repeating Island*, Benítez Rojo returns to the virgin as symbolic of an impossible desire for unity. She represents, moreover, a distinctively feminine "quality of resistance to the patriarchal discourse of the West, because everything creole, in Cuba, had flowed since the beginning from the source that was a Virgin who held everyone in her lap" (55). Her figure, maternal and virginal at once, both reproduces and reverses the earlier image of the splayed and suppurating mother. It is not her genitalia nor her womb that are open but rather her lap; it is not (only) blood and salt water but rather "everything creole" that flows from her body. Unlike her conquered counterpart, she cannot be controlled or pinned down because her image is constantly refracted and multiplied in an endless chain of "medallions, prints, lithographs, printed prayers, songs, popular poetry, and even tattoos" whose purpose is to reclaim and reorder the violated space of the plantation.

Benítez Rojo's Virgen de la Caridad del Cobre thus unfolds as a series of inexact repetitions in much the same way as his Caribbean isles. The role she plays in his poetics, however, is only fully revealed when she is understood in relation to the other female figures he conceives: not only the violated archipelago and the old black women of his introduction, but also the female characters created by other male writers that he analyzes in later chapters. In chapter 1, for example, he quotes from an 1866 description of Cuba published by E. Duvergier de Hauranne, and argues that the French travel writer could not help but focus on "the Negresses of Santiago," moving through the marketplace with "inner rhythms" that demonstrate once again a Caribbean polyrhythm performed by black women in "a 'certain kind of way'" (79). In chapter 7, he stresses the symbolic significance of another black woman, a wizened magical mediator in Carpentier's Viaje a la semilla who, if listened to carefully, may unravel the "labyrinth of Caribbean codes" (232). Chapter 3 underscores the centrality, in Guillén's early poetry, of a concept of "neo-African beauty" (123) incarnated in the flesh of an "everyday black woman who ... carries with her the transcontinental mysteries of the African forest, but also the Antillean mystery of Cuba" (124). Each of these instances reconfirms the "Negress" as a hermetic performer—not dissimilar to Aunt Studney in Delta Wedding and Laura in Garden—who enacts the polyrhythms of the Peoples of the Sea even as she protects a secret knowledge. That knowledge, in turn, is tied to a premodern order ruled by rhythm, magic, and "transcontinental mysteries." Guillén's neo-African beauty, in particular, lays bare a critical relationship between these proliferating dark-skinned female bodies and Benítez Rojo's intensely gendered concept of the poetics that emerges from the plantation.

She is, the critic declares, called up by "the voice of the Negro, which directs itself toward all strata of the Plantation with the intention of investing them with its *desire* and *resistance*. [... Guillén] wishes to impregnate society with the Negro's libido—his own libido—transgressing the mechanisms of sexual censorship that the Plantation imposed on his race" (123, emphasis in original). Benítez Rojo praises "the revolutionary character of this sensuality" (125). Yet the postmodernist critic asserts the limitations of the modernist poet's vision:

> But the desire for mixing (*mestizaje*) that Guillén offered in these poems ... went no further than the dialectical and positivist discourse of modernity. Guillén desired a Cuba that was "*mulata*"; that is, a form of nationality that would resolve the deep racial and cultural conflicts by means of a reduction or synthesis that flowed from the proposal of a creole myth .... (126)

Thus, although Guillén challenges the tangled discourse of gender, race, and sexuality produced by the plantation, he falls short of escaping the "integrationist myth" (126).[9]

Benítez Rojo's assessment of Guillén might be productively compared to Glissant's critique of Faulkner. The latter praises Faulkner for creating a new model for the epic but reproaches him for reinforcing the passivity of marginalized voices and turning his back on the generative potential of creolization. The former, in contrast, extols Guillén for giving an active voice to the previously silenced libido of the black man, but accuses him of replicating old intellectual paradigms. These inverted evaluations draw attention to a subtle but critical distinction between Glissant's notion of creolization and Benítez Rojo's conception of *mestizaje*. The first is the traumatic history of the plantation added to the "unforeseeable consequences" of that history, which can be both destructive and creative (*Faulkner, Mississippi* 88). Like Glissant's concepts of the open word and Relation, it implies a pendular movement between extremes. The second, in contrast, is "a sheaf of different and coexistent dynamics" (*Repeating Island* 126) that exist in parallel to each other, and may even intersect at times, but do not generate anything except more differences. Creolization, potentially, gives rise to something new; *mestizaje*, in contrast, creates only more difference, more resistance, more movement. Benítez Rojo's focus on this endless voyage of difference, which is put into motion by the circular death of the plantation, helps explain why the female bodies rendered by Guillén do not satisfy him: they are fecund and fecundated. Confronted with the "*desire* and *resistance*" of the Negro's voice, they submit rather than offering a resistance of their own. The critic subverts this dynamic by imagining female flesh that flaunts itself but actively resists union with the other by engaging in an endless play of difference rather than surrendering to the desire of the poet who, be he identified with Africa or with Europe, falls prey to the binaries of modernist discourse.

At the same time, however, his own ostentatious display of feminine bodies reveals the limits of his strategy and reminds us once again that he, too, is hemmed in by the modern plantation imaginary. Even as he celebrates its subversive potential, he consistently inscribes (although he does not impregnate) female flesh with his desire and, more importantly, his interpretative authority. The women he invokes do not exhibit themselves nor do they speak for themselves; rather they are exhibited and explicated by an always-disembodied male critic. Moreover, his insistence on their blackness (with the exception of the copper-colored Virgin, who represents the integrationist myth), and his association of that blackness with inaccessible mystery, reinforces essentialist images of African sensuality and harmful stereotypes of the accessible sexuality of the female slave. In this sense, he threatens to reduce the very women whose resistance he praises to a passivity that we have seen repeatedly in the modern plantation imaginary: Glasgow's Memoria, Parra's Gregoria, Loynaz's Laura, Welty's Pinchy, and even Ortiz's Doña Sugar.

Despite these very real problems, however, Benítez Rojo hints at a paradigm shift that permeates the postmodern plantation imaginary. While Guillén longs to "impregnate society with the Negro's libido," Benítez Rojo imagines a male libido that is met, not by a receptive and ultimately passive female sexuality, but rather by a reticent, actively resistant one. That is to say, the imagined community he conjures is predicated upon a non-phallic desire that incorporates both feminine and masculine eroticism in a polyrhythmic dance that is never consummated. As we saw in chapter 1, the final paragraphs of the first part of *Cuban Counterpoint* imagine a union, simultaneously subversive and conventional, between Don Tobacco and Doña Sugar, which gives birth to the revolutionary spirit of alcohol. *The Repeating Island* proposes something very different: a sensual encounter between male poet and female muse whose revolutionary thrust lies in its refusal to give birth to anything at all.

An Indefinite "She": Reticence in *Faulkner, Mississippi*

While the pages of *The Repeating Island* attempt to embody resistance in and through extravagantly displayed female flesh, *Faulkner, Mississippi* focuses on Yoknapatawpha county, which it represents as a starkly segregated, defeminized, and de-eroticized realm in which legitimate lineage is white and male even though the father is almost always an impotent figure. If Benítez Rojo suggests the libratory possibilities of female barrenness, Glissant more modestly proposes fatherlessness as a means of rebellion for some of Faulkner's characters. Within the fictional territory of Yoknapatawpha, the patrilineal family "falls apart" while trying to maintain the genealogical fictions of the plantation order (124). As a result, "to have no father becomes a kind of virtue: it is a way of being cut off from malediction" (125).

Yet Glissant also emphasizes that, in spite of the failure of the masculine, Faulkner's feminine remains symbolically unproductive as well: "Faulkner suggests, throughout his works, that matrilineage is not really lineage at all since it grants no legitimacy" (126). The matriarch, as much or more than the patriarch, is an ineffective figure: "mothers are frail, sickly, absent, invariably beautiful, usually abusive" (128). Non-mothers and surrogate mothers, black and white, are likewise unproductive: "There are others who also have neither power nor mastery over events: women (the Black servants or the White maiden aunts) and children, instinctively close to the fatalistic and confused reasoning that derive from the county's burdensome past" (62). Glissant expresses particular interest in the function of these women and children, about whom he asserts:

> They are preserved and protected from every disruption, held prey to an innocence nothing can reduce, but, when it comes to what concerns the White Aunts and old Black Mammies, they are uncompromisingly clear. Miss Rosa, Dilsey, young Ike McCaslin, young Charles in *Intruder in the Dust*, and young Lucius in *The Reivers*. These are the ones who contaminate the others and who never cease to question, even if they do nothing but finalize their initiation or lament the ruins. They reconstruct what others would have the tendency to misunderstand or overlook and what they "stare at fixedly." They are hallucinated memory, where what is reinforced is their innocence, their stubbornness, and their ability to "endure." (174–5)

Although Glissant focuses his analytical lens on Faulkner, while Benítez Rojo surveys the works of many authors, both reference the imaginative visions of other writers in order to elucidate their own notion of poetics. It is interesting to note, then, that like the fictional black women Benítez Rojo highlights, the Faulknerian characters singled out here are represented as inscrutable and possessing a magical kind of knowledge. Moreover, at first glance their intimate contact with "instinct" seems to tie them to a premodern order, allowing them to comprehend the past with a "confused reasoning" and so emerge, like the women who pass below Benítez Rojo's balcony, as survivors of the apocalyptic history of the plantation.

But these women, or Glissant's portrayal of them, differ fundamentally from those in *The Repeating Island*. Perhaps most obviously, they are not all women; nor are they all dark-skinned. Rather, they represent a heterogeneous mix of "White Aunts," "old Black Mammies," and young boys. Moreover, upon careful consideration, their anti-apocalyptic powers are neither ontological nor the result of some premodern magical or mystical essence. Rather, they are the product of an imposed innocence to which they are "held prey." That is to say, their power is explicitly tied to their powerlessness. In contradistinction to Benítez Rojo, Glissant foregrounds the historical circumstances that bring about female unproductiveness, and emphasizes the fact that, for these women (and boys), sterility is inseparable from the lack of "mastery" bequeathed to them by the modern plantation. Finally, compared with the profoundly corporeal, flamboyantly performative women of *The Repeating Island*, they are almost ascetic in appearance and character. Their force lies not in the exhibition of an unproductive erotic physicality, but rather in their own interpretative gaze, their ability to "reconstruct" the suffering of the South by what they "stare at fixedly."

Indeed, Glissant alleges a general lack of eroticism in Faulkner's oeuvre: "His situations may be extreme (incest, murder, rape) but his manner of dealing with sex is often so neutral as to discourage further interest" (244). Glissant links Faulkner's writerly reticence to "a quiet misogyny and at least a restriction of the roles of women in society, in the family, or in the search for truth," which he understands to be a manifestation, not of "Puritanical detachment" but rather "because of his code as a gentleman" (244). Ironically, Glissant's restrained portrayal of women in *Faulkner, Mississippi* suggests a decision, conscious or unconscious, to emulate Faulkner's gentleman's code by creating a text that avoids sexuality and locates the eroticism of Faulkner's, as well as his own, South, in its natural and man-made landscapes. Rather than displaying female bodies, the Martinican writer indirectly acknowledges the unavoidable contradictions that plague his entanglements with gender through the insertion of sly references to an unnamed, incorporeal "she" who intervenes suddenly, without segue or explanation, half a dozen times in the text, to supplement, critique, or redirect the author's textual meanderings.

Although her appearances are relatively few, and her physical self is never described, the importance of this anonymous female figure is indicated by the fact that she is given, literally, the first and last words. The opening sentence of *Faulkner, Mississippi* reads: "She calls my attention to how much (in the pictures in this magazine) the two writers look alike" (3). As will be the case each time she appears, the passage, with its use of present tense verbs and the modifier "this," conveys a sense of immediacy; while the simplicity of her gesture suggests an intimate, even mundane quality to her relationship with the author. Two other interventions are quite similar: "She shows me the inscription in a book by Albert Camus" (15); and "She gives me a playbill for a ballet by a Native American company ..." (196). In all three instances, "she" acts as an extemporaneous archivist who produces, without fanfare or embellishment, an everyday artifact that suggests zones of contact or Relation for the author to expound upon. Judging from these examples, then, "she" fulfills the familiar role of the female mediator.

At other points, however, her intercessions acquire a more aggressive tone, and operate as reminders that the "imaginary construct of Relation" requires difference as well as linkage. The first takes place early in the second chapter, as a parenthetical digression that recounts a debate between "she" and the author. "It is not long before she points out to me, with a reticent resolve, that there are inherent contradictions in this scheme," the passage begins. Following a brief conversation—"I insist" and "She counters"—the author capitulates: "I concede. ... She smiles serenely" (38). While continuing to withhold any concrete information about his companion, Glissant does provide the reader with a greater knowledge of her by revealing that, rather than admiring his interpretations, she challenges them. He also tellingly describes her as "reticent," and suggests an enigmatic quality in her serene reaction to his discomfort.

This suggestion of sphinx-like inscrutability is confronted directly in her fourth appearance, which also elucidates Glissant's own ambivalence toward the place of the feminine—literally of "she"—in his work. It is hardly insignificant that this appearance takes place only two pages after the gender-inflected examination of the "White Aunts and old Black Mammies," and as part of a longer section contemplating how Faulkner employs such "witnesses" through a " 'continuous stream of consciousness' " in order to testify to the horrors of the plantation past: "The meetings of all these sensibilities are confirmed in the text by an astounding blur of pronouns, almost all of them are indefinite, regardless of the referent ('he,' 'one,' or 'we'), and by first names that are often androgynous" (176). At about this point, "she" brings his lofty ruminations to a halt:

> She tells me frankly as I was thinking out loud that I am speaking nonsense. Oh! no, she says—she does not want to appear in this book I am writing. Her words have nothing to do with what I was saying. Yes, there are indefinite pronouns, she says, such as *one, we, he, she*. I tell her that a pronoun has power even when you do not know who is hidden behind it. Some argue that "she" is Mycea, "the one with whom the poet is enchanted." Others deduce an imaginary identity, if this interests them, perhaps a synthesis of several elements at their command. She tells me she does not want to hide. She laughs. She tells me not to work like that, needlessly, and not to construct my Faulkner out of this pronoun, which, after all, is hers. (176–77)

The reticence of "she" reemerges here as open refusal: she does not *want* to appear in this book. Her words do not merge with his words; they do not mingle in an act of "contamination and interplay." Defiantly, perhaps, she adds "she" to his earlier enumeration of indefinite pronouns, to which he responds, "a pronoun has power even when you do not know who is hidden behind it." In this highly self-reflexive moment, Glissant acknowledges the deliberateness with which he has cloaked "she" in mystery, as well as the important—the powerful—role she plays in his text. At the same time, however, he repudiates her refusal: despite her demand to be excised from his work, he includes her. He even goes so far as to suggest, with the reference to Mycea, a recurrent character in his fiction and poetry, that "she" is not a flesh-and-blood person at all, but rather a figment of his imagination, a muse, or an amalgamation of women he has known or invented. "She" interrupts to complicate her earlier refusal by asserting that "she does not want to hide," indicating that she does not want *him* to hide *her* or, perhaps, that she is complicit after all in her inclusion in the text— although the possibility remains that her complicity, like "she" herself, is an invention of the author's pen. She concludes by asserting an autonomous identity, punctuated by her laughter and her claim that "this pronoun"—that is, indefinitely, "she"—is not indefinite but definite, representing a discrete, concrete, and sexed identity that is not his but hers.

Conclusion

In *The Repeating Island*, Benítez Rojo revels in a play of difference, deferral, and desire between his own voice and the evocative bodies of reticent women. As Vera Kutzinski remarks, however, "the text's erotic investment in visual and olfactory metaphor" means that "what is valued about these women is how they look and smell, not what they might say" (175). In contrast, Glissant portrays the process of Relation in such a way that openness and reticence function in tandem to create linkages that are at once intimate and respectful of difference. In his interactions with "she," what "she" says matters deeply—even though, Glissant admits, he might be putting his words in her mouth. Despite their distinct approaches, both writers inscribe these exchanges as encounters between a male poet and his female muse; yet, whereas Benítez Rojo portrays them through rhythm and performance, Glissant depicts them through language and silence, or as a series of conversations and verbal negotiations. That the female authors of the novels analyzed in the following chapters are not interested in the relationship between male poet and female muse should come as no surprise. Nevertheless, all four strategically draw attention, not only to what their protagonists say, but also to how they look and smell. Words and body, rhythm and performance, language and silence, production and nonproduction: all of these become important means by which to confront the past in the postmodern plantation imaginary.

These strategies, however, are not without risk. Kutzinski, in her critique of Benítez Rojo, warns that the "nonreproductive, and thus nonthreatening, black sexuality" of his women threatens to reproduce damaging stereotypes, such as "the racist belief in the mulata's supposed sterility, a myth perpetuated in Cuba's national cult of the Virgin of Charity on the one hand and in the stylized erotic commodification of white women on the other" (178). And, indeed, the sterility, whether literal or figurative, of the characters discussed in the following chapters is often not self-chosen: Jones's protagonist, Ursa, for example, undergoes what may be a forced hysterectomy, while Santos-Febres' title character, Selena, is biologically male. Yet they and the others struggle to reclaim their unproductiveness as a strategic reticence. In doing so, they differentiate themselves from previous characters we have seen, like Glasgow's Eva Birdsong, whose hysterectomy functions as an endpoint rather than a beginning, or, conversely, Parra's María Eugenia, whose fertility is indispensable to the reproduction of the nation.

In some ways, the late twentieth-century characters introduced in the following pages most resemble Welty's Aunt Studney and Loynaz's Laura, both of whom employ a strategic verbal reticence that forces their white counterparts to recognize them, however briefly, as threats. Yet, unlike those women, these new protagonists also demand the right to speak their stories aloud, on their own terms. Their speech acts, however, may also pose dangers. Writing about Toni Morrison's *Beloved*—another New World text that bears witness to (some of) the histories that disrupt History—Doris Sommer observes, "jeopardy ... is a constant condition of telling this story. Remembering is full of risks. History haunts its survivors. Nothing immediately liberating comes from reliving loss and humiliation" (*Proceed with Caution* 172). Recognizing the dangers they face, the protagonists of these novels must develop a rhythm of approach and withdrawal as they remake History into histories through the bold performances and reticent silences of the open word.

New World Silences, New World Songs

Stairway for Electra and *Corregidora*

The protagonists of Aída Cartagena Portalatín's *Escalera para Electra*, or *Stairway for Electra* (1970), and Gayl Jones's *Corregidora* (1975) are telling stories they do not want to tell, about events that should be forgotten and yet must be remembered. As a result, their recountings are ordered and disordered by a rhythm of speaking and not speaking that constitutes at once the very conditions of trauma and a deliberate resistance to the gripping power of the past. The horrors to which the novels' female narrators testify, while different in important ways, are rooted in a common legacy of New World colonialism and slavery; and their relationship to that legacy, as women of mixed African and European heritage intrinsically marked by its violence, shapes the manifold, variegated strategies they employ to confront it. Although their relationship with the plantation past differs, both novels also denounce the cruelty of a master or *amo* whose influence is still felt long after his death; but they do so without focusing attention on his story. Rather, they examine the lasting effects of his tyranny in their own lives and the lives of their communities. Their narrations thus not only expose the misdeeds of the master, but also shift the focus away from what Benítez Rojo calls the "phallic world in pursuit of the vertical desires of ejaculation and castration" (10), and onto those who have suffered under that world's oppression. To tell about the past, then, becomes a willful and knowing act of defiance.

Yet Cartagena and Jones also reveal the act of bearing witness to be inseparable from trauma and an unavoidable consequence of it. Emphasizing their narrators' reluctance, they demonstrate the need to withhold information, defer telling, and maintain a defensive posture in the face of overwhelming histories. Despite these precautions, however, both novels suggest an unexpected connectivity generated by testimony's dialogic and performative capabilities, and so echo Glissant's insistence that both openness and reticence are fundamental to the process of Relation. More-over, they understand this process to involve, not only the words produced through testimony, but also the bodies of the women who give that testimony, bodies engaged in public performances that enact both suffering and a defiant rejection of suffering. Through their words and their performances the protagonists of these novels reclaim their desire and begin to extricate their bodies, as well as their memories, from the closed circle of the past.

Stairway for Electra, published in 1970, was the first novel written by an already established poet, Aída Cartagena Portalatín. Cartagena, who was born in 1918 to a rural family of mixed racial ancestry and modest means, rose to prominence in the 1940s, and became known for her work as a writer of prose and poetry, a publisher, and a scholar of Greek, Roman, and Dominican art and architecture. Although she traveled extensively, she spent most of her life writing and teaching in the Dominican Republic, where she died in 1994.[1] Appearing nine years after the 1961 assassination of Rafael Trujillo, whose government Cartagena had steadfastly opposed, *Stairway for Electra* grapples with the legacy of his thirty-one year dictatorship and its imme-diate aftermath, which included a military coup, civil war, and direct military intervention by the United States. It does so indirectly, however, by presenting the "biography" of a woman named Swain, as recounted by the novel's narrator, Helene (who, much like Cartagena, is an unmarried, middle-aged Dominican writer of mixed race). Born and raised in the same town as Helene, Swain is the daughter of Don Plácido, the local *caudillo*, or strong man. Conceived during her father's brutal rape of her mother, Rosaura, Swain is seduced by Don Plácido as an adolescent and be-comes his lover and ally against Rosaura. After her mother discovers the incestuous relationship and kills her husband, daughter and mother continue to live under the same roof, until Swain, enraged that Rosaura has found happiness with a new lover, plots to murder her. Shaped by the violent sexual acts of her father, Swain matures into an angry, defiantly promiscuous woman who blindly honors her father's power, refusing to form alliances with her mother or any other member of a community that has likewise been scarred by Don Plácido's rule. As unlikely as it seems, Swain becomes the catalyst for Helene's testimony, and the figure through which the secret traumas suffered by so many are brought to light so that Don Plácido's symbolic grip upon the pueblo might finally be loosened.

Corregidora is also a first novel, although its author, Gayl Jones, was a little-known twenty-seven year old African-American poet and playwright at the time of its 1975 publication. Born in 1949, in Lexington, Kentucky, Jones, like Cartagena, has published in a variety of genres, including poetry, novel, and criticism.[2] Stretch-ing from the nineteenth century to 1969, *Corregidora* is set primarily in the 1940s and 1950s, in Jones's home state. It is narrated by Ursa Corregidora, a blues singer haunted by stories about her great-grandmother and grandmother, who were slaves in Brazil. Although she is born several decades after her grandmothers achieve their freedom and migrate to the United States, Ursa's childhood is defined by constantly repeated stories about the tyranny of their Portuguese master, Corregidora, whose surname they all carry. Like Swain, both of Ursa's grandmothers endure horrific sexual violence at the hands of their master, who forces them into prostitution. Em-ploying frank language, the novel describes how Corregidora impregnated Ursa's great-grandmother and, later, her grandmother—his daughter—as well. Although she never knows Corregidora, Ursa remains bound by his symbolic presence and by her foremothers' mandate to "make generations" in order to recount, and so pass on, their history of suffering. Yet her central dilemma is clear: the first page of the novel relates how her husband, Mutt, in a jealous rage, pushes her down a flight of stairs in the blues bar where she performs. As a result, although she is only twenty-five years old, she is given a hysterectomy. Unable to bear children, she turns to performing the blues as an alternative way to bear witness. Through her song, Ursa testifies not only to the horrors inflicted by Corregidora but also to the struggles of her own life, especially as they relate to her conflicted sexuality, which has been marked in multiple ways by the traumas suffered by her as well as her foremothers.

Trauma, Testimony, and Performance

The self-awareness Cartagena and Jones employ to describe the process by which their protagonists come to accept the task of testifying can be attributed, at least in part, to the moment in which they were writing, which saw the coming-of-age of two American literary genres: the *testimonio* in Latin America and the neoslave narrative in the United States. The former, whose origins George Gugelberger traces to the 1966 publication of Miguel Barnet's *Biografía de un cimarrón*, was initially celebrated as an authentic, unmediated narration of real-life experiences. However, the truth-value of the *testimonio* became a well-known topic of debate in the 1990s, as critics began to question the notion of authenticity and uncover the contradictions and complex strategies that shaped the *testimonio's* apparently straightforward structure. As a work of fiction that flaunts, rather than cloaks, the layers of mediation on which it is constructed, *Stairway for Electra* is not a true *testimonio*, although it reproduces many of its most common features.[3] It is more productively understood as an early example of what Elzbieta Sklodowska calls the pseudo-testimonial novel, which distinguishes itself from the *testimonio*, not because it is "fictional" rather than "factual," but because it enacts "the very process of 'recomposing' the past" so as to emphasize "the failure of the testimonial act" (180). In *Stairway for Electra*, the precariousness of Helene's project is continually emphasized, both in the structure of the novel—its chronological twists and turns, its radically fragmented text—and in the doubts its narrator openly expresses regarding the usefulness of the tale she is telling. As a result, the reader is forced to question not only the veracity of her story, but also, more fundamentally, whether she should be telling it at all. Cartagena thus echoes the question that lies implicit in the oft-quoted final sentence of Toni Morrison's *Beloved*: "This is not a story to pass on" (275). Is this story not to be told (passed on or handed down), or is it not to be ignored (passed on or passed up)?

The point of contact between *Beloved* and the two novels examined here is not coincidental since, like *Corregidora*, Morrison's work is an example of the neoslave narrative that flourished in the 1970s.[4] Although African-American authors have written about the aftermath of slavery since the late nineteenth century, it was only with the development of this genre that a critical mass of fictional texts began to explore systematically the imprint left by slavery in the contemporary U.S.

The neoslave narrative, like the pseudo-testimonial novel, is a highly self-conscious genre concerned with the nature of the past, its continued influence in the present, and the inevitable problems faced when trying to tell about it.[5] Just as Sklodowska differentiates pseudo-testimonial novels from the *testimonio*, so Naomi Morgenstern distinguishes between neoslave narratives and their nonfictional predecessors in terms of literary strategy rather than truth-value: "As *fictional* testimonial literature, *neo*slave narratives both stage a simple return of history and reinscribe it. ... In this sense, they do what all testimonies do: they both return to an event and make it happen for the first time. Their status as self-conscious fiction means that they represent, as well as enact, this process" (103). Both the neoslave narrative and the pseudo-testimonial novel, then, are performative genres, in the sense that the literary and organizational strategies they employ "enact" the complexities of the histories they recall. Their performativity, as we saw in chapter 4, also links them to a postmodern plantation imaginary. Moreover, by foregrounding the artistic performances of their protagonist-narrators, they add yet another layer of metaliterary self-awareness to this formula.[6]

The inconstant rhythm of all of these performances is necessitated by the dangers inherent to the act testifying, whose source can be uncovered by tracing the evolution of the meaning of "trauma." Kai Erikson notes that in its original medical usage it describes "a blow to the tissues of the body—or, more frequently now, to the tissues of the mind—that results in an injury or some other disturbance" (455). That is to say, trauma traditionally refers to the *event* that inflicts injury. More recently, however, its meaning has expanded to include the *effects* of that blow on the injured party. As a result, Erikson argues, "the term has been drifting somewhat ambiguously," alternately referring to the event that brings the injury into being and the condition(s) that result from that injury (456). Such ambiguity is not arbitrary. To the contrary, it lies at the very heart of contemporary conversations about trauma, which stress that traumatic disorders are defined precisely by the way in which their victims repeatedly relive the traumatic experience through thoughts, hallucinations, dreams, and flashbacks. Discussions of trauma regularly employ words such as "concrete" and "literal" to describe the manner in which the traumatic event is reexperienced without being assimilated through the normal functioning of memory. Unable to process the event as a coherent narrative, the victim becomes "haunted" by a past that repeatedly returns to her in all its original, horrible solidity.

The narrators of *Stairway for Electra* and *Corregidora* experience the past in just this way, as a concrete presence that appears, unsummoned, and will not go away. They are, therefore, shaped by history, but in a way that is qualitatively different from protagonists in the novels previously examined. In contrast to the Alonsos of *Iphigenia*, the Archbalds of *The Sheltered Life*, or the Fairchilds of *Delta Wedding*, who actively attempt to preserve an idealized image of the old order, these women do not choose to live in the past. They also differ from *Garden*'s Bárbara, who inhabits a lush natural world in which history has become illusory and fleeting. History has lost meaning for them, too, but it is hardly ephemeral. To the contrary, it is a solid invasive presence.

According to Cathy Caruth, this invasion of the traumatic past into the present results in a paradoxical relationship between "the *elision* of memory and the *precision* of recall," in which "in its repeated imposition as both image and amnesia, the trauma thus seems to evoke the difficult truth of a history that is constituted by the very incomprehensibility of its occurrence" (*American Imago* 48.4, 419). The am-biguous nature of trauma, therefore, extends beyond issues of linguistic usage or even of individual experience, so as to encompass questions of historical knowledge. How is history recorded, or not recorded; experienced or not experienced? What are the limitations, both practical and ethical, of understanding what "really happened" in the past? If official history articulates itself as a whole and wholly accurate record, testimony, as a response to trauma, is partial, made up of fragments that cannot be fitted together into any satisfactory pattern. Caruth asserts, "what trauma has to tell us—the historical and personal truth it transmits—is intricately bound up with its refusal of historical boundaries" (*American Imago* 48.1, 7). Trauma reveals the limi-tations of historical as well as psychological truth, in part, by blurring the lines between official histories and individual experiences, between external events and internal reactions to them. At the same time, it also confuses the temporal divisions that allow an event to be located on a particular point in the timeline of history, and so to be recorded, analyzed, and understood.

Trauma's refusal of historical boundaries is also at least partially responsible for the danger of what has been called its "contagion" (Caruth *American Imago* 48.1, 10). Theory on traumatic repetition has drawn attention to how the initial blow rever-berates in the lives of those who come into intimate contact with its original victim. As psychoanalysts who work with the children of Holocaust survivors have observed, the symptoms of trauma can be passed down from one generation to the next.[7] It can also "spread laterally" by means of what Erikson calls "collective trauma," which he defines as "a blow to the basic tissues of social life that damages the bonds attaching people together and impairs the prevailing sense of community" (460). Thus, trau-ma's disorder moves vertically, penetrating several generations, and laterally, throughout a larger community, with the initial incident repeating itself in the lives of an ever-widening circle.

Its capability to possess its victims through incessant repetition, its fragmentation of historical truth, and its ability to contaminate others: these are the characteristics of trauma that create the conditions under which the protagonists of *Corregidora* and *Stairway for Electra* struggle to understand how they came to be infected by events they did not directly experience. In *Corregidora*, Ursa recalls a childhood spent lis-tening to the stories of her great-grandmother and grandmother's lives under slavery, and proclaims: "I am Ursa Corregidora. I have tears for eyes. I was made to touch my past at an early age" (77). Ursa's identity and way of seeing the world have been shaped by the suffering of the past; but that past, which she refers to as "*my* past," is not truly hers. Rather, it is made up of "their memories, but never my own" (100). Similarly, in *Stairway for Electra*, Helene is made to confront long-suppressed mem-ories of an adolescence dominated by the terrifying story of Swain, which violently bursts forth into her consciousness while she watches a Greek production of Euripi-des's *Electra*: "The shell breaks like a cracked nut or a ripe banana. The shell breaks and Swain is a memory. I throw away the shell and she remains like a nightmare, a thing of strange and damned things" (10). The reemergence of Swain is not just psy-chological but strikingly physical. It is not only a "memory" or "nightmare" vision, but also a solid "thing." The physical nature of the return of trauma—what Nancy

Morgenstern calls its "strangely concrete" character (103)—is emphasized in Jones's novel as well. Ursa is "made to *touch*" her family history as if it were an object that could be held, caressed, passed on. In both novels, the past appears in concrete form and demands to be acknowledged. In response, the narrators must devise a set of strategies that allow them to tell about history without becoming subsumed by it.

The resulting narrations can be frustratingly indirect and fragmented, characteristics that arise from the requirements of bearing witness. According to Dori Laub: "The narrator and [the listener] need to halt and reflect on these memories as they are spoken, so as to reassert the veracity of the past and to build anew its linkage to, and assimilation into, present-day life" (Felman and Laub 76). To respect the risks inherent to the process, testimony must develop a rhythm of approach and withdrawal, which is created, not by the teller alone, but with the active participation of a willing listener. In these novels, however, the dialogic demands of testimony manifest themselves not as an intimate conversation between the traumatized individual and a trained therapist (the scenario described by Laub), but rather as a series of performative moments enacted by the first person narrators, for a public comprised, directly, of members of their communities (the men sitting in the smoky bars where Ursa performs, the friends and family who simultaneously read and help to piece together Swain's story); and, indirectly, of the reading public.

Diana Taylor has described suggestive affinities between trauma and performance: both are characterized by repetition, are experienced "affectively and viscerally in the present," and rely on the interactive process of telling and listening for transmission (*The Archive* 165–67). Yet, as Taylor emphasizes, this last similarity also reveals a significant disparity: while the transmission of trauma is best described as contagion, performance is deliberate and strategic. Moreover, while a victim of trauma cannot separate herself from its effects, a performer can. If trauma isolates people in the pain of the past, performance can transform suffering: "By emphasizing the public, rather than private, repercussions of traumatic violence and loss, social actors turn personal pain into the engine for cultural change" (168). Thus while the affective characteristics of performance resemble those of trauma, its strategic effect is more closely akin to that of testimony: moving trauma out of the private and into the public realm, it makes it a topic of deliberate conversation rather than a taboo subject or rote story. Not a simple narration of history, testimony is a "performative speech act" that pushes at the limits of received notions of truth in relation to the past as well as the present and the future (Felman and Laub, 5). The narrators of *Corregidora* and *Stairway for Electra* produce such speech acts, even as they engage in provocative physical performances that draw attention to bodies that exhibit marks of the physical and sexual violence about which they must testify.

Singing and Silence in *Corregidora*

In *Corregidora*, Ursa must find a new way to remember the past while honoring her foremothers' rejection of the written word as a means by which to do so—a rejection that they trace back to the government-ordered destruction, in 1889, of many documents relating to slavery in Brazil.[8] Reacting to this official erasure of history, Ursa's great-grandmother declares: "And you got to leave evidence too. And your children got to leave evidence. ... That's why they burned all the papers, so there wouldn't be no evidence to hold up against them" (14). For the Corregidora women, the truth can only be kept alive through the womb that bears generations and the voice that bears witness. Pointing to the sexual coercion that shapes their family narrative, Morgenstern observes that their employment of the womb as a site of resistance ultimately traps them in the very past they resist: "To bear witness—literally, to bear witness by bearing witnesses—is to resist and to repeat a history of enslavement" (106–107). This observation is simultaneously affirmed and complicated by the fact that the legitimate (white) wives and daughters of the master employ the same strategy. Despite the fact that they remember the repressed history of slavery rather than reinforce the official history of the plantocracy, the Corregidora women's desire to control their daughter's reproductive capacity is surprisingly comparable to Abuela's manipulation of María Eugenia's romantic desire in *Iphigenia* or General Archbald's selfish adoration of Eva's "eternal" beauty in *The Sheltered Life*.

However, their focus on the voice—that is to say, on oral rather than written history—distinguishes them. For Ursa, bereft of her womb, the voice becomes the sole means of leaving evidence, and critics have tended to focus on two important ways that she employs it: by performing the blues and by maintaining silence. The blues functions as a central mode of expression for Jones and her narrator. The movement and structure of the novel's language, its oral, rhythmic, and even melodic qualities, and its thematic concern with what Jones refers to as the mix of brutality and tenderness that defines "blues relationships," all reveal the extent to which *Corregidora* draws from this musical tradition (Tate "Interview" 147).[9] At the same time, silence pervades the novel's pages. Janelle Collins notes, "silence frequently takes over the storytelling" (8). Ursa alternates telling with not telling and, more specifically, singing with silence in such a way that allows her to withdraw when necessary. Yet, as Collins observes, this defensive strategy also empowers Ursa to "contradict the historical silencing of and silence about black women" and control how her story will and will not be told (8).[10]

The power of the blues, like the power of silence, lies beyond language: the blues, Ursa says, allows her "to explain what I can't explain" (56) and "to explain it in blues, without words, the explanation somewhere behind the words" (66). Pointing to these textual moments, Ashraf Rushdy suggests that the functionality of the blues in *Corregidora* results not from its oral but rather from its performative qualities. In Jones's novel, "history [is] not to be answered through another verbal construct but to be rendered suspect through an extravagant performance" (*Remembering* 63). Performance thus becomes a strategy by which Ursa simultaneously honors and challenges the forms of resistance employed by her foremothers: on the one hand, she questions the official historical record; on the other, like her foremothers, she uses her body and voice to rebel against the restrictive narrative of written history. But while they mounted their opposition through reproduction (of generations of women) and repetition (of stories about the past), Ursa recognizes the limitations of their strategy.

By crafting blues performances that explore connections between body and sexuality, voice and song, and past and present, she attempts to overcome these limitations. Hazel Carby has argued that the female blues singers of the 1920s and 30s—the very singers that Ursa, born in or around 1922, would have heard as a child—"occupied a privileged space; they had broken out of the boundaries of the home and taken their sensuality and sexuality out of the private and into the public sphere" (756). Similarly, Ursa makes public the private discourse of her mothers, who tell their stories only to the female members of their family.

If bringing into the open that which was hidden is an essential part of bearing witness, however, it is also dangerous. The men who watch Ursa sing read her as promiscuous despite her consistent refusals of their sexual advances. Moreover, her flesh is doubly marked by violence—first by a familial history of slavery, rape, and incest that can be read in her mixed-race features; then by the more recent scars inflicted by Mutt's act of jealous rage. After her hysterectomy, Ursa begins to articulate how these histories are bound together in her body—particularly in her "center," her genitals, over which both Mutt and Corregidora claim ownership—as well as in her song:

> [Mutt was t]alking about *his* pussy. ... The center of a woman's being. Is it? No seeds. Is that what snaps away my music, a harp string broken, guitar string, string of my banjo belly. Strain in my voice. Yes, I remember your hands on my ass. Your damn hands on my ass. That vomity feeling when they squeezed my womb out. Is that the way you treat someone you love? Even my clenched fists couldn't stop the fall. That old man still howls inside me. (46, emphasis in original)

Mutt's jealous violence is joined, by Ursa's clenched-fist fury, to the "old man [who] still howls inside" her. They, and the pain they have caused her, are a primary source of her song, which Corregidora helps to generate through his howling and which Mutt, as Ursa reminds him in the closing lines of this passage, demanded that she sing for him: "I came to you, open and wounded. ... I sang to you out of my whole body" (46). As a blues performer, Ursa sings with her *whole* body, and her conflation of Corregidora with Mutt is explained by the fact that neither man can see beyond "*his* pussy ... center of a woman's being." If her grandmothers and mother would reduce her to her womb, Mutt's violence deprives her of that womb even as it values her only for her genitals. In response, Ursa strives for wholeness—that is, to be recognized and valued fully, but also to abandon her reticence and present herself, "open and wounded," without fear of being diminished.

It is not just *her* body, however, that is entangled in the history of slavery. In the final scene of the novel, when Ursa is reunited with Mutt, she confuses her own body with Great Gram's, and his, once again, with Corregidora's: "It was like I didn't know how much was me and Mutt and how much was Great Gram and Corregidora" (184). Just as the men in her life are unable to recognize that she sings from her whole body, so Ursa, like her foremothers, cannot separate male sexuality from the brutality of the master. The bodies of both genders are caught up in a past consumed by Corregidora's abuse.

Face to face with Mutt for the first time since he pushed her down the stairs twenty-two years earlier, Ursa returns with him to their old room in the Drake Hotel.

Abandoning her public act for an intimate one, Ursa begins to perform fellatio on her ex-husband (something she had consistently refused to do when they were married). As she does so, she unexpectedly understands what Great Gram had done to Corregidora decades earlier, an action that enraged him so much that she was forced to flee to the United States: "In a split second of hate and love I knew what it was, and I think he might have known too. A moment of pleasure and excruciating pain at the same time, a moment of broken skin, but not sexlessness, a moment just before sexlessness, a moment that stops just before it breaks the skin: 'I could kill you' " (184). In a moment, Ursa realizes that Great Gram performed the same act of (potential) violence toward Corregidora that she now threatens to do to Mutt. This new comprehension, however, does not bring resolution. Rather, it evokes the brutality and tenderness of the blues relationship, reinforcing the ambivalence that has permeated her story. As Rushdy has observed, her epiphany allows her a choice: "Ursa does not describe a 'moment.' She describes, in the style of a gradation, a set of options" (*Remembering* 53). Ursa finally recognizes that the past, which has since her childhood exerted itself as a dull, repetitive moment from which there is no escape, is not unchangeable. It can be expanded, understood as a series of moments, a series of choices. Because she chooses the "moment that stops before it breaks the skin," because she threatens to kill him but instead brings him pleasure, the closing scene leaves open the possibility of a reconciliation between Ursa and Mutt, and of a future at least partially unburdened by the bitterness of the past.

Deviance and Defiance in *Stairway for Electra*

In *Stairway for Electra*, it is the shock of recognition that Helene experiences while viewing Euripides's *Electra* that compels her to acknowledge Swain's story, but she continually expresses her hesitancy to do so: "Displaying Swain's case is not as easy as arranging its facts in a Tiffany display window. ... I, Helene, her biographer, don't feel comfortable putting her on view like in an auction with no bidding" (50). To tell Swain's story is to betray the members of her community, to give away their secrets, and Helene's reluctance manifests itself in the very structure of her "biography," a kind of collage in which flashes of Swain's story are surrounded by other kinds of writing: travelogues; telegrams to friends back home; sociopolitical diatribes; chaotic interior monologues in which the narrator reflects on her anxieties about writing; and dozens of quotations from Euripides's *Electra*. Fragmenting the facts of Swain's life and scattering them without regard to chronological order, the biographer executes her task through silences—secrets that remain untold or withheld until the end—and silencings—constant interruptions of the biographical narrative. These strategies allow its narrator to retreat when necessary, and so to testify successfully. At the same time, they expand the text, making it more complex and inclusive.

Like *Corregidora*, *Stairway for Electra* features a series of extravagant performances by Helene, who self-consciously assigns herself the role of the reluctant "biographer" and, through her ostentatious use of intertextuality, acts out her desire to be taken seriously as a writer in an international context. As Isabel Zakrzewski

Brown observes, Helene's (and Cartagena's) wide-ranging knowledge of Western intellectual traditions—demonstrated by a flow of references to Cervantes, Shakespeare, Beckett, Freud, and dozens of other major as well as minor literary and intellectual figures—legitimizes her intellectual competence and thus secures her right to participate in the global literary scene (131). While mining the Western canon to prove her identity as an intellectual, however, she undermines the notion that it is an untouchable, unchangeable monolith.

This double-edged strategy is demonstrated through Cartagena's use of Euripides' *Electra*, an explicitly performative theatrical text that is cited at least once in all but two of the thirty-one chapters, often in the form of block quotes that extend half a page or more.[11] The relationship between the novel and the intercalated text is multifaceted. On the one hand, the parallels drawn between the ancient and modern tales sanction the latter by calling upon the canonical status of the former. On the other hand, when read in relation to Cartagena's surrounding text, the citations from the Greek tragedy frequently generate contrasts rather than comparisons. At times, these contrasts reveal themselves in the structure and language of the novel, by comparing the rigid codes that organize classic Greek tragedy with the wide-ranging formal experimentalism that characterizes Cartagena's novel: as Zakrzewski Brown observes, Cartagena's use of both modern Spanish and rural Dominican dialect self-consciously clashes with Euripides' prescribed poetic language (133). Elsewhere, they emphasize different ways of conceiving and embodying female sexuality.[12] Euripides' Electra, although forced to marry a peasant farmer, honors the moral codes of the royalty of the ancient world by remaining a virgin to protect the family bloodline. As the daughter of a *caudillo* and a wealthy mother, Swain also belongs to a landed aristocracy; unlike her counterpart, however, she rejects the similar sexual proscriptions of her community and avenges her father's murder by shaming her mother through her promiscuous behavior. Perhaps most significant, however, are the disparate strategies of bearing witness employed by each protagonist. Electra, often responding to questions posed to her by the Chorus, ceaselessly tells her about her suffering. Swain, in contrast, remains mute, thus forcing the task of telling upon her biographer. In the novel, then, Electra's words do what Swain's silence cannot: they articulate her (their) suffering for the reader.

At the same time, Swain's remarkably nonverbal nature forces attention on her actions, unmitigated by self-justification, particularly her promiscuity, which she flaunts by parading a string of lovers through the home she shares with her mother. Comparing Swain and Electra, Ramón Figueroa notes that both characters break the mold of traditional womanhood: "Owing to her direct participation in punishing the murder of her father, Electra becomes a woman who destroys the models of conduct imposed upon her sex, in the same way that Swain enjoys a freedom that contrasts with the social restrictions suffered by women in Dominican culture, especially in the era in which the novel takes place" (42). Electra's community, however, ultimately understands her unwomanly behavior to be heroic. This is not the case with Swain, who is viewed as such a dangerous and disruptive force that parents forbid their children from speaking her name aloud. Swain, like Electra, participates in the murder of her mother; however, it is not the act of killing that irretrievably stains her. Swain's mother, Rosaura, who embraces traditional notions of female purity, is welcomed back into the community after she butchers her sleeping husband with a machete. It is not murder, then, but rather sexual deviance that makes Swain a threat.

Yet the same sexual deviance, openly performed, draws Helene to Swain. Despite the uneasiness of their relationship, Helene recognizes that they are alike. Both, for example, remain unmarried and childless by choice—Swain, we are told, has had several abortions—and in doing so, embrace a self-chosen sterility by freely refusing the role of motherhood. Although Helene does not describe her own sexual activities the way she does Swain's, she emphasizes the physicality of the act of writing.[13] And just as Swain's ferocious promiscuity strips sex of romantic or reproductive connotations, so Helene's portrayal of her own body at work is without sentimentality: she sweats, suffers from insomnia, drinks too heavily, and wanders endlessly through the steamy streets of Athens.

It is this final activity, streetwalking, that links Helene most directly to Swain. Although they are different kinds of streetwalkers, by moving their bodies outside of the private and into the public realm, they act in defiance of the patriarchal society that shaped them. As Debra Castillo argues within a broader Latin American context:

> Streetwalking, even in its innocent variants, is discouraged as an offense against this ingrained morality; it is appropriate only for racially and socially inferior women who are assumed to be promiscuously impure. Streetwalking as a political activity ... is officially ignored as unintelligible madness, a displacement made possible by the tradition of seeing all deviance from the model of self-restricted, enclosed femininity as insane. (*Talking Back* 16)

Although she describes herself as non-white (literally, as "negrita," or little black one), Helene never identifies her class background. But her childhood memories indicate that, at least at times, her family interacted socially with Swain's, which would suggest that she, like the subject of her biography, would be censured by her community for her "streetwalking." Moreover, although her political motivations for writing remain muted throughout most of the novel, a fear that her work will be judged as "unintelligible madness" permeates it pages and, perhaps for this reason, she refuses to cast final judgment upon Swain. Unlike Swain, however, who performs her rebellion in an incoherent eruption of defiant and (self-) destructive action, Helene does not allow her speech act, her testimony, to be ignored. To the contrary, she draws attention to the deliberate silence that has surrounded Swain's story for so long: "when the small town atmosphere began to kick up winds that threatened to raise a storm, Swain became our only companion: a captivating dream replete with nightmares and violent meditations that filled us with hate, never compassion or forgiveness, because the pressures of our education had deepened a deep dungeon full of taboo things" (37). Helene insists on opening up this deep dungeon; yet, repeatedly, when on the verge of relating an especially important piece of her story, she digresses, and is only able to return to it by literally, physically making herself be quiet: "The biographer bites her tongue" (126). Again and again, the author must bite her tongue in order to stay focused on the subject she has promised to discuss, and her reader, like a good listener, must learn to follow unexpected twists and turns in the narration.

In the closing sentences of the novel, Helene addresses those readers with the following plea, which comes from a loose sheet of paper she has found, containing one of "Scaramelli's Keys": "if at some point this book ends up in the hands of a person who desires to contemplate it for idle reasons, I beg him to reflect upon the hard pincers through which one must pass and the press of numerous sorrows under which one must weep before arriving" ["si este libro llega a caer alguna vez en manos de una persona que aspire a la contemplación por motivos vanos, yo le ruego que reflexione sobre las duras tenazas por las cuales hay que pasar, y la prensa de numerosas penas bajo las cuales hay que llorar antes de llegar" (152)]. A direct quotation from *Il direttorio mistico* (*The Mystic Directory* 1754), a posthumously published treatise by the eighteenth-century ascetical writer Giovanni Battista Scaramelli, in their original context these words are replete with allusions to the severe process of spiritual purification required of the ascetic preparing to encounter God's presence.

Excising this reference from its original context, Cartagena strips it of explicit religious meaning, but preserves its urgency and solemnity. Scaramelli's words become her instructions to the reader, placed at the end rather than, more logically, the beginning of the novel. Thus she does not dictate how *Staircase for Electra* will be read (and risk going unheeded), but rather ensures that the reader thus inclined will have already contemplated it "for idle reasons." In this way, she emphasizes the potentially combative relationship between the biographer and her public. The impersonal "one must" (*hay que*) compounds the ironic nature of the warning by making it unclear who must endure the difficulties described. Is it Swain and the members of her community, or the Dominican Republic as a whole? Is it the author, or perhaps the reader? While these final lines reflect the stubborn, strategic ambiguity of the novel as a whole, the images of pincers and presses evoke not only the self-flagellation implicit in the original context, but also the violent tortures and deaths, alluded to elsewhere in the novel, endured by so many Dominicans who resisted Trujillo's tyranny. At the same time, in the context of this metaliterary novel, the word *prensa*, or press, which in modern Spanish usage refers most often to the printing press and the media, ties physical instruments of torture to the intellectual and emotional act of writing and reading. Idelber Avelar observes that "Latin American postdictatorial texts, and postcatastrophe literature in general, is challenged to subsume the stark, brute facticity of experience into a signifying chain in which such facticity perennially runs the risk of being turned into yet another trope" (211).[14] Through her final words, borrowed from yet another source, Cartagena describes the precarious place of a writer who attempts to witness through storytelling. At the same time, she posits an ideal reader who does not consume her novel for self-centered pleasure or to turn history "into yet another trope," but rather reflects seriously and soberly on the pain it contains. Tellingly, she concludes her advisory, and her novel, with the phrase "antes de llegar," or "before arriving," which signals both the need for continued struggle and the possibility of arrival at a new, unspecified destination.

Writing Across Borders: Cross-Cultural Strategies in Cartagena and Jones

Although the precise destination remains unknown, it is clear from the pages of *Stairway for Electra* that it will be a place at once vitally transnational and distinctively Dominican. Indeed, both Cartagena and Jones tap into a neo- or pseudotestimonial aesthetic that allows them, on the one hand, to tell about specific repressed histories and, on the other, to participate in broader struggles against political, social, and linguistic domination. As commentators on their own work, they self-consciously locate their writing in an emerging postcolonial literary movement that was establishing a place for itself in the global literary market at about the same time their novels were published. *Stairway for Electra*, for example, contains many references to Cartagena's Latin American contemporaries, including Alejo Carpentier (Cuba), Julio Cortázar (Argentina), Beatriz Sarlo (Argentina), Carlos Fuentes (Mexico), and Mario Vargas Llosa (Peru), which reveal the author's awareness that her text would inevitably be read in the context of the "boom" of the Latin American novel. The unease that Helene expresses regarding her book's reception should also be understood in terms of this moment: aware of her doubly marginalized position as a woman and a Dominican within the Latin American literary scene, she also worries about being rejected by the European presses controlling most of the publication and distribution of "boom" literature. Helene (and by extension Cartagena) thus asserts an affinity between herself and other Latin American and postcolonial writers, while underscoring the competitive, market-driven nature of international publication.[15] Unlike Cartagena, Jones does not allow blatantly metaliterary moments to penetrate the enclosed setting of *Corregidora*. In interviews, however, she has claimed "kinship" with Latin American novelists, particularly Gabriel García Márquez and Carlos Fuentes, who, like her, produce a morally responsible and technically inventive literature that grapples with "the particular historical and contemporary nightmares" faced by their communities (Harper 365–66).

At the same time that they acknowledge artistic and political affinity with other postcolonial writers and regions, Jones and Cartagena situate their stories in specifically national contexts, and employ the social and political upheavals of the 1960s as essential backdrops to the personal stories of their protagonists. At certain moments in *Stairway for Electra*, for example, Cartagena openly decries the chaos and repression that followed Trujillo's assassination, including the 1963 deposal of Juan Bosch's presidency, the ensuing civil war, and the 1965 military intervention by the United States. In contrast to these exacting historical references, *Corregidora*, as Rushdy notes, is "understated" in its acknowledgement of the Civil Rights, Black Power, and feminist movements in the U.S. (*Remembering* 56). Rather than addressing them explicitly, Jones (like Welty in *Delta Wedding*) relies on her audience's knowledge of recent history to inform its reading of the novel, particularly of Mutt and Ursa's final reunion, which takes place in the seminal year of 1969, twenty-two years after their marriage in 1947. The two authors thus approach contemporary history from diverse angles: Cartagena utilizes frank rhetoric to denounce political injustice while Jones suppresses direct political discourse but quietly urges her readers to imagine the massive changes her characters would have witnessed during two tumultuous decades.

This difference is complemented by their distinct attitudes toward space and place. Like Ortiz, Loynaz, and Benítez Rojo, Cartagena confronts the challenges posed by island geography, and accentuates the tensions, creative and destructive, generated by the dynamic play between her insular island nation and the outside world.[16] Placing her biographer in the Greek archipelago and her biography in the Dominican Republic, she crafts a text that swings between "inside" and "outside" locations in the same way that, through its multiple intertexts, it swings between original and borrowed words. Jones, in contrast, creates a fictional world that is insular in a different way: it is profoundly closed. Not only do such momentous outside events as the civil rights movement go unmentioned, but the physical world portrayed remains tightly constricted: with few exceptions, it is only through the recollections of others—Great Gram's stories about Brazil, for example—that she leaves the restricted physical spaces (hotel rooms, small bars) that demarcate her life. As has been the case with almost every pairing I have chosen for this study, here again the Caribbean text displays a greater sense of transnational mobility (it is hardly coincidental that the exception to this is chapter 4, where the U.S.-based text is authored by a citizen of the archipelago). Still, in the present chapter and the following one, this pattern begins to break down: although their Caribbean counterparts are still relatively more daring in their border crossings, Jones's *Corregidora* and Morrison's *Paradise* engage a trans-American movement generated by the recognition of a shared plantation past. Specifically, both authors turn to Brazil, which, although it remains geographically secondary in their storytelling, is symbolically foregrounded as a space that functions, simultaneously, as an alternative to and an uncanny double of the United States.

Imagining "Our Greece": Nationalism and Transnationalism in *Stairway for Electra*

In his seminal 1891 essay, "Nuestra América," or "Our America," José Martí asserts that Latin America must learn to claim its own narrative: "The history of America, from the Incas to the present, must be taught in clear detail and to the letter, even if the archons of Greece are overlooked. Our Greece must take priority over the Greece which is not ours" (114). *Stairway for Electra* is, in many ways, Cartagena's attempt to imagine "our Greece" in a specifically Dominican context; it represents, as one critic has expressed it, "a complete critical revision" of her nation's history as it transpired after Trujillo's assassination (Figueroa 41).[17] In the tradition of such canonical Dominican national romances as Manuel de Jesús Galván's *Enriquillo* (1882), Federico García Godoy's "patriotic trilogy" (*Rufinito, Alma dominicana, Guanuma*; 1908–1914), and Tulio Cestero's *La sangre* (1914), it allegorizes Swain's incestuous relationship with her *caudillo* father in order to critique the corrosive effects of the kind of unfettered authoritarian rule his character represents, and to facilitate the articulation of an alternative, autonomous national identity—what Martí calls "our Greece."[18] At the same time, as we have seen, Swain's story only emerges because

Helene is traveling in the *other* Greece, where she is inspired by a performance of a tragic text that belongs to a past that is not hers but that she claims for herself. In *Stairway for Electra*, then, the history of "our Greece" is, ironically, inseparable from that of "the Greece that is not ours."[19] In this sense, Cartagena's ambitious novel incorporates two distinct projects that, like the two Electras struggling in Helene's imagination, do not always fit comfortably together. On the one hand, it is a national novel concerned with telling the story of Swain and, by extension, the Dominican Republic. On the other, it places those stories in an intertextual and transnational context that threatens to undermine the very notion of national autonomy. Like Loynaz's *Garden*, Cartagena's novel participates in Caribbean debates about insularity by playing upon the tension between the need to look inwards in order to strengthen an independent identity, and the benefits to be gained by moving beyond its circumscribed island sphere. Yet while Loynaz avoids directly engaging political debates, Cartagena charges headfirst into them. Furthermore, unlike her Cuban counterpart, who ultimately privileges the inward-looking gaze, Cartagena insists, perhaps paradoxically, that leaving the island sphere is not just useful but necessary.

Put differently, Cartagena suggests that "the Greece that is not ours" is in fact indispensable to "our Greece." Indeed, the Greece that Helene tours in 1969 is portrayed, not precisely as an ally, but rather as an uncanny double of the Dominican Republic. Each is an isolated, economically depressed island nation living under a repressive government and being invaded by an endless stream of *gringos* in the guise of soldiers or tourists. Moreover, each possesses a rich cultural inheritance marred by a traumatic past. For Helene, the recognition of these parallels provokes intellectual vertigo: "Everything shakes me at once, you could say it is a cocktail: Athens: Electra: my pueblo: Swain: these people I just met: my friends since forever in Dominicana" (131). The distinctions she purports to make here—between new acquaintances, for example, and life-long friends—are undermined by the colons, which create a visual sense of continuity and even equivalence. Likewise, the image of the cocktail evokes a mixture impossible to separate back into its original elements. Although here she stresses correspondence or fusion, elsewhere she asserts that it is cultural and geographical *distance* that allows her to tell her story: "from a distance, I think it is much easier for what has been seen and rummaged through to manifest itself in an objective light. I should intercalate the word perspective" (69). Yet both sameness and difference are integral to the transnational strategies of the novel, which repeatedly interrupts its Dominican-centered narrative with references to Greece as well as Iran, South Africa, and a host of other countries. At the same time, however, the narrative and narrator remain circumspect. They are aware, not only that such strategies might distract from the true intent of the novel, but also of the potential dangers posed to their island nation by the outside world. Contact with the other can generate growth and imagination, but it can also contaminate and destroy.

For this reason, Helene relies upon the familiar tactic of deferral, asserting a comparison only to cut it short. In one scene, for example, while dining with an Iranian archaeologist, she brings up guerilla warfare: "Mr. Mahuad, all that about guerrilla fighters gets people excited today" (70). Mahuad, in response, confesses that he once belonged to an organization that attacked English oil refineries in Iran. Before he can finish telling his story, however, Helene interjects: "I interrupt him again: Mr. Mahuad, my country is in America: Dominicana. That is where the first anti-colonialist guerrilla fighter appeared ..." (71). Deliberately broaching the topic of guerrilla warfare as a form of resistance to imperial domination, Helene allows Mahuad to tell just enough of his story to emphasize the global context in which such conflicts are taking place. Almost immediately, however, she redirects the discussion to the heroism of the sixteenth-century indigenous leader, Enriquillo. This reference, in turn, reminds the reader of a long history of underground resistance on her island, up to and including guerrilla groups that fought in the 1965 Dominican civil war and beyond.[20] Although she implies a need for international solidarity, Helene continues to redirect the reader's attention to the specific story that she is telling.

In doing so, she reminds us of the risks inherent to the process of building cross-cultural alliances, a theme that reappears in the novel's final chapter. Responding to an imaginary reader who asks for her opinion on the current state of relations between European nations and their ex-colonies, she invokes a South African novelist: "I am going to let Peter Abrahams respond by recounting one of his adolescent adventures. Abrahams? Yes, the black African author of *Es roja la sangre negra*. He was trapped by and subjected to the laws that govern *l'apartheid*. A cruel monologue" (151). Quoting from Abrahams's novel, originally published in English under the title *Mine Boy*, Helene claims to cede her voice to his. The reader's expectation is that he will speak in a clear and pointed manner. This does not happen, in the first place, because Cartagena quotes directly from a French translation of the text, *Rouge est le sang des Noirs* (*Es roja la sangre negra* or *Black Blood is Red*). Before analyzing the *meaning* of its words, therefore, the reader must translate them from French into Spanish. Thus, a "cruel monologue" becomes a frustrated multilingual and multinational conversation. At the same time, this passage emphasizes the increasingly complicated web that ties once disparate regions of the world together: Asians and Africans fill the streets of Paris, South African writers speak for a Dominican biographer, and readers from around the world must maneuver labyrinths of cultural and linguistic difference in order to understand text and context.

At other moments, however, the novel's digressions serve, not to complicate its transnational perspective but rather to sharpen its nationalist focus by shedding its allegorical layers in order to speak directly about the Dominican experience. After narrating the climatic moment in which Swain's mother murders her husband, Helene abruptly shifts focus to ponder her own life story: when she was an infant, a bullet from the gun of a U.S. soldier passed one inch over her body, sparing her but killing a Dominican soldier. She immediately links this incident, which took place during the 1916 U.S. invasion of the Dominican Republic, to more recent events:

> I, Helene,
> Swain's biographer,
> sufficiently mature,
> have been rewarded. I have watched one of the cruelest tyrants on earth govern for thirty-one years.
>   In 1963 I saw the military overthrow the Substantive Law; in April of 1965 my friends: professionals, artists, writers, students, workers, artisans, and peasants closed ranks like heroes and rose up in order to restore the Law. Immediately: the second occupation of my country by the gringos. (125)

In her conversation with Mahuad, Helene refers to Enriquillo, a sixteenth-century indigenous leader who rebelled against the Spanish; here, she proclaims the heroism of her friends who took up arms in the 1965 civil war. In doing so, she confronts the immediate traumas that are more often absent from her narration. She also laments the fact that, just as the murder of Swain's father does not end the cycle of injustice, so the assassination of the dictator and the bravery of her friends mark, not a fresh beginning, but rather another phase in a history of oppression—one in which the U.S. represents the greatest current threat. This story, which lies at the heart of Helene's rage and drives her to tell the many other stories that fill her narration, serves as a warning of the dangers posed to those who are vulnerable to penetration from the outside. It also reminds us that Martí's essay, "Our America," is not primarily concerned with defining "our Greece" in opposition to "that Greece which is not ours." Rather, as its title suggests, it grapples with the problem of how to define "our America" when constantly confronted with the aggression of the United States of America. As we have seen, Cartagena ultimately configures the relationship between the two Greeces as one of productive tension. The same cannot be said for her depiction of the two Americas. Like Ortiz and Benítez Rojo before her, she defines that relationship in purely oppositional terms and proposes the need, not simply for defensive reticence, but for clear opposition to the other America's imperialistic projects.

Below all of these narrations lies another story, one that never quite emerges and that is indelibly linked to the plantation past. To understand it, however, one must first recognize the unique history of the plantation—and the tangled discourse of race, gender, and sexuality it produces—in the Dominican Republic. Despite efforts, in the sixteenth century, to establish a plantation economy on the lands surrounding Santo Domingo, the region's fortunes quickly declined as Spain began to conquer and settle other New World lands. While the French territories in the western regions of Hispaniola did succeed, in the eighteenth century, in building a thriving sugar industry, the Spanish-speaking citizens of the other half remained impoverished. Richard Turits, among others, has argued that a perhaps surprising result of this chronic economic stagnation was the development of a relatively colorblind, racially equal society, in which no large-scale slave labor was required and even legally enslaved peoples of African descent were granted comparative autonomy. Nevertheless, some Dominican scholars suggest that by the end of the nineteenth and into the twentieth century, the dominant ideology of colorblind citizenship and raceless national identity gave way to a new controlling myth of cultural and racial whiteness. They argue that the development of mechanized sugar production and, with it, U.S. intervention in Dominican affairs and the arrival of Haitian and Afro-Antillean workers to labor in cane fields and sugar mills, "challenged the economic and ideological foundations of racial equality and colorblind citizenship" (Mayes n.p.).[21] That is to say, in the Dominican context the emergence of a race-conscious, and racist, discourse of national identity can be tied, at least in part, to the postslavery rise of the kind of mechanized, large-scale plantation that Ortiz calls the super-central.

Describing this late emerging myth of cultural and racial whiteness, Pedro San Miguel emphasizes the centrality of Haiti:

The definition of "Dominican" became "not Haitian." This dichotomy could be seen
in nearly every sphere: Haitians practiced voodoo, Dominicans Catholicism; Haitians spoke Creole, Dominicans Spanish; Haitians were black, Dominicans were of
mixed race or white. More than this, Haitian culture and society were seen as an
extension of Africa, whereas Santo Domingo clung to its pure Spanish origins. (39)

Rejecting Haiti as the forbidden other, the Dominican nation denied its own historical and cultural links to Africa. This denial, and the "racist, anti-Haitian discourse"
that reinforced it, "reached the apex of its ideological and political expression during
the long dictatorship of Rafael L. Trujillo" (40). That is to say, it was a fundamental
characteristic of the very *caudillo* legacy that Cartagena denounces. Yet she never
directly confronts this part of that legacy, or its long-lasting consequences. She
openly condemns racism in the U.S. and South Africa. Why does she avoid an equal
condemnation of her own country's history of racism?

Her reticence can perhaps be explained by her recognition, conscious or otherwise, that the nationalist project of her novel would be undermined by the inclusion
of a blunt presentation of this problem. As San Miguel notes, "once the nation is
identified with 'Spanishness,' a term that carries all sorts of cultural and racial bag-
gage, then by extension everything that is 'black' and identified with Haiti becomes
antinational" (64). As we saw in chapter 4, Benítez Rojo maintains an "uncanny"
silence regarding Castro's legacy, a silence that Colás attributes to a "fear of 'being
cut off' from the utopian culture of the People of the Sea" ("There's No Place" 213).
This fear of castration serves as a reminder that not all reticence is productive or
creative—it is not always one movement in a pendular swing. Sometimes silence is
motivated by fear, powerlessness, or a fear of being rendered powerless. Just as
Benítez Rojo is anxious about being severed from the culture he has left, so, I would
argue, Cartagena worries about being cut off if she says too much.

Although submerged, however, the problem of anti-Haitianism and Dominican
identity is not entirely absent. It appears, for example, when Helene subtly claims her
African heritage by suggesting that *negrita* might be a name the reader would choose
to call her (130). It surfaces most clearly, however, when she recalls a conversation
overheard as a young girl, in which Agliberto, a peasant who worked for her family,
refers to Haitians as "unos tragones de hombrecitos," literally "gluttons for" or
"guzzlers of little men." Agliberto continues: "they are strong black people. Every
day they cut several cords of sugar cane. They spend any free time they have fighting,
gossiping, and barbequing sweet potatoes and little men (*hombrecitos*); they almost
always finish up at midnight with a celebration of witchcraft: a vodu dance" (90).
The older man enumerates, with a mixture of admiration and disgust, the customs of
the Haitian migrants who work in local sugarcane fields. In the process, he underscores their blackness and religious practices, which, as San Miguel notes above,
implicitly mark them as non-Dominican. As she listens to his words, the young
Helene imagines rituals in which primitive Haitians gorge themselves on tiny human
bodies: "My imagination goes wild: I think of dwarves, as well as of very small
normal men: swallowed: digested: defecated by Haitians" (90). Voicing her concern,
Helene is quickly informed that *hombrecitos* is a local word for herring. Nevertheless, the image of Haitians devouring, digesting, and defecating their helpless human

victims, knowingly reflects Dominican prejudices and fears. This is confirmed by the narrator's admission that, much later, she would discover that "what they did with the Haitians is called: the exploitation of man by man" (91). Upon going to bed that night, the adolescent Helene sleeps deeply and awakens smiling at her own gullibility: "It was impossible then to give that any credit, all that about being a *machetero*" (91). Often used as generic term to describe those who work cutting sugar cane, the word *machetero*—literally, "machete wielder"—is deeply implicated in the history of the plantation but also contains more violent implications. Using humor and the innocence of childhood to disarm her readers, Cartagena employs a deceptively simple digression to condemn the belief that Haitians are machete-wielding cannibals and to denounce the economic exploitation of Haitian workers in Dominican sugar plantations. Her reference to the *machetero* also serves as an oblique reminder of the Haitian Revolution, in which the machete was wielded against the master rather than for him. Even more subtly, and more daringly, it quietly recalls a shameful and long repressed episode in Dominican history: the 1937 massacre of tens of thousands of Haitians, ordered by Trujillo, in which Dominican soldiers and civilians became the *macheteros*, and Haitian peasants their victims.[22]

Cartagena would more fully explore some of these themes in *Culturas africanas: rebeldes con causa* (*African cultures: Rebels with a Cause*, 1986) which she published sixteen years after *Stairway for Electra*. A loose combination of essays, memoir, and literary anthology, it describes the author's personal awakening, in the 1940s—that is to say, more than two decades *before* the publication of *Stairway for Electra*—to the importance of Africa in Caribbean literature, and her subsequent investigations of the cultural and artistic production of the African Diaspora. The book includes sections on the work of Léopold Sédar Senghor (Senegal), Aimé Césaire (Martinique), Richard Wright (United States), and Nicolás Guillén (Cuba), among others, as well as two chapters extolling Haiti's role in the development of Caribbean cultural expression. Perhaps because of the politically delicate period in which it was written, *Stairway for Electra* displays markedly more reticence when establishing connections between the Dominican Republic and other nations of the Caribbean, the African Diaspora, and the postcolonial world. Choosing Greece as its principle point of comparison, it perhaps contradictorily lays claim to a Western tradition while opposing the colonial legacy of Western nations. In *Culturas africanas*, Cartagena would suggest different paths of connection that hint at the intra-Caribbean circuits explored by both Benítez Rojo *The Repeating Island* and, although differently, Mayra Santos-Febres in *Sirena Selena*.

Straddling the Mediterranean and Caribbean archipelagos, Cartagena and her alter ego Helene play fiercely, but not quite fearlessly, in an international and intertextual world that blurs the borders separating nations, centuries, archipelagos, and cultural canons. Yet their play has purpose: to bring a deeper understanding to the plight of their own nation. They do not desire to displace or discount the stories of other peoples who have endured similar suffering. To the contrary, they deliberately draw attention to them, while at the same time reminding us that *their* story must be the focus of this novel. The resulting conflict between the novel's cross-cultural and nationalist visions remains, perhaps necessarily, unresolved and so generates a creative tension that raises important questions about the place of the local and the global in a poetic imaginary that is at once Dominican and American, postslavery and post-colonial, national and transnational.

A New World Song: The Black Aesthetic and Blues Aesthetics in *Corregidora*

If *Stairway for Electra* constitutes an extravagantly intertextual performance, Ursa's blues performances in *Corregidora* take place in much smaller, more intimate settings. In sharp contrast to Helene, Ursa intentionally reduces her world to the enclosed, repetitive space of the hotel room and the bar. Its lack of flamboyant border crossing, however, is not the only thing that distinguishes Jones's novel. Cartagena's work is also pervaded by a dedication to the nation that *Corregidora* flatly denies. More specifically, Jones engages in a subtle but insistent critique of the Black Nationalist movements that flourished in the sixties and seventies. As Madhu Dubey warns, however, "the term 'black nationalist discourse' is ... problematic in its con-flation of various, often conflicting, strands of nationalism into a single, simplified, homogenous ideology" (14). In an attempt to categorize its diverse manifestations, historians have tended to recognize two broad divisions: revolutionary nationalism, which emphasized class struggle as the root cause of racial oppression; and cultural nationalism, which, according to William L. Van Deburg, "proposed a black cultural renaissance as a key component in the revolutionary struggle for Black Power" (170). Despite their differences, each of these strands, as well as their various offshoots, shared what Van Deburg describes as a "collective thrust ... toward racial pride, strength, and self-definition" (2). Although Jones is hardly hostile toward these goals, she is deeply critical of the inflexible, authoritarian perspectives perceptible in much official Black Nationalist discourse. Indeed, in a collection of academic essays published 16 years after *Corregidora*, Jones compares Black Aesthetics, a cultural nationalist theory of artistic production, to totalitarian Communism (*Liberating Voices* 30).

Jones's rejection of Black Nationalism in general, and Black Aestheticism in particular, links her work to those of other African-American women writers of the 1970s, as Dubey has shown. In her critique of the Black Aesthetic doctrine, Jones stresses that it impinges on artistic freedom. Dubey expands this analysis in femi-nist terms: the rejection, by African-American women writers, of Black Aestheti-cism's formal restrictions is inseparable from their critique of Black Nationalism's "womb-centered definition of black women" as carriers of a new generation of "rev-olutionary warriors" (19).[23] Wahneema Lubiano has similarly understood this reductive view of women in terms of "a hysterical black nationalist revision of a patriarchal family romance" (240). In order to implement its version of the "patri-archal family romance," Black Aestheticism demanded that African American art-ists produce models of what Deborah McDowell describes as "a 'positive' black self, always already unified, coherent, stable, and known" (57). This positive repre-sentation of black subjectivity, however, was to be conceived of, not through the lens of radical individuality but in the context of a cohesive, authentic black community that expresses itself through a "univocal oral collectivity" (Dubey 86). Moreover, it should be represented, in terms, not of the traumatic past, but of a triumphant future often imagined as the recovery of lost origins located in a mythically unblemished Africa.[24]

Black Nationalist rhetoric thus inverts, rather than overturns, the dichotomous logic of the plantation. In contrast, African-American women writers offer a "unique," and uniquely subversive, perspective. Yet, a glance at the strategies that, according to Dubey, they employ reveals clear points of contact with other postslavery literatures of the Americas: like Loynaz and Welty, they exploit "a structural tension between cyclic and linear time;" like Benítez Rojo and Glissant, they emphasize "communal narrative frames and oral cultural modes." To what extent, then, are they truly distinctive? The final characteristic listed by Dubey offers some insight into this question: they trace "a figuration of black feminine subjectivity as absent." On the one hand, we have seen that black feminine subjectivity is glaringly absent in all of the texts we have studied up until now. And, as Dubey stresses, in the 1970s not only Black Nationalism but also white feminism continued to deny this subject position: "black women's sense of their exclusion from the two liberationist discourses of the period is eloquently expressed by the phrase, 'all the women are white, all the Blacks are men'" (16). On the other hand, in recent fiction by and about African-American women, this ongoing absence is neither denied nor taken for granted. Instead, it becomes a place of strategic intervention. Rather than asserting a coherent and unified subject position that establishes yet another inversion of old binaries, they struggle to define a different kind of subjectivity, one that Sally Robinson has described as functioning "both within and against the discourses which place them in positions marginal to subjectivity" (135).

Corregidora grapples with this conundrum by insisting on the need to testify in a way that complicates all sides of the argument. Although respectful of the Corregidora women and their suffering, Jones is profoundly critical of their mandate to "make generations." She condemns Mutt's violence against Ursa, showing how it echoes Corregidora's brutal treatment of Great Gram, but also hints in the novel's final scenes that Mutt, like Ursa, has undergone a difficult journey toward knowledge and transformation. In other words, she replaces the Black Aesthetic, which inverts the old binaries of the plantation, with a blues aesthetic that draws on the dialogic and performative capacity of music.[25]

Dubey affirms that by "challenging the univocal oral collectivity postulated by the Black Aesthetic, Ursa's blues voice signifies black feminine subjectivity as the 'more' that exceeds the reproductive terms of the nationalist discourse on black women" (86). As we have seen, it is not only Black Nationalist rhetoric that would limit women to "reproductive terms." The white master and even Ursa's own foremothers attempt to do the same. Yet through her vocal performances, Ursa is able to transform her lack—of a womb, of the capacity to have children—into subversive excess. It is not only, however, through her invocation of the blues that Jones confronts monolithic discourses. Like Cartagena, although in a quieter fashion, she challenges official histories through transnationalist strategies. Specifically, by placing Brazil at the historical and symbolic heart of Ursa's story, she stages a conception of personal and collective identity that, like the blues, generates a web of connections that extends the length of the Americas.

Throughout her literary career, Jones has evinced an enduring interest in exploring the possibilities, not only of a trans-American history, but also of a trans-American—and, more broadly, a postcolonial—ethics and aesthetics. In a chapter from *Liberating Voices* entitled "Multiple-Voiced Blues," for example, she compares texts by the U.S. African-American poet, Sherley Williams, and the Mexican writer, Carlos Fuentes. Arguing that their common "merging of the poet's voice and history with other voices has moral-aesthetic connotations" she affirms that they demonstrate "an essential connection among all Third World voices" by creating a "freer form" that shapes "a sense of communal wholeness out of multiple fragments and juxtapositions of voices" (42–3). In her own work, she has sought to convey this "freer form" not only through her employment of the blues and other exemplars of African-American folk and oral culture, but also by asserting historical, spiritual, and cultural connections between the U.S. and Latin America. Just as she claims creative "kinship" between herself and various Latin American novelists, so too, her earlier work suggests a multivalent affiliation between the United States and Brazil. Jones, of course, shares her abiding interest in Brazil with many other U.S. Americans, particularly those of African descent who, for many years, saw the racially mixed Brazil as a kind of "racial paradise."[26] Although *Corregidora* resoundingly rejects such utopian notions, Jones nevertheless can be seen as participating in a larger tradition in which, as we saw in the introduction, Brazil has long "played the role of foil to the U.S. system" (Coser 123). The following chapter shows that Toni Morrison, too, taps into this tradition in her novel *Paradise*.

Jones's interest in Brazil manifests itself not only in *Corregidora* but also in other works, including her long form poems *Song for Anninho* (1981) and *Xarque* (1985), both of which recount the history of Palmares, Brazil's most famous *quilombo*, or settlement for runaway slaves, which was founded in the early seventeenth century. By returning repeatedly to this site, Jones indicates that, like Glissant and Benítez Rojo, she perceives New World communities established by runaway slaves to be central to the postslavery imagination. Moreover, by commemorating Palmares in not one but several imaginative texts, she recalls Glissant's assertion of a link between "historical" and "creative *marronage*" (*Poetics of Relation* 71), or Benítez Rojo's claim that "the Caribbean's 'other' history had begun to be written starting from the palenque and the maroon" (254). It is, then, hardly insignificant that Palmares also appears, however fleetingly, in *Corregidora*.[27]

Brazil's role in the novel, however, is more clearly signaled by the author's choice of title. In Brazil, the word *corregidor* dates back to the colonial era and refers to a judicial magistrate or local judge. By equating the slave owner with an arbiter of justice, Jones comments on power structures established in Brazil and across the Americas during the age of conquest and colonization. By giving the word a feminine ending, however—by turning *corregidor* into *corregidora*—she turns the tables and implies, as Marvin Dixon has observed, that it is now Ursa who "must bring justice to bear" upon the past (239). More than an inversion, however, the commentary implicit in the title functions ironically: how does one "bring justice to bear" when the papers have been burned and the victims of injustice reside in a country thousands of miles away from the victimizer?

The author also draws attention to differences between slavery in Brazil and the United States in order to develop key aspects of her narrative argument. For example, because Brazilian slaves were not freed until 1888, Ursa, born in 1922, is only one generation removed from enslavement. Without claiming that the ongoing impact of slavery is felt less by blacks in the United States, Jones employs Ursa's generational closeness to the experience to heighten the dramatic intensity of her situation. Likewise, her reference to the 1889 destruction of many Brazilian records related to slavery not only explains Great Gram's distrust of the written word but also provides a powerful historical example of how official archives can be manipulated to erase the voices of the exploited while protecting the interests of the exploiters.

It is, however, the well-documented Brazilian practice of prostituting female slaves that most profoundly links the historical and contemporary concerns of the novel. Although the sexuality of female slaves was systematically exploited throughout the Americas, the aboveboard form this took in Brazil distinguished it from its quasi-secretive status in the United States. Carl Degler writes: "A number of Brazilian sources, both during the colonial period and under the Empire in the nineteenth century ... speak of the use of female slaves as prostitutes. In some cases their masters even lived off the earnings of such slaves" (70). Degler explains this practice by observing that Brazilian plantations did not need female slaves to reproduce, since the slave trade with Africa remained legal in Brazil for decades after it was formerly outlawed elsewhere. To the contrary, they were more likely to benefit financially from slave women who did not reproduce: "Masters had little incentive to breed slaves, which required that women be released from work to rear children, so long as the foreign slave trade promised to supply labor needs for the future" (69).[28] By creating a female character who has intimate contact with the legacy of slavery in both Brazil and the United States, Jones is able to emphasize the multiple ways in which the sexual and reproductive capacities of black women across the Americas have been exploited.

Her novel's contemporary context additionally allows her to engage more recent polemics surrounding black women's bodies in U.S. society. For example, Ursa's hysterectomy, presented as a medically necessary consequence of Mutt's act of violence, would likely have raised the suspicion of a reader in the 1970s, for it was during this period that the media exposed the forced sterilization, by the U.S. government, of poor and minority women.[29] Contemporary readers might also have been influenced by the controversial 1965 "Moynihan Report," as well as the Black Nationalist response to it. The former argued that the black family was in crisis due, in part, to a high rate of female-headed households and a lack of strong father figures. The latter publically denounced the report's findings but paradoxically embraced the notion that female usurpation of male power was a root problem within the African American community and, in response, called for a restoration of patriarchal order.[30] By highlighting the particular history of the forced prostitution of female slaves in Brazil, Jones offers a pointed condemnation of the control exerted over black women's bodies under slavery while also suggesting that Ursa's mothers repeat the same pattern by demanding that their daughters "make generations." At the same time, she extends her critique to contemporary rhetoric from the white establishment, which denigrated black motherhood as pathological and excessive, and the Black

Nationalist rejoinder, which demanded that black women submit to male authority and (re)produce a new generation of revolutionaries.

Although she relies on the specificity of the slave system in Brazil, Jones resists the temptation simply to oppose the histories of U.S. and Brazilian slavery to each other. Instead, she places them in dialogue with each other to expose a continuum of suffering that respects both similarities and differences and to generate a multiplicity of stories that counters the numbing repetition that Ursa experiences as a child. For example, even though she focuses on Gram and Great Gram's horrific experiences as slaves in Brazil, she gestures toward the lives of other characters who suffered under slavery in the United States. She tells the tale of Mutt's grandfather, who labored to win the freedom of his wife only to see her forced back into slavery; or that of the bartender, Sal, whose mother was abandoned as a child because her dark skin made it impossible for her to pass as white with the rest of her family. Through these stories and others, Jones affirms that the traumas of New World slavery are varied and complex, and have no respect for national boundaries.

While bedridden and recovering from her hysterectomy, Ursa longs to perform a new song for herself and her foremothers: "I wanted a song that would touch me, touch my life *and* theirs. A Portuguese song, but not a Portuguese song. A new world song. A song branded with the new world" (59). About twenty pages later, Ursa will remind us, "I was made to touch my past at an early age" (77). In this moment, however, she imagines a different possibility: to be touched by song rather than history, to find an experience of the New World that does not conflate her life with her mothers' but rather embraces each one separately and all at once. Her first instinct is to sing a Portuguese song infused, perhaps, with old man Corregidora's howling. But she quickly amends her desire: she will sing a song that is simultaneously Portuguese and not Portuguese, "branded with the new world" just as her family, for four generations, has been branded, literally and figuratively, by their experiences of slavery. She immediately links this song to her foremothers' suffering: "I thought of the girl who had to sleep with her master and mistress. Her father, the master. Her daughter's father. The father of her daughter's daughter. How many generations? Days that were pages of hysteria" (59). Repeating the story she has heard since childhood, she recognizes that the page (Corregidora's means of telling about the past) and the womb (Great Gram and Gram's) have become entangled in time: "Days that were pages of hysteria." The master's seed fills their wombs and his words their mouths. A few paragraphs later, Ursa describes her fascination with a snapshot of herself with Mutt: "I'd always thought I was different. *Their* daughter, but somehow different. Maybe less Corregidora. I don't know. But when I saw that picture I knew I had it. What my mother and my mother's mother before her had. The mulatto women. Great Gram was the coffee bean woman, but the rest of us ..." (60). What ties her to her family is her mixed blood. What separates her is her inability to bear children. Yet she also underscores an important difference: her great-grandmother does not have Corregidora's blood running through her veins. Brought to Brazil from Africa, she was called the coffee-bean woman because of her dark skin. A few pages earlier, Ursa sees this difference as a possible sign of salvation: "let me witness the only way I can. I'll make a fetus out of grounds of coffee to rub inside my eyes" (54). She envisions creating a fetus, a new generation, from coffee beans, seeds that recall Corregidora's pet name for Great Gram and the sweat of the slaves who grew them on Brazil's plantations, but that also embody the pre-slavery origins that Great Gram's dark skin represents. Although tempted by this return to impossible origins, however, she ultimately accepts the devastating fact of her blood, while posing a new difference: "But I *am* different now, I was thinking. I have everything they had, except the generations. I can't make generations" (60). Ursa's hope for escaping the traumatic past thus lies, ironically, in her inability to reproduce and in the space that this creates between her and the family history she has inherited.

If Cartagena uses the geographical distance between the Mediterranean and the Caribbean so that her narrator may better understand the Greece that is her own, Jones gives Ursa a history that straddles the Americas in order to underscore her distance from any geographical place or national identity.[31] Born and raised in the southern United States, speaking English and deeply immersed in the blues tradition, Ursa is not Brazilian. A black woman living in the pre-Civil Rights South, she is denied many of the basic rights of a U.S. citizen. Because of her light skin and Portuguese features, other black Americans see her as someone who could "pass" or who looks "Spanish." Indeed, Fiona Mills, noting that the label "Spanish" is given to Ursa by various characters in the book, argues that by underscoring Ursa's Spanish or Portuguese background, Jones hints at the possibility, not just of a "kinship" between the U.S. and Brazil, but more broadly of "an Afro-Latino/a heritage" that encompasses the Americas (92).[32] Thus Jones does not finally portray Ursa as hopelessly alienated from all forms of community; rather, through her she imagines a new "New World," one that extends beyond national boundaries and links together long divided lands in one scarred body that struggles to sing out the pain of the past in order to remake it. As such, Coser affirms her as a symbol of the New World: she is "a hybrid and thoroughly American, mixing two races, two hemispheres, and several continents in her memory and her blood" (138). Ursa, however, knows too much to celebrate her own mixture and the unfixed identity it helps to shape. Mixture was forced upon her. It is only through the treacherous work of testimony that it can be used as a means of resistance, and so become a source of strength as well as weakness, a path to liberation as well as a reminder of the past.

Conclusion

As we have seen, about fifteen years after the respective debuts of their novels, Cartagena and Jones published essays articulating their desire to establish transnational connections through a politically engaged, libratory poetics. In the final pages of *Culturas africanas*, Cartagena urges her fellow Latin Americans to embark on a search for origins. She speaks, however, of "roots" in the plural and further complicates the notion of a unified beginning by stressing, "We nations of the strange isles are mestizo and mulatto" (124). She thus describes not a single origin but rather a network of roots that extends throughout the Americas, across the Caribbean archipelago, and all the way to Africa and even Europe. Likewise, in her conclusion to *Liberating Voices*, Jones argues, "the problems of the freed voice apply not only to African American literature and criticism, but to all the world's literatures and criticisms ... " (192). Both authors thus express a yearning for unity, but nuance that yearning with reminders of the multivalent contexts of which they write.

In *Corregidora*, Jones explores Ursa's struggles to free her voice from the tyrannical frame of the master's outlook; and in *Stairway for Electra*, Cartagena does the same through the character of Helene. As we have seen, they are not equally concerned with the plantation legacy *per se*: while Jones focuses explicitly on a family that has lived through slavery, Cartagena speaks to the problem of the *caudillo* who seeks to control an ostensibly free population. Yet both authors ground their stories in a New World place and employ the strategies of the open word to show, on the one hand, how the legacy of the master continues to impact men and women in the most intimate areas of their lives; and, on the other, how strategies of resistance can be forged from the physical and spiritual dislocations imposed by that same traumatic history. Through her corporeal performances of song and silence, Ursa links stories of slavery in Brazil and the United States. Helene makes dizzying references to the histories, literatures, and artistic productions of the Caribbean, Latin America, and Africa, as well as Asia, Europe, and the Middle East in an attempt to transform Swain's furious silence into a composition that will command the world's attention.

Analyzing female-authored American fictions written in the last decades of the twentieth century, George Handley notes a common tendency to "imagine a plural and shifting conception of identity and call into question the individualist assumptions by which postslavery imaginings have revised plantation and colonial discourses" (*Postslavery* 144). To a degree, these tendencies are evident in *Stairway for Electra* and *Corregidora*. Both employ transnational movement, dynamic performance, and fractured or nonlinear structures to rework official narratives and create new spaces for negotiation. Yet the plurivocal nature of their texts is inherently limited because it is filtered through the single voice of a protagonist narrator. Helene and Ursa, displaying themselves with reluctance but also defiance, denounce the historical violations of the master while fiercely protecting the autonomy of their own persons—and in the case of Helene, the autonomy of her nation as well. Relation in the Glissantian sense—that is, "the possibility for each one at every moment to be both solidary and solitary" (*Poetics of Relation* 131)—is desired, but remains almost impossible to negotiate. The novels discussed in the following chapter reinforce the longing for Relation, but do so in narratives that are intensely fractured by multiple voices and a transnational vision that presses aggressively against the circumscriptions of unified national or personal boundaries.

Redressing the Big House

Paradise and *Sirena Selena*

Toward the end of the penultimate chapter of Toni Morrison's *Paradise* (1998), a sixty-year-old named Consolata describes a dimly remembered childhood in a Brazilian metropolis. After living in the United States for half a century, the memory she narrates is saturated with the language of nostalgia:

> Piedade had songs that could still a wave, make it pause in its curl listening to language it had not heard since the sea opened. Shepherds with colored birds on their shoulders came down from mountains to remember their lives in her songs. Travelers refused to board homebound ships while she sang. At night she took the stars out of her hair and wrapped me in its wool. Her breath smelled of pineapple and cashews .... (285)

Consolata describes a bustling port city, perhaps Rio de Janeiro, and recalls how, as a young girl, she was cared for by a woman, perhaps her mother, named Piedade, whose beautiful voice won them coins and leftovers from passersby. But she infuses what might be a tale of urban survival with the jewel tones of a tropical landscape and a mythological resonance generated by a powerful gift of song. Earlier in the novel, however, we are given a much grittier version of the same story. In 1925, at the age of nine, Consolata was "kidnapped" by Mary Magna, a white nun who plucked her from the street and brought her to the United States: "By anyone's standard the snatching was a rescue, because whatever life the exasperated, headstrong nun was dragging [her] to, it would be superior to what lay before [her] in the shit-strewn paths of that city" (223). We are also informed, a few pages later, that young Connie was the victim of sexual abuse: "One of the reasons she so gratefully accepted Mary Magna's hand, stretching over the litter like a dove's wing, was the dirty pokings her ninth year subjected her to" (228). As happens repeatedly in its multilayered pages, the novel offers competing versions of the past: did Connie's childhood take place in a vital paradisiacal realm or a "shit-strewn" city? Did Mary Magna save Connie, or dispossess her of a maternal inheritance of love and miraculous song?

The first pages of the second chapter of Mayra Santos-Febres' *Sirena Selena vestida de pena*, translated as *Sirena Selena* (2000), describe the eponymous protagonist, a delicate fifteen-year-old street hustler, homeless and high on cocaine, picking through the garbage for aluminum cans while singing a bolero in a voice that is "a sorrowful murmur, a heartbreaking agony" (4). The song leaves a nearby group of transvestite prostitutes unable to negotiate with potential clients: "They couldn't do anything except remember what made them cry" (4). Selena Sirena's soon-to-be mentor and manager, Martha Divine, is also bewitched, "like all the other *dragas*, like all the *clientes*, stunned, like all the people driving cars along the street" (4). Like Piedade, Sirena Selena possesses an uncanny gift of song that halts the movement of everyday life and lures listeners, helpless, into a timeless, wordless space of primordial dreams and impossible memories. At the same time, like Consolata, Sirena inhabits an urban Caribbean space—specifically, the Santurce district of San Juan, Puerto Rico—and struggles with poverty and sexual abuse from an early age, until being "rescued" from the streets by Martha Divine, an experienced drag performer who transforms the young hustler into a gorgeous *bolerista* whose performances in the luxurious hotels of the Dominican Republic will, she hopes, bring them both fame and fortune.

These brief vignettes suggest initial points of contact between *Paradise* and *Sirena Selena*, ones that also link them to the texts studied in the previous two chapters: the fracturing of official narratives, the privileging of marginalized perspectives, the strategic power of voice and song, and the vital need for transnational crossings. Yet, in most ways, these turn-of-the-century novels are profoundly dissimilar. Notwithstanding the compelling mythological allure of Piedade in its final paragraphs, most of *Paradise* occurs a world away from the urban Caribbean environs of Consolata's childhood, in the big-sky country of rural Oklahoma. Its principal action unfolds between 1968 and 1976 in Ruby, a deeply conservative all-black farming hamlet founded after World War II, and in the nearby "Convent," a decaying mansion built in the 1920s and currently inhabited by Consolata and the vulnerable, traumatized young women to whom she recites her memories. The densely woven narrative of *Paradise* employs lyrical, somber, and frequently theological language to examine specific historical conundrums of the U.S. African-American experience, while also self-consciously addressing questions of far-reaching philosophical and ontological import. Both its published title and its working one, *War*, underscore the comprehensive scope of its ambitions.[1] In contrast, the rhyming, singsong title, *Sirena Selena vestida de pena* (literally *Sirena Selena Dressed in Pain*), announces playfulness, even as its reference to *pena*—sadness, pain, or shame—hints at more serious intentions. Set in the 1990s, its action shifts between San Juan and Santo Domingo and focuses on the picaresque adventures of Martha Divine and Sirena Selena, even as it frequently spirals outward to encompass a constellation of intersecting stories. Employing tones that reflect its own calculated transience, it underscores the artificial and the superficial. One reviewer complains that its characters' thoughts "rarely go deeper than the details of forks and table cloths, wardrobe, wigs, makeup, nail polish and petty rivalries," but this is hardly accidental (Stuhr 118). The novel's deliberate superficiality and campy humor allow it to explore, challenge, and redefine the often-grim circumstances confronted by its protagonists.

Why do two such different novels pivot on such similar descriptions of miraculous songs emanating from mysterious female bodies that dwell at urbanized edges of American seas? Certainly, that both evoke the mythological figure of the siren is no coincidence. In *Sirena Selena*, this connection is made explicit by the titular character's name as well as her hybrid body, at once female and not female, which inflames desire that, like the longing awakened by her song, can never be satiated.[2] In *Paradise*, Piedade's siren identity is revealed through her voice, which, like Selena's, reduces the powerful and dispossessed alike to tears, and bewitches seafarers so that they, like Odysseus, are in danger of forgetting their vow to return home. Although the immortal fame of Homer's sirens makes his *Odyssey* an inevitable intertext, the siren songs of Sirena and Piedade in fact generate a more extensive chain of associations forged by literary, mythological, and religious traditions that have shaped the Caribbean regions of the Americas. This is especially true when one takes into account the common, if erroneous, conflation of sirens and mermaids.[3] Singing for travelers journeying to Caribbean ports, Sirena and Piedade recall the mermaids who purportedly greeted Christopher Columbus off the coast of Haiti. With their divine countenances and dark complexions—we are told that Sirena has cinnamon-colored skin while Piedade is "black as firewood"—they also resemble an *orisha*, or African deity, who was originally associated with the Ògùn River in present-day Nigeria, but in the Americas became known as the patroness of the ocean.[4] Called by many names—including Yemayá in Cuban and Puerto Rican Santería, Yemanja in Brazilian Candomblé, Yemalla in New Orleans Hoodoo, and Le Siren in Haitian Vodou—this globe-spanning goddess is linked to creation, motherhood, and the moon, and is often depicted as a mermaid. Thus the siren, already physically hybrid, becomes a potent symbol of the oceanic crossings and transculturations that have produced the Caribbean world. In these novels, however, the bodies that produce siren songs are simultaneously described in terms of divine immortality, on the one hand, and poverty, violence, and trauma, on the other. Sirena Selena may emerge from her dressing room "the living image of a goddess" (34), but she is also an orphaned boy who has witnessed the deaths of two surrogate mothers, scratched out a living on the streets, and survived a horrific rape. Piedade, while more mysterious, is associated with Consolata's painful childhood, similarly shaped by poverty, orphanhood, and sexual violation.

Paradise and *Sirena Selena* create indelible images of twentieth-century singing women, New World sirens who emerge from the "shit-strewn" streets of (post)modern cities, but who, despite their gifts, are judged by those around them to be, as the opening scene of Morrison's novel expresses it, "detritus: throwaway people that sometimes blow back into the room after being swept out the door" (*Paradise* 4). Like *Stairway for Electra* and *Corregidora*, these novels examine the problem of trauma through an exploration of testimony's performative dimensions. More particularly, they emphasize the latter's corporeal and rhythmic manifestations, which are able to disrupt the closed boundaries of the plantation past and, like the open word, trace new circuits of Relation that are "both solidary and solitary" (*Poetics of*

Relation 131). That is to say, they attempt to articulate a notion of identity that functions within a radically corporate, although hardly cooperative, framework. Rather
than testifying through the voice of a single character, as happens in the novels analyzed in chapter 5, they incorporate the voices and perspectives of multiple characters: half a dozen major ones in *Sirena Selena* plus as many minor ones, and well
over a dozen in *Paradise*. Although all of them speak from the margins of mainstream society, they do not articulate a consistent critique of the center, nor do they
provide a coherent counternarrative, even though some individuals may attempt to do
so. Instead, through their intersections, overlappings, and contradictions, they reveal
the contingencies through which communities are imagined. Compared with the
novels by Cartagena and Jones, these texts are less interested in confronting official
history than in exploring the possibilities, and the limits, of multiple unofficial histories. As a result, although reticence, silence, and sterility are not absent from these
novels, they are not employed with the same strategic force. Rather, Santos-Febres
and Morrison explore dynamic movements permit the reimagining of communities.
Like Cartagena and Jones, they emphasize geographical and, especially, cross-cultural
and transnational movement; additionally, they compose multi-voiced, nonlinear
narratives that enact, at the level of form and structure, the very crossings they describe. Yet Morrison examines traversals through what she has called "a very interior
terrain," and reveals how movements that promise freedom—be they geographical or
racial, revolutionary or religious—can stagnate and fester (Denard 12). Santos-Febres,
in contrast, dwells on the surface, drawing attention to how strategic cross(-dress)
ings can manipulate the appearance of things in a way that simultaneously provides
a means of self-defense and brings into question static notions of the self.

Transvestism and Traversals in *Sirena Selena*

Published in 2000, *Sirena Selena* foregrounds its strategies of crossings—of open-
endedness, fragmentation, and multivocality—in an elaborate narrative structure.
Divided into fifty chapters ranging in length from one paragraph to ten pages, it is
filled with flashbacks, dream sequences, and monologues whose speakers are often
deliberately difficult to identify.[5] The first novel published by its Afro-Puerto Rican
author, like *Paradise*, it locates its action in a realm apart from the dominant culture:
just as the protagonists of Morrison's novel are "throwaway people," so too are the
domestic workers, street hustlers, drag performers, child brides, and closeted homo-
sexuals highlighted here.[6] Yet in *Paradise*, as we shall see, the citizens of the town of
Ruby strive to create a permanent utopian society to shelter them from the outside
world. In contrast, the characters in *Sirena Selena* embrace impermanence, imperfec-
tion, mobility, and disguise. Shunning the stability of home, they inhabit transitory
spaces: hotels, airplanes, and bars are common settings in this novel. Thus, while
Morrison highlights the longing for an enduring home, Santos-Febres does just the
opposite: she plunges the reader into a volatile world filled with gleaming surfaces that
act like fun house mirrors, reflecting a reality at once familiar and unrecognizable.

Her novel, as one critic has put it, is built upon the tropes of transvestism
and traversals (De Maeseneer 538); but although traversals appear in many guises,

transvestism, perhaps unsurprisingly, dominates early criticism of the novel, much of which focuses on how the text enacts and enables what Judith Butler has called the "critical promise of drag" (237).[7] While Butler's ideas are not irrelevant to my inquiries, I am more directly interested in how Santos-Febres uses the performative, parodic, and allegorical qualities of transvestism to comment on Caribbean identity, past and present. Put more simply, (how) can a teenaged transvestite bolero singer help us to re-imagine Caribbean identity? The theories of two Latin American critics, Nelly Richard and Jossianna Arroyo, speak directly to my concerns.

Richard, who focuses on a broadly Latin American, rather than specifically Caribbean, context, argues that, when confronted with artistic representations of transvestism, the difficulties the spectator faces go "beyond sexual titillation" and "have to do with the concealment of truth: with privileging the falsehood of appearance over the truth of essences, with letting oneself be mesmerized by the brilliance of the artificial" (*Masculine/Feminine* 51). This brilliance, in turn, exposes the precariousness of coherent notions of identity through a parodic pose that reveals such notions to be rooted in "strategies of appearance" rather than ontological truth (51). Within a Latin American context, Richard asserts, such parodies serve an additional function by enacting a "hyperallegorization of *identity as a mask*" that is generated by and speaks to the region's postcolonial condition:

> Viewed from the center, the peripheral copy is a diminished double, a devalorized imitation of an original that enjoys the added value of being a metropolitan reference. But viewed from itself, that copy is also a postcolonial satire of how First World fetishism projects onto the image of Latin America false representations of originality and authenticity (the primitivist nostalgia of the virgin continent), which Latin America again falsifies into a caricature of itself as Other to satisfy the other's demands. (*Masculine/Feminine* 46–7)

Richard's description of how the "peripheral copy" is interpreted differently from the center (what we might call the North) versus itself (or the South) is reminiscent of Benítez Rojo's assertion, in *The Repeating Island*, that the West's understanding of Caribbean literature is fundamentally limited. Although both assert that one's critical perspective changes depending on one's location, Benítez Rojo insists on the existence of "codes that the Caribbean people alone can decipher ... that refer us to traditional knowledge" (220). Richard eschews such a possibility of authentic knowledge and emphasizes an "artificial" performance that disrupts, rather than creates, meaning.

Writing about *Sirena Selena*, Arroyo similarly cites the ability of the transvestite performance to call into question concepts of transcendental being and cultural authenticity, and furthermore argues that Sirena and her mentor, Martha Divine, should be understood as enacting a postcolonial Latin American and Caribbean discourse that she calls "cultural transvestism" or "cultural drag." According to Arroyo, by making visible the performative nature of gender, race, and sexuality, cultural drag generates an "intermediate space" in which the body, rather than achieving wholeness, "remains in that place of negotiation and agency" ("Sirena canta boleros" 42). Emphasizing the generative as well as the symbolic capacity of this intermediate space, she affirms that the national cultures of Latin America and the Caribbean can be understood analogously: rather than inherent and authentic, they become, like the body caught up in a transvestite pose, "a constant 'becoming' (*hacerse*) of the performative gesture or gestures of a cultural imaginary in which elements that are 'difficult' to apprehend or assimilate are negotiated" ("Sirena canta boleros" 42).[8] In the pages of *Sirena Selena*, the interpretative difficulties posed by the transvestite and parsed by Richard are inseparable from the "'difficult' elements" to which Arroyo makes reference: cultural, racial, sexual, and gender differences that are constantly in play.

While providing a dynamic framework in which to negotiate the cultural imaginary of the nation, however, "cultural drag" also questions the limits of that imaginary and so encourages transnational crossings, supplying a model by which to read the ongoing historical effect of what Ortiz called transculturation, as well as the more contemporary consequences of current forms of economic and technological globalization. The transvestite performances in *Sirena Selena* are thus inseparable from its geographical traversals. For example, Santos-Febres' novel locates its characters in a multigenerational web of relations, and reveals how the geographical displacements of parents and grandparents have affected the sense of home and community experienced by newer generations. The migratory patterns of previous generations largely conform to conventional expectations: Sirena's grandmother, for instance, recalls her family's move from the countryside to the capital city. However, Santos-Febres complicates predictable patterns—country to city, Puerto Rico to New York, the Dominican Republic to Puerto Rico—by moving Martha Divine and Sirena in the opposite direction: from Puerto Rico to the Dominican Republic.[9]

The novel's present action begins on the plane ride that takes Martha and Sirena from San Juan to Santo Domingo and afterward takes place entirely within the Dominican Republic. Yet its flashbacks are centered primarily in Santurce, a district in San Juan known not only for its vibrant gay nightlife but also as a gathering place for recent Dominican arrivals (a fact alluded to in descriptions of the Dominican-owned diner where Serena and her companions often gather). By reversing the usual direction of migration—by having Puerto Ricans search for fame and fortune in the Dominican Republic, for example, instead of New York—Santos-Febres simultaneously highlights and complicates the social and economic forces that drive Caribbean migratory patterns. At the same time, however, she does not deny the lure of more established patterns of migration. Martha and Selena may arrive in Santo Domingo on a plane, but two Dominican boys, Leocadio and Migueles, plan to travel to San Juan in a *yola*; Martha may embrace new opportunities in the Dominican Republic, but Selena still dreams of conquering New York.[10]

The novel's crossings, however, go beyond the gendered and the geographical to emphasize the complexity of everyday interactions: its characters constantly cross paths or cross lines, double-cross each other, and find themselves at cross-purposes. Soon after she arrives in Santo Domingo, for example, it becomes apparent that Serena plans to leave her "mentor" to seek fame, fortune, and "luxury" on her own. To this end, she quickly abandons Martha after being approached by Hugo Graubel, a wealthy Dominican businessman who offers to pay her a considerable sum to perform in his lavish seaside villa. The narrative thus begins to splinter, dividing its attention between the shrewd game of seduction played by Hugo (a closeted homo-sexual with a predilection for teenaged boys) and Selena, on the one hand; and Martha's adventures in Santo Domingo, on the other. Into this mix, it adds yet an-other subplot: the tale of Leocadio, a young Dominican who, like Selena, is born into poverty but possessed of a beautiful and sexually ambiguous physical appearance. Although he has no intimate interactions with either Selena or Martha, Leocadio comes into brief contact with each: first, with Selena when they cross paths on the beach; then, in the novel's penultimate chapter, with Martha, when she spots him dancing with a friend on the abandoned dance floor of a gay bar. The fleetingness of these moments is typical of *Sirena Selena*, whose characters pass in and out of each others' lives with startling velocity.

Selena functions as an elusive focal point in this fluid network of identification, misidentification, and desire, although she does not comprise an absolute center. Rather, other characters recognize themselves in her ambiguous appearance. Leoca-dio, for example, when he spots her on the beach, realizes she is "a boy who looked like a girl. Just like him" (41). In an analogous moment, Hugo Graubel understands that she is not only the "woman of his dreams" but also a version of his adolescent self, "that feeble white boy who looked like a girl" (103). Hugos' wife, Solange, more reluctantly sees herself in the competitor she thinks of as an *engendro*—a fetus, malformed person, or misfit. Specifically, she fears that Sirena's powerful voice will destroy her own carefully constructed performance of ladylike decency and so "turn her into the [*engendro*] she was before; into the milky child held captive for the high-est bidder, transformed into a lady only in her dreams, returned to earth again like an ordinary victim" (135). Like the mythical siren, Selena and Solange are hybrid crea-tures, and Solange is all too aware that the "meaning" of their inhuman qualities can change in an instant: in one moment they are ethereal seductresses, in the next they are half-formed freaks. It is fitting that Solange's name contains the word "sol," or sun, while Selena shares hers with the goddess of the moon: just as the sun generates its own light while the moon reflects that of other astral bodies, so Solange's gender identity would seem to be innate, as her wide hips and multiple pregnancies confirm. Yet the novel resists such a neat division, and insists that neither possesses an immanent identity. Rather, each must make and remake herself through a series of strategic performances.

These performances are literalized when Sirena sings her boleros. Although they are interpreted by her transfixed public as magical and transcendent, for the per-former music functions first and foremost as a "weapon" that allows her to "mark her space" (Cuadra 158). The boleros are sung from a necessary pose of reticence and self-defensive resistance because they are inherently linked to two traumatic events in the protagonist's life: the death of her grandmother and her brutal rape by a cus-tomer. The long forgotten lyrics of the boleros return to her on the first night that she returns to the streets after the attack: "'Distancia,' 'Miseria,' 'Dime capitán,' then, suddenly, 'Bajo un palmar,' 'Silencio,' 'Teatro,' and it wasn't that he liked any of those songs, he simply heard them sung in his head by his [grandmother]" (69). Like Piedade's song in *Paradise*, the boleros link Sirena to a lost maternal inheritance that serves as a protective shield. After she meets Martha Divine, they also come to sig-nify the potential for economic stability and freedom from prostitution. Throughout the novel, the tension between these practical functions and the bolero's transcendent power remains unresolved. On the one hand, like the rhythmic movement described by Benítez Rojo, Sirena's boleros are capable of expressing profound truths that cannot be put into words. On the other hand, they are strategic: songs Selena doesn't even like, but performs to get what he wants.

The profound effect of Sirena's songs on those who hear them suggests a third function—one that, like the transvestite performance, is allegorical (although not parodic) and arises from the particular place that the bolero occupies in popular culture. Invented in Cuba in the late nineteenth century, the bolero is an urban romantic ballad that quickly gained popularity throughout Latin America.[11] Its discourse of love shares with the *modernista* poets of the same era an "abstract yet sensual and refined imagery and lexicon" and an "ethereal, idealizing and mythifying textualization of Woman as divine seductress" (Aparicio, *Listening to Salsa* 126). As such, it affirms a patriarchal, heterosexual model of romantic love. Yet, because it is a libidinal genre, its conservatism can be subverted, especially when it is performed.[12] In answer to the question, "what is the bolero?," Iris Zavala responds, it is "a lyric of pleasure" that "eludes all secure relationships, in truth, all domineering discourses (family, marriage); it evades the discourse of any power that is not seduction, with the promise of forever" (125). The vertiginous affect of the bolero's desire is compounded by the gender-bending potential of its performance: because the meaning of a song changes according to the gender of its singer, as well as that of its listener, it foments a game of desire based on the ambiguity generated by the recipient of the song, who acts as "a familiar *you* [*tú*] ... that can always metamorphosize into *she* [*ella*] or *he* [*él*]" (Zavala 126). In the novel, this effect is, of course, compounded by the indefinite gender of the singer, but it is also complicated by the collective nature of the response to Selena's songs. It is not just borders between genders that blur, but between individuals. When she sings at Hugo's house, for example, the audience members are described as *testigos*, or witnesses, and their response is described in almost entirely plural terms: "The witnesses remember hearing the tossing sea behind the notes of the piano" (164) ["Los testigos recuerdan haber oído al mar enredado en aquel piano de visión" (205)]. Mixing the language of erotic desire with images like that of the sea intertwined with the piano, the novel underscores its island setting and suggests a deep link between private and communal desire. The bolero's trans-American history, its open and circular form, its ability to blur the borders of identity, and its evocation of an as-yet unconsummated yearning: all of these factors allow it to function as a vital trope of crossing in the novel. Because it "traverses social classes, generations, genders, and race boundaries," Aparicio calls the bolero "metaphorically speaking, the body of Latin America" (*Listening to Salsa* 127). Likewise, when she performs the bolero, Sirena becomes the allusive, elusive body of the Caribbean, an incarnation of its past and present, of its individual and collective desires.

The Cross and the Crossroads in *Paradise*

While Santos-Febres' protagonist embodies a transvestite Caribbean, Morrison affirms that she too uses fiction to give flesh to a new kind of nation. Since the beginning of her literary career, she has endeavored "to move away from the unstated but overwhelming and dominant context that was white history and to move into another one" (Denard 5). Published in 1998, *Paradise* is the third and final install-ment of Morrison's celebrated trilogy of novels that places African-American experi-ences at the center of a radical re-visioning of U.S. national mythology. Like *Beloved* (1987) and *Jazz* (1992) before it, *Paradise* is inspired by historical fact: namely, the Exoduster Movement of the late nineteenth century, during which more than 20,000 African Americans departed Louisiana and Mississippi to settle in more westerly states.[13] As a result of these migrations, more than sixty all-black towns were estab-lished, primarily in Kansas but also in Colorado, Nebraska, and Oklahoma. Nomi-nally basing her narrative on this history, Morrison tells about the founding of two such towns: Haven, in 1890, and its direct successor, Ruby, in 1950. Like the histori-cal Exodusters, the seventy-nine individuals who build Haven arrive in Oklahoma in the post-Reconstruction era, after a long journey out of the U.S. South, where their ancestors had lived since before the Revolutionary War, first as slaves and then as freed men and women. When the third generation of Haven men returns from World War II, they detect signs of economic, physical, and spiritual deterioration creeping into their town, and so retreat "deeper into Oklahoma, as far as they could climb from the grovel contaminating the town their grandfathers had made" (16). In this way, Ruby is born. A chain of migrations thus generates the novel's plot: from Africa to the New World, from the U.S. South to the U.S. West, from Oklahoma to deeper into Oklahoma. As is the case in *Stairway for Electra, Corregidora*, and *Sirena Selena*, geographical movement therefore comprises a first important category of crossing in *Paradise*.

However, echoing the first forced passage from Africa, the subsequent geograph-ical crossings of this multigenerational group do not bring liberation but rather a se-ries of refusals, one of which comes, in the towns' collective memory, to eclipse and encapsulate all the others. As they journey west, the founders of Haven are refused entrance by the light-skinned residents of the all-black town of Fairly, Oklahoma be-cause of their dark complexions. This moment is commemorated as the "Disallow-ing," a foundational trauma that reshapes their understanding of their community: "for ten generations they had believed the division they fought to close was free against slave and rich against poor. Usually, but not always, white against black. Now they saw a new separation: light-skinned against black. ... The sign of racial purity they had taken for granted had become a stain" (194). Here, migratory movement becomes entangled with the racial and racist ideologies that emerge from the fact of racial mix-ing, and both of these tropes of crossing congeal into signs of oppression which are then reversed, rather than rejected, by the citizens of Haven and Ruby: the "stain" of their "racial purity" is reconfigured into an inviolable sign of their special status, and they become fiercely protective of their "eight-rock" blood: "a deep deep level in the coal mines. Blue-black people, tall and graceful, whose clear, wide eyes gave no sign of what they really felt about those who weren't 8-rock like them" (193). Reacting to the virulent racism, not only of whites but also, more devastatingly, of lighter-skinned blacks, they embrace an inverted ideology of racial purity that allows them to fashion a community of people whose physical appearance acts as a visible reminder of their suffering as well as a symbol of the prophesied triumph of their lineage.

After the founding of Ruby, the story of the Disallowing is preserved and passed on by the Morgan twins, Deacon and Steward, descendants of the "Old Fathers" of Haven. Self-styled "New Fathers" of Ruby, the twins not only control most of the town's economy but are also possessed of "powerful memories" that endow them with the ability to "remember the details of everything that ever happened—things they witnessed and things they have not" (13). The novel's critical attitude toward the veracity of the twin's memories, implied in the ironic assertion that they remember events they have not witnessed, allows it to interrogate how alternative histories, like physical and racial crossings, can continue to function within the binary logic of the plantation. As Marni Gauthier asserts, "by illustrating the subjectivity, distortions, and abuses of power to which oral history is vulnerable, Morrison applies to oral history the precise critical examination to which written history has been particularly subject in recent decades" (398). In this way, *Paradise* differs from *Corregidora*. It is true that Jones shows how the stories repeated by Ursa's foremothers become implicated in an unproductive repetition of the traumatic past. Nevertheless, she presents orality—I am thinking especially of the blues—as a necessary corrective to the official written record of the past. In *Paradise*, in contrast, oral history as configured through the Morgans' "powerful memories" becomes another kind of official history.[14]

The novel's examination of the processes by which living history fossilizes into rigid doctrine, is further complicated by its chronology: it opens and closes in July of 1976, at the peak of U.S. bicentennial celebrations, an ironic commentary on Morrison's intention to move away from the (white) heroic narratives of U.S. history. Here and elsewhere, the author's self-conscious exploration of dominant mythologies of U.S. nationhood, such as the Puritan jeremiad and the Western myth of the frontier, signals both the impossibility of completely escaping hegemonic narratives and the fundamental inextricability of black and white experience in the United States.[15] Yet, Morrison has emphasized that *Paradise* is not a novel about white U.S. America. Rather, it is "about conflicts within the race": "it's a very interior terrain. What that one town becomes after very revolutionary and hardworking activity to build it with no help. They're very separatist people" (Denard 12). These words reveal important tensions that underlie the novel's attitude toward the "separatist people" of Haven and Ruby: on the one hand, Morrison extols the "revolutionary" nature of their project; on the other, she intimates that its eventual corruption is linked to its separatism—and, we might add, its subsequent refusal to engage in any kind of crossing at all. The novel's focus on the experiences of U.S. African Americans, in general, and the separatism of Haven and Ruby in particular, along with its setting in the late 1960s and early 1970s, suggests that, like *Corregidora*, it engages the rhetoric of Black Nationalism. Unlike Jones's novel, however, Morrison's reflects on the successes as well as the failures of this movement.

In particular, she underscores what Lubiano has called Black Nationalism's "commonsensical" value, which lies in its ability to articulate what racism has silenced. Not only does it help fashion political, critical, and aesthetic narratives, it also generates "a utopian narrative—a rallying cry, an expression of desire" (233). Black Nationalism thus facilitates a language, not only of resistance and critique, but also of imagination and aspiration. In this sense, the "very revolutionary and

hardworking activity" that builds Haven and Ruby is rooted in a yearning for freedom that encompasses all dimensions of human existence. This yearning is expressed,
with seductive beauty, in the first pages of the novel: "From the beginning its people
were free and protected. A sleepless woman could always rise from her bed, wrap a
shawl around her shoulders and sit on the steps in the moonlight. And if she felt like
it she could walk out in the yard and on down the road. No lamp and no fear" (8).
Linking Haven and Ruby to a history that extends back to 1755 and the plantations
of Louisiana, *Paradise* reveals a people's struggle to live fearlessly and freely in
community. Moreover, it explores the importance of black identity to that community and acknowledges, as Lubiano asserts, that "despite our necessary awareness
that race is not a given but an explanation fought over across a specific history, black
identity is also a sign for remembering our specificity and aestheticizing our resistance to racist trauma" (237–38). Yet *Paradise* also shows how Ruby, founded on
revolutionary zeal, hardens over time into an exclusionary realm. Thus, even as it
honors the constructive possibilities of Black Nationalism, it critiques its authoritarian tendencies.

In particular, like *Corregidora*, it exposes the ways in which Black Nationalism
reinforces patriarchal values and so begins to resemble that which it opposes. As
Lubiano asserts, a "black nationalist revision of a patriarchal family romance" is the
means by which "black nationalism most thoroughly coalesces into a conventional
master narrative" (240). Indeed, the description of Ruby quoted above, seductive
though it may be, is so strongly gendered as to elicit suspicion: it immediately substitutes a woman for the "people," and suggests, moreover, that a free woman is,
simply put, a protected one. In doing so, it betrays what one critic calls "a patriarch's
view of women's freedom" (Patell 183).

It is important to note, however, that although the novel implicitly critiques
Black Nationalism, the residents of Ruby do not identify with the organized Black
Nationalist or Black Power movement. To the contrary, the town leaders are deeply
suspicious of it and of the Civil Rights movement in general. Although they occupy
the ideological position of an authoritarian Black Nationalist rhetoric, their separatist
beliefs are equally rooted in a Christian theology that some critics have described as
"Old Testament"—that is, a theology that privileges the "old covenant" of the law
rather than the "new covenant" initiated by Christ's self-sacrifice on the cross.[16] The
novel explores Ruby's religious *and* revolutionary zeal and draws attention to the
diversity of faith that persists in this small community. It probes the legacy of Protes-
tantism for U.S. African Americans by recounting theological debates between
Ruby's three churches, and also refers to other religious influences: the Convent,
for example, was previously used as a Catholic boarding school for Arapaho girls, a
history that recalls the Catholic church's role in colonizing the Americas; and
Consolata as well as Lone Dupres, Ruby's midwife, engage in the practice of
African-based folk religions.

Emphasizing the wide range of belief systems that thrive even within the
"very interior terrain" of *Paradise*, Morrison expands her inquiries beyond both the
"Old Testament" and "New Testament" versions of African-American Christianity
and ultimately advocates a New World spirituality that embraces the grace epitomized in Christian iconography by the cross, but that also, as Linda Krumholz notes,

understands the same cross "as a symbol of doubleness, of human and divine love, of multiplicity and movement rather than purity and singularity" (26). In the symbolic matrix of the novel, then, the cross becomes (con)fused with the crossroads, a place linked to choice and possibility and, not coincidentally, one that features prominently in West African and African diaspora belief systems. The poet Yusef Komunyakaa has written, "the crossroads is a real place between imaginary places—points of departure and arrival. It is also a place where negotiations and deals are made with higher powers. In the West African and Haitian traditions of Legba, it is a sanctified place of reflection. ... The crossroads is a junction between the individual and the world" (n.p.). In *Paradise*, this charged place is located, not at the "Cross" streets of Ruby—residential lanes that bear the prefix "Cross" to differentiate them from older streets—but rather in the Convent, which, although not a road at all, becomes a route toward change or transformation.

Perhaps because of their association with this symbolic crossroads, the five women who live in the Convent are accused of being "sluts" and "heifers" "who chose themselves for company, which is to say not a convent but a coven" (276). They are a "new and obscene breed of female" characterized by "streetwalkers' clothes and whores' appetites" (279). As women who move freely, they are—like Ursa in *Corregidora* and Swain in *Stairway for Electra*—understood to be literal and figurative streetwalkers who refuse to be protected and sheltered, and therefore pose an immediate threat. *Paradise* begins at its end, at the moment when the men of Ruby decide to do away with this threat by carrying out a surprise attack against the un-armed women. Yet, as the narrative pulls back to recount the entangled histories of victims as well as aggressors, it reveals, little by little, how dangerous these women really are: through them, the novel's tropes of crossing—among them, migration, racial hybridity, and a diasporic spiritual syncretism represented by the cross and the crossroads—are activated in ways that directly oppose the binary logic upon which the community of Ruby has been built.

For example, the novel's notorious first sentence, "They shoot the white girl first," immediately elicits a question—which girl is white?—that it refuses to answer (3). Mavis, Gigi, Seneca, and Pallas are the four young women who arrive, one by one, at the Convent. But although we come to know many intimate details about their traumatic lives, we are never told their racial identities. Morrison's withholding of this information generates what she has called a "race-specific, race-free language," which not only acts as a corrective to the rhetoric of eight-rock purity, but confronts the reader's entrenched notions of black and white ("Home" 9). As she remarks in an interview published in *Time* magazine, "I wanted the readers to wonder about the race of those girls until those readers understood that their race didn't matter" (Gray n.p.). Unlike the other U.S.-based writers analyzed in this book, but like many of the Spanish-American ones, Morrison creates language that directly confronts the black-white dichotomy. By employing racial ambiguity to call attention to how we rely on racial markers to categorize, judge, and even empathize with those around us, Mor-rison utilizes a strategy that recalls Arroyo's notion of "cultural drag": she exposes the performative nature of race and so opens up an intermediate space in which the body—a body simultaneously racialized and raceless—"remains in that place of negotiation and agency" ("Sirena canta boleros" 42). However, if in *Sirena Selena* the protagonist's performances activate this strategy, in *Paradise* it is the reader who performs race when he or she struggles to identify the white girl by scouring the text for clues, dressing each character up in white, black, or, perhaps, white-and-black skin. Faced with the absence of the supposedly clear marker of race, "whiteness loses its potency, its power of judgment, but the nomadic circulation of whiteness and blackness among the women prevents blackness from replacing whiteness as gaze and judgment" (Krumholz 28).

Krumholz's phrase, "nomadic circulation," captures, not only Morrison's deliberate unmooring of the black-white binary, but also the way in which the women of the Convent conceive of space and movement, as well as community and home.[17] The townspeople of Haven understand migration as an endless search for unsullied territory on which to build their fragile Eden. In *Faulkner, Mississippi*, Glissant identifies this kind of movement as "territorial conquest," to which he opposes "wandering." The former "is systematic ... like an arrow, a forward projection," the latter "a confused setting down of roots" (117). Elsewhere, Glissant elaborates a particular kind of wandering he calls errantry:

> The thought of errantry is not apolitical nor is it inconsistent with the will to identity, which is, after all, nothing other than the search for a freedom within particular surroundings. If it is at variance with territorial intolerance, or the predatory effects of the unique root ... , this is because, in the poetics of Relation, one who is errant (who is no longer traveler, discoverer, or conqueror) strives to know the totality of the world yet already knows he will never accomplish this—and knows that is precisely where the threatened beauty of the world resides. (*Poetics of Relation* 20)

Neither a relentless forward projection nor an aimless journey, errantry is a deliberate refusing of vertical rootedness. Its horizontal linkages long to be all embracing but recognize this as impossible. Although errantry favors movement, it also privileges Relation, and so becomes a means through which to configure different notions of community and home. As we shall see, the women of the Convent must learn to be errant, and their initial arrival to the symbolic crossroads of the Convent is but the first step in the process. For it is in the Convent, whose imposing architecture and exploitative history would make it seem more a symbolic Big House than "a sanctified place of reflection," that the cross and the crossroads meet to remake the revolutionary zeal and sacred love on which Haven was originally founded (Komunyakaa n.p.).

Redressing the Big House: Transvestite Mansions and Plantation Hotels in *Sirena Selena*

In an essay entitled "Caribe y travestismo," or "The Caribbean and Transvestism," Santos-Febres describes a different kind of symbolic Big House, an ornately decorated mansion inhabited by her bolero-singing protagonist. She claims that it was precisely the image of this house, paired with the contrasting vision of "a young boy, high out of his mind, singing boleros and picking up cans," which inspired *Sirena Selena*:

> In the beginning it was Sirena, a siren, gliding down the stairs of a Caribbean mansion. The mansion was transvestite. Its patio furniture of Philippine rattan, its floors of marble, the air conditioning exhaling a fresh breeze like those of other latitudes, its calla lilies twice reflected in the mirror built into the wall: all these bore witness to the sorcery. Sirena was another decorative element. Her face made up to perfection, her curls, the evening gown with embroidered arabesques: everything was made of fantasy. (*Sobre piel* 128)

Mixing the biblical language of origins ("In the beginning") with references to sorcery and fantasy, Santos-Febres identifies this "transvestite mansion" as the genesis of her own work of fiction. Its rich adornments act as visual confirmation of a history of exploitation: the Philippine wicker suggests Spain's expansive colonial days while the air conditioning bespeaks a more recent connection to the "latitudes" of the North. In its center, however, she places Sirena, at first glance another exotic gilding, but one possessing a siren song that calls forth the tragic history that the rest of the decor can only simulate: "Sirena's voice was the only true thing. With that voice she would bewitch the audience, she would transport it toward the regions of the unnamed, toward the place where sorrows originate, which springs forth from the first violence. The foundational violence, the first lash of desire" (*Sobre piel* 128). The truth-value of Sirena's boleros thus lies in their ability to "bewitch" their *testigos*, or witnesses, returning them to a "foundational violence" or original trauma that, although it can be sung, remains impossible to put into words. Santos-Febres links this trauma to a longing that is both libidinal and historical: the phrase "lash of desire" (*latigazo del deseo*) suggests the existential ache of love lost as well as the scarred backs of slaves.

But what of the mansion in which Sirena performs? Like the mysterious protagonist and the Caribbean itself, it is identified as "transvestite," but it does not bear the scars of a traumatic past. Rather, it displays the triumphant signs of the profits gained from the violent legacy of slavery. Like the manor houses in *Garden* and *Delta Wedding*, it is made from and filled with foreign materials, expensive collectibles, and a variety of international objects that, as Ileana Rodríguez affirms, "connote epoch and history" (102). Yet it is not a "Big House" *per se*, but rather a cross-dressed or redressed version of the Big House, which functions as a "hyperallegorization" of the plantation past toward which it gestures.

As we saw briefly in the introduction to this book, in the Puerto Rican context the "Big House" is known as the *casa solariega*, or patrician house, and it stood for many decades at the center of a discourse that strove to create a national family, unified and homogenized through its submission to a patriarchal order that valorized the Spanish inheritance to the exclusion of all others. Although the *casa solariega* does not need to be located on the plantation, it was built by and for Puerto Rico's landowning elite, as Juan Gelpí reminds us (22). In his influential 1934 essay, *Insularismo*, Antonio Pedreira, perhaps the most famous advocate of the *casa solariega*, laments that "the old *casas solariegas*, with the spaciousness of a warehouse, have given way to the hermetic apartment," and urges his country's leaders to return to the former model of dwelling: "We do not fit in our own house and this discomfort intervenes painfully in the measure of euphoria to which every people has a right" (82).

Pedreira's essay was published four years after *I'll Take My Stand* and features similar rhetoric and imagery to that of the Twelve Southerners, one of whom, for example, waxes nostalgic about "the beauty and stability of an ordered life" expressed by the architectural features of "old country homes, with their pillared porches, their simplicity of design, their sheltering groves, their walks bordered with boxwood shrubs" (Donald Davidson 55). Both works draw from the repertoire of the modern plantation imaginary to envision the Big House as an ample and sheltering space in which a national family may thrive.

If for Pedreira a return to the *casa solariega* symbolized a future of amplitude and euphoria, however, for recent generations of Puerto Rican intellectuals the reverse has been true. As Arnaldo Cruz-Malavé writes, by the 1970s "it seemed incredible that Puerto Ricans had for so long lived within the paradoxical confines of the *casa solariega* ... of our colonial modernity" (139). In reaction, writers who came of age during this period began dismantling the Big House. Their textual assault on the myth of the unified national family is undertaken, in part, through a critical reconfiguration and recuperation of what, in *Insularismo*, Pedreira identifies as the principle source of Puerto Rico's "inferiority complex": namely, the fact that it is mired in a prolonged state of adolescence. As Cruz-Malavé explains, Pedreira understood this state to be one of "effeminacy and impotence, or what he also terms the Island's 'medio patológico,' both its pathological and *pato*logical milieu of depressed and unproductive men" (150). Cruz Malavé defines "*pato*logy"—a play on the word *pato*, a derogatory term for homosexual—as a pathology brought about by Puerto Rico's colonial condition, which traps the nation, not only between immaturity and maturity, but between Puerto Rican and North American cultural identities (148). It is precisely this *pato*logy, this ambivalence and in-betweenness, that Puerto Rican writers began to embrace, rather than lament, in the 1970s by choosing "to speak not from the space of a stable, 'virile,' and 'mature' identity but from that '*patological* milieu' of castration and gender-crossing, superfluity and equivocalness that ... Pedreira ... display[s] and condemn[s]." Like other writers we have seen in this study, these authors suggest the strategic value of an identity shaped by excess (androgyny, ornate performance, promiscuity) as well as lack (withdrawal, refusal, sterility). More specifically, rather than censuring effeminacy and impotence, they envision an "ambivalent *pato* [who] opts instead for his *locura* [madness] and blossoms into a self-conscious drag queen" (151).

By imagining Sirena Selena—a "self-conscious drag queen" if ever there was one—as "another decorative element" in Hugo's mansion, Santos-Febres does not simply bring the effeminate adolescent into the *casa solariega*, but also identifies him as a part of it and it of him. The Big House is thus redressed as a gaudy parody of a parody, in which, as Nelly Richard reminds us, Latin America poses as the "authentic" and "virginal" paradise of First World fantasies, reaffirming and undermining its exotic image with the same transvestite gesture (*Masculine/Feminine* 46–47). Even as she exploits its parodic potential, however, Santos-Febres attempts to move beyond the destructive cruelty of parody, on the one hand, and the emotional ambivalence of nostalgia, on the other.[18] Arguing that these two discourses have dominated Caribbean poetics for too long, she posits a third way, which she terms *guachafita monga*. In an interview given after the publication of *Sirena Selena*, she describes *guachafita monga* as a "discourse of laughter and pleasure" that "presents a larger space in which to see, analyze, visit, and explore a reading of the Caribbean, without mocking and without melancholy. That reading recuperates, to a small extent, the pleasure of discovering our own Caribbean, which is a Caribbean that always escapes us" (Peña-Jordán 119). Imagining "a larger space," ample but disconnected from the traditional *casa solariega*, in which to (re)discover the Caribbean with a sense of joy, *guachafita monga* resembles Serena's performances of the bolero in its evocation of origins. But, just as it sidesteps the derision of parody, it avoids the painful nostalgia of the bolero and, instead, approaches the past through humor. Israel Reyes suggests that this humor "is not incompatible with other, more aggressive species of the comic. ... Yet humor goes beyond ridicule, exaggeration, mimicry, negation, or nonsense and seeks an affirmation from those who laugh at life's cruelties" (2). Referring to the particular shapes that humor acquires in Puerto Rican literature, Reyes explains that *guachafita*, defined as levity or lack of seriousness, "deflates the seriousness of everything and everyone as a self-defense mechanism, since the most fervent practitioners of *guachafita* ... represent the most exploited and marginal members of society" (54).[19] Santos-Febres' addition, to *guachafita*, of the modifier *monga*, which means weak but also connotes softness or flaccidity, underscores not only the gentler nature of the humor she deploys, but also her intention to deflate phallocentric logic and redefine pleasure and desire.[20]

While mapping out freer patterns of circulation between bodies and islands, however, Santos-Febres continues to interrogate the fixed space of the plantation. As we have seen, she does this first and foremost through her presentation of the transvestite mansion. However, it is important to recognize that, even as she self-consciously challenges the Puerto Rican *casa solariega*, she also pointedly engages Dominican history and discourse. The novel's Big House is not a *casa solariega* in Puerto Rico, after all, but rather Hugo Graubel's beachfront estate in the wealthy Dominican enclave of Juan Dolio.[21] The scene of Selena's arrival to this glamorous residence opens from the perspective of the host, who attempts to discern the "true" identity of the young person whose goal, he knows, is "to seduce away his entire fortune if possible, everything he had accumulated through blood and [lashes]" (83). From the beginning, the great estate is configured as a place of desire, as the stage on which Serena—but also Hugo (and also Solange)—will perform her carefully choreographed seduction.

Yet, the reference to blood and lashes ("sangre y latigazos") hints at *another* story, whose presence is confirmed when the narrative shifts briefly to Serena's point of view, only to interrupt itself in order to tell, obliquely, the history of the Dominican Republic:

> The meeting in the magnate's house helped her to visualize her performance. Glamour always made Sirena feel good. She hadn't known that there were millionaires like this in the Dominican Republic. On the news they only talked about Dominicans fleeing in boats—encrusted with salt, or gnawed at by sharks and floating belly up in the Mona Passage. She didn't know about the acres and acres of sugarcane that had paid for her host's [humble] estate. She didn't know about the Haitians toiling over pots [*los haitianos tirados a las calderas*] to ensure that the sugarcane syrup achieved

the perfect consistency; she didn't know about the peasant leaders [shredded in sug-arcane fields] in San Pedro de Macorís, fertilizing the red earth stolen from the sea, nor about the succulent *cocolos* always served as a snack to hungry children in the Graubel household. (84)

Paid for with the fortune of Hugo's sugar magnate father, the mansion tells a history of the Dominican Republic that, with its circuitous presentation and its images of cannibalism, uncannily resembles that of *Stairway for Electra*. At the same time that it acknowledges the specificity of this past, however, the passage emphasizes how, by viewing it only as a site of glamour, seduction, and performance, Sirena effectively dehistorizes the space of the mansion. On the one hand, her lack of aware-ness functions as a trenchant reminder of Puerto Rico's willful ignorance about its neighbor's past. On the other hand, by making it the stage of Sirena's performance, the novel unmoors the Big House from its always-tragic foundation and allows it to take on the freer movement of the open word. Through its contact with the libidinous desire of the transvestite Caribbean, it begins to be transformed.

Hugo's house, however, is not the only space linked to the plantation legacy that comes under scrutiny. To the contrary, *Sirena Selena* continuously draws attention to such non-domestic places as airplanes, bars, and hotels. Hugo and Selena's game of seduction, for example, is consummated in a Juan Dolio hotel, and two Santo Domingo hotels, the Conquistador and the Colón, are featured prominently. The first of these, which provides luxury accommodations to a mostly European clientele, may have been built with international capital rather than the "blood and lashes" of Dominican sugar fortunes (although Hugo is a primary investor), but like Hugo's mansion it is decorated with mahogany furniture, marble columns, and expensive works of art. The second is a kitschier, humbler space that serves gay tourists from around the world. While it attracts a different clientele, however, it is no coincidence that, like its more "legitimate" counterpart, its name commemorates the European conquerors of the Caribbean. Its guests may be homosexual, but they are still mon-eyed "northerners" in search of cheap thrills. The prominence given to both the Conquistador and the Colón, and the subtle parallels drawn between them and Hugo's transvestite mansion, suggests another way in which the plantation might be said to creep into the novel's pages: namely, in the form of what Ian Strachan has called the "plantation hotel," which should not be conflated with the historical institution but rather understood as an iteration of Benítez Rojo's plantation machine.

Surveying the contemporary Caribbean, Strachan asserts: "Benítez Rojo imag-ines the plantation as a repeating machine ... but he does not discuss the Caribbean travel industry as an extension of this reality. Is it part of the plantation's time-tested process of wealth extraction?" (7). Answering with a qualified but firm yes, Strachan asserts that, like the plantation, tourism is an "export industry" in which a "Caribbean 'product' is marketed and sold to consumers in the North Atlantic;" it monopolizes and exploits the land while exacerbating Caribbean dependence on metropolitan centers; and it tends to reinforce racial and class hierarchies established during the colonial period (7–10). At the same time, he reminds us of the many factors that can complicate this neat formula: not only do the men and women demeaned by the conditions of the tourist industry practice subtle strategies of resistance, but the interactions between tourists and their hosts are complicated as more non-white travelers are able to choose the Caribbean as their destination.

Sirena Selena teases out these complications by offering a sustained critique of the role of tourism in the lives of its characters. Through the always self-aware Martha Divine, for example, we see the Dominican Republic from the perspective of a Caribbean citizen masquerading as a First World tourist.[22] Dressed as a "rich *señora*," Martha revels in the performative power of her drag queen's disguise and the (relative) economic power afforded to her by her status as a Puerto Rican. As a result, she interprets Santo Domingo through the superior pose of a first-world traveler: "All dressed up like a rich *señora* out for a walk in the capital of this dirty island, which is well below her level of taste, a little below the level of her own island" (89). It is not until she discovers the city's gay underworld that her view is modified. On the one hand, she is prompted to ask herself why she had imagined that "this island would be different from her own" (180). On the other hand, she realizes that in the Dominican Republic "things for *locas* [homosexuals] weren't as advanced ... as in Puerto Rico" (182). In *Corregidora*, Jones uses Ursa's epiphanic moment to argue that the past can be understood as a series of moments or choices. Similarly, Martha's shifting understanding of her position in the Dominican Republic suggests that the *present* relationship between the isles of the Caribbean should be understood as range of possibilities. Mockery, empathy, exploitation, opportunity, mutual interdependence: all of these options are put into play as Martha schemes to make her fortune and, at the same time, longs for greater justice and equality in both her native Puerto Rico and her temporary home.

Sirena Selena does not propose, through Martha's character, a definitive delineation of intra-Caribbean relations, nor does it praise or condemn tourism absolutely. Rather, it presents the tourist industry as an inexorable force of globalization that shapes the lives of the protagonists; which is to say, it is a machine that, like Benítez Rojo's, cannot be conquered. The novel also suggests, however, that this same force can be manipulated for the benefit of those who live within its realm of influence.[23] This potential is particularly apparent in the story of the Dominican protagonist, the preadolescent Leocadio, who obtains a low-level job at the Hotel Colón. If Martha becomes a proxy for the tourist, Leocadio represents the labor force that makes the tourism machine run, and his work undoubtedly provides him with immediate financial opportunities and the promise of more to come: his older friend, Migueles, offers intimate services on an unofficial basis to some of the guests at the Colón, and receives gold jewelry and generous tips in return.[24] Migueles' forays into sex tourism dramatize the tension between the exploitation and opportunities generated by tourism, a tension also inscribed in the hotel's architecture, which Leocadio explores, beginning with the roof, from which "he could see the city, breathing, alive, and complete, and then he would descend into its intestines, the service areas of the Hotel Colón, full of detergent and white sheets" (178). The expansive view from the roof draws attention to the ways in which his connection with the tourist industry endows Leocadio with a larger vision of the world and a new sense of power. At the same time, the description of the hotel's "intestines" serves as a reminder of the industry's exploitative nature—its dirty laundry, so to speak.

It is, however, the hotel's bar, which he has been prohibited from entering, that acquires the greatest symbolic meaning in Leocadio's story, for it is there that he dances with Migueles and reflects upon what it means to be a man, *un hombre*, or a woman, *una mujer*. According to the more experienced Migueles: "*El hombre* is the one who leads, the one who decides. The other one is *la mujer*, the woman" (203). Leocadio's interior response to this definition is presented in a self-contained chapter toward the novel's end:

> There are many ways to rule, many [ways] to be *un hombre* or to be *una mujer*, for each person can decide for himself. Sometimes you can even be both. Without having to choose one or the other. Money, a big car, the *billetes* to go far away, to go into the best bars, the ones with the most lights. That's what the man has. And if he dances and the other one leads, then he's *la mujer*. And if she decides where to go, then she's *el hombre*, but if he stays there in the arms of Migueles, who is leading, he's *una mujer*. (208)

> Hay muchas maneras de mandar, muchas formas de ser hombre o ser mujer, una decide. A veces se puede ser ambas sin tener que dejar de ser lo uno ni lo otro. Dinero, el carrazo, los chavos para irse lejos, para entrar en las barras más bonitas, más llenas de luces. Eso le toca al hombre. Y si se baila y otro dirige, entonces es la mujer. Y si ella decide adónde va, entonces es el hombre, pero si se queda entre los brazos de Migueles, que dirige, es una mujer. (258)

Here, Leocadio articulates the transvestite strategies of the novel in what Debra Castillo calls a utopian "dream of love" (22). He does not imagine a world in which disguises are imposed or taken on as a means for survival, nor does he express the anxiety articulated by Martha, who longs to complete her sex-change operation so as "to rest in a single body" (11). Rather he envisions an entirely flexible identity in which "una decide," one decides who one is in every moment, not in isolation but in communion with others, in a dance of love and mutual respect. The elastic nature of the gendered self he imagines is reinforced by the mutability of the passage's language, particularly in the original Spanish, which switches easily from feminine forms (ending in "a," like *una* or *ambas*) to masculine ones (ending in "o," such as *uno* or *otro*).

Both of the novel's young, ambiguously gendered protagonists thus conceive of themselves and their relationships to others in terms of fluidity and movement; but whereas Leocadio speaks in idealized terms, Selena responds to a simpler edict: "a ti no te clava nadie más," which translates, very roughly, as "don't let anyone nail you again" (89). After she is raped and left for dead, Selena promises Valentina Frenesí, who rescues her from the street after her grandmother's death, that she will never again allow herself to be *clavado*—that is to say, penetrated or fucked by a customer, but also nailed or pinned down, and so immobilized.[25] The chapter immediately preceding Leocadio's utopian dance with Migueles depicts Selena's final meeting with Hugo. In the consummation of their long dance of desire, Selena keeps her promise to Valentina and, reversing conventional power dynamics, penetrates Hugo. Just before entering him, however, she reflects upon the temptation of opening herself, physically and emotionally, to him: "She would like to say so many things to those arms. ... But to speak she would have to let go of who she really is, who it took her so much work to become" (206) ["Quisiera decirle a esos brazos tantas cosas ... Pero para hablar tendría que deshacerse de quien es ella en realidad, de quien tanto trabajo le ha costado ser" (256).] Leocadio imagines a fluid and changing identity that is not incompatible with intimacy and community. Sirena's lived reality, in contrast, plays out very differently: whispering her story to a lover, spilling her guts to a confidante, or becoming rooted to one place, amounts to a betrayal of her disguise, which has become her truer identity. Thus she remains faithful to her oath and, after penetrating Hugo, steals his wallet and watch and flees. Although critics have emphasized the sexual connotations of *clavar*, both the word's meanings are important.[26] Selena is not penetrated, nor does she allow herself to be nailed down, crucified to Hugo's all-consuming desire or to the traumas of the past. Recognizing that the Caribbean is "founded on violence," Santos-Febres asks: "what do we do with this violence? Lament it all the time, carry it like a cross all the time, minimize it, or learn to laugh at it while knowing it deeply?" (Peña-Jordán 120). In response to this question, she produces a protagonist who refuses to carry, like a cross, the burden of the past, or to be martyred to it. Instead, she redresses the Big House through her powerful performances and then simply vanishes from the pages of the novel.

Finding "Home" in *Paradise*

While a transvestite mansion provides a self-consciously decentered place of origins for Santos-Febres' novel, the Convent casts a long shadow over Morrison's *Paradise*. A labyrinthine structure, its peculiar architecture is revealed over the course of many chapters, but its centrality is established from the first pages, when it is invaded by the men of Ruby, who "have never been this deep in the Convent ... only a few have seen the halls, the chapel, the schoolroom, the bedrooms. Now they all will. And at last they will see the cellar and expose its filth" (3). In these initial pages, the novel describes the Convent in psychosexual terms that evoke both a vulnerable female sexuality and the Jungian concept of the house as collective unconscious. Yet the same space is also presented as a historical artifact whose meaning is found in layers and accretions. It is, as Krumholz observes, a palimpsestic structure in which past and present, and feeling and fact, comingle. As soon as the men enter, they are startled by its "grandeur," which reminds them that, "before it was a Convent, this house was an embezzler's folly. A mansion where bisque and rose-tone marble floors segue into teak ones" (3). Like the transvestite mansion in *Sirena Selena* and other Big Houses we have seen, the Convent's physical appearance immediately reminds those who enter it of the economic plunder that allowed it to be built. The architecture and decor of this house, however, also convey a masculine sexuality that is at once aggressive and withdrawing. On the one hand, it is filled with frolicking nymphs, penis-shaped bathroom fixtures, and doorknobs shaped liked breasts. On the other, the narrator observes: "Fright, not triumph, spoke in every foot of the embezzler's mansion. Shaped like a live cartridge, it curved to a deadly point at the north end where, originally, the living and dining rooms lay" (71). Thus, although it strives to engage in the unfettered pursuit of what Benítez Rojo calls "the vertical desires of ejaculation and castration" (*Repeating Island* 10), it ultimately expresses a paranoid, defeated masculinity, underscored by the sexless feminine name by which it is now known: the Convent.

It receives the name, more accurately a misnomer, because of the second phase of its history, when it served as a Catholic boarding school "where stilled Arapaho girls once sat and learned to forget" (4). The embezzler's paranoia, it turns out, was justified: after throwing his first orgiastic party, he was arrested, and his dream house purchased by a wealthy woman who founded the "Christ the King School for Native Girls." Upon their arrival, the nuns shatter plaster nymphs, replace phallic fixtures, and remove explicit artwork from the walls. They fail, however, to erase the presence of the embezzler. Thus, when the men of Ruby enter the Convent, both its erotic masculine and chaste feminine histories are immediately visible, the icons of the lustful pagan and the pious nuns having become hopelessly intertwined: "Now the armed men search rooms where macramé baskets float next to Flemish candelabra; where Christ and His mother glow in niches trimmed in grapevines" (4). Pressed up against these heterogeneous objects are others that denote the house's most recent history: a Modess box in the bathroom, an empty Doublemint wrapper, a bedroom with "strange things nailed or taped to the walls or propped in a corner" (7). Neither embedded into the house's structure nor attempting to erase its previous histories, these disposable, casually abandoned objects seem to indicate a different, more transient, kind of feminine presence. Yet, seen through the eyes of the men of Ruby, they take on perverted significance, and the Convent itself becomes an evil gothic mansion that, as the sun rises, "float[s], dark and malevolently disconnected from God's earth" (18). As such, it contrasts, violently and vilely, with the sheltered town of Ruby.

In an address published under the title "Home," Morrison articulates a desire "to think of a-world-in-which-race-does-*not*-matter as something other than a theme park, or a failed and always-failing dream, or as the father's house of many rooms. I am thinking of it as home" (3). Distinguishing between house and home, Morrison asserts, allows for a strategy that "domesticates the racial project, moves the job of unmattering race away from ... an impossible future or an irretrievable and probably nonexistent Eden to a manageable, doable, modern human activity" (3–4). No one in the modern world can fully escape the confines of the racial house; yet, Morrison argues, "it was important, at the least, to rebuild it so that it was not a windowless prison into which I was forced, a thick-walled, impenetrable container from which no cry could be heard, but rather an open house, grounded, yet generous in its supply of windows and doors" (4). How does one make the racial house into "a race specific yet nonracist home" (5)? This question is central to both novels under examination in this chapter. In response, Santos-Febres imagines a transvestite mansion, redressed and so revealed to be not a home nor even a house, but rather a funhouse, a collection of distorted images whose authentic forms cannot, and, perhaps, should not, be recovered. Morrison's strategy is different, but in order to understand it, it is necessary to note that Morrison's notion of "domestication" does not conform to contemporary connotations of the verb "to domesticate," which include "to naturalize" or "to civilize," and often imply a negative form of "feminization," an emasculating gesture. Morrison instead draws from what, according to the *Oxford English Dictionary*, is an obsolete meaning of the word: "To live familiarly or at home (*with*); to take up one's abode." Within the novel, the process of domestication is understood to be chosen— that is, freely taken up—with the purpose of creating a beloved communion with oneself and others. Moreover, it unfolds in relation to a multivalent but specific past that connects the histories of the mansion, the women who reside within it, and the community of Ruby. The complexity of this last relationship, between the racial house of the Convent and town of Ruby, is suggested by the following excerpt from Morrison's address, which closes with a brief passage from *Paradise* that I have cited previously:

> In my current project I want to see whether or not race-specific, race-free language is both possible and meaningful in narration. And I want to inhabit, walk around, a site clear of racist detritus; a place where race both matters and is rendered impotent. . . . I want to imagine not the threat of freedom, or its tentative panting fragility, but the concrete thrill of borderlessness—a kind of out of doors safety where "a sleepless woman could always rise from her bed, wrap a shawl around her shoulders and sit on the steps in the moonlight. And if she felt like it she could walk out in the yard and on down the road. No lamp and no fear." (9)

What I want to highlight in this passage is the ambiguity it establishes between Ruby and the Convent. On the one hand, given its history, it would seem that the Convent provides the negative space implied in Morrison's comments, a site decidedly *not* clear of racist detritus, while Ruby, the product of "very revolutionary and hardwork- ing activity," offers the opposite (Denard 12). On the other hand, as we have seen, the idealized description of Ruby that Morrison cites turns out to be a manifestation of the collective imagination of the "New Fathers." As such, it represents, not "border- lessness," but a patriarchal vision of paradise.[27] It is, then, the Convent that, despite its dual history of oppression, becomes an "open house." This transformation is facilitated by at least three factors suggested in the above quotation. The first two, intimately linked to the novel's strategies of crossing, have been touched upon in an earlier section of this chapter: they are Morrison's use of "race-specific, race-free language" to describe the women of the Convent, and her depiction of the Convent as a crossroads capable of generating a "nomadic circulation" of bodies, histories, and meaning that overcomes the limitations imposed by its violently paranoid architec- ture. The third factor, in turn, is achieved by the intentional actions of the women themselves, who work to rid themselves of not just racist but all manner of psycho- logical and historical "detritus."

This is no small task, since they begin their time in the Convent as captives and exiles, victims and vagabonds, fugitives and refugees. Mavis, Gigi, Seneca, and Pal- las are the four young women who appear, one by one, at the Convent to be taken in by Consolata. Each has her own traumatic story, but, once gathered under the roof of the dilapidated mansion, they form a makeshift community that is flexible, tolerant, and comforting. All come and go as they please. Those who remain cook, drink, and eat together; tend the garden and sell its produce; listen to the radio, talk, and dance. On occasion, they care for a resident of Ruby who arrives in a moment of crisis. And the younger women find in Consolata, as her name would suggest, a profound source of solace: she is an "ideal parent, friend, companion in whose company they were safe from harm" (262). Their little household, however, is no paradise: Mavis and Gigi fight constantly; Connie falls into an alcoholic stupor; Seneca carves lines into her body; and Pallas refuses to accept her pregnancy. Although they live together, they remain isolated in individual pain. As Connie, drunk and depressed, uncharitably thinks: "the timbre of each voice told the same tale: disorder, deception and, what Sister Roberta warned the Indian girls against, drift. The three *d*'s that paved the road to perdition, and the greatest of these was drift" (222). Like the "Peoples of the Sea" imagined by Benítez Rojo, these drifters wander on an endless voyage that evinces no more than the "will to persevere through flight" (*Repeating Island* 25). It is only in the final three chapters, when they take intentional action, that they cease drifting and become, to paraphrase Glissant, ones who are errant (*Poetics of Relation* 20).

This action is set in motion when Consolata remakes herself as a spiritual leader. Although her transformation is dramatic, it represents the culmination of a long process of awakening that begins at a precise moment, shortly after Ruby's founding in 1951, when the town gathers for an impromptu celebration, which Connie witnesses while on a shopping excursion:

> As Consolata watched that reckless joy, she heard a faint but insistent Sha sha sha. Sha sha sha. Then a memory of just such skin and just such men, dancing with women in the streets to music beating like an infuriated heart, torsos still, hips making small circles above legs moving so rapidly it was fruitless to decipher how such ease was possible. These men here were not dancing, however; they were laughing, running, calling to each other and to women doubled over in glee. And although they were living here in a hamlet, not in a loud city full of glittering black people, Consolata knew she knew them. (226)

Triggered by "reckless joy" and the call of "sha sha sha," Consolata's epiphany resonates compellingly with the collective desire inflamed by Selena's boleros, and also with Benítez Rojo's "in a certain kind of way," which he defines as "something remote that reproduces itself and that carries the desire to sublimate apocalypse and violence" (*Repeating Island* 16). Once again, music acts as a force that somehow is produced by history and simultaneously stands outside of it. Like the open word, it is capable of tracing a different kind of path toward the past and then again away from it. Drawn into an ecstasy that reproduces the rhythms of her forgotten childhood in Brazil, Consolata reawakens to the sensual pleasures of carnival, and her fresh desire takes on physical, spiritual, and (trans)cultural dimensions.

Initially, her reawakening leads her to embark on an intense but short-lived sexual affair with Deacon Morgan. Later, it enables her to begin "practicing" forms of both traditional and magical healing. Both of these activities comprise serious acts of rebellion against the orthodox Catholicism of Mary Magna, the "rescuer" to whom she remains devoted. They also, for similar reasons, are inextricable from her struggle to articulate and reclaim her lost cultural identity. When she repents of her affair with Deacon, she longs to tell her mentor "Sha sha sha ... meaning, he and I are the same." Mary Magna, however, silences her: "Sh sh sh. ... Never speak of him again" (241). By reducing "sha sha sha" to "sh sh sh," Mary Magna cuts her off from the rhythm of her African and New World heritages, figuratively reenacting her earlier "snatching" of nine-year-old Consolata from the streets of her homeland.

Yet Consolata's relationship with Catholicism and, especially, Mary Magna remains ambiguous. Far from breaking with her, she spends months extending her mentor's life by employing her magical healing powers. The novel's only detailed description of Mary Magna comes in chapter 1, where she is depicted, quite literally, as a blinding vision of white light: "The whiteness at the center [of the bed] was blinding. It took a moment for Mavis to see the shape articulated among the pillows and the bone-white sheets ... " (46). The light emanating from the dying nun is later explained as an effect of Connie's use of magic; yet Morrison's own insistence, in *Playing in the Dark* and elsewhere, on the inescapable symbolism of whiteness in the U.S. imaginary, points to a racial meaning as well: a well-intentioned "rescuer" of native girls from across the Americas, Mary Magna is the white mother *par excellence*. As such, she is opposed to Consolata's first mother, the siren-like Piedade: if the former has "a face paler than the white cloth wrapped around [her] head" (46), the latter is "black as firewood" (318). Despite their racial difference, however, both are represented in terms of divinity: Mary Magna, called "Mother," is surrounded by a halo-like circle of light and "sees everything in the universe" (47); Piedade is "a black face framed in cerulean blue" which Consolata's "emerald eyes adore" (318). Because these descriptions employ the language of Christian iconography, it could be argued that Mary Magna and Piedade represent a White and a Black Madonna, respectively. However, Consolata's relationship to each complicates what might be a straightforward parallel. The novel, for example, draws attention to her racial difference from both mothers. On the one hand, it describes her "brown fingers gentling the white ones" when she is at Mary Magna's side (48). On the other, it accentuates how her "tea brown hair" and her face, which contains "the colors of seashells— wheat, roses, pearl," contrasts with Piedade's dark complexion (318). Connie's racial and cultural in-betweenness marks her similarity to Ursa in *Corregidora*, who is also "a hybrid and thoroughly American" (Coser 138). Although their stories are distinct—Ursa, for example, is not only closer to the slave experience but also to African-American cultural traditions—both women uneasily embody a trans-American identity that extends from Brazil to the United States. If *Paradise* disrupts the black-white binary of U.S. race discourse by refusing to identify the "white girl," it pushes this racial and cultural uncertainty further through Consolata, whose transnational hybridity suggests the need for what Mills, in the context of Jones's fiction, calls an "Afro-Latino/a heritage" (92). Indeed, Consolata's shifting alliances between the novel's two mother figures suggest that she represents an alternative Mary, one who fuses black and white, and North and South, together. This theory is further validated by the fact that she shares a name with Our Lady Consolata, a revered saint whose ancient icon still attracts devoted pilgrims. Despite these correspondences, however, the novel implies that she is in fact a Christ figure.[28]

Perhaps more accurately, she is a New World transfiguration of Christ; for she explicitly rejects the Christian God and bids "Him" farewell with the words "I'll miss You ... I really will" (251). Immediately after this, she is approached by another kind of divinity, a stranger who speaks in broken English and claims to come from "far country." When he removes his hat and sunglasses, he is revealed to be a young, male version of Consolata: "Fresh, tea-colored hair came tumbling down, cascading over his shoulders and down his back. He took off his glasses then and winked, a slow seductive movement of a lid. His eyes, she saw, were round and green as new apples" (252). The God she learned to love under the tutelage of Mary Magna demanded she leave her homeland, reject her culture, and forget her language for a chance at salvation. This god, in contrast, returns from "far country" in order to reveal himself to her *as* her.

Her rejection of Mary Magna's God and subsequent encounter with her own divine nature mark the culmination of Consolata's personal transformation and the beginning of the intentional, collective efforts of the women of the Convent. She prepares a meal for the younger women, a First rather than a Last Supper during which she announces, in language that echoes both the broken English of her divine self and the biblical call of Christ: "I call myself Consolata Sosa. If you want to be here you do what I say. Eat how I say. Sleep when I say. And I will teach you what you are hungry for" (262).[29] This invocation is followed by an exhortation to integrate "bones" and "spirit": "Hear me, listen. Never break them in two. Never put one over the other. Eve is Mary's mother. Mary is the daughter of Eve" (263). Rejecting the traditional dichotomy between Mary and Eve, virgin and whore, she urges the women to embrace themselves and each other as unbroken body and soul.

The process in which they are engaged, however, demands not only a reconciliation of body and spirit, but also a theological and cultural realignment that represents, not so much a syncretic fusion of European and African traditions, as a reclamation of the New World African traditions previously represented only vaguely as "sha sha sha." The cultural, or cross-cultural, dimension of the transformation of the Convent women is further underscored by the passage that immediately follows Consolata's admonition to reject the spirit-body binary:

> [S]he told them of a place where white sidewalks met the sea and fish the color of plums swam alongside children. She spoke of fruit that tasted the way sapphires look and boys using rubies for dice. Of scented cathedrals made of gold where gods and goddesses sat in the pews with the congregation. Of carnations tall as trees. Dwarfs with diamonds for teeth. Snakes aroused by poetry and bells. Then she told them of a woman named Piedade, who sang but never said a word. (263–64)

This passage is the first to mention Piedade; and its colorful rendering of Brazil serves as a gateway that allows the younger women to embrace Consolata's vision of paradise as a carnivalesque world that reproduces the "reckless joy" of her childhood. Moreover, although it describes an ornate cathedral, it infuses that typically Christian location with a polytheistic and pagan iconography, in which gods and goddesses worship alongside human beings, snakes are holy, and music takes precedence over the Word.

Significantly, all of these elements—the direct participation of gods in worship experiences, the sacredness of the snake, the overwhelming importance of music—are identifying features of many New World religious practices rooted in West African belief systems. Indeed, a number of critics have suggested that, given her Brazilian origins, Consolata's spiritual transformation should be read as a return to

Candomblé.[30] Morrison has spoken more obliquely of presenting, in *Paradise*, "organized religion and unorganized magic as two systems" (Donahue n.p.). Morever, she refrains from identifying Consolata's practices with a specific theology, just as she refuses to specify her homeland as Brazil—and, we might add, just as she refuses to name the "white girl." In spite of her lack of geographical or anthropological detail, however, she clearly encodes the novel's "unorganized magic" as African in origin and New World in practice. Thus Ruby's midwife, Lone Dupres, who was adopted in Louisiana, implicitly owes her knowledge of herbs and belief in her own and Consolata's spiritual "giftedness," to the hoodoo practices of her native state. And, as we have seen, Piedade's siren qualities link her to the powerful West African orisha of the ocean, known as Yemayá, Yemalla, or Yemanja. Similarly, Consolata's green-eyed visitor can be associated with Eshu-Elegbara, an orisha of African origins worshipped, like Yemanja, throughout the Americas. His flirtatious manner, peculiar but exacting use of language, and guise as a traveler suggests this correlation, for Eshu is a messenger and trickster, as well as the god of communication and spiritual language. He is also the guardian of the crossroads and, according to Robert Farris Thompson, one of his key functions is to "cultivate the art of recognizing significant communications ... or else the lessons of the crossroads—the point where doors open or close, where persons have to make decisions that may forever effect their lives—will be lost" (19). Thompson's definition of the crossroads as "the point where doors open or close," resonates with Morrison's allusion, in "Home," to "an open house, grounded, yet generous in its supply of windows and doors" (4). But what is the relationship between home, with its connotations of fixedness and stability, and the crossroads, a place of mobility and change?

The answer to this question is hinted at in the final chapter of *Paradise*, after the attack on the Convent, when the Baptist minister, Richard Misner, and his fiancée, Anna Flood, drive from Ruby to the scene of the crime to try to understand what has transpired. Wandering the rundown mansion's abandoned grounds, they see or sense something, a door or a window, move:

> They expanded on the subject: What did a door mean? what a window? focusing on the sign rather than the event; excited by the invitation rather than the party. ... Anything to avoid reliving the shiver or saying out loud what they were wondering. Whether through a door needing to be opened or a beckoning window already raised, what would happen if you entered? What would be on the other side? What on earth would it be? (305)

The Convent—first an "embezzler's folly;" then a boarding school where "Arapaho girls once sat and learned to forget;" and finally, briefly, a home broken apart by vengeful violence—is now, perhaps, a haunted house, where windows blink open and doors mysteriously swing shut. Then again, despite the "shiver" it induces, it is not haunted, for it has no ghosts: the women who were attacked have disappeared, body and soul. It is a beckoning crossroads, an earthly place where history is not erased—the artifacts representing all of its histories remain solidly in place—but through which the Big House has nevertheless been reconfigured, if only for the briefest of moments, into an open home.

Conclusion

The night before they are attacked, the women of the Convent dance outside of the mansion in a cleansing ritual described as "the rapture of holy women dancing in hot sweet rain," during which each of the younger characters finally lets go of the traumas of her past and Consolata becomes "fully housed by the god who sought her out in the garden" (283). The latter description, in particular, calls to mind Morrison's evocative suggestion of "the body as consummate home" ("Home" 5). The untitled epilogue, with which *Paradise* concludes, depicts the women as inhabiting a reality between life and death: like the post-resurrection Christ, they are not ghosts but fully physical beings who visit family members in order to make amends or seek vengeance. Despite the necessary role of the Convent throughout, the women's redemption is not finally dependent upon that, or any, geographically fixed place. Rather, they discover that their bodies—their "bones" and their "spirits"—are their true homes. If the novel's final pages advocate "the body as consummate home," its last paragraph articulates a vision, at once soaring and grounded, of an earthly paradise presided over by Consolata and Piedade, who occupy a site that joins together the novel's contradictory versions of Consolata's childhood home: the jewel-toned paradise and the "shit-strewn" inferno. They rest on a beach, on which "sea trash gleams. Discarded bottle caps sparkle near a broken sandal. A small dead radio plays the quiet surf" (318). Fantastical visions of sapphires, rubies, and diamonds are here displaced by the mundane dregs of modern life, "sea trash" that nevertheless takes on the "gleam" of jewels, for Piedade's song transforms her surroundings:

> There is nothing to beat this solace which is what Piedade's song is about, although the words evoke memories neither one has ever had: of reaching age in the company of the other; of speech shared and divided bread smoking from the fire; the unambivalent bliss of going home to be at home—the ease of coming back to love begun.
>
> When the ocean heaves sending rhythms of water ashore, Piedade looks to see what has come. Another ship, perhaps, but different, heading to port, crew and passengers, lost and saved, atremble, for they have been disconsolate for some time. Now they will rest before shouldering the endless work they were created to do down here in Paradise. (318)

Piedade's song, like Sirena's boleros or Leocadio's dance, expresses an impossible transcendent dream of love, of an "unambivalent" return to uninterrupted origins, a return that is not a return but rather a continuous being and unbroken sharing. This dream, however, coexists with the constant and constantly different coming and going of ships—a stream of movement that calls to mind the voyages of conquistadors, slave traders and slaves, tourists on pleasure cruises, and migrants in *yolas*, but that also symbolizes the possibility of change and transformation. The identity of the passengers, too, remains ambiguous: they are conquerors and conquered, lost and saved, disconsolate and consoled. They are, like those who hear Serena's boleros, *testigos*, witnesses to Piedade's voice, which beckons them "to remember their lives in her songs" (*Paradise* 284). Yet they are also active participants in the construction and destruction of an earthly paradise that is constantly remade.

Despite the siren songs that resonate between these novels, the last two chapters of *Sirena Selena* offer a different vision of paradise, and of home, than the last paragraphs of *Paradise*. Following Serena's disappearing act and Leocadio's utopian dance, the final pages return to the perspective of Miss Martha Divine; and it is, appropriately, this most earth-bound and undivine of characters that recapitulates the novel's light-hearted, hardnosed preference for the artificial and the superficial. The final chapter reproduces one of Martha's stand-up comedy routines, which are scattered throughout the novel and comprise, alongside Serena's concerts, a second category of performance. Indeed, it is telling that the narrative closes, not with one of Sirena's miraculous performances, but rather with comic patter that ends in a cliché-ridden bit about a program entitled "Positive Thinking," which has inspired Martha with formulaic mantras like "'Desire creates ability.' 'He who perseveres accomplishes.' 'Don't go backward even to get a head start'" (214). Urging her audience members to stay positive and keep on believing in their lucky stars, even though they may live "in a tiny room filled with cockroaches," she concludes by expressing the undying hope that her own lucky star is within reach: "I can already see mine, just beyond my grasp. I can almost reach it. I swear, there are days when I believe I can touch it with my fingertips" (214). *Paradise* ends with the elusive but beautiful vision of Consolata, gazing adoringly at the holy face of Piedade, and "going home to be at home." *Sirena Selena* concludes with a string of tongue-in-cheek truisms that culminates in the even more impossible promise of catching a "lucky star," or a lucky break, that will allow for the making of a better home, one with far more luxury and glamour than can be provided by a cramped, roach-filled room. Morrison's earthly paradise is finally a place of "endless work," but one that holds the promise of home. In *Sirena Selena*, in contrast, the very concept of paradise is inextricable from the colonial condition of the "transvestite Caribbean" whose paradisiacal glamour is a necessary disguise, and a strategic means of exposing and redressing (although perhaps not escaping) the legacy of the plantation.

Conclusion

Open Words, Known Worlds

The coda to Edward P. Jones's 2003 Pulitzer Prize-winning novel, *The Known World*, begins with a letter, postmarked April 12, 1861, from "The City of Washington." The letter is written, on the first day of the Civil War, by Calvin, a free black man whose prosperous southern family owns slaves. Calvin writes to his sister, Caldonia, who lives with her second husband, in the fictional county of Manchester, Virginia, on the plantation that she inherited from her deceased first husband, Henry.[1] Calvin narrates his arrival "in a City that will either send me back in defeat to Virginia or will give me more Life than my Soul can contain" (383). His first impressions of Washington, however, are familiarly unsettling: "The City is one mud hole after another, and there is filth as far as the eye can see. Virginia green has been reduced to a memory. . . . I am more than afraid of being lost in the City" (383). Like many of the protagonists we have seen, Calvin is torn between the promised freedom of the modern metropolis, and the hazards of what, in *Paradise*, Morrison calls its "shit strewn paths" (223).

Despite a fleeting ache for the "Virginia green" of his known world, he finds his way to an idyllic community tucked into the squalor of the urban landscape, a hotel where Washington's elite sleeps and dines alongside "people of our Race because that was the way the owners and proprietors wanted it" (384). Those "owners and proprietors" turn out to be black men and women, many of them runaway slaves, including three from Caldonia's plantation. The novel soon reveals that this hotel epitomizes the alternative space of the *palenque* or maroon communities imagined by Benítez Rojo and Glissant: it is a space of resistance as well as creation, where what Glissant calls "creative *marronage*" flourishes (*Poetics of Relation* 71). Such creativity is evident in the artwork of Alice Night, a fugitive from Caldonia's plantation who has crafted two large wall hangings that are displayed in the hotel, each of which Calvin describes as "a grand piece of art that is part tapestry, part painting, and part clay structure—all in one exquisite Creation" (384). The first is "a kind of map of the life of the County of Manchester," which shows "what God sees when he looks down" (384). The second, perhaps "even more miraculous," depicts Caldonia's plantation in such detail that "there is nothing missing, not a cabin, not a barn, not a chicken, not a horse" (385):

> Each person's face, including yours, is raised up as though to look in the very eyes of God. I look at all the faces and I am more than glad now that I knew the name and face of everyone there at your home. The dead in the cemetery have risen from there and they, too, stand at the cabins where they once lived. So the slave cemetery is just plain ground now, grass and nothing else. It is empty, even of the tiniest infants, who rest alive and well in their mothers' arms. In the cemetery where our Henry is buried, he stands by his grave, but that grave is covered with flowers as though he still inhabits it. (385–86)

Alice's composite "Creation" generates a "miraculous" and undeniably moving image of the plantation past redeemed. More specifically, it rescues a single plantation from oblivion, emancipating every life lived in it, however fleeting and fragile, through a divine and loving gaze. Here, New World history—which, Handley reminds us, is "fragmented, partial, and while undeniable, ultimately unknowable" ("A New World Poetics" 26)—is whole and wholly known.

Yet several details in Calvin's letter suggest intentional limits to Alice's redemptive vision. First, even as he proclaims that there is nothing missing from her depiction, Calvin notes that neither Alice nor her two runaway companions are present: Alice's art is only possible because of her act of rebellion—her escape to the city—and, in her art, that act is represented only as an absence, a hole in the historical record. Second, Calvin's emotional response to Alice's handiwork is motivated by more than simple gladness at the sight of his sister's "home." It is also provoked by the fear of being "cast out" of the new, urban Eden to which he has arrived: "What I feared most at that moment is what I still fear: that they would remember my history, that I, no matter what I had always said to the contrary, owned people of our Race" (386). His fear, in turn, generates another gap. So that they will allow him to stay, he tries "to make myself as indispensable as possible and yet … to stay out of the way, lest someone remember my history" (386). Just as Henry, the dead master, is shunted to the edges of Alice's wall hanging, so too Calvin clings silently to the margins of his new community, hoping his history of complicity will simply be forgotten.

What is the nature of communities? How are they imagined, and re-imagined? What materials do we use to construct them? What are the roles of history and memory in this construction, and what is the role of art? How much should be remembered, how much forgotten? How, and where, do we find redemption in or from the past? Who deserves to be redeemed and, alternatively, who deserves to be cast out, or cut off? These questions accumulate, intersect, and collide, at times violently, in this brief vignette from *The Known World* and also in each of the texts examined in the preceding chapters; and they are not generated by universal or abstract ponderings. Rather, as the title of Jones's novel makes clear, they are attached to specific places—to the known worlds of Manchester County or the Mississippi Delta, of Caracas or

Swain's pueblo in the Dominican Republic. Yet we have seen, as well, that they ac-quire different weight and nuance as they circulate through these places, then beyond them, and at times back to them. The voyage between known and unknown worlds sets the imaginary of the open word into motion, dislodging thorny questions from old contexts and so fragmenting official narratives while introducing new ones.

Migratory crossings are essential to the postmodern imaginary: just as Alice Night's transformation from mute slave to witness-bearing artist is made possible only by her daring journey to the city, so the stories told in *Corregidora, Stairway for Electra, Paradise* and *Sirena Selena* are facilitated by the often risky voyages of those who tell them. Thus the Corregidora women escape from Brazil to the United States, Helene travels from the Dominican Republic to Greece, Consolata is "snatched" from Brazil and brought to Oklahoma, and Selena and Martha shuttle between San Juan and Santo Domingo. Such movement is not, of course, absent from the modern imaginary. To the contrary, it pervades the Spanish-language novels we have examined: in *Iphigenia*, the narrator spends her formative years in Europe; in *Garden*, the protagonist flees her insular island to travel the world. Yet, both of these novels intimate the liberating power of movement only to deny it: María Eugenia, unable to accept Mercedes' invitation to return to Europe, finds herself forced to marry a man she despises; while Bárbara finally returns to her island, and so to her death—or, rather, her eternal stagnation. Perhaps ironically, it is *Delta Wedding*, whose journeys are limited by the boundaries of the plantation, which successfully articulates a landscape in flux, capable of disrupting—to a point—the dichotomous logic of the past.

In general, however, the modern plantation imaginary—even when it declares, as Ortiz's *Cuban Counterpoint* so forcefully does, the creative potential of move-ment—stresses the difficulty of escaping immurement and stagnation, as well as the comfort that, for some, such changelessness provides. The postmodern imaginary, in contrast, presents the strategic necessity of movement. At the same time, however, it does not shrink from its dangers, and even, at moments, suggests that it might be nothing more than a new form of entrapment. This is the case with the nightmarishly endless flight from the plantation described by Benítez Rojo; and it is also implicit in Glissant's unsettling comparison of Rowan Oak (Faulkner's plantation-like house in Oxford, Mississippi) to New York City, which we first saw in chapter 4: "This is characteristic of the United States, both North and South: glitter and glamour are always side by side with ruin and dilapidation. (Tourists in New York, for example, expect to be awed.) As if even in famous places, like Rowan Oak, the ephemeral lies in wait, as if the building were about to be dismantled only to be rebuilt and placed on view somewhere else" (*Faulkner, Mississippi* 10). Glissant's assertion brings to-gether the northern and southern United States as well as the plantation and the city. Both are places of disguise and decay, but they are also moveable centers of power, all the more dangerous because they are ephemeral: like a film set, they can be taken apart and relocated at a moment's notice. Interestingly, the last scenes of *Paradise* and *Sirena Selena* invoke a similar juxtaposition, of glamour and dilapidation; unlike Glissant, however, Morrison and Santos-Febres focus on how this juxtaposition may be generated and employed by the powerless rather than the powerful. In her final vision of an earthly paradise, Morrison imagines the miraculous voice of Piedade transforming urban beach trash in Brazil—bottle caps, a broken sandal, a dead radio—into glittering gems. Santos-Febres, in contrast, uses Martha's closing comedy routine to underscore the simulative, but also vital, nature of her own, and her island's, glitzy poses. If the former highlights the transformative power of song, the latter emphasizes the strategic use of disguise. Despite their difference from each other, however, both suggest that, in an age of consumption and globalization, "glitter and glamour are always side by side with ruin and dilapidation," not just in the U.S. North and South, but in every corner of the New World. In doing so, they raise questions about the relationship between the powerful and the powerless, as well as between the city, the plantation, and community.

Contemporary critical discourse about community in the Americas (and elsewhere) has tended to privilege the heterogeneous, dynamic, globalizing space of the city; yet, more recently, some have suggested that the emphasis on the urban too often exaggerates the freedom and flexibility offered by the city. These critics propose, not a return to the plantation, but rather a reassessment of both the inevitable egalitarianism of placelessness and the inevitable despotism of rural landscapes and rooted communities. Sarah Casteel, for example, asserts "the failure of deterritorialized models of identity to supersede more traditional, rooted models" (192) and, in response, considers the work of artists and writers who simultaneously refuse notions of stable identity *and* of libratory placelessness: "To insert oneself into a landscape or to plant a garden is to lay claim to a sense of place, but place is understood as an ongoing, laborious, and always provisional process" (193).[2] In order to complicate the monotonously pendular swing between plantation and city—in order to call upon the eccentric spiraling that is also part of the movement of the open word—Casteel invokes an alternative "sense of place," one we have seen in many guises in this study: Ortiz's global paradise, which "included the whole world, which must be completely made over if we are to find and enjoy it once more" (202); Benítez Rojo's vital *palenque* or Glissant's creative maroon; Morrison's transcendently earth-bound paradise. Casteel's emphasis on the laborious and provisional nature of these landscapes suggests that to invest any of them with too much power—be it destructive or constructive—is perilous. Rather, it is through the study of the interplay of urban and rural, placelessness and place, mobility and fixedness, paired with a careful interrogation of how each of these is deployed, and with what intention, that different kinds of community can be imagined.[3] If, in the first part of the twentieth century, the open word of the plantation imaginary reassesses notions of community primarily from within the domesticated realm of the plantation, in the latter part it exits the master's house and enters a global arena in which old debates and old memories must be reevaluated on new, dangerously unstable ground. In doing so, it alters the predictable contours of the plantation landscape, remembers its tragedies even as it reevaluates their meanings, and ponders the possibility of a final exit from its grounds.

NOTES

Introduction

1. Brathwaite and Muñiz Varela are especially critical of "plantation system studies," which Brathwaite traces back to "the work, first of social anthropologists, then of economists dealing with the Caribbean contribution and reaction to mercantilism," beginning with a 1957 seminar organized by the Research Institute for the Study of Man at Columbia University. He also cites Lloyd Best's "A Model of Pure Plantation Economy" (1968) and George Beckford's *Persistent Poverty* (1972). Muñiz Varela additionally mentions Sidney Mintz's *Caribbean Transformations* (1984), but the focus of her article is *The Repeating Island*, which I analyze in chapter 4.

2. A third term of significance, "hacienda," is discussed in chapter 2 of this book.

3. Throughout this study, I use the English word "plantation" flexibly. It may refer to the notion of the "rooted" institution, or acquire the different nuances contained in the words *ingenio* or *hacienda* (see chapter 2). Moreover, it will frequently retain one of the final definitions listed by the *OED*: "any institution regarded as exploitative or paternalistic, esp. in fostering an environment of inequality and servitude reminiscent of slavery." While this definition also fails to draw attention to the capitalistic aspects of the plantation venture, it does underscore its negative institutional qualities and "environmental" impact.

4. See chapter 6 for a more in-depth discussion of the *casa solariega* in Puerto Rico. With reference to Ferré, I am alluding to the short stories collected in *Papeles de Pandora*, translated as *The Youngest Doll*. In "Cuando las mujeres quieren a los hombres" ("When Women Love Men"), for example, an elegant mansion is transformed into a gaudy but lucrative whorehouse. "Amalia" is narrated by a young girl, the product of an incestuous relationship, who describes how her father/uncle's servants dismember him and burn down his house. The narrator of "La caja de cristal" ("The Glass Box") flees after blowing up his grandparents' elegant home. The protagonist of "De tu lado al paraíso" ("The Other Side of Paradise") describes how he slowly destroys his employers' house.

5. See also Davis and Gray White for key analyses of the historical development and sociocultural consequences of this discourse.

6. Regarding Pike's reference to the U.S. West, see chapter 4 of Adams.

7. "Trans-American" is the preferred term of this book because it emphasizes the crossings that are necessary to comparative work, and also retains the uneven, irregular, and multiple forms such crossings can take. These include, as the *OED* definition of "trans-" reminds us, not only "across," but also "through, over, to or on the other side of, beyond, outside of, from one place, person, thing, or state to another." By contrast, "Inter-American" implies the existence of a neutral zone between ("inter") the Americas and "Hemispheric" invokes a shared, static space.

8. On the curricular challenges posed by trans-American studies, see Fitz "In Quest" and "Inter-American Studies."

9. See Bérbubé and Kadir.

10. For a variety of perspectives on the tensions between Latin American (and Latino) Studies in the U.S. versus Latin America, see de la Campa *Latin Americanism* and "Latin, Latino, American;" Colás "Of Creole Symptoms;" Richard "Intersectando Latinoamérica;" Fox and Sadowski-Smith; Tinsman and Shulka; and Mignolo as well as other essays in the Poblete volume. On the place of cultural studies in Latin America, see the debate between Moreiras "Order of Order," and Sarlo "Cultural Studies."

11. Taylor, in "Remapping Genre," calls for a similar dialogue, and discusses practical methods for, as well as considerable obstacles to, achieving it.

12. In addition to Loichot and Handley, recent publications on trans-American topics include Casteel, DeLoughrey, and Strachan; as well as anthologies edited by Adams, Bibler, and Accilien; Smith and Cohn; Levander and Levine; Peacock, Watson, and Matthews; and Shukla and Tinsman.

Chapter 1

1. The highly literary style of many of the essays in *I'll Take My Stand* should be attributed to the fact that, "at the center of the group were four poets who during the early 1920's had been active in one of the most important and influential literary groups ever to exist in American letters, the Nashville Fugitives," as Rubin notes (xxiv). My analysis follows the lead of Kreyling and Limón, both of whom show how the Twelve Southerners employ poetic language to construct imaginary communities. With regards to the literary qualities of Ortiz's text, Pérez Firmat notes its "lively, often humorous, and sometimes lyrical style" and asserts its fundamentally poetic character (48–49). More generally, late twentieth-century critics of *Cuban Counterpoint* affirm a decentered poetics that "recognizes the play of desire," as Coronil points out in his introduction to the English translation of the text (xiv).

2. Along with Kreyling, recent works by Conkin, Murphy, and Bingham and Underwood have sought to revise so-called neo-Agrarian evaluations of *I'll Take My Stand*, which dominated critical discourse from the 1950s into the 1980s. See Bone for a thorough overview of this body of revisionist criticism as it has developed since the late 1980s.

3. As Smith and Cohn demonstrate, by evoking the European roots of southern culture and opposing North to South, Tate participates in a long tradition of claiming the "exceptionality" of the U.S. South ("Introduction" 1–3).

4. Guillén and Carpentier are also crucial to Benítez Rojo's analysis of Cuban cultural production; see chapter 4. González Echevarría makes special reference to Ortiz's first book, *Hampa afrocubana*, a criminological "study of witchcraft among Cuban blacks, written with the clear intention of understanding this phenomenon in order to eliminate it." Rooted in nineteenth-century positivism and theories of eugenics, Ortiz's early work "perceived blacks as

people with a primitive mentality and strong inclination to lust and violence. It was a race that had to be 'civilized' to ensure the country's progress and well being" (210). For more on this aspect of Ortiz's work, see chapter 1 of Rodríguez-Mangual.

5. See especially Conkin and Murphy.

6. Kreyling argues that Tate played a key role in suppressing any disagreement amongst the twelve contributors, providing "a tentative table of contents for the Agrarian book; his controlling idea was that the Agrarians could recoup through intense coherence what they stood to lose through tardiness [because two rival intellectual groups had also published volumes in 1930].... Nothing less than cultural survival was at stake: 'for this end we must have a certain discipline; we must crush minor differences of doctrine under a single idea'" (14).

7. See, for example, the "frail" personage of Caroline, the wife in Wade's character sketch, "The Life and Death of Cousin Lucius" (279). The symbolic role played by the southern lady is looked at in detail in chapter 2 of this book.

8. See Murphy, 206–10, for a discussion of the contradictions inherent in Warren's evolving views on race and segregation in the decades following the publication of *I'll Take My Stand*.

9. However, Kreyling notes that Warren's essay was viewed by Davidson as not conservative enough, and surmises that this judgment was due, not only to Warren's relatively moderate views on race, but also because "his understanding of 'the negro problem' was historical, far from Tate's preference for relegating it to the frame of cultural 'image.' Moreover, Warren's analysis directly challenged the southern utopian ideology that Tate, Ransom, and Davidson had agreed to impose on the ranks" (17–18).

10. Coronil similarly observes: "Tobacco tends to be masculine and to represent the more desirable features in Cuban culture; sugar, in contrast, stands for the feminine and represents the most destructive features of foreign capitalism." (xxii).

11. For a thorough and thoughtful analysis of trans-American representations of mixed-race women since the nineteenth century, see Bost.

12. Relevant here is Tate's classic definition of the so-called "Southern renaissance," which he penned fifteen years after the publication of *I'll Take My Stand*: "With the war of 1914–1918, the South reentered the world—but gave a backward glance as it slipped over the border: that backward glance gave us the Southern renascence, a literature conscious of the past in the present ...." ("The New Provincialism" 292).

Chapter 2

1. On *Iphigenia*, see Aizenberg, Garrels, and Moya-Raggio. On *The Sheltered Life*, see Manning, Levy, and Matthews. Although Aizenberg employs the term "failed *Bildungsroman*" to describe Parra's novel, I would tend to agree with those critics who reject the category of *Bildungsroman* altogether when referring to what Abel, Hirsch, and Langland call "fictions of female development." Arguing that the *Bildungsroman* employs a limited model of development that is unable to accommodate stories about women, these critics have turned to psychoanalytical theories to formulate alternative models of development that emphasize the distinctive patterns of sexual and psychological development experienced by women. Alternatively, they have focused on the problem of female education, which has relied on female innocence/ignorance as a sign of good character.

2. The themes emphasized by Parra and Glasgow are relevant to the study of a wide range of early twentieth-century trans-American fictions of female development; as Chevigny affirms, the "pioneering classics [written by women in the Americas] all tell a single tale of a woman who awakens to her condition and imagines a freed self she is powerless to realize" (147). In addition to *Iphigenia*, "The Awakening," and *La última niebla*, Chevigny mentions

Edith Wharton's *House of Mirth* (1905) as exemplifying this kind of fiction. Yet to say simply that these texts "tell a single tale," is to erase the range of stylistic, thematic, cultural, and contextual differences that mark them. Their common preoccupations are revealing, but should be understood in terms of the variations that emerge with each telling.

3. Fraiman argues that critics of *all* fictions of development, be they male- or female-centered, should focus "less on the progress of an alienated individual than on his or her constitution by manifold social relations" in order to free themselves from the model of the *Bildungsroman*, which is rooted in experiences that are not only typically male, but also grounded in a specific class and culture (xiii).

4. See Scura 321–52.

5. Glasgow was a vocal supporter of female suffrage and, in a 1913 interview, praised the broader women's movement as well: "It is the splendid growth of the whole world in its attitude toward women that is the beauty and the glory of our century" (*Ellen Glasgow's Reasonable Doubts* 23). Parra similarly advocated for social, intellectual, and economic equality between the sexes: "woman should be free in her own eyes, conscious of both dangers and responsibilities, useful to society even if she is not a mother, and financially independent" (*Influencia* 58). In the same breath, however, Parra claimed to be "neither a defender nor a detractor of suffragism" (58). For more on the contradictions in *Influencia*, see Rosa and Sommer and Russ. For an in-depth analysis of Parra's ambivalent attitudes regarding gender politics, see Garrels.

6. In this, she echoed the viewpoint of the Venezuelan elite at large, which largely supported Gómez in the hopes that he would reinstate order, stimulate the economy, and restore the glory of the nation, as Winthrop Wright has observed (80). Parra's attitudes toward the Venezuelan political situation, and Gómez's regime in particular, have generated considerable critical debate and speculation. See Garrels, Rosa and Sommer, and Russ. Although Parra publicly supported the dictator, and relied on his government for a portion of her income, recent criticism of *Iphigenia* argues that an underlying anti-Gómez sentiment pervades the novel; see Gomes and Lerner.

7. The citation is from a letter dated December 12, 1929; Fain and Young published this letter as part of a series of correspondence between Tate and Davidson. For more on the relationship between Glasgow and the Twelve Southerners, see Caldwell and Watson.

8. Both writers did publish novels with rural settings, for example Parra's *Las memorias de Mamá Blanca* (1929) and Glasgow's *Barren Ground* (1925).

9. For more on the plantation or hacienda in the Venezuelan context, see Herrero 23–34 and Ríos de Hernández. On the distinction between the hacienda and the plantation, see Keith, *Haciendas and Plantations*.

10. See Keith, "Encomienda, Hacienda" 438. Although the most intense debates surrounding the hacienda and the plantation took place in the 1960s and 1970s (see Keith, *Haciendas and Plantations*), some literary and cultural critics have recently renewed the discussion (see the section of Smith and Cohn titled "From Plantation to Hacienda: Greater Mexico and the U.S. South").

11. Sommer argues that Latin American women writers have been particularly adept at exploiting such gaps: "By dramatizing the incommensurability between experience and expression, they keep pointing to a gap between available words and the world" (*Foundational Fictions* 313). Writing in a language that frequently fails to describe accurately the lived experience of women, they identify the "maladjustments between desire and meaning," subvert symbolic orders, and present alternative possibilities (300). Lerner argues that in *Iphigenia*, such silences mask a political story: "The author, for reasons of caution, style, or both, wraps her ironic political testimony concerning Gómez's regime in the happy, enveloping cellophane paper of a love story" (par. 6).

12. For Parra, politics and history are inherently masculine activities. As Garrels observes, they "are associated with violence, conflict, and oppression, which makes them antagonistic to the feminine, which is all forgiveness, love, and reconciliation" (63). More generally, Garrels contends that all of Parra's writing relies on a reductive male-female binary. While I agree that she does label certain values and institutions consistently as either masculine or feminine, my reading of *Iphigenia* focuses on how the male-female binary, like the black-white binary examined in the second part of this chapter, is frequently and deliberately disrupted.

13. Rodríguez similarly describes the "ideological function" of black servants in *Iphigenia* and other white-authored novels of the Caribbean: "[they] give us the other (the decaying) side of the family history.... They are points of view, at times alternative to those expressed by a member of the family clan—the profile, hint, and blueprint of a possible revolutionary modern subjectivity and alternative epistemology" (82). The abstract nature of Rodríguez's vocabulary is telling: "points of view," "profiles," and "hints." They remain incomplete, mere "blueprints" rather than fully constructed characters.

14. Rodríguez asserts: "The white, oligarchic *Mantuana* nation is always the focus of discussion. The mulatta nation is an absurdity, a nightmare, the grotesque. The black nation, a 'sympathetic' illiteracy" (80).

15. See Wright, chapter 3.

16. Goodman argues that this is the precise moment at which the protagonist "aligns herself with the white Southern matriarchy flourishing in Queenborough," which suppresses "Memoria's unacknowledged history." Prohibited from speaking about this history, they cling to "the dominant myths of chivalric manhood and romantic love" ("Memory and Memoria" 245–6).

17. Matthews cautions: "Focusing primarily (or even exclusively) on Glasgow's blindness to subtleties of her own racism ... can in turn blind us to Glasgow's criticism of a generalized oppression that gives rise to its more specific forms, such as racism" (161).

18. Garrels similarly observes: "many times, María Eugenia finds herself on the brink of a discovery that would reveal a way to escape from her situation, but she takes a step backward in the face of the enormity of the discovery" (53).

Chapter 3

1. See Freedman, 18 and 279.

2. Friedman asserts that lyrical strategies held special appeal for women novelists during the first half of the twentieth century because they enabled the avoidance of the tragic plot by allowing for a dynamic interpenetration of "masculine" and "feminine" time. That is to say, lyrical novels "partake of linearity, change, evolution, birth. But this linear process ultimately depends ... on circling back into lyric timelessness, into a gynopoetic gestalt that breaks the tyranny of traditional plots against women" (179). Friedman analyzes the use of lyrical strategies in the work of Virginia Woolf, an author that Welty read and admired, and to whom she has frequently been compared.

3. The lyrical quality of Welty's writing was first suggested to me in a private conversation with Louise Cowan. Weston also analyzes lyrical aspects of Welty's writing in "Eudora Welty as Lyric Novelist" and *Gothic Traditions*.

4. Devlin continues: "While there is no evidence that Welty specifically assimilated any of these contemporary sources, it is clear that she seeks to satisfy the demands of verisimilitude by evoking both the superficial aspect of Delta life and its informing myth of timeless bounty" (91). See Devlin, as well, for a detailed analysis of the interplay between *Delta Wedding* and the conventions of the Plantation School.

5. Grammer notes that the broad conventions of plantation fiction were established by the eighteenth century and includes, as early examples of the plantation novel, George Tucker's *The Valley of Shenandoah* (1824) and John Pendleton Kennedy's *Swallow Barn* (1832). Mackethan, who focuses on the development plantation fiction from 1861 to 1920, similarly singles out *Swallow Barn*, noting that it portrays the Big House as a "social and moral center of order;" imagines the figure of the planter as a "generous, unmaterialistic" master; and underscores the dichotomy between the pastoral plantation and the industrial modern city. Mackethan also confirms the rise, in the post-bellum era, of "the voice of the black slave, brought forward to authenticate a version of the plantation system as tragic Eden" (211). Gardner identifies the same central features of the genre, but affirms an unbroken alternative tradition that provided a critical understanding of the plantation, and includes Glasgow in this dissenting tradition.

6. García Marruz alludes to *La vorágine*, by José Eustasio Rivera (Colombia, 1924); *Don Segundo Sombra*, by Ricardo Güiraldes (Argentina, 1935); *Doña Bárbara*, by Rómulo Gallegos (Venezuela, 1929); and *Los pasos perdidos*, by Alejo Carpentier (Cuba, 1953). The first three, published just before or during the seven-year period that Loynaz was writing *Garden*, are well-known examples of the *novela de la tierra*, or novel of the land. Sommer, in the final chapter of *Foundational Fictions*, compares the "masculine" strategies employed in *Doña Bárbara* with the "feminine" ones used by Parra in *Las memorias de Mamá Blanca* (1929). Many of her observations may also be fruitfully applied to Loynaz.

7. As Rodríguez observes: "To oppose garden to bush, mountain, plain, as a locus of meaning and as a space for male/female interaction ... undertakes a new definition of national space as garden house, an enclosed feminine space and the place of reproduction" (103).

8. The discourse of insularity in the Caribbean varies greatly from author to author, and the historical, social, and cultural experiences of individual islands play a role in shaping this variety. For an analysis of insularity in Cuban poetry, see Vitier, *Lo cubano en la poesía*. For a discussion of insularity in Loynaz, see Sedeño Guillén. For a comparison of the discourse of insularity in Cuba versus Puerto Rico, see Pérez Firmat 2–7.

9. Smith similarly argues that Loynaz "advocates periods of quietude or spiritual withdrawal in which the individual can dream and grow in ways which cannot be discerned on the surface" ("Dwarfed" 141).

10. Loynaz's depiction of what Handley has called "the postslavery placelessness of the white Creole woman" (*Postslavery* 151) finds a strong echo in her celebrated 1958 work, *Últimos días de una casa* (*Last Days of a House*). This long poem is narrated by an ancestral house that, deemed obsolete by the urbanizing society around her, describes her glorious past, abrupt decline, and imminent demolition.

11. Following clues from the novel, Davies creates this detailed timeline for the novel; see 88.

12. The Cuban sugar industry benefited enormously from the Haitian Revolution (1791–1804) and its aftermath. According to Pérez, "Between 1778 and 1846, the number of sugar mills in Cuba increased from 424 to 1,442" (60) and "between 1763 and 1862, an estimated 750,000 slaves were introduced into Cuba" (63).

13. Rodríguez observes that, while Loynaz "intends to erase" history, "iconography, objects, things, letters, furniture, style, and décor bring it back. They connote epoch and history" (102). As García Marruz notes, Loynaz's language and style often serve the same purpose, such as in the love letters, which create an atmosphere evocative of nineteenth-century Romanticism (592).

14. Cabrera discusses the importance of maize in *santería* in *El monte*, 561–72.

15. This was the case because during the 1840s, the newly wealthy elite feared a repeat of the Haitian Revolution and so preferred to remain under the protection of the

Spanish colonial government. Nevertheless, a growing discontentment with the status quo manifested itself through secret movements agitating for annexation to the U.S. or independence. However, the 1843 slave rebellion, known as the Ladder Conspiracy, served as a reminder that slavery and racial divisions remained an obstacle to independence (see Gott 59–67).

16. Reading *Garden* as a Gothic Romance that ultimately switches from the conventions of the female gothic to those of the male, Davies asserts that A ... and the garden are vampiric. *Delta Wedding* similarly contains many elements of the Gothic, although I would argue that neither novel is Gothic in the proper sense. On *Delta Wedding*, see Weston, *Gothic Traditions*.

17. De Jongh similarly observes that the garden "represents the patriarchal text which frames Bárbara's (and by extension, female) existence" (423). She does not, however, link garden to nation, nor does she discuss its dual nature—although she hints at the latter, observing: "Bárbara's final journey [back to the garden] constitutes a symbolic return to the beginning, to the origin/womb" (425). For more on the garden's dual nature, see Davies.

18. Loynaz references fairy tales throughout *Garden*, most explicitly in a chapter entitled "El cuento" ("The Story"), which compares Bárbara to Sleeping Beauty. For more, see Smith "Dwarfed."

19. Smith argues that these chapters are fundamentally flawed: "their tone is strident and hectoring. As a lyric poet, Dulce María is here assuming a social voice which does not ring true; the rhetoric is cliché–ridden and unconvincing" ("Dwarfed" 140). Many early reviewers, in contrast, laud this section as an example of trenchant, soaringly poetic, social critique (see Simón). Although I would tend to agree with Smith, I nevertheless read Loynaz's change of tone as strategic.

20. López Lemus observes a similar shift, but reads the detached narration of the final part as omniscient and independent rather than imperialistic and patronizing. For him, the initial narrator is neither feminine nor empathetic, but rather co-opted by Bárbara: "the sick girl takes over the tale so that her perspective and the narrator's become confused" (35). In the final section, the narrator "recovers the thread of the story," resulting in a renewed narrative momentum, but also in greater distance between reader and protagonist (36).

21. The ending has generated considerable debate, although most critics read it as pessimistic and tragic, including recent feminist analyses. Davies, for example, contends that *Garden*'s final message is that "for woman, there is no escape" (81).

22. García Marruz identifies the fisherman, not as A ... but rather as a Christ-figure who conquers the dragon painted on the wall above Bárbara's bed. Smith also identifies him as a "new Adam," although she concludes, "humanity's sins impede the recreation of the Biblical Garden" (" 'Eva sin paraíso' " 266).

23. See Cobb 142.

24. See Cobb 197.

25. Numerous critics have examined how the contexts of the thirties and forties play out in *Delta Wedding*. Devlin summarizes, "the emergence of the new woman, the new Negro and the efficient, modern plantation exists in tense counterpoint with the communal world of Shellmound Plantation" (111). See Patterson for an analysis of gender unrest and Costello for an examination of class and race in the novel.

26. The novel observes that the "throb of the compress had never stopped. Laura could feel it now in the handle of her cup, the noiseless vibration that trembles in the best china, was within it" (17). Of this scene, Yaeger writes, "What is vibrating in this china is not just the cotton compress, ceaselessly at work binding the just-picked cotton into bales, but the ceaseless vibrations of the pickers and the house servants, a vibration that trembles through the silverware and the best linens and every other expensive item in this house" (98).

27. Weston perceives the "dual nature of the family wilderness: like its counterpart, the real forest, it is diverse and yet a single entity; it both isolates and protects, gives privacy and hides the light. Its tangled undergrowths are frightening but, as both the frontiersman and the incarcerated prisoner knew well, the opposite is also dangerous; for, as Foucault remarks, 'visibility is a trap'" (*Gothic Traditions* 99).

28. Griffin archly observes, "Marmion was built ... when the legend of the Old South was at its height. It is to be expected that its builder would be killed in a duel, that his wife would die of a broken heart, and that the children would be raised, pampered and spoiled by two adoring, widowed aunts" (531).

29. The scenes at Marmion illustrate Westling's argument that *Delta Wedding* "rejects the heroic code of southern patriarchy" by creating a feminine realm "in determined opposition to the exclusively masculine rituals of violence expressed on the local scene as coercion of blacks or individual conflicts over cotton or women, and on the public scale as wars" (37).

30. See Smith, "'Eva sin paraíso,'" and López Lemus for different takes on this issue.

Chapter 4

1. Benítez Rojo was born in Cuba in 1939. He published his first collection of short stories in 1967, while working for Castro's government, and was an established writer when he left Cuba in 1980 to settle in the United States, where he taught at Amherst College until his death in 2005. While in the U.S., he continued producing scholarly as well as fictional work, including the novels *El mar de las lentejas* [*Sea of Lentils*] (1979) and *Mujer en traje de batalla* [*Woman in Battle Dress*] (2001). Born in Martinique in 1929, as a young man Edouard Glissant was taught by Amié Césaire, the poet and leader of the Negritude Movement. In 1946, he moved to France to study at the Sorbonne, and since then he has lived in Martinique, France, and the U.S. He has published numerous works of poetry and fiction, as well as influential essay collections, including *Le discours antillais* [*Caribbean Discourse*] (1981) and *Poétique de la relation* [*Poetics of Relation*] (1990). Although Glissant is the only Francophone Caribbean writer included in this study, his longstanding interest in defining, not only a Caribbean, but more broadly a New World or American, poetics makes his inclusion here not only probable but necessary.

2. Deleuze and Guattari develop their theory of the machine in their two-volume work, *Capitalism and Schizophrenia.*

3. See Durán.

4. I have been unable to pinpoint with confidence the point at which these changes were made. However, I do know that the change from "in 'another way'" to "in a 'certain way'" was incorporated into later Spanish editions; and, I would argue, this change makes the text more consistent in its overall usage of the phrase, "in a 'certain way.'" Kutzinski alludes to additional changes made to the English translation between its original publication in 1992 and its later editions (see 174–78).

5. Much debate has surrounded the precise cultural meaning of *métissage*. This is also true of *mestizaje* in Spanish America, and *mestiçagem* in Brazil. For a brief overview of the polemics surrounding these terms, see Rahier. With regards to creolization, Glissant opposes this notion to *creolité*, a movement founded in the 1980s by the Martinican writers Patrick Chamoiseau, Jean Bernabé, and Raphaël Confiant. See *Poetics of Relation* 89 and Tirthankar.

6. The author's commitment to this scientific discourse is reiterated in his epilogue, which carries the title, "Bibliographical Notice Concerning Chaos." Jarrett Bromberg and Ritchie analyze his employment of chaos theory in more detail. Jarrett Bromberg elucidates the particular theories of quantum mechanics from which he draws, while Ritchie critiques, more generally, his use of scientific rhetoric.

7. This passage has provoked considerable critical attention. See de la Campa 543–44, Kutzinski 175, and Torres-Saillant 239.

8. The novel referred to is *L'âge de raison, roman* (1945).

9. Benítez Rojo focuses this portion of his analysis of Guillén on two of his early collections of poetry: *Motivos de son* (1930) and *Sóngoro cosongo* (1931). He argues that the poet's "desire [for mixing] is most clearly seen in his next book, *West Indies, Ltd.* (1934)" (126).

Chapter 5

1. Between 1944 and 1970, Cartagena published seven collections of poems, including *Víspera del sueño* (1944), *Una mujer está sola* (1955), and *La voz desatada* (1962); and edited the journals *La Poesía Sorprendida* and *Brigadas Dominicanas*. After the publication of *Stairway for Electra*, she continued to publish poetry as well prose, including the experimental novel *La tarde en que murió Estefanía* (1983) and the essay collection *Culturas africanas: rebeldes sin causa* (1986).

2. In addition to *Corregidora*, Gayl Jones has published the following novels: *Eva's Man* (1976), *The Healing* (1998), and *Mosquito* (1999). She has also written collections of poetry, including *Xarque & Other Poems* (1985) and the book-length poem, *Song for Anninho* (1981). She has also published a volume of criticism, *Liberating Voices: Oral Tradition in African American Literature* (1991), among other works.

3. Early definitions describe *testimonio* as a first person account characterized by its popular or subaltern nature and political urgency, and a resulting authenticity that gives it value as a truth-telling document (Gugelberger 9). Helene writes as a first-person witness to the traumatic events she documents, stresses the urgency of her task, and incorporates the testimony of marginalized members of her community. However, she is also a self-aware intellectual who distrusts her potential readers, particularly the European publishers who may reject her. These latter elements allow *Stairway for Electra* to be read productively through the lens of the critical debates surrounding *testimonio* that arose in the 1990s (see Gugelberger and Arias).

4. Bell originated the term "neoslave narrative" in 1987 (285, 289). See also Rushdy *Neo-Slave Narratives* and Morgenstern.

5. Although *testimonio* and neoslave narratives flourished in the 1960s and 1970s, a significant body of criticism exploring the complexities involved in the literary production of testimonial language did not develop until the 1980s and 1990s, the same period in which the disciplines of psychology, psychoanalysis, and sociology showed a renewed interest in the "problem of trauma" in an effort to understand survivors of war suffering from post-traumatic stress syndrome (see Caruth *American Imago* 48.1).

6. Handley observes a generalized trend toward "an imagined re-creation of testimonial language to counter the metaphorical reach of traditional narratives that have justified plantocratic authority" (37) and argues that the importance of this turn lies in the metonymical function of testimony. This stands in contrast to the "metaphorical reach of traditional narratives," which erases difference by claiming to speak for all. Handley follows Sommer, who defines metaphor as "a murderous trope that reduces two to one" (*Proceed with Caution* 22).

7. See Fresco and Grubrich-Simitis.

8. This element of the novel makes reference to the burning of many official papers related to slavery, ordered in 1889 by Ruy Barbosa, the Brazilian Minister of Finance. Although this event is well documented, historians have varied in their accounts of its purpose and impact. Barbosa himself, a strong proponent of the abolition of slavery, claimed he did it so as to symbolically erase the corrupting influence of slavery from the national consciousness (Herring 92). But many historians have, like the Corregidora women, read it as "an act of

'willful forgetting'" and a "practice of whitening records" (Winddance Twine, 111). The overall impact of Barbosa's order was limited, as most documents related to slavery in Brazil were not destroyed.

9. For more on the blues in Jones, see Allen, Dixon, Fraile-Marcos, Gottfried, and Claudia Tate "*Corregidora.*"

10. See also Cognard-Black.

11. There are thirty numbered chapters, plus one "chapter without number." It is surely not by chance that Trujillo's dictatorship ended in its thirty-first year.

12. For more on female sexuality in the novel, see Williams.

13. Like her narrator's, Cartagena's sexual life remains cloaked in silence. She never married or had children, and did not discuss her sexual preferences publicly.

14. There are significant political, geographical, and chronological differences between the postdictatorial texts and contexts that Avelar discusses and the Dominican situation out of which Cartagena wrote. Nevertheless, Avelar's emphasis on trauma and mourning, as well as the relationship between economic modernization and the Latin American "boom," makes his analysis useful here.

15. *Stairway for Electra* was a finalist for the prestigious literary prize, the Premio Biblioteca Breve, awarded by the Spanish publishing house Seix Barral, which launched or enhanced the international careers of many Latin American "boom" writers. Cartagena ultimately lost the prize and, years later, expressed continuing ambivalence about this loss and, more generally, her relationship to the European publishing machine. See Rosario Candelier 50.

16. Glissant, of course, is also profoundly interested in island geography and insularity, although this is not his focus in *Faulkner, Mississippi.*

17. See also Rodríguez Guglielmoni 149.

18. The term "national romance" refers to Sommer's assertion, in *Foundational Fictions,* that the "national novels" of Latin America present "an interlocking, not parallel, relationship between erotics and politics" (43). In an interview with Rosario Candelier, Cartagena contrasts the novels of Galván, Cestero, and García Godoy with the late twentieth-century Dominican novel, and praises them for being "more historical, more dramatic" (49). *Stairway for Electra,* too, is deeply concerned with themes of *caudillismo;* however, it avoids the straightforward historicity and dramatic tones that Cartagena claims to appreciate in her predecessors. Although not lacking nationalist sentiment, it also refuses to privilege heterosexual desire in its vision of the nation.

19. In associating Greece with the Dominican Republic, Cartagena participates in a long tradition of comparing the Mediterranean and Caribbean archipelagos. See Lewis 16–20, and Dash, *The Other America,* 82–106.

20. Enriquillo was a cacique (indigenous tribal leader) on the island of Hispaniola who alternately rebelled against and collaborated with European invaders in the sixteenth century. His story was immortalized in Galván's novel, *Enriquillo.* According to Moya Pons, at least some of the leftist guerrilla groups who participated in the Civil War of 1965 were still active in 1970 (391).

21. See also Inoa and José del Castillo.

22. Trujillo "traveled to the frontier at the beginning of October 1937, and there gave a speech announcing that the occupation by Haitians of the frontier territories must not continue. Afterwards, he ordered that all Haitians remaining in the country be exterminated. In the days following October 4, 1937, the army assassinated all Haitians on sight. Eighteen thousand Haitians were killed" (Moya Pons 368).

23. In addition to Dubey, see Athey and Verge. All of these critics emphasize the intellectual context in which Jones wrote, as well as the sustained critique made by many black women writers during and after the 1970s, of both Black Nationalist and white feminist discourse.

24. See Dubey 24–28.

25. Jones's embrace of the blues represents a critical engagement with Black Aesthetics, which proposed guidelines for the creation of transformative art, within which black folklore, especially the blues, constituted an area of ideological ambiguity. See Dubey 83–84.

26. See Coser 203–204 and Hellwig.

27. See Rushdy, *Remembering* 49–54, for an analysis of the role of Palmares in the novel.

28. Robinson similarly notes, "it was the white woman who was responsible for providing children, as heirs, while the black woman functioned almost entirely as a sexual partner whose reproductive capacities would be more of a threat than an asset to her function as prostitute" (152). See also Coser 123 and Rushdy, *Remembering* 47.

29. See Athey 178.

30. See Dubey 72–78 and Athey 176–81. The Moynihan Report was officially entitled, *"The Negro Family: The Case For National Action,"* and published by the United States Department of Labor.

31. See Robinson 135.

32. Mills argues that Jones can be productively understood "as an Afro-Latino/a writer" and traces her development as a trans-American writer from earlier works about Brazil to her 1999 novel, *Mosquito*, which explores the relationship between peoples of color living in the U.S. Southwest and Mexico (92).

Chapter 6

1. See Marcus.

2. As Delgado-Costa observes, Cirlot's *A Dictionary of Symbols* describes sirens as incarnating "both the inferior characteristics of woman, like her corrupt imagination, and also the torment and desire that lead to self-destruction, 'for their abnormal bodies cannot satisfy the passions that are aroused by their enchanting music and by their beauty of face and bosom' (284)" (69).

3. The *OED* indicates that "siren" was "in early use frequently confused with the mermaid." The dictionary of the *Real Academia Española* similarly calls attention to this error in its definition of *sirena.*

4. See Clark 59–60.

5. The English translation, however, adds clarifying phrases to many of these chapters. For example, in the Spanish, chapter 11 begins in the middle of a conversation: " … Es que aquella noche la calle estaba floja" (70). The reader only later learns, due to a single intervention by an anonymous listener, that the speaker's name is Balushka. The translation reworks the first sentence in order, not only to place Balushka's story into a specific context, but also to identify the unnamed interloper: "'That night the street was slow,' Sirena remembered Balushka telling one of her many stories about Valentina" (52). The effect is to foreclose the sensation of dislocation and confusion purposely generated in the original.

6. Sandoval-Sánchez draws attention to the novel's "enthusiastic academic reception" and "instant canonization" inside its country of origin (6–7). Before the publication of *Sirena Selena*, Santos-Febres published well-received collections of poetry and short stories. Since then, she has published two additional novels, *Cualquier miércoles soy tuya* (2002) and *Nuestra Señora de la Noche* (2006), as well as a collection of essays, *Sobre piel y papel* (2005).

7. Butler argues that this critical promise "does not have to do with the proliferation of genders … but rather with the exposure or the failure of heterosexual regimes ever fully to legislate or contain their own ideals" (237). Critics who apply Butler's theories to *Sirena Selena* include Castillo "She Sings," González-Allende, and Morell.

8. Arroyo develops her concept of cultural drag more fully in *Travestismos culturales*.

9. Although it makes references to Cuba, Haiti, and New York, the novel's geographical crossings focus on the relationship between Puerto Rico and the Dominican Republic. Barradas, who interprets *Sirena Selena* as a postmodern allegory of pan-Hispanic Caribbean unity, suggests reasons for Cuba's relative absence in the novel.

10. For more on the inversion of conventional migratory patterns in *Sirena Selena*, see Arroyo "Silena canta boleros." For a broader analysis of migration in the Spanish Caribbean, see Martínez-San Miguel.

11. See Zavala 124.

12. For an analysis of how this tension plays out in the novel, see Cuadra.

13. See Painter and Ravage for historical documentation of the Exodusters.

14. Written history fares little better: in a move that Yukins compares to the destruction of documents about slavery in Brazil, Pat Best burns her subversive genealogy in "an act of historical aggression," and so allows the town's oral traditions to go uncontested (236). For more on Pat Best, see Gauthier and Rob Davidson.

15. The extent to which *Paradise* invokes U.S. nationalist rhetoric is much debated. See, for example, Fraile-Marcos "Hybridizing," Dalsgard, and Jenkins. The latter, in particular, contends that the founding of Ruby should *not* be read as a "neat inversion" of mainstream rhetoric, but rather as a critique of the "authenticity discourse" prevalent in U.S. Black Nationalism (277). Although I would argue that the histories of blacks and whites in the U.S. are impossible to separate so neatly, Jenkins is correct in asserting that Morrison privileges a specifically black experience.

16. The description of Haven's annual Christmas pageant underscores how the town's self-mythology conflates the Old Testament story of the Israelites' exodus with the New Testament story of Mary and Joseph being refused lodging in Bethlehem. Bouson, Jessee, Romero, Stave, and Terry provide a variety of perspectives on the role of Christianity and other religious or theological discourses in the novel.

17. The phrase "nomadic circulation" alludes to Braidotti's concept of "nomadic subjects," which resonates with Glissant's notion of errantry, although it also differs from it, most obviously in its focus on Europe and its overtly feminist application. Like Glissant, Braidotti draws from Delueze and Guattari's notion of the rhizome (Deleuze and Guattari), which, she argues, "stands for a nomadic political ontology that ... provides movable foundations for a post-humanist view of subjectivity" (23). It should be noted, however, that Glissant frequently underscores the futility of certain kinds of nomadic movement, and the goal of conquest implicit in others.

18. I am not the first to note that Santos-Febres attempts to move beyond this oppositional discourse, which dominates much of the literature produced in Puerto Rico during the 1970s. See also De Maeseneer and Díaz.

19. Because of its association with marginalized and oppressed groups, and its posture of self-defense, *guachafita* may be associated with *el arte de bregar* and *jaibería*. On the former, see Quiñones; on the latter, see Grosfoguel et al 30–31. Reyes additionally links *guachafita* "to [the Mexican notion of] *relajo* and [Bakhtin's concept of] the carnivalesque" (54).

20. The dictionary of the *Real Academia Española* defines *mongo* as *débil*, or weak. The word also calls to mind the term *salsa monga*, a derisive nickname that opposes a sentimental form of salsa to classic salsa, in turn heralded as *salsa gorda* or *salsa dura*. The sexual connotations of these terms—limp or flaccid salsa versus fat or hard salsa—can be extended to Santos-Febres' anti-phallocentric concept of *guachafita monga*.

21. Arroyo observes that most critics have ignored the Dominican context of the novel, which she attributes to the social malaise caused in Puerto Rico by the growing presence of Dominican migrants, which marks "a 'dangerous' frontier through which the Puerto Rican is

drawn closer ... to the Afro-Antillean and Caribbean parts of his or her own identity" ("Sirena canta boleros" 41). That this frontier is "dangerous" because of the racial and cultural *similarities* it uncovers (particularly, that both islands share an African inheritance that Puerto Rican discourse has repressed) is especially ironic given that a discourse of cultural and racial whiteness has long prevailed in the Dominican Republic as well (see chapter 5). While Arroyo refers to Puerto Rican critics of the novel, it is interesting to note that several reviews of the novel's English translation simply collapse Puerto Rico and the Dominican Republic together by conflating the characters of Sirena and Leocadio into a single person. See Mujica and Nyren.

22. Martha's role is both vital and ambiguous. For Delgado-Costa, she is a "female vampire, the great tyrant" (73). In contrast, Castillo argues that she serves as the novel's "anchoring vision" ("She Sings" 23).

23. See Arroyo 47, Van Haesendonck 87, and Barradas 59.

24. Chapter 35 (34 in the English translation) comprises a monologue, spoken by a Canadian tourist in English (no Spanish translation is provided in the original version of the novel), which provides a candid perspective on sex tourism in the Caribbean. The speaker argues of the young boys he seeks out, "Most really need the money, and I'm happy to oblige. It must be so tough to be gay in this country" (152 in the English translation). The commodification of young male flesh functions as one of several intriguing points of contact between the unidentified Canadian and Martha, who recognizes in Leocadio a potential for profit: "He has something, that boy. Just like what Sirena had" (211). The former pays for it while the latter sells it, but both recognize it as source for pleasure and profit.

25. The English version of the novel fails to translate the nuanced meaning of *clavar*, opting instead for broadly worded phrases like "nobody is going to touch you ever again" (67), which capture neither the sexual aggression implicit in the Spanish phrase nor its warning against being "nailed down" or immobilized by intimacy.

26. Although most critics read this scene as transgressive, some have argued that, despite upsetting the dichotomy feminine-as-penetrated versus masculine-as-penetrator, the novel ultimately reinforces the power of the phallus, and therefore the heteronormative model. See González-Allende and Morell.

27. See also Krumholz's excellent reading of the novel.

28. Sweeney, Fraile-Marcos "Hybridizing" and Stave all identify Connie as a Christ figure, although Stave asserts "the redemption she offers differs radically from that of her New Testament counterpart" (222). Page argues that all the Convent women are Christ figures "who must die so that others may soar" (646).

29. Stave identifies this supper as a First Supper, "a beginning of a life in the body that for these women does not end with the massacre" (224).

30. See Terry and Bouson for specific parallels between the practices of Candomblé and the rituals that Consolata performs.

Conclusion

1. Although his novel was inspired by the historical fact of free blacks owning slaves in the U.S. South, Jones has stated in numerous interviews that not only Manchester County but all of the historical records cited in the novel are of his own invention.

2. In "Area Studies Beyond Ontology," McClennen likewise questions the unconditional usefulness of deterritorialized models of identity, arguing "that dominant power has historically depended on an interplay between strategic territorializations and deterritorializations" and asserting that "it is not the use of space that holds political potential" but the reasons for which particular groups or individuals "use space in particular ways" (181).

3. Like Casteel, DeLoughrey *Routes and Roots* and Martínez-San Miguel offer useful reconsiderations of space and place. Although both embrace models that privilege fluid movement, they emphasize the provisional nature of land and seascapes. As the main title of her book, *Caribe Two Ways*, suggests, Martínez-San Miguel emphasizes a multi-directional circulation of people, ideas, and culture through the Spanish Caribbean world. DeLoughrey focuses on both Caribbean and Pacific Island literatures, and examines the ways in which ocean insularity can be reinscribed as "'tidalectics,' a methodological tool that foregrounds how a dynamic model of geography can elucidate island history and cultural production" (2).

WORKS CITED

Abel, Elizabeth, Marianne Hirsch, and Elizabeth Langland, ed. *The Voyage In: Fictions of Female Development.* Hanover: University Press of New England, 1983.

Abrahams, Peter. *Mine Boy.* New York: Collier Books, 1946.

———. *Rouge est le sang des Noirs. (Mine Boy.)* Trans. Denise Shaw-Mantoux. Tournai: Casterman, 1960.

Adams, Jessica. *Wounds of Returning: Race, Memory, and Property on the Postslavery Plantation.* Chapel Hill: University of North Carolina Press, 2007.

Adams, Jessica, Michael Bibler, and Cécile Accilien. *Just Below South: Intercultural Performance in the Caribbean and the U.S. South.* Charlottesville: University of Virginia Press, 2007.

Aizenberg, Edna. "El *Bildungsroman* fracasado en Latinoamérica: el caso de *Ifigenia* de Teresa de la Parra." *Revista Iberoamericana* 51.131–2 (1985): 539–46.

Allen, Donia Elizabeth. "The Role of the Blues in Gayl Jones's *Corregidora.*" *Callaloo* 25.1 (2002): 257–73.

Ammon, Elizabeth. *Conflicting Stories: American Women Writers at the Turn into the Twentieth Century.* New York: Oxford University Press, 1991.

Aparicio, Frances R. *Listening to Salsa: Gender, Latin Popular Music, and Puerto Rican Cultures.* Hanover: University Press of New England, 1998.

———. "Performing the Caribbean in American Studies." *American Quarterly* 50.3 (1998): 636–44.

Arias, Arturo, ed. *The Rigoberta Menchú Controversy.* Minneapolis: University of Minnesota Press, 2001.

Arroyo, Jossianna. "Sirena canta boleros: travestismo y sujetos transcaribeños en *Sirena Selena vestida de pena.*" *CENTRO Journal* 15.2 (2003): 39–51.

———. *Travestismos culturales: literatura y etnografía en Cuba y Brasil.* Pittsburgh: Editorial Iberoamericana, 2003.

Athey, Stephanie. "Poisonous Roots and New World Blues: Rereading Seventies Narration and Nation in Alex Haley and Gayl Jones." *Narrative* 7.2 (1999): 169–93.

Avelar, Idelber. *The Untimely Present: Postdictatorial Latin American Fiction and the Task of Mourning.* Durham, NC: Duke University Press, 1999.

Bachelard, Gaston. *The Poetics of Space. (Poétique de l'espace.)* Trans. Maria Jolas. Boston: Beacon, 1964.

Barnet, Miguel. *Biografía de un cimarrón.* Havana: Instituto de Etnología y Folklore, 1966.

——. *Biography of a Runaway Slave. (Biografía de un cimarrón.)* Trans. W. Nick Hill. Willimantic: Curbstone Press, 1995.

Barradas, Efraín. *"Sirena Selena vestida de pena* o el Caribe como travestí." *CENTRO Journal* 15.2 (2003): 53–65.

Beckford, George L. *Persistent Poverty: Underdevelopment in Plantation Economies of the Third World.* Kingston: University of the West Indies Press, 1999.

Bell, Bernard W. *The Afro-American Novel and Its Tradition.* Amherst: University of Massachusetts Press, 1987.

Benítez Rojo, Antonio. *El mar de las lentejas.* Havana: Editorial Letras Cubanas, 1979.

——. *Sea of Lentils. (El mar de las lentejas.)* Trans. James Maraniss. Amherst: University of Massachusetts Press, 1991.

——. *La isla que se repite: El Caribe y la perspectiva posmoderna.* Hanover: Ediciones del Norte, 1989.

——. *The Repeating Island: the Caribbean and the Postmodern Perspective. (La isla que se repite: El Caribe y la perspectiva posmoderna.)* Trans. James E. Maraniss. Durham, NC: Duke University Press, 1992.

——. *Mujer en traje de batalla.* Madrid: Santillana, 2001.

Bérubé, Michael. "American Studies without Exceptions." *PMLA* 118.1 (January 2003): 103–13.

Best, Lloyd. "Outlines of a Model of Pure Plantation Economy." *Social and Economic Studies* 17.3 (1968): 283–26.

Bingham, Emily S. and Thomas A. Underwood. Introduction. In *The Southern Agrarians and the New Deal: Essays after I'll Take My Stand.* Ed. Emily S. Bingham and Thomas A. Underwood. Charlottesville: University Press of Virginia, 2001. 1–33.

Bombal, María Luisa. *La última niebla.* Buenos Aires: Sur, 1935.

——. *The House of Mist. (La última niebla.)* Trans. María Luisa Bombal. New York: Farrar, Strauss and Giroux, 1947.

Bone, Martyn. "Were Farms Necessary?: The Agrarian Question." *Mississippi Quarterly* 56.3 (2003): 421–37.

Bost, Suzanne. *Mulattas and Mestizas: Representing Mixed Identities in the Americas, 1850–2000.* Athens: University of Georgia Press, 2003.

Bouson, J. Brooks. *Quiet as it's Kept: Shame, Trauma, and Race in the Novels of Toni Morrison.* Albany: State University of New York Press, 2000.

Braidotti, Rosi. *Nomadic Subjects: Embodiment and Sexual Difference in Contemporary Feminist Theory.* New York: Columbia University Press, 1994.

Brathwaite, Edward Kamau. "Caribbean Man in Space and Time." *Savacou* 11–12 (1975): 1–11.

Bunting, Charles T. "The Interior World: an Interview with Eudora Welty." In *Conversations with Eudora Welty.* Ed. Peggy Prenshaw. Jackson: University Press of Mississippi, 1984. 40–73.

Butler, Judith. *Bodies that Matter.* New York: Routledge, 1993.

Cabrera, Lydia. *El Monte.* Havana: Letras Cubanas, 1993.

Caldwell, Ellen M. "Ellen Glasgow and the Southern Agrarians." *American Literature* 56.2 (1984): 203–13.

Carby, Hazel. "It Jus Be's Dat Way Sometime: The Sexual Politics of Women's Blues." In *Gender and Discourse: The Power of Talk.* Ed. Alexandra Dundas Todd and Sue Fisher. Norwood: ABLEX, 1988. 227–42.

Carpentier, Alejo. *Viaje a la semilla.* Havana: Ucar, García y Cía, 1944.

———. "Journey Back to the Source." (*Viaje a la semilla.*) In *War of Time.* Trans. Frances Partridge. New York: Knopf, 1970. 105–31.

———. *Los pasos perdidos.* Mexico City: Edición y Distribución Ibero Americana de Publicaciones, 1953.

———. *The Lost Steps.* (*Los pasos perdidos.*) Trans. Harriet de Onís. New York: Knopf, 1956.

Cartagena Portalatín, Aída. *Víspera del sueño: Poemas para un atardecer.* Ciudad Trujillo: La Poesía Sorprendida, 1944.

———. *Una mujer está sola.* Ciudad Trujillo: La Isla Necesaria, 1955.

———. *La voz desatada.* Santo Domingo: Brigadas Dominicanas, 1962.

———. *Escalera para Electra.* Santo Domingo: Brigadas Universitarias, 1970.

———. *La tarde en que murió Estefanía.* Santo Domingo: Taller, 1983.

———. *Culturas africanas: Rebeldes con causa.* Santo Domingo: Ediciones de la Biblioteca Nacional, 1986.

Caruth, Cathy. Introduction. *American Imago* 48.1 (1991): 1–12.

———. Introduction. *American Imago* 48.4 (1991): 417–24.

Casteel, Sarah Phillips. *Second Arrivals: Landscape and Belonging in Contemporary Writing of the Americas.* Charlottesville: University of Virginia Press, 2007.

Castillo, Debra A. *Talking Back: Toward a Latin American Feminist Literary Criticism.* Ithaca, NY: Cornell University Press, 1992.

———. "She Sings Boleros: Santos-Febres' *Sirena Selena.*" *Latin American Literary Review* 29.57 (2001): 13–25.

Castillo, José del. "La inmigración de braceros azucareros en la República Dominicana, 1900–1930." *Cuadernos del CENDIA* 262.7, 1978.

Celebration Tours, LLC. Advertisement. http://www.celebrationtoursllc.com/plantationtour.htm (accessed 15 Nov. 2006).

Cepero Bonilla, Raúl. *Azúcar y abolición: apuntes para una historia crítica del abolicionismo.* Havana: Editorial Cenit, 1948.

Cestero, Tulio M. *La sangre.* Paris: Ollendorf, 1914.

Chevigny, Bell Gale. Introduction. In *Reinventing the Americas: Comparative Studies of Literature of the United States and Spanish America.* Ed. Bell Gale Chevigny and Gari Laguardia. Cambridge: Cambridge University Press, 1986. 137–57.

Chopin, Kate. *The Awakening.* 1899; repr. Mineola: Dover Publications, 1993.

Cirlot, J. E. *A Dictionary of Symbols.* New York: Philosophical Library, 1962.

Clark, Mary Ann. *Santería: Correcting the Myths and Uncovering the Realities of a Growing Religion.* Westport: Praeger, 2007.

Cobb, James C. *The Most Southern Place on Earth: The Mississippi Delta and the Roots of Regional Identity.* New York: Oxford University Press, 1992.

Coffey, David W. "Ellen Glasgow's *In This Our Life:* The Novel and the Film." In *Regarding Ellen Glasgow: Essays for Contemporary Readers.* Ed. Welford Dunaway Taylor and George C. Longest. Richmond: Library of Virginia, 2001. 117–26.

Cognard-Black, Jennifer. " 'I Said Nothing': The Rhetoric of Silence and Gayl Jones's *Corregidora.*" *NWSA Journal* 13.1 (2001): 40–60.

Cohn, Deborah N. *History and Memory in the Two Souths: Recent Southern and Spanish American Fiction.* Nashville, TN: Vanderbilt University Press, 1999.

Colás, Santiago. "Of Creole Symptoms, Cuban Fantasies, and Other Latin American Postcolonial Ideologies." *PMLA* 110.3 (May 1995): 382–96.

———. " 'There's No Place Like Home'; or, the Utopian, Uncanny Caribbean State of Mind of Antonio Benítez Rojo." *Siglo XX* 31.2 (1995): 207–17.

Collins, Janelle. " 'Intimate History': Storyteller and Audience in Gayl Jones's *Corregidora.*" *CLA Journal* 47.1 (2003): 1–31.

Conkin, Paul. *The Southern Agrarians.* Knoxville: University of Tennessee Press, 1988.

Coronil, Fernando. "Introduction to the Duke University Press Edition." In *Cuban Counterpoint: Tobacco and Sugar.* By Fernando Ortiz. Durham, NC: Duke University Press, 1995. ix–lvi.

Coser, Stelamaris. *Bridging the Americas: the Literature of Paule Marshall, Toni Morrison, and Gayl Jones.* Philadelphia: Temple University Press, 1995.

Costello, Brannon. "Playing Lady and Imitating Aristocrats: Race, Class, and Money in *Delta Wedding* and *The Ponder Heart.*" *Southern Quarterly* 42.3 (2004): 21–54.

Cruz Malavé, Arnaldo. "Toward an Art of Transvestism: Colonialism and Homosexuality in Puerto Rican Literature." In *¿Entiendes? Queer Readings, Hispanic Writings.* Ed. Emilie L. Bergmann. Durham, NC: Duke University Press, 1995.

Cuadra, Ivonne. "¿Quién canta? Bolero y ambigüedad genérica en *Sirena Selena vestida de pena* de Mayra Santos-Febres." *Revista de Estudios Hispánicos, U.P.R.* 30.1 (2003): 153–63.

Dalsgard, Katrine. "The One All-Black Town Worth the Pain: (African) American Exceptionalism, Historical Narration, and the Critique of Nationhood in Toni Morrison's *Paradise.*" *African American Review* 35.2 (2001): 233–48.

Dash, J. Michael. *The Other America: Caribbean Literature in a New World Context.* Charlottesville: University Press of Virginia, 1998.

———. "Martinique/Mississippi: Edouard Glissant and Relational Insularity." In *Look Away!: The U.S. South in New World Studies.* Ed. Jon Smith and Deborah Cohn. Durham, NC: Duke University Press, 2004. 94–109.

Davidson, Donald. "A Mirror for Artists." In *I'll Take My Stand: the South and the Agrarian Tradition.* By Twelve Southerners. New York: Harper, 1930; repr. Baton Rouge: Louisiana State University Press, 1977. 28–60.

Davidson, Rob. "Racial Stock and 8-Rocks: Communal Historiography in Toni Morrison's *Paradise.*" *Twentieth-Century Literature* 47.3 (2001): 355–73.

Davies, Catherine. *A Place in the Sun: Women Writers in Twentieth-Century Cuba.* London: Zed, 1997.

Davis, Angela. *Women, Race and Class.* New York: Vintage, 1981.

de Jongh, Elena M. "Intertextuality and the Quest for Identity in Dulce María Loynaz's *Jardín.*" *Hispania* 77.3 (2004): 416–26.

de la Campa, Román. *Latin Americanism.* Minneapolis: University of Minnesota Press, 1999.

———. "Latin, Latino, American: Split States and Global Imaginaries." *Comparative Literature* 53.4 (Fall 2001): 373–88.

———. "Mimicry and the Uncanny in Caribbean Discourse." In *The Latin American Cultural Studies Reader.* Ed. Ana Del Sarto, Alicia Ríos, and Abril Trigo. Durham, NC: Duke University Press, 2004. 535–60.

DeLoughrey, Elizabeth M. *Routes and Roots: Navigating Caribbean and Pacific Island Literatures.* Honolulu: University of Hawai'i Press, 2007.

DeLoughrey, Elizabeth M., Renée K. Gosson, and George B. Handley. Introduction. In *Caribbean Literature and the Environment: Between Nature and Culture.* Ed. Elizabeth M. DeLoughrey, Renée K. Gosson, and George B. Handley. Charlottesville: University of Virginia Press, 2005. 1–30.

De Maeseneer, Rita. "Los caminos torcidos en *Sirena Selena vestida de pena* de Mayra Santos-Febres." *Revista de Estudios Hispánicos* 38.3 (2004): 533–53.

Degler, Carl. *Neither Black nor White: Slavery and Race Relations in Brazil and the United States.* New York: Macmillan, 1971.

Deleuze, Gilles, and Félix Guattari. *Anti-Oedipus: Capitalism and Schizophrenia.* (*L'anti-Oedipe: Capitalisme et schizophrénie.*) Trans. Robert Hurley. New York: Penguin Classics, 2009.

———. *A Thousand Plateaus: Capitalism and Schizophrenia.* (*Mille Plateaux: Capitalisme et schizophrénie.*) Trans. Brian Massumi. Minneapolis: University of Minnesota Press, 1987.

Delgado-Costa, José. "Fredi Veláscues le mete mano a *Sirena Selena vestida de pena.*" *CENTRO Journal* 15.2 (2003): 67–77.

Denard, Carolyn. "Blacks, Modernism, and the American South: an Interview with Toni Morrison." *Studies in the Literary Imagination* 31.2 (1998): 1–16.

Devlin, Albert J. *Eudora Welty's Chronicle.* Jackson: University Press of Mississippi, 1983.

Díaz, Luis Felipe. "La narrativa de Mayra Santos y el travestismo cultural." *CENTRO Journal* 15.2 (2003): 25–36.

Dixon, Melvin. "Singing a Deep Song: Language as Evidence in the Novels of Gayl Jones." In *Black Women Writers (1950–1980): A Critical Evaluation.* Ed. Mari Evans. New York: Anchor, 1984. 236–48.

Donahue, Deirdre. "Morrison's slice of 'Paradise': Nobel laureate's personal exploration of pain and peace." *USA Today*, Jan 8, 1998. http://pqasb.pqarchiver.com/USAToday (accessed July 21, 2007).

Dubey, Madhu. *Black Women Novelists and the Nationalist Aesthetic.* Bloomington: Indiana University Press, 1994.

Durán, Michelle. "Antonio Benítez Rojo: Un caribeño irrepetible." In *Voces de América: entrevistas a escritores americanos.* Ed. Laura P. Alonso Gallo. Cadiz: Editorial Aduana Vieja, 2004. 99–121.

Duvergier de Hauranne, Ernest. "Cuba et les Antilles." *Revue de Deux Mondes* 65 (Sept.–Oct. 1866): 140–175, 619–54, 852–92.

Erikson, Kai. "Notes on Trauma and Community." *American Imago* 48.4 (1991): 455–72.

Fain, John Tyree and Daniel Young. "The Agrarian Symposium: Letters of Allen Tate and Donald Davidson, 1928–1930." *Southern Review* 8 (1972): 845–82.

Felman, Shoshana and Dori Laub. *Testimony: Crisis of Witnessing in Literature, Psychoanalysis, and History.* New York: Routledge, 1992.

Ferré, Rosario. *Papeles de Pandora.* Mexico City: Joaquín Mortiz, 1976.

———. *The Youngest Doll.* (*Papeles de Pandora.*) Trans. Rosario Ferré. Lincoln: University of Nebraska Press, 1991.

Figueroa, Ramón. "Nacionalismo y universalismo en *Escalera para Electra.*" *Areito* 10.38 (1984): 41–43.

Fitz, Earl. "In Quest of 'Nuestras Américas.'" *Ameriquests* 1.1 (2004), http://ejournals.library.vanderbilt.edu/ameriquests/viewarticle.php?id=14 (accessed Oct. 17, 2007).

———. "Inter-American Studies as an Emerging Field: The Future of a Discipline." *Vanderbilt e-journal of Luso-Hispanic Studies* 1 (2004), http://ejournals.library.vanderbilt.edu/lusohispanic/viewissue.php?id=1 (accessed Oct. 17, 2007).

Fox, Claire F. and Claudia Sadowski-Smith. "Theorizing the Hemisphere: Inter-Americas Work at the Intersection of American, Canadian, and Latin American Studies." *Comparative American Studies* 2.1 (2004): 5–38.

Fraile-Marcos, Ana María. "Lady Sings the Blues: Gayl Jones' *Corregidora.*" In *Literature and Music.* Ed. Michael J. Meyer. Amsterdam: Rodopi, 2002. 203–27.

———. "Hybridizing the 'City upon a Hill' in Toni Morrison's *Paradise.*" *MELUS* 28.4 (2003): 3–33.

Fraiman, Susan. *Unbecoming Women: British Women Writers and the Novel of Development.* New York: Columbia University Press, 1993.

Franco, Jean. *Plotting Women.* New York: Columbia University Press, 1989.

Freedman, Ralph. *The Lyrical Novel.* Princeton, NJ: Princeton University Press, 1963.

Fresco, Nadine. "Remembering the Unknown." *International Review of Psychoanalysis* 11 (1984): 417–27.

Freyre, Gilberto. *Casa-grande & senzala: formação da família brasleira sob o regime da economia patriarcal.* Rio de Janeiro: Maia & Schmidt, 1933.

———. *The Masters and the Slaves.* New York: Knopf, 1946.

Friedman, Susan Stanford. "Lyric Subversion of Narrative in Women's Writing: Virginia Woolf and the Tyranny of the Plot." In *Reading Narrative: Form, Ethics, Ideology.* Ed. James Phelan. Columbus: Ohio State University Press, 1989. 163–85.

Gallegos, Rómulo. *Doña Bárbara.* Barcelona: Editorial Araluce, 1929.

———. *Doña Bárbara.* Trans. Robert Malloy. New York: Peter Smith, 1948.

Galván, Manuel de Jesús. *Enriquillo, leyenda histórica dominicana (1503–1533).* Santo Domingo: García Hermanos, 1882.

———. *The Cross and the Sword. (Enriquillo.)* Trans. Robert Graves. Bloomington: Indiana University Press, 1954.

García Godoy, Federico. *Rufinito: sucedido histórico.* Santo Domingo: La Cuna de América, 1908.

———. *Alma dominicana: novela histórica.* Santo Domingo: La Cuna de América, 1911.

———. *Guanuma: novela histórica.* Santo Domingo: La Cuna de América, 1914.

García Marruz, Fina. "*Jardín:* una novela inatendida." In *Dulce María Loynaz.* Ed. Pedro Simón. Havana: Ediciones Casa de las Américas y Editorial Letras Cubanas, 1991. 548–94.

Gardner, Sarah E. "The Plantation School: Dissenters and Countermyths." In *A Companion to the Regional Literatures of America.* Ed. Charles L. Crow. Malden: Blackwell, 2003. 266–85.

Garrels, Elizabeth. *Las grietas de la ternura: nueva lectura de Teresa de la Parra.* Caracas: Monte Avila Editores, 1986.

Gauthier, Marni. "The Other Side of *Paradise:* Toni Morrison's (Un)Making of Mythic History." *African American Review* 39.3 (2005): 395–414.

Gelpí, Juan. *Literatura y paternalismo en Puerto Rico.* San Juan: Editorial de la Universidad de Puerto Rico, 1993.

Genovese, Eugene. *The World the Slaveholders Made.* New York: Pantheon, 1969.

Glasgow, Ellen. *Barren Ground.* Garden City: Doubleday, Page, 1925.

———. *The Sheltered Life.* Garden City, NY: Doubleday, Doran, 1932; repr., Charlottesville: University Press of Virginia, 1994.

———. *Ellen Glasgow's Reasonable Doubts: A Collection of Her Writings.* Ed. Julius Rowan Raper. Baton Rouge: Louisiana State University Press, 1988.

Glissant, Edouard. *Le discours antillais.* 1981; repr. Paris: Gallimard, 1997.

———. *Caribbean Discourse: Selected Essays. (Le discours antillais.)* Trans. J. Michael Dash. Charlottesville: University Press of Virginia, 1989.

———. *Poétique de la Relation.* Paris: Gallimard, 1990.

———. *Poetics of Relation (Poétique de la Relation.)* Trans. Betsy Wing. Ann Arbor: University of Michigan Press, 1997.

———. *Faulkner, Mississippi.* Paris: Stock, 1996.

———. *Faulkner, Mississippi.* Trans. Barbara Lewis and Thomas C. Spear. New York: Farrar, Straus and Giroux, 1999.

Goldstein, Laurence. "Our Faulkner, Ourselves." *Michigan Quarterly* 42.4 (2003): 724–37.

Gomes, Miguel. "*Ifigenia* de Teresa de la Parra: Dictadura, poéticas y parodias. *Acta Literaria* 29 (2004): 47–67.

González Echevarría, Roberto. "The Counterpoint and Literature." In *Cuban Counterpoints: The Legacy of Fernando Ortiz.* Ed. Mauricio A. Font and Alfonso W. Quiroz. Lanham and New York: Lexington Books, 2005. 209–16.

González-Allende, Iker. "De la pasividad al poder sexual y económico: el sujeto activo en *Sirena Selena.*" *Chasqui* 34.1 (2005): 51–65.

Goodman, Susan. *Ellen Glasgow: A Biography.* Baltimore: Johns Hopkins University Press, 1998.

———. "Memory and Memoria in *The Sheltered Life.*" *Mississippi Quarterly* 49.2 (1996): 243–54.

Gott, Richard. *Cuba: A New History.* New Haven, CT: Yale University Press, 2004.

Gottfried, Amy S. "Angry Arts: Silence, Speech, and Song in Gayl Jones's *Corregidora.*" *African American Review* 28.4 (1994): 559–70.

Grammer, John M. "Plantation Fiction." In *A Companion to the Literature and Culture of the American South.* Ed. Richard Gray and Owen Robinson. Malden: Blackwell, 2004. 58–75.

Gray, Paul. "Paradise found." *Time,* January 19, 1998, http://www.time.com/time/magazine/article/0,9171,987690,00.html (accessed July 16, 2007).

Gray Line New Orleans. Advertisement. http://www.graylineneworleans.com/plantation.shtml (accessed Nov. 15, 2006).

Gray White, Deborah. *Ar'n't I a Woman? Female Slaves in the Plantation South.* New York: Norton, 1985.

Greene, Roland. "Wanted: A New World Studies." *American Literary History* 12.1 (2000): 337–47.

Griffin, Dorothy. "The House as Container: Architecture and Myth in Eudora Welty's *Delta Wedding.*" *Mississippi Quarterly* 39.4 (1986): 521–35.

Grosfoguel, Ramón, Chloé S. Georas, and Frances Negrón-Muntaner. "Beyond Nationalist and Colonialist Discourses: The *Jaiba* Politics of the Puerto Rican Ethno-Nation." In *Puerto Rican Jam: Essays on Culture and Politics.* Ed. Francés Negrón-Muntaner and Ramón Grosfoguel. Minneapolis: University of Minnesota Press, 1997. 1–36.

Grubrich-Simitis, Ilse. "From Concretism to Metaphor: Thoughts on Some Theoretical and Technical Aspects of the Psychoanalytic Work with Children of Holocaust Survivors." *The Psycho-analytic Study of the Child* 39 (1984): 301–19.

Guerra y Sánchez, Ramiro. *Azúcar y población en las Antillas.* Havana: Cultural S.A., 1927.

Gugelberger, Georg M., ed. *The Real Thing: Testimonial Discourse and Latin America.* Durham, NC: Duke University Press, 1996.

Guillén, Nicolás. *Motivos de son.* Havana: Rambla & Bouza, 1930.

———. *Sóngoro cosongo: poemas mulatos.* Ucar, García y Cía, 1931.

———. *West Indies, Ltd.* Havana: Ucar, García y Cía, 1934.

Güiraldes, Ricardo. *Don Segundo Sombra.* Buenos Aires: Proa, 1926.

———. *Don Segundo Sombra.* Trans. Patricia Owen Steiner. Pittsburgh: University of Pittsburgh Press, 1995.

Gullón, Ricardo. *La novela lírica.* Madrid: Cátedra, 1984.

Handley, George. *Postslavery Literatures in the Americas: Family Portraits in Black and White.* Charlottesville: University Press of Virginia, 2000.

————. "A New World Poetics of Oblivion." In *Look Away!: The U.S. South in New World Studies*. Ed. Jon Smith and Deborah Cohn. Durham, NC: Duke University Press, 2004. 24–51.

Harper, Michael S. "Gayl Jones: an Interview." In *Chant of Saints: A Gathering of Afro-American Literature, Art, and Scholarship*. Ed. Michael S. Harper and Robert B. Stepto. Urbana: University of Illinois Press, 1979. 352–75.

Hellwig, David J., ed. *African-American Reflections on Brazil's Racial Paradise*. Philadelphia: Temple University Press, 1992.

Herrero, Rafael. *The Colonial Slave Plantation as a Form of Hacienda: A Preliminary Outline of the Case of Venezuela*. Glasgow: Institute of Latin American Studies, University of Glasgow, 1978.

Herring, Hubert Clinton. *A History of Latin America from the Beginnings to the Present*. New York: Knopf, 1961.

Inoa, Orlando. *Azúcar, árabes, cocolos y haitianos*. Santo Domingo: Editora Colé, 1999.

Isfahani-Hammond, Alexandra. "Writing Brazilian Culture." In *The Masters and the Slaves: Plantation Relations and Mestizaje in American Imaginaries*. Ed. Alexandra Isfahani-Hammond. New York: Palgrave Macmillan, 2005. 34–49.

Jarrett Bromberg, Shelly. "The New Story of the Caribbean: Quantum Mechanics and Postmodern Theory in Antonio Benítez Rojo's *La isla que se repite: El Caribe y la perspectiva posmoderna*." *Ometeca* 3–4 (1996): 142–53.

Jenkins, Candice M. "Pure Black: Class, Color, and Intraracial Politics in Toni Morrison's *Paradise*." *Modern Fiction Studies* 52.2 (2006): 270–96.

Jessee, Sharon. "The 'Female Revealer' in *Beloved, Jazz* and *Paradise*: Syncretic Spirituality in Toni Morrison's Trilogy." In *Toni Morrison and the Bible: Contested Intertextualities*. Ed. Shirley A. Stave. New York: Peter Lang, 2006. 129–58.

Jones, Anne Goodwyn. *Tomorrow Is Another Day: The Woman Writer in the South, 1859–1936*. Baton Rouge: Louisiana State University Press, 1981.

Jones, Edward P. *The Known World*. New York: HarperCollins, 2003.

Jones, Gayl. *Corregidora*. Boston: Beacon, 1975.

————. *Eva's Man*. New York: Random House, 1976.

————. *Song for Anninho*. Detroit: Lotus, 1981.

————. *Xarque and Other Poems*. Detroit: Lotus, 1985.

————. *Liberating Voices: Oral Tradition in African American Literature*. Cambridge: Harvard University Press, 1991.

————. *The Healing*. Boston: Beacon, 1998.

————. *Mosquito*. Boston: Beacon, 1999.

Kadir, Djelal. "Introduction: America and its Studies." *PMLA* 118.1 (January 2003): 9–24.

Keith, Robert G. "Encomienda, Hacienda and Corregimiento in Spanish America: A Structural Analysis." *The Hispanic American Historical Review* 51.3 (1971): 431–46.

————, ed. *Haciendas and Plantations in Latin American History*. New York: Holmes & Meier, 1977.

Kennedy, John Pendleton. *Swallow Barn, or A Sojourn in the Old Dominion*. Philadelphia: Carey & Lea, 1832; repr. Baton Rouge: Louisiana State University Press, 1986.

Klein, Herbert S. *Slavery in the Americas: A Comparative Study of Virginia and Cuba*. Chicago: University of Chicago Press, 1967.

Komunyakaa, Yusef. "Crossroads (Introduction)." *Ploughshares* 23.1 (1997), http://www.pshares.org/issues/article.cfm?prmArticleID=4190 (accessed June 30, 2008).

Kreyling, Michael. *Inventing Southern Literature*. Jackson: University Press of Mississippi, 1998.

Kristeva, Julia. "Women's Time." In *Women, Knowledge, and Reality: Explorations in Feminist Philosophy*. Ed. Ann Garry and Marilyn Pearsall. New York: Routledge, 1996. 61–83.

Krumholz, Linda J. "Reading and Insight in Toni Morrison's *Paradise*." *African American Review* 36.1 (2002): 21–34.

Kutzinski, Vera. *Sugar's Secrets: Race and the Erotics of Cuban Nationalism*. Charlottesville: University Press of Virginia, 1993.

Ladd, Barbara. "'Coming Through': The Black Initiate in *Delta Wedding*." *Mississippi Quarterly* 41.4 (1988): 441–51.

Lerner, Elisa. "La desazón política en Teresa de la Parra." *Venezuela Analítica*, http://www.analitica.com/bitblioteca/elerner/teresa.asp (accessed Nov. 7, 2006).

Levander, Caroline F. and Robert S. Levine, ed. *Hemispheric American Studies*. New Brunswick, NJ: Rutgers University Press, 2008.

Levy, Helen. "Clothes Make the Mannequin: Covering Up the Female Body in *The Sheltered Life*." *Mississippi Quarterly* 49.2 (1996): 255–67.

Lewis, Gordon K. *Main Currents in Caribbean Thought: The Historical Evolution of Caribbean Society in its Ideological Aspects, 1492–1900*. London: Heinemann, 1983.

Limón, José E. *American Encounters: Greater Mexico, the United States and the Erotics of Culture*. Boston: Beacon, 1998.

Loichot, Valérie. "Glissant, Yoknapatawpha." *Mississippi Quarterly* 57.1 (2003–2004): 99–111.

———. *Orphan Narratives: The Postplantation Literature of Faulkner, Glissant, Morrison, and Saint-John Perse*. Charlottesville: University of Virginia Press, 2007.

Lombardi, John V. *The Decline and Abolition of Negro Slavery in Venezuela 1820–1854*. Westport: Greenwood, 1971.

López Lemus, Virgilio. *Dulce María Loynaz: Estudios de la obra de una cubana universal*. Tenerife and Grand Canary: Centro de la Cultura Popular Canaria, 2000.

Loynaz, Dulce María. *Juegos de agua: versos del agua y del amor*. Madrid: Editora Nacional, 1947.

———. *Jardín*. Madrid: Aguilar, 1951; repr., Barcelona: Seix Barral, 1993.

———. *Últimos días de una casa*. Madrid: Soler Hermanos, 1958.

———. *A Woman in Her Garden: Selected Poems by Dulce María Loynaz*. Ed. and trans. Judith Kerman. Buffalo, NY: White Pine, 2002.

Lubiano, Wahneema. "Black Nationalism and Black Common Sense." In *The House that Race Built: Black Americans, U.S. Terrain*. Ed. Wahneema Lubiano. New York: Pantheon, 1997. 232–52.

Lúdmer, Josefina. "Tricks of the Weak." In *Feminist Perspectives on Sor Juana Inés de la Cruz*. Ed. Stephanie Merrim. Detroit: Wayne State University Press, 1991. 86–93.

Lytle, Andrew Nelson. "The Hind Tit." In *I'll Take My Stand: the South and the Agrarian Tradition*. By Twelve Southerners. New York: Harper, 1930; repr. Baton Rouge: Louisiana State University Press, 1977. 201–45.

Mackethan, Lucinda. "Plantation Fiction, 1865–1900." In *The History of Southern Literature*. Ed. Louis Rubin. Baton Rouge: Louisiana State University Press, 1985. 209–18.

Manning, Carol S. Afterword. In *The Sheltered Life*. By Ellen Glasgow. Charlottesville: University Press of Virginia, 1994. 293–329.

Marcus, James. "This Side of Paradise." Amazon.com, http://www.amazon.com/exec/obidos/tg/feature/-/7651/ (accessed June 27, 2008).

Marrs, Suzanne. *Eudora Welty: A Biography*. Orlando, FL: Harcourt, 2005.

Martí, José. "Nuestra América." 1891; repr. *Obras completas* vol. 6. La Habana: Editorial Nacional de Cuba, 1964. 15–22.

————. "Our America." ("Nuestra América.") In *José Martí Reader: Writings on the Americas.* Ed. Deborah Shnookal and Mirta Muñiz. Melbourne: Ocean, 1999. 111–20.

Martínez-San Miguel, Yolanda. *Caribe Two Ways: cultura de la migración en el Caribe insular hispánico.* San Juan: Ediciones Callejón, 2003.

Matthews, Pamela R. *Ellen Glasgow and a Woman's Traditions.* Charlottesville: University Press of Virginia, 1994.

Mayes, April. "The Mulatto Republic: Dominican National Identity in the Age of Sugar, 1860s–1940s." Unpublished manuscript.

McClennen, Sophia A. "Area Studies Beyond Ontology: Notes on Latin American Studies, American Studies, and Inter-American Studies." *A Contracorriente* 5.1 (Fall 2007): 173–84.

————. Review of *Look Away! The U.S. South in New World Studies. Comparative Literature Studies* 44.1–2 (2007): 186–89.

McDowell, Deborah. "Boundaries: Or Distant Relations and Close Kin." In *Afro-American Literary Study in the 1990s.* Ed. Houston A. Baker, Jr. and Patricia Redmond. Chicago: University of Chicago Press, 1989. 51–70.

Mignolo, Walter. "Capitalism and Geopolitics of Knowledge: Latin American Social Thought and Latino/a American Studies." In *Critical Latin American and Latino Studies.* Ed. Juan Poblete. Minneapolis: University of Minnesota Press, 2003. 32–75.

Mills, Fiona. "Telling the Untold Tale: Afro-Latino/a Identifications in the Work of Gayl Jones." In *After the Pain: Critical Essays on Gayl Jones.* Ed. Fiona Mills. New York: Peter Lang, 2006. 91–115.

Mintz, Sidney Wilfred. *Caribbean Transformations.* Chicago : Aldine, 1974.

Molloy, Sylvia. "Disappearing Acts: Reading Lesbian in Teresa de la Parra." In *¿Entiendes? Queer Readings, Hispanic Writings.* Ed. Emilie L. Bergmann and Paul Julian Smith. Durham, NC: Duke University Press, 1995. 230–56.

Moreiras, Alberto. "The Order of Order: On the Reluctant Culturalism of Anti-Subalternist Critiques." *Journal of Latin American Cultural Studies* 8.1 (1999): 125–45.

Morell, Hortensia. "Las paradojas de la masculinidad en *Sirena Selena vestida de pena.*" *Caribe* 8.2 (2005): 7–18.

Moreno Fraginals, Manuel. *El ingenio: Complejo económico cubano del azúcar.* Havana: Comisión Nacional Cubana de la UNESCO, 1964.

————. *The Sugarmill: The Socioeconomic Complex of Sugar in Cuba 1760–1860. (El ingenio.)* Trans. Cedric Belfrage. New York: Monthly Review Press, 1976.

Morgenstern, Naomi. "Mother's Milk and Sister's Blood: Trauma and the Neoslave Narrative." *Differences* 8.2 (1996): 101–26.

Morrison, Toni. *Beloved.* New York: Knopf, 1987.

————. *Jazz.* New York: Knopf, 1992.

————. *Playing in the Dark: Whiteness and the Literary Imagination.* New York: Vintage, 1993.

————. "Home." In *The House that Race Built: Black Americans, U.S. Terrain.* Ed. Wahneema Lubiano. New York: Pantheon, 1997. 3–12.

————. *Paradise.* New York: Alfred A. Knopf, 1998.

Moya Pons, Frank. *The Dominican Republic: A National History.* Princeton: Markus Wiener, 1998.

Moya-Raggio, Eliana. "El sacrificio de *Ifigenia:* Teresa de la Parra y su visión crítica de una sociedad criolla." *La Torre* 2.5 (1988): 161–71.

Mujica, Barbara. "Into the Labyrinth of Truth and Fiction." *Américas* 53.2 (2001): 60.

Muñiz Varela, Miriam. "The Caribbean: Archeology and Poetics." *Social Text* 39 (1994): 105–10.

Murphy, Paul. *The Rebuke of History: The Southern Agrarians and American Conservative Thought.* Chapel Hill: University of North Carolina Press, 2001.

Nyren, Ron. "Scooped from the Gutter to Become a Drag Queen." Review of Mayra Santos-Febres, *Sirena Selena*. Trans. Stephen Lytle. *San Francisco Chronicle*, August 27, 2000, http://www.sfgate.com/cgi-bin/article.cgi?file=/chronicle/archive/2000/08/27/RV88233. DT (accessed August 29, 2006).

Ortiz, Fernando. *Hampa afrocubana: Los negros brujos*. Madrid: Librería de Fernando Fé, 1906.

———. *Contrapunteo cubano del tabaco y el azúcar*. Havana: Jesús Montero, 1940; repr. Madrid: Cátedra, 2002.

———. *Cuban Counterpoint: Tobacco and Sugar. (Contrapunteo cubano del tabaco y el azúcar.)* Trans. Harriet de Onís. Durham, NC: Duke University Press, 1995.

Owsley, Frank Lawrence. "The Irrepressible Conflict." In *I'll Take My Stand: the South and the Agrarian Tradition*. By Twelve Southerners. New York: Harper, 1930; repr. Baton Rouge: Louisiana State University Press, 1977. 61–91.

Page, Philip. "Furrowing all the Brows: Interpretation and the Transcendent in Toni Morrison's *Paradise*." *African American Review* 35.4 (2001): 637–49.

Painter, Nell Irvin. *Exodusters: Black Migration to Kansas after Reconstruction*. New York: Norton, 1992.

Parra, Teresa de la. *Ifigenia*. 2 vols. Caracas: Las Novedades, 1924; repr. Caracas: Monte Avila, 1990.

———. *Iphigenia: The Diary of a Young Lady Who Wrote Because She Was Bored. (Ifigenia.)* Trans. Bertie Acker. Austin: University of Texas Press, 1993.

———. *Las memorias de Mamá Blanca*. Paris: Editorial "Le Livre libre," 1929.

———. *Mama Blanca's Memoirs. (Las memorias de Mamá Blanca.)* Trans. Harriet De Onís and rev. Frederick H. Fornoff. Pittsburgh: University of Pittsburgh Press, 1993.

———. *Influencia de las mujeres en la formación del alma americana*. R. J. Lovera De-Sola, prologue. Caracas: Fundarte, 1991.

———. *Obra escogida*. 2 vols. Caracas: Monte Avila Latinoamericana; Mexico City: Fondo de Cultura Económica, 1992.

Patell, Cyrus R. K. *Negative Liberties: Morrison, Pynchon, and the Problem of Liberal Ideology*. Durham, NC: Duke University Press, 2001.

Patterson, Laura Sloan. "Sexing the Domestic: Eudora Welty's *Delta Wedding* and the Sexology Movement." *Southern Quarterly* 42.2 (2004): 37–59.

Peacock, James L., Harry L. Watson, and Carrie R. Matthews, ed. *The American South in a Global World*. Chapel Hill: University of North Carolina Press, 2005.

Pedreira, Antonio S. *Insularismo: ensayos de interpretación puertorriqueña*. Madrid: Tipografía Artística, 1934; repr., Río Piedras: Editorial Edil, 1992.

Peña-Jordán, Teresa. "Romper la verja, meterse por los poros, infectar: una entrevista con Mayra Santos-Febres." *CENTRO Journal* 15.2 (2003): 117–25.

Pérez, Louis A. Jr. *Cuba: Between Reform and Revolution*. 3d. ed. New York: Oxford University Press, 2006.

Pérez de la Riva, Juan. *El barracón: esclavitud y capitalismo en Cuba*. Barcelona: Crítica, 1978.

Pérez Firmat, Gustavo. *The Cuban Condition: Translation and Identity in Modern Cuban Literature*. Cambridge: Cambridge University Press, 1989.

Pike, Frederick B. *The United States and Latin America: Myths and Stereotypes of Civilization*. Austin: University of Texas Press, 1992.

Poblete, Juan, ed. *Critical Latin American and Latino Studies*. Minneapolis: University of Minnesota Press, 2003.

Quiñones, Arcadio Días. *El arte de bregar: Ensayos*. San Juan: Ediciones Callejón, 2000.

Rahier, Jean Muteba. "*Mestizaje, Mulataje, Mestiçagem* in Latin Ideologies of National Identities." *Journal of Latin American Anthropology* 8.1 (2003): 40–51.

Ransom, John Crowe. "Reconstructed but Unregenerate." In *I'll Take My Stand: the South and the Agrarian Tradition*. By Twelve Southerners. New York: Harper, 1930; repr. Baton Rouge: Louisiana State University Press, 1977. 1–27.

Raper, Julius Rowan. *From the Sunken Garden: The Fiction of Ellen Glasgow, 1916–1945*. Baton Rouge: Louisiana State University Press, 1980.

———. "Ellen Glasgow: Gaps in the Record." In *Regarding Ellen Glasgow: Essays for Contemporary Readers*. Ed. Welford Dunaway Taylor and George C. Longest. Richmond: Library of Virginia, 2001. 127–37.

Ravage, John W. *Black Pioneers: Images of the Black Experience on the North American Frontier.* Salt Lake City: University of Utah Press, 1997.

Reyes, Israel. *Humor and the Eccentric Text in Puerto Rican Literature*. Gainesville: University Press of Florida, 2005.

Richard, Nelly. "Intersectando Latinoamérica con el latinoamericanismo: saberes académicos, práctica teórica, y crítica cultural." *Revista Iberoamericana* 63.180 (1997): 345–61.

———. *Masculine/Feminine: Practices of Difference(s)*. (*Masculino/femenino: prácticas de la diferencia y cultura democrática.*) Trans. Silvia R. Tandeciarz and Alice A. Nelson. Durham, NC: Duke University Press, 2004.

Ríos de Hernández, Josefina. *La Hacienda Venezolana: Una visión a través de la historia oral.* Caracas: Serie Agricultura y Sociedad, 1988.

Ritchie, Susan J. "Constructing an Archipelago: Writing the Caribbean." *Postmodern Culture* 3.2 (1993), http://muse.jhu.edu.proxy.libraries.smu.edu/journals/postmodern_culture/v003/3.2r_ritchie.html (accessed May 31, 2007).

Rivera, José Eustasio. *La vorágine*. Bogota: Camacho Roldan & Cia, 1924.

———. *The Vortex. (La vorágine.)* Trans. Earle Kenneth James. New York: TVRT, 1979.

Robinson, Sally. *Engendering the Subject: Gender and Self-Representation in Contemporary Women's Fiction.* Albany: State University of New York Press, 1991.

Rodríguez, Ileana. *House/Garden/Nation: Space, Gender, and Ethnicity in Post-Colonial Latin American Literatures by Women.* Durham, NC: Duke University Press, 1994.

Rodríguez Guglielmoni, Linda. "El texto perdido del boom latinoamericano." Afterword to *Escalera para Electra*. By Aída Cartagena Portalatín. Santo Domingo: Editorial Letra Gráfica, 2004. 145–59.

Rodríguez-Mangual, Edna M. *Lydia Cabrera and the Construction of an Afro-Cuban Cultural Identity.* Chapel Hill: University of North Carolina Press, 2004.

Romero, Channette. "Creating the Beloved Community: Religion, Race, and Nation in Toni Morrison's *Paradise*." *African American Review* 39.3 (2005): 415–30.

Rosa, Richard and Doris Sommer. "Teresa de la Parra: America's Womanly Soul." In *Reinterpreting the Spanish American Essay: Women Writers of the Nineteenth and Twentieth Centuries*. Ed. Doris Meyer. Austin: University of Texas Press, 1995. 115–24.

Rosario Candelier, Bruno. *Coloquio literario: estudios y entrevistas*. Santo Domingo: Banreservas, 2000.

Rubin, Louis D. "Introduction to the Torchbook Edition (1962)." *I'll Take My Stand: The South and the Agrarian Tradition*. By Twelve Southerners. New York: Harper, 1930; repr. Baton Rouge: Louisiana State University Press, 1977. xxiii–xxxv.

Rushdy, Ashraf H. A. *Neo-slave Narratives: Studies in the Social Logic of a Literary Form.* New York: Oxford University Press, 1999.

———. *Remembering Generations*. Chapel Hill: University of North Carolina Press, 2001.

Russ, Elizabeth. "Disordering History, Denying Politics: Performative Strategies in Teresa de la Parra's *Influencia de la mujer en la formación del alma americana*." *Latin American Literary Review* 34.67 (2006): 161–69.

San Miguel, Pedro L. *The Imagined Island: History, Identity, and Utopia in Hispaniola.* (*La isla imaginada : historia, identidad y utopía en La Española.*) Trans. Jane Ramírez. Chapel Hill: University of North Carolina Press, 2005.

Sandoval-Sánchez, Alberto. "*Sirena Selena vestida de pena:* A Novel for the New Millennium and for New Critical Practices in Puerto Rican Literary and Cultural Studies." *CENTRO Journal* 15.2 (2003): 5–23.

Santos-Febres, Mayra. *Sirena Selena vestida de pena.* Barcelona: Mondadori, 2000.

———. *Sirena Selena. (Sirena Selena vestida de pena.)* Trans. Stephen Lytle. New York: Picador U.S.A., 2000.

———. *Cualquier miércoles soy tuya.* Barcelona: Mondadori, 2002.

———. *Sobre piel y papel.* San Juan: Ediciones Callejon, 2005.

———. *Nuestra señora de la noche.* Madrid: Espasa Calpe, 2006.

Sarlo, Beatriz. "Cultural Studies and Literary Criticism at the Crossroads of Values." *Journal of Latin American Cultural Studies* 8.1 (1999): 115–24.

Sartre, Jean Paul. *L'âge de raison, roman.* Paris: Gallimard, 1945.

Scaramelli, Giovanni Battista. *Il direttorio mistico.* Venice, 1754.

———. *A Handbook of Mystical Theology.* (*Il direttorio mistico,* abridged.) Trans. D. H. S. Nicholson. Newburyport: Red Wheel/Weiser, 2005.

Scott, Ann Firor. *The Southern Lady: From Pedestal to Politics 1830–1930.* Chicago: University of Chicago Press, 1970.

Scura, Dorothy, ed. *Ellen Glasgow: The Contemporary Reviews.* Cambridge: Cambridge University Press, 1992.

Sedeño Guillén, Kevin. "La insularidad en la obra de Dulce María Loynaz: ausencia de agua rodeada de agua." In *Dulce María Loynaz: Cien años después.* Ed. Humberto López Cruz and Luis A. Jiménez. Madrid: Editorial Hispano Cubano, 2004.

Shukla, Sandhya and Heidi Tinsman, ed. *Imagining Our Americas: Toward a Transnational Frame.* Durham, NC: Duke University Press, 2007.

Simón, Pedro, ed. *Dulce María Loynaz.* Havana: Ediciones Casa de las Américas y Editorial Letras Cubanas, 1991.

Sklodowska, Elzbieta. *Testimonio hispano-americano: historia, teoría, poética.* New York: Peter Lang, 1992.

Smith, Jon and Deborah Cohn. "Introduction: Uncanny Hybridities." In *Look Away!: The U.S. South in New World Studies.* Durham, NC: Duke University Press, 2004. 1–24.

———, ed. *Look Away!: The U.S. South in New World Studies.* Durham, NC: Duke University Press, 2004.

Smith, Verity. "Dwarfed by Snow White: Feminist Revisions of Fairy Tale Discourse in the Narrative of Maria Luisa Bombal and Dulce Maria Loynaz." In *Feminist Readings on Spanish and Latin-American Literature.* Ed. S. M. Hart and L. P. Condé. Lewiston: Edwin Mellen, 1991. 137–47.

———. "'Eva sin Paraíso': una lectura feminista de *Jardín* de Dulce María Loynaz." *Nueva Revista de Filología Hispánica* 41.1 (1993): 263–77.

Sollors, Werner. Introduction. In *Interracialism: Black-White Intermarriage in American History, Literature, and Law.* Ed. Werner Sollors. Oxford: Oxford University Press, 2000. 3–16.

Sommer, Doris. *Foundational Fictions: The National Romances of Latin America.* Berkeley: University of California Press, 1991.

———. *Proceed with Caution When Engaged by Minority Writing in the Americas.* Cambridge: Harvard University Press, 1999.

Spitta, Silvia. "Transculturation, the Caribbean, and the Cuban-American Imaginary." In *Tropicalizations: Transcultural Representations of Latinidad.* Ed. Frances R. Aparicio and Susana Chávez-Silverman. Hanover: University Press of New England, 1997. 160–80.

Stave, Shirley A. "The Master's Tools: Morrison's *Paradise* and the Problem of Christianity." In *Toni Morrison and the Bible: Contested Intertextualities*. Ed. Shirley A. Stave. New York: Peter Lang, 2006. 215–23.

Strachan, Ian Gregory. *Paradise and Plantation: Tourism and Culture in the Anglophone Caribbean*. Charlottesville: University of Virginia Press, 2002.

Stuhr, Rebecca. Review of *Sirena Selena*, by Mayra Santos-Febres, trans. Stephen Lytle. *Library Journal* 15 (June 2000): 118.

Sweeney, Megan. "Racial House, Big House, Home: Contemporary Abolitionism in Toni Morrison's *Paradise*." *Meridians* 4.2 (2004): 40–67.

Tate, Allen. "Remarks on the Southern Religion." In *I'll Take My Stand: the South and the Agrarian Tradition*. By Twelve Southerners. New York: Harper, 1930; repr. Baton Rouge: Louisiana State University Press, 1977. 155–75.

———. "The New Provincialism." 1945; repr. *Collected Essays*. Denver: Alan Swallow, 1959. 282–93.

Tate, Claudia C. "*Corregidora*: Ursa's Blues Medley." *Black American Literature Forum* 13.4 (1979): 139–41.

——— "An Interview with Gayl Jones." *Black American Literature Forum* 13.4 (1979): 142–48.

Taylor, Diana. *The Archive and the Repertoire: Performing Cultural Memory in the Americas*. Durham, NC: Duke University Press, 2003.

———. "Remapping Genre through Performance: From 'American' to 'Hemispheric' Studies." *PLMA* 122.5 (October 2007): 416–30.

Terry, Jennifer. "A New World Religion? Creolisation and Candomblé in Toni Morrison's *Paradise*." In *Toni Morrison and the Bible: Contested Intertextualities*. Ed. Shirley A. Stave. New York: Peter Lang, 2006. 192–214.

Thompson, Robert Farris. *The Flash of the Spirit*. New York: Vintage, 1983.

Tinsman, Heidi and Sandhya Shulka. "Introduction: Across the Americas." In *Imagining Our Americas: Toward a Transnational Frame*. Ed. Sandhya Shulka and Heidi Tinsman. Durham, NC: Duke University Press, 2007. 1–33.

Tirthankar, Chanda. "The Cultural 'Creolization' of the World: Interview with Edouard Glissant." *Label France* 38 (January 2000), http://www.diplomatie.gouv.fr/label_france/ENGLISH/DOSSIER/2000/15creolisation.html (accessed May 28, 2007).

Torres, Sonia. "U.S. Americans and 'Us' Americans: South American Perspectives on Contemporary American Studies." *Comparative American Studies* 1.1 (2003): 9–18.

Torres-Saillant, Silvio. "The Unity of Caribbean Literature: A Position." In *Sisyphus and Eldorado: Magical and Other Realism in Caribbean Literature*. Ed. Timothy J. Reiss. Trenton: Africa World Press, 2002. 225–48.

Trilling, Diana. "Fiction in Review." In *The Critical Response to Eudora Welty's Fiction*. Ed. Laurie Champion. Westwood: Greenwood, 1994. 103–05.

Tucker, George. *The Valley of Shenandoah*. New York: C. Wiley, 1824; repr., Chapel Hill: University of North Carolina Press, 1970.

Turits, Richard. *Foundations of Despotism: Peasants, the Trujillo Regime, and Modernity in Dominican History*. Stanford: Stanford University Press, 2003.

Twelve Southerners. *I'll Take My Stand: the South and the Agrarian Tradition*. New York: Harper, 1930; repr. Baton Rouge: Louisiana State University Press, 1977.

———. "Introduction: A Statement of Principles." In *I'll Take My Stand: the South and the Agrarian Tradition*. By Twelve Southerners. New York: Harper, 1930; repr. Baton Rouge: Louisiana State University Press, 1977. xxxvii–xlviii.

United States Department of Labor, Office of Policy Planning and Research. *The Negro Family: The Case For National Action*. (The Moynihan Report.) Washington, DC: Government Printing Office, 1965.

Van Deburg, William L. *New Day in Babylon: The Black Power Movement and American Culture, 1965–1975.* Chicago: University of Chicago Press, 1992.

Van Haesendonck, Kristian. "*Sirena Selena vestida de pena* de Mayra Santos-Febres: ¿transgresiones de espacio o espacio de transgresiones?" *CENTRO Journal* 15.2 (2003): 79–96.

Verge, Shane Trudell. "Revolutionary Vision: Black Women Writers, Black Nationalist Ideology, and Interracial Sexuality." *Meridians* 2.2 (2002): 101–25.

Vitier, Cintio. *Lo cubano en la poesía.* Havana: Instituto del Libro, 1970.

Wade, John Donald. "The Life and Death of Cousin Lucius." In *I'll Take My Stand: the South and the Agrarian Tradition.* By Twelve Southerners. New York: Harper, 1930; repr. Baton Rouge: Louisiana State University Press, 1977. 265–301.

Wallace, Michele. *Black Macho and the Myth of the Superwoman.* New York: Dial, 1978.

Warren, Robert Penn. "The Briar Patch." In *I'll Take My Stand: the South and the Agrarian Tradition.* By Twelve Southerners. New York: Harper, 1930; repr. Baton Rouge: Louisiana State University Press, 1977. 246–64.

Watson, Ritchie. "Ellen Glasgow, the Nashville Agrarians, and the Glasgow-Allen Tate Correspondence." *Mississippi Quarterly* 44.1 (1990–1991): 35–47.

Welty, Eudora. *Delta Wedding.* San Diego: Harcourt Brace Jovanovich, 1946; repr. 1974.

———. *The Eye of the Story.* New York: Random House, 1977.

Westling, Louise. "Food, Landscape, and the Feminine in *Delta Wedding.*" *Southern Quarterly* 30.2–3 (1992): 29–40.

Weston, Ruth. *Gothic Traditions and Narrative Techniques in the Fictions of Eudora Welty.* Baton Rouge: Louisiana State University Press, 1995.

———. "Eudora Welty as Lyric Novelist: The Long and the Short of It." In *The Late Novels of Eudora Welty.* Ed. Jan Nordby Gretlund and Karl-Heinz Westarp. Columbia: University of South Carolina Press, 1998. 29–40.

Wharton, Edith. *The House of Mirth.* New York: Charles Scribner's Sons, 1905.

Williams, Lorna V. "The Inscription of Sexual Identity in Aída Cartagena's *Escalera para Electra.*" *MLN* 112.2 (1997): 219–31.

Williamson, Joel. *New People: Miscegenation and Mulattoes in the United States.* New York: The Free Press, 1980.

Winddance Twine, France. *Racism in a Racial Democracy: The Maintenance of White Supremacy in Brazil.* New Brunswick: Rutgers University Press, 1997.

Wolf, Eric. "Specific Aspects of Plantation Systems in the New World: Community Sub-Cultures and Social Classes." In *Plantation Systems of the New World.* Research Institute for the Study of Man and the Pan American Union. Washington: Pan American Union, 1959. 136–47.

Wright, Winthrop R. *Café con leche: Race, Class, and National Image in Venezuela.* Austin: University of Texas Press, 1990.

Wynter, Sylvia. "Novel and History: Plot and Plantation." *Savacou* 5 (1971): 95–102.

Yaeger, Patricia. *Dirt and Desire: Reconstructing Southern Women's Writing, 1930–1990.* Chicago: University of Chicago Press, 2000.

Young, Stark. "Not In Memoriam, But In Defense." In *I'll Take My Stand: the South and the Agrarian Tradition.* By Twelve Southerners. New York: Harper, 1930; repr. Baton Rouge: Louisiana State University Press, 1977. 328–59.

Yukins, Elizabeth. "Bastard Daughters and the Possession of History in *Corregidora* and *Paradise.*" *Signs* 28.1 (2002): 221–47.

Zakrzewski Brown, Isabel. "Autora en busca de expresión en *Escalera para Electra.*" *Cincinnati Romance Review* 12 (1993): 130–38.

Zavala, Iris M. "De héroes y heroínas en lo imaginario social: El discurso amoroso del bolero." *Casa de las Américas* 30.179 (1990): 123–29.

INDEX